Turning the Pages
of American Girlhood

Turning the Pages of American Girlhood

The Evolution of Girls' Series Fiction, 1865–1930

EMILY HAMILTON-HONEY

McFarland & Company, Inc., Publishers
Jefferson, North Carolina, and London

LIBRARY OF CONGRESS CATALOGUING-IN-PUBLICATION DATA

Hamilton-Honey, Emily.
    Turning the pages of American girlhood : the evolution of girls' series fiction, 1865–1930 / Emily Hamilton-Honey.
      p.   cm.
    Includes bibliographical references and index.

    ISBN 978-0-7864-6322-0
    softcover : acid free paper ∞

    1. Children's stories, American—History and criticism. 2. Girls in literature. 3. Girls—Books and reading—United States—History—19th century. 4. Girls—Books and reading—United States—History—20th century. 5. Children's literature in series—History and criticism. 6. Serialized fiction—United States—History and criticism. 7. American fiction—19th century—History and criticism. 8. American fiction—20th century—History and criticism. I. Title.
PS374.C454H36 2013
813'.5099282—dc23   2012049419

BRITISH LIBRARY CATALOGUING DATA ARE AVAILABLE

© 2013 Emily Hamilton-Honey. All rights reserved

No part of this book may be reproduced or transmitted in any form or by any means, electronic or mechanical, including photocopying or recording, or by any information storage and retrieval system, without permission in writing from the publisher.

On the cover: Girls from 1800s with book (iStockphoto/Thinkstock)

Manufactured in the United States of America

McFarland & Company, Inc., Publishers
* Box 611, Jefferson, North Carolina 28640*
*   www.mcfarlandpub.com*

For Nick.
I never would have made it
this far without you.

Table of Contents

Acknowledgments ix
Introduction 1

ONE. Learning to Be an Angel: Religion and Reading for
    Nineteenth-Century American Girls 25

TWO. Angels in the House: Christian Womanhood and
    Community Power in Postbellum Girls' Series 54

THREE. A Revolution in Series Production: Edward Stratemeyer
    and the Commodification of Series Books 84

FOUR. Communities of Friends: Series Heroines as Consumers,
    1901–1930 104

FIVE. Two Miles Forward, One Mile Back: Gender Battles
    During the Great War 135

SIX. Running the Gamut and the Gauntlet: World War I
    Series Fiction as a Catalyst for Change in the
    Cultural Landscape of American Girlhood 169

SEVEN. Taking Advantage of New Markets: Ruth Fielding as a
    Motion Picture Screenwriter, Producer, and Executive 201

Conclusion: Nancy Drew and a New Era 223
Appendix: Series Books in Order of Publication 233
Bibliography 237
Index 251

Acknowledgments

Deborah Carlin, Joyce Berkman, Laura Lovett, and Randall Knoper, of the University of Massachusetts, Amherst, deserve more thanks than I can ever express in such a small space. They believed in this project from the beginning, they let me run with it and reshape it several times over, they reined me in when necessary, and most importantly, they made me a better and more careful writer and scholar. They willingly helped me negotiate the difficult balance of rigorous literary analysis and historical proof that is often required of American Studies researchers; they also allowed me to find creative ways of documenting and dealing with this mostly-uncharted territory of nineteenth-century series. Thank you all for being such a supportive and enthusiastic dissertation committee.

I am grateful to Northern Illinois University for providing me with a Horatio Alger, Jr. Fellowship to travel to their collection. Their monetary support allowed me to spend a wonderful week examining original Alcott, Finley, and Champney volumes, as well as the William Thayer advice manual that came in handy at a crucial moment. The NIU curator, Lynne Thomas, has been a wonderful source of support and information as well as a lovely new friend.

Thanks must also be given to the librarians of the Manuscripts and Archives Division at the New York Public Library, Stephen A. Schwarzman Building. They were incredibly helpful both before and during my week-long stay in New York, and helped me navigate the mountains of material from the Stratemeyer Syndicate with a great deal of patience and many smiles.

James Keeline has been unfailingly kind and generous with both his own work and his critiques during the writing of this project. His research on Edward Stratemeyer (much of it unpublished) has been absolutely invaluable, and he took the time to point out many small errors and clarify many details about Stratemeyer's methods and the operations of the Syndicate.

Acknowledgments

Deidre Johnson of Westchester University cheerfully provided me with a great deal of information on nineteenth-century women authors and publishers' marketing methods. I am so thankful for her expertise. The other members of the Popular Culture Association's Dime Novels and Series Book Area were incredibly welcoming and helpful to a newcomer, particularly Kathleen Chamberlain, Pamela Bedore, and Lydia Schurman.

Susan Ingalls Lewis of SUNY New Paltz read through many drafts of the Great War chapters of this book, providing much useful criticism and enthusiasm at a critical period in the writing process. She has expanded my thinking about Great War series books, collaborated with me on conference panels, and is a wonderful colleague and friend.

Gwen Tarbox of Western Michigan University deserves as much credit as I can give her for putting me on this path, for mentoring me, being a lifeline when I needed one, and being a cherished friend. I hope that I can live up to her sterling example.

Jennifer McFarlane-Harris of Messiah College has been a discerning and enthusiastic reader throughout countless drafts. Her extensive knowledge of nineteenth-century women's spiritual autobiography, the Bible, and other religious texts has made this a much better product. Her friendship is irreplaceable.

Brian Johnson of Case Western Reserve University was my co-conspirator throughout the American Studies program at the University of Massachusetts Amherst. His brilliance, humor, encouragement, scholarly work, and friendship made the journey to our doctorates much more enjoyable.

Finally, these acknowledgments would not be complete unless I thanked my wife, Nicole Hamilton-Honey, who has been a tireless critic, editor, and sounding board as well as an unwavering pillar of faith, love, and encouragement throughout the last nine years. Her endless work for the two of us, her patience, and her devotion have made this book possible.

Introduction

As a fourteen-year-old, I found an old volume entitled *Beverly Gray, Sophomore* at a Boy Scout used book sale in my hometown. When I first read about Beverly and her group of girl friends attending the fictional Vernon College, it was their camaraderie that attracted me, as well as their thirst for adventure and their professions as actress, playwright, and photographer (among other vocations). These girls felt entitled to an education that would allow them to pursue the careers of their dreams, and they worked through their problems with the help of friendship and loyalty that was both highly appealing and comforting to me, a shy teenager who hoped that college would bring her similar friends and opportunities.

That one book was the beginning of a collecting obsession; I have spent the past eighteen years putting together sets of girls' series books from the late nineteenth and early twentieth century by scrounging antique shops, used bookstores, and online book dealers. However, as I continued to collect and read these early series and began to study them as a scholar, an array of questions opened up that demanded answers. First, why was it that series books that were published for my own generation (which included the lengthy *Baby-Sitters Club* and *Sweet Valley High* series, as well as the later paperback *Nancy Drew* books published by Simon & Schuster) didn't include narratives about college and careers, even when they depicted groups of girlfriends? Why was it that series girls after Nancy never aged? Why, as readers, did we never get to see the career that someone as intelligent and self-driven as Nancy surely would have had? Why had appearance, romance, and competition between friends become the key components of fictional girlhood? Why was it that even entrepreneurs like the girls of the Baby-Sitters Club created a business around something as traditional and feminized as caring for children?

The series fiction from the turn of the century contained many of the traits that I, as an adolescent, felt were notably absent from series books of the 1980s and 1990s. These antique series for girls fascinated me as a reader. Here were girl heroines who, like their successor Nancy, were brave, resourceful, self-motivated, independent, and eager to explore the world. Unlike Nancy, they grew up, went through high school and college, chose professions, and had to contend with the tricky balance between careers and romantic relationships. The historical elements contained in some individual series added another element of interest; for example, volumes published during and after American involvement in World War I offered a particularly rich and detailed window into the activities of American women during the Great War. Historical specificity is another characteristic of series books that has since fallen by the wayside. Publishers discovered that historical facts quickly "dated" the books; plots and characters that could exist in any timeframe meant better sales.

As I began finding older series from the postbellum and Progressive eras, including *Patty Fairfield*, *Elsie Dinsmore*, the *Chautauqua Girls*, the *Three Vassar Girls*, and *Witch Winnie*, my questions only multiplied. Why was it that series from the nineteenth century contained so much about religion and the positive moral influence that women could exert in the world, while in the twentieth century girl heroines became a focal point for the consumption of material goods? Social activism and benevolence in the nineteenth century gave way to consumerism and careers in the twentieth. Stranger still, what had been a decades-long historical progression in reality was an abrupt change in the world of series, with religion evaporating from series narratives completely within about twenty years, roughly between 1895 and 1915.

This last set of questions concerning the shift from religious benevolence to women as consumers interested me the most, and this study is the result. Series books from the end of the Civil War through the 1920s both reflect and encourage a cultural shift in beliefs about the role of young women in U.S. society. While series from the postbellum period still tend to concentrate on women as religious and moral figures, similar to Barbara Welter's antebellum "Cult of True Womanhood," they also open up more space for women's social and political activism, empowering women to reform society based on their cultural status as moral enforcers.[1] National religious and reform groups like the Chautauqua Institute and the Woman's Christian Temperance Union allowed women to learn political skills, while still remaining within the boundaries of their cultural designation as moral leaders. Welter's "True Women" were no longer confined to the home; they took their moral authority into the city slums and the political arena, into the Reconstruction South and the New York tenements, doing their best to alleviate the effects of poverty, hunger, poor sanitation, and illness. Postbellum series books narrated this new, wider work that women were accomplishing. Sometimes the books were even intentionally written to help recruit young women readers into national reform organizations.

Girls' reading in the nineteenth century was often seen as a tool for reinforcing proper religious and moral behavior. Chapter One examines the ways in which church membership and reading were often overlapping activities for postbellum girls, the latter intended to emphasize the responsibilities of the former. Parents expected their female children, particularly, to attend church and to exhibit a certain level of faith, although the level and expression of that faith varied from denomination to denomination. In the first half of the chapter, I give a brief picture of nineteenth-century girls and the expectations surrounding their religious beliefs and church membership, the community functions of women's antebellum benevolence organizations, the backlash against women speaking or preaching in church, and the emergence of postbellum organizations that gave women a voice in important moral and political issues like temperance and abolition. The second half of the chapter examines girls' postbellum reading habits, the conflicts between educational and novel reading, and parents' worries and expectations about their daughters' reading. Middle- and upper-class girls read primarily to educate themselves, and fiction was often carefully chosen and sometimes even rationed. Postbellum series were performing a particular kind of cultural work by teaching girls about "correct" (read "Protestant" or "Protestant evangelical") religious behavior while also explicating the empowering possibilities of benevolence.[2] Since women were eventually expected to be the spiritual heads of the home, reading was one form of self-improvement that helped girls define their faith and morality. Drawing on the scholarship of Joseph Kett, Jane Hunter, Lori Ginzberg, Andrew Reiser, and others, I demonstrate that while parents relied upon reading to ensure the proper behavior of their daughters, that same reading also allowed girls to glimpse a means for personal agency — the religious social reform organizations which gave women an outlet for meaningful, if often unpaid, work. Girl readers may have internalized not only the social expectations around Christian wifehood and motherhood, but also the possibilities for activism in large movements such as the Women's Christian Temperance Union, the Chautauqua Institute, and the suffrage movement. The first two organizations, in particular, gave women a voice that allowed them to criticize public institutions and social customs without appearing to step beyond the boundaries of the private sphere.

Chapter Two looks at the *Little Women*, *Elsie Dinsmore*, and *Chautauqua Girls* series as prime examples of postbellum texts that encourage young women to become progressively more involved in social benevolence and political activism. Each series helps map the progression from local community benevolence to national political activism. Through individual charity as well as group efforts, series heroines are able to improve the lives of their neighbors, influence the policies of their churches, prevent the sale of liquor, and alleviate poverty on a large scale. In addition, the books highlight assumptions about class and race that often permeated both series literature and historical organizations; benevolence becomes a vehicle for converting the working-class to Christianity and ensuring their adherence to middle-class social norms.

I argue that these postbellum series modeled a proto–New Womanhood that was based first on individual acts of charity, next on overlapping networks of benevolent organizations and reform societies, and finally on political and social reform organizations that aimed to create national change through local, state, and federal legislation. Series books provided insight into postbellum women's organizations that were altering the way women functioned in the public sphere. Series heroines take advantage of their social status as moral, pious individuals to assist the poor in their communities and to extend their moral reach. While it is difficult to know how many girls actually read the series examined here, series book authors were clearly trying to spread awareness of women's organizations and their methods to a younger generation.

While upper- and upper–middle class young women were being trained in the principles of benevolent Christianity and leading the fights for temperance reform and suffrage, a revolution was happening in the world of publishing. Better printing technology, mandatory schooling laws, and an increase in literacy rates all helped increase the demand for books. The emergence of story papers and dime novels had a profound effect on series books in particular. Both the content and the production of series books changed drastically at the turn of the century. While the postbellum series studied in Chapter Two were all created and written by individual women authors, ghostwriters most often wrote the series that were produced after about 1905, and each book in a series would be published under a single pseudonym, creating the illusion of one author where there were often several.

The most influential series creator at the turn of the century was undoubtedly Edward Stratemeyer, who formed the Stratemeyer Syndicate in 1906. In Chapter Three, I trace the history of Stratemeyer's involvement with story papers and dime novels, cheap periodicals and paperbacks that sold in the millions during the second half of the nineteenth century. Using better and faster printing technology, both story paper and dime novel publishers took advantage of a swift increase in literacy and increased demand for reading material. They paid writers flat fees to produce manuscripts and always had multiple stories in production, so that there was a new story chapter or dime novel on a weekly or biweekly basis. Stratemeyer adopted dime novel production techniques in order to increase the number of series books that he could produce and to simultaneously lower their prices. The work of ghostwriters allowed Stratemeyer to continually produce and sustain new series when they were selling well, since stories could be written and printed much more quickly. The content of his series books was new and exciting as well. He combined the dynamic, action-filled plots of dime novels with the secular middle-class values of honesty, patriotism, and hard work in order to create a new kind of fiction that was marketed specifically for middle-class readers. He made his books inexpensive enough for adolescents to purchase on their own, and he used all the modern selling methods that he could muster, including mailed catalogs, dust jackets, department store displays, and printed advertisements. Thanks to Stratemeyer's innovations, his Syndicate still stands as the most successful producer of juvenile books in U.S. history. Not everyone appreciated his books or his success, though, particularly newly minted professional librarians, who regarded his books as morally corrupt and socially dangerous. The last part of Chapter Three examines Stratemeyer's lengthy correspondence with several professional librarians and his publisher (Lothrop, Lee, & Shepherd) over the way his books and the Syndicate's were catalogued and the way librarians characterized his series. Some libraries even refused to carry anything put out by Stratemeyer or the Syndicate. While their boycotts did not hurt the Syndicate in terms of sales, Stratemeyer vigorously and indignantly defended the quality of his books.

Production techniques were not the only area in which series books were changing at the turn of the century. A new emphasis on woman-as-consumer appears, focusing on responsible consumption as a means for individual female agency. Series books were only one of many products designed to "hook" young people, especially young women, into making repeated and steady purchases of a particular item. In Chapter Four, I examine the *Patty Fairfield*, *Grace Harlowe*, and *Outdoor Girls* series for the ways they communicate both excitement and anxiety about the new culture of consumption. Girl heroines exercised agency as consumers and developed individuality through their purchases. Since food and goods were sold in public space, whether in a town or a city, the consumption of those goods and the shopping trips to obtain them allowed girls more access to traditionally male public spaces, enabling them to define their personalities through buying power. It also gave them the opportunity to utilize economic judgment, even when they were shopping with friends or family members. As consumers they could form their own social groups and appreciate each other as individuals, away from the control and oversight of parents and older siblings. They gained a considerable amount of individual autonomy, while they lost some community influence and some of their status as spiritual leaders. Even new inventions like motor cars and airplanes assist heroines in their search for independence and adventure. Series heroines and their friends develop individual taste, create social space, and form group bonds through their consumption of all kinds of goods, especially food, clothing, and souvenirs. While girl readers are encouraged to develop a distinct personality through choosing and consuming products, tasteful and practical consumption becomes the new hallmark of domesticity.

On the other hand, overindulgence in material goods could lead to selfishness and moral degeneration. Individuality could go too far. Girl heroines like Patty Fairfield and Grace Harlowe learn to be responsible consumers and enjoy the pleasures of individual consumption, but series authors also warn against desiring money and material goods simply for their own sake.[3] If money becomes the sole marker of class status in the new capitalist economy, then the door is open to criminals and swindlers who have not earned their class status through work and industry. Girls, too, can be caught up in the desire for social status and forget the middle-class morals they have been so carefully taught.

The natural development of the new consumer economy, and its possibilities for women, was abruptly interrupted by the advent of the Great War and its intrusion into American life. Although the United States did not officially enter the war until 1917, American women did much to help the European soldiers and civilians who were fighting and suffering. In Chapter Five, I present a brief history of the activities of U.S. women in the Great War, both on the home front and on the battle lines, in the armed services and out of them. It has only been in the last two decades that the extent of women's participation in the First World War has been thoroughly researched and documented, and the extent to which the images and activities of women war workers influenced the popular culture of the U.S. is still not fully understood. Women participated in much smaller numbers in 1917 and 1918 than they would during World War II, not least because U.S. involvement in the war was half as long and because the government and the armed services were reluctant to accept women. However, women performed many varied services during the war, despite the best efforts of Congress and their male supervisors to keep them out of the war and away from the front. The story of their service is one of advance and retreat, progress and regression.

This history is necessary to understand the radical break that appeared in series fiction during the war. Even though the number of American women who managed to make it to the battlefields was small, it was enough to capture the imagination of series book writers and readers alike. Heroines from popular series, like Ruth Fielding, Grace Harlowe, and the Girls of Central High, put aside their schooling and professions to answer the call to service, often overseas and away from home. Other, new heroines appeared in print just for the duration of the war, like the Red Cross Girls and the Khaki Girls. Like their real-life counterparts, series heroines performed important services that had lasting effects — and also like real women, they encountered barriers, prejudice, and bureaucratic limits on their work. However, women war workers and series heroines alike often found ways to overcome those supposed limits. Through intelligence, daring, and not a little rule-breaking, they stayed with the soldiers until the very end, until injury or the Armistice forced them home.

What makes series fiction from the Great War so unique is that it suspends all other cultural ideologies in favor of patriotism, democracy, and service. The heroines in these series do not reflect either the benevolent woman of the nineteenth century or the educated consumers of the turn of the century. They become, instead, fierce patriots devoted to serving the Allied cause. The war offered girl heroines a unique opportunity to participate in masculine public spaces, particularly the armed forces, the battlefield, and military espionage. The patriotic service of girl heroines provided an example to readers of the capabilities of U.S. women if they were given the opportunity to exercise their full talents.

In Chapter Six, I examine four series that dealt with women's participation in the war: *The Outdoor Girls*, *Ruth Fielding*, *Grace Harlowe*, and *The Khaki Girls*. The responses of writers and publishers to women's participation in the war, as represented in their fiction, ran the gamut from conservative to liberal. The four Outdoor Girls stay within the United States and primarily do work for the YWCA canteens, and they are the most conservative representation of women in the war that I have found. Ruth Fielding ventures a little further afield; she performs Red Cross work overseas and undertakes an espionage mission to save her friend (and eventual sweetheart) Tom Cameron. Although she assumes both male and female personas in the course of her spying, however, she is kept firmly within the boundaries of feminine ideals. Grace Harlowe, in the six volumes that comprise her war experience, manages to perform almost every kind of war work, including Red Cross aide, ambulance driving, canteen service, and military intelligence. Grace is noteworthy for her problem-solving skills. While she *is* brave in physically dangerous situations, her most notable contributions to the war involve catching spies, using her intelligence to help capture enemies of the Allied powers. The Khaki Girls, Valerie Ward and Joan Mason, are at the farthest liberal end of the spectrum, driving ambulances, carrying revolvers, and rescuing the wounded from the front lines. Series fiction in this period upsets gender norms to an extent that has rarely happened since.

However, once the war was over, series fiction retreated as rapidly as civilian life back to the expected cultural and gender norms. Women war workers returned home, and so did their fictional counterparts — yet, doors had been open for women that would never be shut again. Women had proven their ability to be independent, to work on an equal footing with men, and with their participation in the war and their achievement of the vote, they gained civic equality that would never be completely rescinded. The Roaring Twenties brought back the consumer economy and offered everyone, male and female alike, a chance to drown the sorrows and afflictions of the war in a prosperous consuming frenzy. The emphasis on consumerism in girls' series returned, and a great deal of the focus was on a new and glamorous commodity: motion pictures.

In Chapter Seven, I examine a single series that focuses on a heroine who is both a consumer and a producer, who exercises her talents to take advantage of an emerging market for leisure and entertainment and who finds herself frequently caught between her roles as a film company executive and a devoted fiancé and wife. Ruth Fielding is unique in many ways as a series heroine. Her series ran for thirty volumes from 1913 to 1934, an unusually long run for a pre–Nancy Drew series, and covered her experiences in high school, college, during World War I, and as a screenwriter, movie producer, and finally motion picture company executive. Here is a young woman who not only consumes products and enjoys her leisure by consuming with friends, but who also produces items for the capitalist market. Ruth is perhaps the earliest example of a series heroine who becomes a professional woman, participating and succeeding fully within a capitalist world dominated by men. Although many series heroines both before and after Ruth attend college, and even engage in organized benevolence or part-time work, not many of them continue on to be full-time professionals producing marketable goods. Ruth takes advantage of the new business of motion pictures and the new culture of leisurely consumption in order to make a career for herself. Unlike most other series heroines, she does not stay solely in the occupation of discerning consumer; she also takes an active role in producing items to be consumed by others.

Ruth clearly corresponds historically with the early women of motion pictures, including screenwriter Frances Marion, actress Marion Davies, and actress/director Mary Pickford; contemporary readers would have been familiar with these new and glamorous women.[4] In a more general sense, she would also correspond with female department store buyers, who dictated the tastes of the public through choosing what to sell in their stores. Women did manage to work on the other side of the consumption world, procuring and producing goods that were sold to the public. Ruth's success as a heroine lies in her ability to negotiate the capitalist market on a level that is equal to her male counterparts, and at the same time to continue to exert the moral influence expected of her gender on her closest family and friends. She cannot always affect the welfare of an entire community, as her earlier counterparts would have done, but she can and does impact the well-being of those closest to her, as well as the prosperity of a larger circle of acquaintances. While Ruth has lost the religious influence of an earlier generation, her influence on those around her still retains its moral strength. Ruth is the exemplary outcome of the long evolution from postbellum Christian heroines to plucky individual consumers, and this book is, ultimately, an attempt to understand that progression.

In undertaking a study that encompasses such a long historical period and contends with a literature that is directed toward the continuously changing, amorphous group of "girls," there were other methodological problems that had to be addressed, including the difficulty of defining a "series" as a genre of literature; race, class, and religion in series fiction; and the development of "adolescence" as a scientific term, a social transition, and a market category. Failing to look at these multiple methodological issues and themes throughout these texts would mean missing many of the cultural assumptions and biases that have a direct bearing on the way series narratives are constructed.

The Problem of Defining a Series

Defining "series book" is a problem in itself. Thanks to Stratemeyer and his complete victory in the juvenile books market, series that were produced from the turn of the twentieth century onward tend to have similar plot structures and even the same "assembly line" type of syndicate production. One adventure follows another, with all of the main characters introduced in the first book making appearances in subsequent volumes. Twentieth century series also deliberately avoided didacticism and favored action and excitement. This definition, however, eliminates many earlier works that were not produced through the same process. Nineteenth-century series were usually written by one person, not through ghostwriters. The books could not be produced as quickly, but they were still intended to be read as related volumes. Often the stories are quite openly didactic. Not all of the characters in a first volume necessarily appear in subsequent volumes, even though one or two characters may reappear, and the plots do not conform to the publishing syndicate standard of short, sweet, and action-packed. Alcott's *Little Women* books and Isabella Alden's *Chautauqua Girls* series are prime examples of these earlier types of series; while the content and some of the characters in the series are related, the plots are lengthy and the works could stand alone almost as easily as they could be read together.

There are other differences as well; girls' culture and series book scholar Sherrie Inness explains the complications of distinguishing between "books in a series" and "series books":

> The biggest problem comes in differentiating between books in a series (the Little House books) and series books (Nancy Drew and her ilk). There are some typical stylistic differences between the two. Series books are more apt to take place in a timeless world where the characters never grow any older or only grow older in the most gradual fashion (think of Nancy Drew); in books in a series, the characters generally age as real people do. The plots of series books are likely to be more formulaic that those of books in a series. In series books, characters are typically less fully developed, less rounded, than characters in books in series. These are a few of the distinctions that may be drawn between series books and books in a series, though a hard and fast distinction between the two types should not be made, since books have a disturbing fashion of slipping over the lines [Inness, *Nancy Drew and Company* 2].

Inness goes on to say that perhaps it is most helpful to study the way that the two styles intermingle and influence one another. While some of the points she makes about stylistic differences are certainly valid and important, I find the distinction between "books in a series" and "series books" unhelpful when one is trying to determine how they function culturally. Regardless of whether a series conforms to the "series book" style or the "books in a series" guidelines, they are still written with the intention that readers will read them as a set, that if they enjoy a particular character or characters, they will continue to buy books that involve those characters. In addition, we seem to have come full circle when it comes to having characters who age as a series progresses. While letting characters age over the course of a series was a commonplace in the nineteenth century, it disappeared almost completely by the middle of the twentieth century. The last of L. M. Montgomery's *Anne of Green Gables* series, *Anne of Ingleside*, was published in 1939, while the last of the *Chronicles of Narnia* series was published in 1956. In both these series, the main characters age considerably, and Anne even has children and grandchildren of her own. However, after the 1950s there were not many girls' series that featured aging characters; the most popular followed the "series books" guideline that had characters aging very little or not at all. Therefore, within this study I draw freely from both "books in a series" and "series books," in the belief that they all are part of the same genre and publishing tradition, and certainly part of the same world of reading for girls.

Issues of Race, Class, and Religion

The series books examined in this study clearly represent a very specific segment of the population. The books themselves were all produced in the Northeast; the female heroines depicted in the stories are almost all Northeastern, white, Protestant, and middle or upper class. Elsie Dinsmore is an exception; she is a Southerner but still an Evangelical Protestant. There are occasional depictions of immigrants, Irish or otherwise, and African Americans, particularly in the *Elsie* series, but most often they are stereotypically described as less intelligent than whites and permanently consigned to the lower classes. Series books were unequivocally promoting a white, Protestant, middle-class standard that would have been unreachable for a significant portion of the population, including anyone who was not native born and anyone with dark skin. The books themselves were intentionally produced for adolescent members of the white upper classes.[5] While it is possible that some immigrant and African American girls read the volumes, it would be very difficult to come up with solid historical proof of their readership. Literacy among African Americans was slowly improving during Reconstruction, but the vast majority of former slaves and their children still worked excruciatingly long hours for meager pay. When they could, parents sent their children to school — and evidence suggests that they sent their female children for longer periods of time than their male children — but black families had little opportunity for the kinds of leisure activities that were common among the white middle class, including reading, since it took the work of everyone in the family to eke out a living (Jones, *Labor of Love* 96–99).

When one considers that white writers and publishers produced series books for other white readers, it is not surprising that racial prejudices are reproduced and for the most part left unquestioned in the narratives. Assumptions about the intelligence of African Americans and Irish immigrants, the demeaning dialect that was often written for these characters to speak, and the indifference that white characters sometimes display toward racial and ethnic Others are all profoundly uncomfortable reminders of a systemic discrimination that was grounded in slavery, nativism, and eugenics. What is surprising, however, are the occasions when white characters do reach out to characters of other races and ethnicities and attempt to alleviate social and economic inequalities. Religious faith is usually the motivation for white characters who assist the less fortunate, and while their efforts are appreciated by their intended recipients, the texts make it clear that the unspoken condition of benevolence is conformity to middle-class faith, hygiene, and manners.

The fictional immigrants, poor whites, and blacks who are on the receiving end of charity in these texts are glad to embrace some of the markers of middle-class respectability: clean bodies and neatly kept clothes, for example, or more schooling for their children. Anne Scott MacLeod points to this same phenomenon in the works of Horatio Alger, Jr., and links it to the widespread American belief that ambition, hard work, and morality would allow anyone to become economically successful, no matter what their class origins:

> Alger's heroes want respectability much more than they want wealth or any particular achievement or position. But acceptance by a respectable middle class requires that these boys, who have been independent, however poor, give up their freedom and take on the coloration of those whose ranks they wish to join. And they do. Not reluctantly but eagerly, these aspiring lads correct their speech, discipline themselves to regular hours, and relinquish their spontaneous and spendthrift ways [*American Childhood* 79; see also 81–82].

While MacLeod mourns the loss of independence that Alger's boy heroes undergo in order to gain a foothold in the middle class, the postbellum female authors studied here persuasively illustrate that independence is a fallacy if you are a poor female or a child with little to no regular income, an uncertain food supply, and worn clothes that might not protect you from the elements. If you are a boy or a man, like Ragged Dick and his fellows, fate might be a little kinder; you can earn enough to at least keep yourself fed, and you have a cohort of friends/workers who will look out for you. Those who receive benevolence in postbellum series are most often women and girls who lack male providers or whose male family members are conspicuously absent or abusive. Louisa May Alcott, Isabella Alden, and Martha Finley, authors of the *Little Women*, *Chautauqua Girls*, and *Elsie Dinsmore* series, respectively, are acutely aware of the social and economic biases that made complete independence almost impossible for women and children of any race, even when their own racial and social prejudices are clearly on display in the text.

Strangely, religious denomination proves to be one of those prejudices, especially in Finley's case. Religious faith and faith-based benevolence, which give women a great deal of community power in postbellum narratives, can also foster divisiveness and open hostility between Protestants and non–Protestants. Protestantism (whether Evangelical or liberal) is the uncontested religious denomination in series books from this period. The denunciation of those who practice other religions is often far more bitter and forthright than racial and ethnic prejudice; while the latter may have been unconscious manifestations of widely shared attitudes, the former was a conscious assault on denominations that were seen as threats to Protestantism. The *Elsie Dinsmore* series contains the most prominent examples of arguments with individuals who do not practice Protestantism, particularly Catholics and Mormons;

author Martha Finley repeatedly constructed conversations between her characters as theological debates, with Protestantism the predetermined winning side. As discussed in Chapters Two and Three, girl heroines were often the messengers who proselytized to those who practiced a different religion or no religion at all. On the page, they are usually successful in persuading others to convert to their Protestant theology.

In order to understand the place that girls and their religious convictions held in postbellum society, however, I first had to grapple with several interrelated problems: defining what "adolescence" meant to medical and social science practitioners in the nineteenth century, the ages encompassed by that term, and the emergence of adolescents as a distinct social category in the U.S.

Defining Adolescence

Adolescence was not defined as a separate period of life for much of the nineteenth century, and so trying to determine how society thought about the teen years during Reconstruction can be difficult. Even establishing an age range for adolescence can be hard. Joseph Kett and Jane Hunter have found that the "adolescents" or "youth" of the mid- to late nineteenth century were typically older than the children we now think of in those categories, ranging anywhere from fourteen or fifteen to twenty. Changing patterns of schooling account for part of this age discrepancy. Antebellum schooling had worked around the planting and harvest seasons on farms, in order to allow children of all ages to help with the intensive work. School was only held for a few months out of the year, so completing grades took a longer period of time. Students might be nineteen or twenty before they finished a full course of study. Starting in the 1850s, however, compulsory education laws were slowly put into place and school years were steadily lengthened, allowing both students and teachers to cover more material. At the same time, urban schools were gradually systematized so that younger children from six or seven to thirteen were placed in one building and older children were taught separately in a high school. In rural areas, however, the older model of schooling remained through much of the second half of the century, and rural schools still had students ranging in age from four to twenty-one (Kett 122–127).

Initially, the longer school years along with the extra grades established in high schools meant, in practice, that it was harder for some children to receive an education beyond primary school. Public high schools frequently had entrance examinations, and their student body was often quite small. For those who could not or did not wish to pass the exams, school through the age of fourteen was enough (Kett 127–129). Gender was also a consideration; boys often left high school after a year or two so they could work and provide additional family income. Families were more willing to forgo the lower wages of girls in order for their daughters to attain a high school education. Education meant refinement, and refinement meant more secure class standing for an entire family, achieved through the young female(s) of the house. A high school diploma could serve as a teaching credential, and many families saw teaching as helpful economic insurance for their daughters, a respectable profession in which a girl could make a living either before she married or if she did not marry (J. Hunter 170–174).

In general, as more and more schooling was required of young people by law, adolescence became more and more entrenched as a transitional period of life that allowed for greater emotional and intellectual maturity while preserving freedom from adult responsibility. However, education was not the only factor that shaped social perspectives on adolescence, nor were adolescent behaviors then necessarily the same as they are now. While Kett finds that the age between childhood and marriage has been considered a unique period of life at least as far back as the 1840s, the typical markers that we associate with modern adolescence (social awkwardness, parental resentment, a social preference for friends and peers over family, defiance of adult authority, etc.) were not usually present.

In her study of nineteenth-century children's fiction, in which she quotes many females who wrote memoirs of their childhoods, Anne Scott MacLeod finds no trace of the alienation from family that we now take for granted as part of the adolescent experience. Using memoirs of women who grew up before 1875, MacLeod observes that there was much more freedom and much less sex differentiation for girls than is generally supposed. Girls learned trapping and hunting along with housework and were often permitted to play with their brothers and other neighborhood boys as well as other girls. They climbed trees, explored the outdoors, and invented games for their indoor amusement. The memoirs also suggest that housework was not solely assigned to female children; boys were expected to help, too, and tasks were often assigned based on a child's preference rather than any assumptions about their gender. Girls were not asked to give up their freedom until they were at least thirteen, often fifteen, and sometimes even older (*American Childhood* 6–13). Hunter finds that this same ideal of an extended period of freedom for girls held true for girls growing up in the 1880s. A girl's transformation to adulthood was gradual, often signified in incremental steps like the lengthening of her dresses, the arrangement of her hair, and the wearing of corsets. Most parents did not ask girls to completely give up their more undignified forms of recreation until they were sixteen, and eighteen seems to have been the most significant age, signaling legal maturity and eligibility for marriage (J. Hunter 140–145).

So adolescence in the postbellum period was a process of maturation, and parents prolonged that period of freedom as much as possible for their daughters. What is more, girls in particular seem to have been fairly happy, in most cases, to enjoy the freedom they were given and not revolt against parental requests or social boundaries. MacLeod speculates that girls must have been highly aware of their limited options if they refused to conform to the expectations for young ladies once they reached sixteen or eighteen. While they may have resented the loss of their freedom (and they frequently expressed that resentment and grief in memoirs and fiction),[6] most of them opted to follow the prescriptions for a woman's behavior that would gain them comfortable lives in good economic circumstances (MacLeod, *American Childhood* 12–14 and 27–29).

Adolescence as we understand it today is actually a relatively new phenomenon, emerging in the last two decades of the nineteenth century and the first two decades of the twentieth. Kathy Peiss and Sarah Chinn argue that the children of immigrants were actually the first segment of the population to embrace the teen years as a period of independence from and even rebellion against adult authority. Child labor laws in the major Northeastern and Midwestern cities meant that childhood, the period of life when children attended school and were free from wage-earning responsibilities, was extended to age fourteen, fifteen, or sixteen. Immigrant young people who were legally old enough to work therefore dominated urban factory jobs, and they claimed new urban leisure spaces as their own, particularly dance halls, amusement parks, movies, and department stores. As wage earners who contributed a significant portion of the family income, young people argued with their immigrant parents that retaining part of their wages was their due for the work they performed. Keeping a portion of their paychecks gave them a small disposable income that they happily spent in mixed-sex social spaces, away from their parents and any neighborhood chaperones who might have tried to enforce traditional gender divisions and behavior (Peiss 34–55; Chinn 4–12). Peiss demonstrates that working, unmarried immigrant girls had many opportunities for social interactions both at work and after hours, but that conflict with parents often erupted when girls refused to turn over all of their paycheck or did not help with housework and the care of younger siblings (67–72). Chinn shows that dance halls in particular were just as important to young immigrant men as to young women, for dance halls provided a secluded space that was removed from the normal gossip networks of the street, the church, and the workplace. Young people could engage in the new, risqué dances like the turkey trot and the shimmy, drink, smoke, and sometimes engage in sexual activities without fear of being discovered by their parents or other community authorities (103–129). Ultimately, Chinn says, the adolescent identity and culture of urban working-class youth made their way into the American mainstream through middle-class intellectuals like Emma Goldman, Margaret Mead, and Randolph Bourne, all of whom disseminated changing ideas about youth thanks to their intersecting social circles of immigrants, workers, students, and bohemians (11).

Margaret Mead's work was particularly important in defining scientific and cultural ideas about adolescence. Her three anthropological studies, *Coming of Age in Samoa*, *Growing Up in New Guinea*, and *Sex and Temperament in Three Primitive Societies*, all focused specifically on rites of adolescence and sexual maturity in tribal societies that Mead researched. Chinn and literary critic Kent Baxter both agree that the thrust of Mead's argument was that norms of adolescence and sexuality are socially constructed rather than biologically determined. That larger truth applied as much to the United States as it did to the tribes of Samoa and New Guinea. The expectations surrounding youth were highly variable and diverse depending on one's country of residence. The prescriptions being put forth by scientists, social commentators, and reformers about the young people of the U.S. were not the sole "truths" about adolescent development; they were truths and anxieties specific to a particular time, place, and population. Those anxieties included worries about premature sexual development, juvenile delinquency, and familial conflict between parents and children (Baxter 44–72; Chinn 142–151).

The other major player who both promoted the study of adolescence and fueled the worries about it was psychologist Granville Stanley Hall, president of Clark University from 1888 to 1920. Hall wrote a massive two-volume treatise entitled *Adolescence* that was published in 1904 and covered every topic from physical and sexual development through religious conversion, education, and juvenile delinquency. Hall was primarily concerned with the effects of industrialization on the physical and mental development of adolescents. In practical terms, Hall feared that juvenile delinquency and sexual permissiveness, which were already perceived as contagious vices of urban working-class youth, would spread among middle-class youth. Hall saw the emotional turmoil of adolescence as biological in nature, while Mead saw it as cultural (and Mead was actively revising and rebutting Hall's ideas a generation later), but they shared worries about adolescent culture, teenage independence, juvenile delinquency, and sexual activity (Baxter 44–46 and 61–71; Chinn 16–28 and 142–151).

Fears about adolescent sexuality were actually nothing new by the time Hall and Mead produced their work, particularly when it came to girls. Chinn places the earliest date of her study at 1880, but in 1873, Harvard Medical School professor Dr. Edward Clarke wrote a book titled *Sex in Education; Or, A Fair Chance for the Girls* that inflamed the debate over female sexuality and intelligence. Opponents and advocates of women's rights, historians of women and education, and feminist theorists have repeatedly referenced Clarke's study since the time of its publication.[7] Hall himself cited Clarke in his chapter on female education. Clarke's basic argument ran thus: Young women who ignored their menstrual cycles and attempted to function normally during their periods were actually ruining their health and reproductive organs. In particular, girls who spent too much time and mental power on their schoolwork were in danger of becoming sterile, invalids, or mental patients because they were draining necessary energy away from their uterus and ovaries. Girls' reproductive capacity meant that they had less stamina than men and were more susceptible to illness (Brumberg, *Body Project* 8). Excessive study would only increase the potential for problems in an already delicate biological system. Female fertility thus became a justification of social conservatives for denying young women a college education, though the existence of Mount Holyoke Seminary, Vassar, Wellesley, and Smith Colleges testified that society's objections to college diplomas for women were already eroding.

Ultimately, current concepts of adolescence were shaped by a number of overlapping historical changes: industrialization, child labor laws, and large populations of immigrants and their children in major cities, the systematization and grading of common schools, the addition of high schools, opportunities for mixed-sex socializing both in school and in commercial venues of leisure, and the interests and fears of anthropologists, psychologists, and educators as they strove to understand a newly visible and growing segment of the population.

Harnessing the Spending Power of Adolescents

Like adolescents themselves, adolescent literature remained broadly and loosely defined throughout much of the nineteenth century, depending on the opinions of parents, teachers, and critics to mark its shifting boundaries. Ilana Nash and Grace Palladino have both suggested that awareness of teens as a discrete social group and capitalist market category did not emerge until sometime between the 1910s and the 1930s, when the solid emergence of the high school as a transitional institution for young people marked them as a specific segment of the population. Although members of the medical and social science communities had recognized adolescence as a biological phase, the recognition of adolescents as a distinct group by other cultural institutions was slow and uneven (Nash 17; Palladino 3–6). However, the work of historian Lisa Jacobson shows that children and teens, grouped largely under the rubric of "youth," were primary targets for advertising as early as the 1890s. The beginnings of this advertising trend can be found in the trade cards of the 1870s and 1880s, which were collected by children and young people for their bright color images. Trade cards were one way to expose children to brand names, and promoting attachment to particular brands in children meant, advertisers hoped, brand loyalty once those children reached adulthood (Jacobson 19–20; see also Garvey 16–50).

By the 1900s, children were frequently featured in periodical ads, and the ads appealed as much to adult consumers as to children themselves. Children were often associated with purity and innocence, and using them as spokespersons for a product promoted the idea that the product in question was also pure and healthy (Jacobson 20–23). On the other hand, children in advertisements who openly expressed their preferences for a particular brand, even to the extent of misbehaving, appealed to adults for a completely different reason: "[T]he naughty, cunning prankster figured as an emblem of the spiritedness and spontaneity that many found lacking in middle-class culture. Simply put, parents preferred a little spunk in their child" (Jacobson 26). Images of children helped to sell products to adults because they were culturally associated with both purity and play, innocence and mischief.

Some of the periodicals published in the 1900s and 1910s were wildly popular with children and teens. *St. Nicholas* is the most obvious and longest-running example, but *Boys' World*, *Girls' Companion*, and *American Boy* are other periodicals that prominently featured advertisements directed toward their young readers. Interestingly, it was the publishers of periodicals who were promoting children-as-consumers to the advertising industry, not the other way around. Periodical publishers actively sought to convince advertising firms that placing ads in periodicals for children and youth would pay off both in the short and long term. Children would want to purchase the items advertised for their own homes, and the earlier children learned brand names and associated them with leisure and fun, the longer they would be a loyal purchaser of particular brands. Jacobson locates a shift in thinking about children's potential as consumers in these turn-of-the-century periodicals:

> A generation of magazine readers and trade card collectors had encountered images of children, if not actual real-life children, who actively identified with branded goods and incorporated trade names into their memories and their play.

Eager to build on that legacy, children's magazine publishers began to push for a broader view of children's marketing significance — one that more firmly acknowledged children as consumers with distinct needs and interests, and the power to influence the spending of family and peers [26–27].

In other words, periodical publishers were the major force behind the recognition of children and adolescents as a consumer group. By the 1920s, the magazine publishers had the advertisers convinced. Children became a separate market, one that was to be capitalized on as much as possible. More and more middle-class youths had money of their own to spend on whatever they liked, and what was more, they often influenced the buying decisions of their parents. Consumption became a leisure activity that middle-class adolescents could indulge in, like the working-class immigrant youths who preceded them.

In this particular case, magazine and periodical publishers were ahead of book publishers in singling out children as a market category. Beverly Clark argues that the category distinctions and readership divisions between "children's" and "adult" literature did not emerge until the turn of the twentieth century and the separation was fostered primarily by the white male editors of the *Atlantic*, the *Nation*, and other journals, who also had a vested interest in defining the emerging canon of American literature (Clark, *Kiddie Lit* 55–59). Books in the nineteenth century were enjoyed by adolescents *and* their parents; a family's collection of books was often communal and used to entertain multiple generations of readers. Separate categories of literature for children and teens had not yet been developed or marketed by publishers. Literature that was read to the family had to accommodate all ages, and parents often supervised the private reading of their daughters. While I talk more extensively about the social purposes of girls' reading in Chapter One, it is worth saying here that postbellum series books often featured girls who went through all stages of life: childhood, adolescence, courtship, marriage, motherhood, and beyond. In some cases, the series would start when a heroine was in childhood or adolescence and then follow her through the rest of her life. Series heroines, like their readers, aged in the seventy-five years between the Civil War and the Great Depression. Not until the advent of Nancy Drew would publishers begin to understand that heroines who *never* aged (or aged very little) were the key to an almost limitless shelf life.

Publishers' advertisements for nineteenth-century series books bear out Clark's assertion; they frequently do not distinguish between books for adults and teens, or even books for adults and children. Nor is there any consistent recognition of children or adolescents as a unique advertising group, although they are occasionally singled out. A quick search for the ads of Dodd, Mead, and Co. in the *American Periodicals Series* database turned up four advertisements covering the years from 1870 to 1894.[8] Dodd, Mead, and Co. was responsible for printing Finley's *Elsie Dinsmore* and *Mildred Keith* series as well as Elizabeth Champney's *Witch Winnie* series, all of which appear at some point in the advertisements.

The earliest advertisement, a full page from 1870 that appeared in the *American Literary Gazette and Publishers' Circular*, specifically classifies the books advertised as "Juvenile Books," but their intended audience is "the Trade and the Public," not adolescents in particular. The page contains blurbs about *Elsie Dinsmore* and *Holidays at Roselands* among others, both of which had already reached their fifth edition. The reference to "the Trade" suggests that the ad was meant to catch the attention of booksellers, while "the Public" could encompass anyone from eight to eighty who had sufficient vocabulary to read the books described.

The second and third advertisements were published in 1880 and 1894, respectively, and both include one or two books in Finley's *Elsie* or *Mildred Keith* series. In neither ad are Finley's books described as being for juveniles; they are listed alongside other adult titles and the only notations concern the edition, previous titles in the series, or the popularity of the series.

Finally, the last ad consists of two consecutive pages in volume 48.6 of *Century Illustrated Magazine*, published in October of 1894. While the first page contains volumes that are clearly all meant for adults, including memoirs, travel narratives, literary criticism, and fiction by Dickens and Josiah Allen's Wife, the content of the second page is more ambiguous. A volume of Welsh poetry is followed by a book of elegiac sonnets that commemorates childhood, and those are followed by a book of literary essays. Fully half the page is taken up by an ad for a fifteen-volume encyclopedia. However, the rest of the list consists mostly of books that we would identify as "juveniles": *The Sherburne Cousins*, part of a series by Amanda M. Douglas, *Witch Winnie at Shinnecock*, *Elsie at the World's Fair*, and *First in the Field*, a novel for boys. Interestingly, the description of the latter contains the only mention of a specifically juvenile audience, and in this case the audience is male. The author, George Manville Fenn, is lauded "as a writer of the most wholesome and engrossing stories for boys" who "mingles adroitly information with incident and adventure." Why Dodd, Mead, and Co. would choose to highlight this single story as a boys' book is hard to know. Perhaps they felt that women and girls alike would read the novels by Douglas, Finley, and Champney but thought it unlikely that boys and grown men would want to read the same things. On the other hand, their ad from 1870, twenty-four years before, seems to promote juvenile literature as a particular class of books. The publishing company's ideas about audience were not consistent; in some ads they promoted books as specifically intended for juveniles, while in others, books that would now be grouped as juvenile series were placed among other adult publications without comment.

While book publishers may not have had a solid grasp on the idea of adolescents as a distinct group of readers, there is considerable evidence to suggest that they understood the importance of girlhood as a stage of life and a topic of cultural interest. Even if the readers of Finley and her contemporaries were adult women, girlhood played a prominent part in the narratives they were purchasing. Literary critic Peter Stoneley makes a solid case that the book publishing industry recognized much earlier than most other commercial institutions that female adolescence or girlhood was a distinct social category with its own set of cultural norms. While he concentrates primarily on individual novels like *An Old-Fashioned Girl, Hans Brinker, Rebecca of Sunnybrook Farm, Daddy Long-Legs,* and *A Girl of the Limberlost,* the postbellum series fiction that I examine in Chapter Two confirms his claims. Although most of these series feature heroines who eventually grow up, girlhood is still central to their spiritual development and their future as social activists. Authors and publishers understood the cross-generational appeal of American girlhood as a subject, even if they didn't yet see girls themselves (or youth in general) as a powerful group of consumers.

By the turn of the century, Stratemeyer and other series book producers would fully grasp the importance of girls as economic consumers and American symbols of youth and vitality. "New Girl" heroines joyfully embraced their new consuming power and reveled in the new independence and individuality offered by commodities like Parisian fashions and motor cars. Series books reveal profound cultural shifts in attitudes toward girls, their education, their spirituality, their community influence, their independence, and their buying power from the end of the Civil War through the Progressive Era. These texts are one part of a cultural discourse about what it means to be an adolescent girl in the U.S.; they help us see how girls' role slowly changed from one of spiritual leadership and community influence after the Civil War to one of independent, responsible consumers by the turn of the century.

Notes

1. It should be noted that the ideal of True Womanhood was almost exclusively applied women who were white and middle class. It was believed that working class white women, black women, and immigrants were incapable of adhering to the chaste sexual and high moral standards required of middle-class white women. These assumptions about other racial and class groups, no matter how false they were, provided a foil for the white middle class that allowed them to believe in their own mental and

moral superiority. See Barbara Welter, "The Cult of True Womanhood, 1820–1860," *American Quarterly* 18 (Summer 1966): 151–175; Nancy F. Cott, *The Bonds of Womanhood: Woman's Sphere in New England, 1778–1835*; Carroll Smith-Rosenberg, "The Female World of Love and Ritual: Relations Between Women in Nineteenth Century America" in *Disorderly Conduct: Visions of Gender in Victorian America*; Jeanne Boydston, "The Pastoralization of Housework," reprinted in *Women's America: Refocusing the Past*, 6th ed., ed. Linda K. Kerber and Jane DeHart; Jeanne Boydston et al., *The Limits of Sisterhood: The Beecher Sisters on Woman's Rights and Women's Sphere*; Ann Douglas, *The Feminization of American Culture*; Barbara Leslie Epstein, *The Politics of Domesticity: Women, Evangelism, and Temperance in Nineteenth Century America*; Lori Ginzberg, *Women and the Work of Benevolence: Morality, Politics, and Class in the Nineteenth-Century United States*.

2. The concept of cultural work is drawn from Jane Tompkins, in her book *Sensational Designs: The Cultural Work of American Fiction 1790–1860*. On page 200 she offers this definition: "I see [novels'] plots and characters as providing society with a means of thinking about itself, defining certain aspects of a social reality which the authors and their readers shared, dramatizing its conflicts, and recommending solutions. It is the notion of literary texts as doing work, expressing and shaping the social context that produced them, that I wish to substitute for the critical perspective that sees them as attempts to achieve a timeless, universal ideal of truth and formal coherence." For further explanation of the term, see xii–xviii and 38.

3. It is difficult to know how girls might have received the social and cultural messages that series authors wrote for them. Asserting causality between reading and action has long been a tricky issue for historians and literary critics. Working in the past makes finding that connection between reading, thought, and action even more difficult. In the absence of written proof that girls read particular books and then changed their behavior, all one has to go on are authorial intentions (which, like readers' reactions, are not always recorded), sales figures, and the texts of the books themselves. Those who study the reading habits of living women and girls have had some success in establishing the links between reading and behavior. Meredith Cherland, a professor of literacy education, has extensively studied the reading patterns of twentieth-century sixth-grade girls, and finds that when girls read about and act upon models that help them articulate their desires and needs, whether in school or with their families, it is a political act in the sense that it will help determine what kind of women the girls will grow up to be. Girls' actions help shape their psychology by either constructing or removing cultural and social barriers. Even when books are trying to socialize girls into certain behaviors, readers choose among the options presented to them and appropriate what is useful and encouraging, rejecting strategies that do not work in their particular circumstances. Literary critic Janice Radway makes a similar observation about adult women romance readers, who mostly read to escape their everyday lives but nevertheless feel that they are sometimes changed for the better by reading romance novels and assessing their own domestic situations. What these scholarly observations indicate is that women of all ages can, and often do, find strategies for personal and social change in their reading.

Because the books studied here are one hundred years old or more, finding actual reader responses to these texts would be extraordinarily difficult, if not impossible. While thinking about the ways girls might have responded to these texts is intriguing, in this study I chose to focus on the interplay between textual representations of girlhood in series books and the changing nature of girlhood in the U.S.

4. For more information on Marion, Pickford, and Davies, see Kevin Brownlow, *The Parade's Gone By*; Eileen Whitfield, *Pickford*; Jeanine Basinger, *Silent Stars*; Cari Beauchamp, *Without Lying Down*. For connections between motion pictures and consumer culture, see Lary May, *Screening Out the Past*.

5. The Stratemeyer Syndicate did not even attempt a series featuring a black family until 1967, and even then it was a short-lived three volumes (Johnson, *Stratemeyer Pseudonyms* 220–221).

6. Anne MacLeod (*American Childhood*) discusses Susan Coolidge's *What Katy Did*, Alcott's *Jack and Jill*, and Carol Brink's *Caddie Woodlawn* as primary examples of girls' novels in which the heroines are "tamed" out of their wildness and forced to become accommodating, grown-up young ladies. Alcott, of course, also expressed her dissatisfaction with growing up through her most famous heroine, Jo March. The heroine of Alcott's *Moods*, Sylvia Yule, goes through a similar kind of taming.

7. See Hall, vol. 2, 569–570 for the reference to Clarke. The rebuttal to Clarke's publication was immediate and indignant. Books included *The Education of American Girls*, an essay collection edited by Anna C. Brackett and published in New York; *Sex and Education*, an essay collection edited by Julia Ward Howe and published in Boston, and *No Sex in Education*, a book by Eliza B. Duffey published in Philadelphia. All three volumes were published in 1874. Clarke's impact was lasting enough that the Association of Collegiate Alumnae commissioned a study in 1885 detailing the health statistics of female college graduates. Subsequent historical and theoretical examinations of Clarke include Bederman, *Manliness & Civilization*; Brumberg, *Body Project*; Horowitz, *Alma Mater*; Lowe, *Looking Good*; Palmieri, *Adamless Eden*; Russett, *Sexual Science*; and Solomon, *Educated Women*.

8. My heartfelt thanks to Dr. Deidre Johnson for locating the ads discussed here and sending them to me. Her quick and insightful response to my query about the way nineteenth century series were advertised was incredibly helpful. In addition, she suggested reviewing Anne Scott MacLeod's work, which added a highly informative layer to my thoughts about the evolution of female adolescence.

ONE

Learning to Be an Angel
Religion and Reading for Nineteenth-Century American Girls

In order to understand the potential impact of postbellum series books on white, middle-class girl readers, one must understand the places of both religion and reading in the lives of girls. Religion was a significant part of most late-nineteenth century series books, and religious faith was often bound up in the expectations and aspirations of parents, peers, and family. Parents expected their female children, particularly, to attend church and exhibit a certain level of piety, although the expression of that faith varied from Christian denomination to denomination. Since women were eventually expected to be the spiritual heads of the home, it was essential that girls develop some kind of religious faith and moral standards. Conversion to Christianity and membership in the Christian (preferably Protestant) church thus became one of the major goals of female adolescence. Reading, as girls' primary method of self-improvement and education, helped them accomplish this goal.[1] Parents generally monitored the reading of their female children and would often choose novels that were explicitly moral or religious. Despite this self-reinforcing system, however, reading also exposed young women to new social possibilities for themselves. This chapter will examine the roles that religion and reading played in the lives of postbellum girls, and the ways that both had the potential to shape social behavior and activism.

Girls and the Church

What work of kindness or charity is prosecuted without the aid of woman? Is not the cooperation of the female sex considered indispensable to success in all

> benevolent movements? Without their sympathies all such cases languish, while with them they flourish. Indeed, such is woman's influence, we may add, that she decides social morality. If her standard of excellence is high, the society in which she moves will be elevated. If otherwise, the morals of the community will be loose.... So great is the power of her precepts and example! No community is ever better than its females. With them it rises or falls in the sense of moral character [Thayer 53–55].

William Thayer wrote this passage in 1858 in a conduct manual for young women called *The Good Girl and True Woman; or, Elements of Success Drawn from the Life of Mary Lyon and Other Similar Concerns*. The book was still in print in 1863, in the middle of a war that was tearing the country apart and in which women were participating as nurses, spies, and occasionally soldiers, or doing their best to keep together their families and homes while most of the country's men were on the battlefields. However, Thayer's commentary on women's role as the moral standard bearers of society shows that the antebellum social expectations surrounding women had, rhetorically at least, stayed in place despite the upheaval of wartime. Morality was one of the cardinal virtues of womanhood, fitting hand-in-glove with piety, and the social expression of those virtues took place in church and benevolent organizations. Religion was seen as the "natural" arena of women, something that their inherently refined characters were particularly suited to. Thayer reiterates this belief in the idealized, essential virtue of women:

> Religion appears to be peculiarly adapted to the nature and condition of women. Hence the fact, that more females than males become the followers of Christ.... That so many of this class have embraced religion is a compliment to their intelligence, wisdom and moral convictions. It is due to woman more than to man that the Gospel has been preserved and advanced in the world. She has kept the fire burning upon its altar, when otherwise it would have expired [Thayer 345].

Thayer extols the abilities of women to "preserve and advance" the Gospel in the world. Their "natural" ability to do so both preserves the morality of the community and enhances their abilities to keep benevolence organizations "flourishing." Those natural abilities clearly carried enough social weight, even in the middle of a war, for Thayer's book to go through multiple editions. Women were still expected to be the moral and religious center of the nation, and they put that moral credibility to good use through the benevolence organizations that allowed them to enact community reform.

While considerable work has been done on women in various sects of the nineteenth-century Christian religion, particularly women within Evangelical Protestantism, sorting out how girls fit into the church is a bit more difficult. The picture becomes even muddier when one considers that by the time female children reached their late teens they were bordering on adulthood in the eyes of society, and so may have participated along with married women in church benevolence societies and other organizations. During the postbellum period, the idea of the "adolescent" or "teenager" as an age category had not yet been defined. This age fluidity in contemporary accounts and current historical studies makes it hard to determine exactly how girls were brought into the church or what their function was.

However, some scholarship in this area has been attempted and sheds light on the possibilities for girls. In his pioneering study of adolescence, historian Joseph Kett asserts that girls who experienced religious conversion during the Second Great Awakening (roughly 1790–1840) and joined a church often felt conflict between their girlish ambitions and pleasures and the self-submission and humility they saw as conditions of piety. Their anxiety was often long-standing, until they could find some way to resolve the seeming contradictions between pleasure and duty. Fortunately, the effects of the Second Great Awakening provided them with a way to do just that: "[It] indirectly provided an entrée for them into a legitimate form of female activity through the various mission and education societies which appeared in its wake" (Kett 76). Protestant benevolence organizations were particularly important in this regard, but some young women became missionaries, while others became Sunday School teachers. Young women also participated in prayer meetings, Bible study, and church fundraising. The variety of activities that were open to young women in churches gave them plenty of opportunities to be useful, active members of the community.[2] Being known as a church member was also highly important in terms of marriage; a girl who would raise her children as Christians fulfilled one of the main qualifications of True Womanhood: "Young men were exhorted to select mates of religious character, and a public profession of faith was the most visible seal of inner worthiness" (Kett 78). Girls who were known to have converted were more marriageable in the eyes of their communities, although it is probable that young men were not held to the same standard.

Protestant benevolence societies were a significant source of agency for women; such societies served several functions for upper- and middle-class white women beyond helping the poor. Barbara Berg argues that the female benevolent societies formed between 1797 and 1860 allowed women to articulate their frustrations with the fashionable expectations imposed upon them, to recognize common experiences with women of their own class, and finally to become aware of economic privations and hardships endured by women of lower classes. They formed friendships and developed their abilities as managers and workers. They asserted themselves in the face of sometimes active hostility from cultural authorities, particularly clergymen, councilmen, and husbands:

> [T]he multiplicity of societies and positions provided women with the opportunity to recognize and utilize their diverse abilities while permitting them to express their individuality through a unity with other women.... As women banded together to help impoverished females, they began to understand their personal thralldom. From this grueling and gradual recognition of their own tyrannized status, the volunteers eventually came to identify with females entirely different from themselves. Ultimately they would articulate a kinship with all women as the victim's of society's oppression [Berg 174–75].

Berg is also careful to point out that although piety was a primary motivating factor for the women involved in benevolence, and was often reflected in the literature of their associations, it was in fact the churches that often put up the greatest resistance to women working in benevolent societies. Clergymen feared that such public work among the lower classes would roughen women, damage their innocence, and interfere with their obligations to act as social ornaments. Some even feared corruption and moral degradation for women who were foolish enough to expose themselves to working men and women, many of whom were immigrants. Religious belief may have been a personal motive for many of the women, but the work of benevolence was often objected to or only cautiously sanctioned by the churches (Berg 146–154).

Lori Ginzberg disagrees with this assessment somewhat, arguing that women were often prompted to start a society by a sermon or a minister's appeal for charitable funds, and that the Protestant Church hardly objected to their formation. Likewise, Joseph Kett refers to Protestant benevolence as "an industry in itself" that "threw up relatively few barriers to female involvement" (76). However, whether or not the Protestant churches fully embraced women's participation in benevolence, it is clear that women did participate in large numbers.

The open hostility that Berg mentions may have had to do with one particular focus of many antebellum women's organizations: prostitution. Not only did men object to respectable women having contact with prostitutes, they resented women's efforts to control male solicitation and hold both sexes to an equal (and chaste) moral standard outside of marriage. By using reform organizations to try and lift women out of prostitution, upper-class women were not only attempting to reduce poverty and disease among women, but also uniting with lower-class women against sexual exploitation: "They did *not* emphasize differences between the prostitutes, the criminals, and themselves ... the volunteers stressed the similitude of all women. And as they labored to restore their beneficiaries to social acceptability, they simultaneously implied their dissatisfaction with the conventional feminine role" (Berg 218; emphasis Berg's). In other words, benevolence not only allowed upper- and middle-class women active, purposeful lives, but also gave them a way to articulate the problems inherent in their own social positions.

Mary Ryan argues in her landmark study of antebellum Oneida County, NY, that female benevolence and reform organizations were not solely meant to reduce the effects of poverty and help prostitutes regain their respectability. For the women of this New York county, the Moral Reform Society served other purposes as well: girls working as servants were frequently rescued from abuse by male employers and placed in better, more respectable homes; men who were known to be sexually promiscuous were shunned and had their misdeeds publicized to the city at large; and young people were encouraged to adhere to premarital celibacy for their own health as well as to avoid social scandal and illegitimate children (116–127). By using public opinion against sexual offenders and doing their best to enforce celibacy among single men as well as women, women who participated in moral reform began to create a specifically middle-class moral code that was not only about religious virtue, but also about respectability: "[T]he temperance and moral reform organizations performed a function that would later be assumed by the family, the socialization of children and young adults to the traits of character necessary to secure a comfortable social and economic niche..." (Ryan 142). In extending their moral responsibilities beyond the home and working to eliminate poverty and social vices, Protestant women were key players in articulating and enforcing the values of the newly-forming middle class, including chastity, piety, and temperance.

Ruether and Keller, Berg, Ryan, and Ginzberg all agree that organized benevolence allowed women to not only gain administrative and political skills, but also to gain a greater understanding of women of other classes. There were frequently blind spots in their perceptions concerning racial and religious differences, but that did not prevent upper-class women from feeling sympathy for others who were in worse circumstances than themselves. In many ways it was remarkable that white women of the upper classes were able to connect with women of other classes and races on such an emotional level. They helped other women who were in need of material assistance and learned about their own needs in the process, all while maintaining a perfectly respectable, moral status within their communities.

More recently, Anne Boylan has argued against this position, stating that the efforts of women in antebellum benevolence organizations actually managed to solidify class and racial lines in Boston and New York by placing clear borders around the religious and social behavior of the middle and upper classes. This was particularly true in Boston, where Unitarianism was the chosen denomination of most of the city's upper class, and Evangelical Protestantism became a social marker of the emerging middle class. Boylan thus complicates the idea that benevolence organizations were always vehicles for diminishing class and racial divisions; at least some of the time benevolence workers managed to reinforce those barriers. For the purposes of this study, however, her scholarship is undeniably important because it details the ways in which reform organizations recruited adolescent girls to continue their work and create multi-generational associations. Most often, adult women's societies formed junior auxiliaries that were expressly meant to encourage girls' involvement:

> Beyond collecting contributions, making clothing, or distributing tracts, subsidiary organizations served the important function of training and recruiting potential new members. Most were peopled with young women, often the single daughters of parent society leaders.... Formally organized with constitutions, lists of officers, and (sometimes) published annual reports, "juvenile" auxiliaries effectively propagated the ideals and practices of evangelical womanhood. Less formal practices, such as encouraging girls' and young women's charitable donations, had a comparable effect [Boylan 29].

Boylan details the lives of several young women who underwent conversion and joined women's organizations as a method of socially expressing their new faith and putting their religious convictions into practice. Such a move not only allowed girls to demonstrate their piety in the public arena, but also gave them new avenues for self-expression and personal fulfillment.

An additional benefit of undergoing conversion and accepting church membership was the agency that was given to women members to bring others into the church. A young woman who underwent a religious experience, either at a revival or through an organized church class, could then carry her religion into her family and community: "Because women were understood to be more religious than men, they were seen as the natural subjects of revivalism and as more effective evangelists in their homes and immediate communities" (Ruether and Keller x). Not only could they instruct or reprimand the males of their household as well as the females, but once they became a little older they could also be community leaders in conversion and church membership. Being able to claim converts was often a source of empowerment for women, albeit in an indirect way: "Women often regarded revivals, and especially the conversions of formerly irreligious men, as victories, though they were careful to point out that in scoring such triumphs they were acting only as the agents of Christ and not for themselves" (Epstein 48).

The power to bring others into the church (either through informal conversation, revivals, or Sunday School classes) would have become particularly important to women by mid-century. It became increasingly difficult after 1830 for women to gain permission to preach from any denomination. Churches that were originally open to women preachers, such as the Methodists, African Methodists, and Freewill Baptists, began to doubt the wisdom of allowing women to preach even in an informal capacity: "Besides fearing that female preaching had begun to gain acceptance within their own churches, mainline ministers also worried — with good reason — that it had paved the way for more radical kinds of women's activism" (Brekus 278). Revivalist Charles Finney came in for a good share of clerical wrath due to his extensive encouragement of female preaching during revivals and prayer meetings. He also taught woman's rights activist Antoinette Brown Blackwell while she attended Oberlin College, and she became the first woman to be officially ordained by a church (in her case, the Congregationalist church).[3]

It is worth noting that preaching was an activity distinct from the tradition of "exhorting," in which a congregant, male or female, would tell the story of their own conversion and urge other members of a congregation or participants in a revival to become part of the Christian faith. Women had served as exhorters in the revivals of the First (1730–1760) and Second Great Awakening and had often been encouraged to do so by the newly-emerged denominations they served. Lay exhorters, however, did not have the authority to deliver sermons or preach. Preaching was specifically defined as explaining Biblical texts and conferred an institutional authority on the speaker that was never given to lay exhorters, especially to women (Berg 44–61, esp. 48). There was a small group of female exhorters who made careers out of evangelism and believed they had as much authority as clergymen, but most women saw preaching as something beyond their authority and skills (Berg 52–55).

In order to stem the tide of female preaching and the potential for political activism, many churches began to discourage female speech and refused to grant women licenses or permission to preach in the second third of the nineteenth century. Instead, they emphasized women's ability to serve the community and society through church benevolence, abolitionist organizations, and temperance work, along with church fundraising and Sunday School teaching. It was a woman's responsibility to raise a family of Christians through a moral and pious example, not to preach in front of strangers.[4] These other kinds of work, including the possibility of bringing other members into the church through social and emotional influence, could still give women a great deal of status in the church even though they were no longer allowed to preach. Women responded to this forced redirection of their faith by moving into all other areas of church work with enthusiasm and large numbers. Ministers perhaps did not expect women to take over the day-to-day functioning of the church so thoroughly. Although we have little numerical evidence concerning the proportions of male and female members in Protestant congregations, the underlying issue for ministers may have been a loss of power in their own church:

> What is clear is that they felt increasingly dominated by their women members who had in the proliferating "societies" new arenas of activity available to them in the church; the ministers also perhaps felt increasingly drawn to their feminine congregation, and an issue of power or of attraction which was decidedly present became confused with an issue of numerical change which may or may not have been valid [Douglas 99].

In other words, whether or not the number of male congregants actually did decrease in the nineteenth century, male clergymen *perceived* their churches as mostly made up of women members, and it was those women who kept all of the various church "societies" organized and running. While plenty of ministers clearly appreciated the accomplishments of their female congregants both individually and collectively, a predominance of female activity in the church was also cause for anxiety. Ministers feared that their churches were in danger of becoming completely feminized and therefore divorced from the "male" public sphere of action and commerce. To make matters worse, women writers were often addressing issues of faith and morality in their work, encroaching further on the space that was meant for male preaching (Douglas 97–117). If those anxious preachers of the 1830s and '40s had been able to see how women would transform their social benevolence into national activism by the 1870s, their anxiety might have turned into full-blown panic. True Womanhood would extend its reach after the Civil War, moving from local organizations to national ones like the Chautauqua Institute and the Woman's Christian Temperance Union.[5]

The traditional distinction in U.S. women's history between the antebellum and postbellum periods, between "True Womanhood" and "New Womanhood," begins to break down when we consider the chain of events within Protestantism that shaped women's responses to both religion and social reform. Historians have often argued that the "Cult of True Womanhood," as Barbara Welter christened it in her 1966 essay, ended before the Civil War. Welter herself defined the period of True Womanhood as lasting from 1820 to 1860. Berg sees the height of Protestant female benevolence and the "woman-belle" ideal as spanning 1800 to 1860, moving back a little in time but not forward. Nancy Cott pushes the beginnings of the True Womanhood philosophy back to 1780. Nancy Woloch also sees 1860 as the crucial dividing year, dividing relevant chapters on the history of U.S. women into

"Promoting Woman's Sphere, 1800–1860," "Benevolence, Reform, and Slavery, 1800–1860," "Women at Work, 1860–1920," and "The Rise of the New Women, 1860–1920." Out of these scholars, only Cott suggests that True Womanhood and domestic ideals did not necessarily fade, but were put to different purposes in the latter half of the century:

> [T]he discourse of domesticity evolved (especially during the half-century of national consolidation after the Civil War) into a national standard, used to understand, measure, and invite in or cast out cultural and racial groups such as Mormons, Asians, and freed blacks, as well as diverse Europeans. It figured prominently in philanthropy and reform of many sorts.... Throughout the surges of immigration in the late nineteenth and early twentieth century, immigrants' adherence to standards of domesticity was judged a principle criterion of their suitability for American life [Cott, *Bonds of Womanhood* xxiv].

Even Cott was working in retrospect; this excerpt comes from the preface to the second edition of *The Bonds of Womanhood*, which was issued twenty years after the book's initial publication. Very little has been written to dismantle the idea that two utterly different conceptions of womanhood existed before and after the war. As easy as it is to use the beginning of the Civil War as the general dividing line between True Womanhood and New Womanhood, the New Woman did not truly emerge as a cultural idea until the 1890s. Nancy Woloch points this out in her introduction to "The Rise of the New Women," noting that the New Woman "had antecedents in the 1870s and 1880s" (275) but was not fully formed until the Progressive Era. The thirty years between 1860 and 1890 are crucial to understanding how the antebellum ideal of True Womanhood changed and expanded, creating the conditions for the emergence of the New Woman. The change from True Woman to New Woman was not so much a radical break as a gradual shift that emerged from both conservative and liberal possibilities. Women who had attempted to preach in the church in the antebellum period had been accepted and then silenced. Women who were committed to benevolence formed a great many charitable organizations, but often had to work against misconceptions about the safety and morality of their work, as well as sometimes fighting the male pastor and male members of their congregations. Postbellum women would continue these organizations after the war, but found new ways to combine religious beliefs and social reform efforts, expanding their efforts to the national level rather than working strictly on a local scale. Thus, "True Womanhood" as a cultural ideology did not disappear entirely after the war, but was reshaped and expanded to include larger social and political issues. Girls who came of age in the postbellum period reaped the benefits of this shift to national reform movements.

Jane Hunter has done the most extensive work thus far on girls and religion after the Civil War. Through her exhaustive search of diaries and letters, she finds that postbellum girls were susceptible to many of the same doubts and anxieties as their antebellum counterparts, as well as some of the same social expectations. They felt the potential consequences of displeasing their parents and other adults of their community; they knew the spiritual importance of joining the church, even if the pressure to have a "conversion experience" had eased: "By midcentury ... the expectation of a moment of sudden epiphany had been muted a bit; it was no longer necessary to have a moment of mystical communion to signify an indwelling Christ. Nonetheless, the anticipation of a mature coming-to-God pervaded and sometimes shaped the experience of youth" (J. Hunter 146). Depending on the faith of one's parents, active belief in God could be an expectation from childhood, constantly shaping everyday life as a girl grew up. Parents who were less stringent about religious faith often still hoped that their daughters would make some kind of commitment to the church. Hunter finds that by the 1880s, at least, religious faith was something that was supposed to be acquired during the teen years, so that girls often felt increasing pressure from family and friends to convert as they neared twenty. One girl diarist, Annie Cooper, joined the church on December 7, 1884, and noted, "I shall be 20 this week. I am so glad I have taken this step while I can say I am in my teens" (qtd. in J. Hunter 184).[6]

The prospect of vocalizing religious feelings in front of their parents, minister, and congregation was often stressful and embarrassing, for it contradicted all girls had been taught about "being good" and *not* speaking in public, *not* expressing forceful opinions, doing their best to be cheerful diplomats of the home: "Just when girlhood's lessons had been learned, religious profession required that they be overturned in a potentially embarrassing confession of religious enthusiasm. Coming in the context of a life defined by being good and subordinating selfish desires, such public self-revelation was anathema" (J. Hunter 149). The churches had done their work well in discouraging women's preaching; combined with other social strictures against women speaking in mixed public gatherings, speaking about newly-found faith in church had the potential to profoundly embarrass girls. A formal declaration of faith was not the only instance of public speaking that could send a girl into a crisis of confidence, either; smaller gatherings could be just as traumatic. Annie Cooper was asked by her minister to help with a female prayer meeting and exclaimed in her diary, "*Oh! My God! How can I?* ... I, who can not even, to save my life, say a single word at home, how can I brake through the barriers of timidity and natural diffidence to *such an extent as that?*" (qtd. in J. Hunter 148; emphasis Cooper's). If Cooper was so worried about her ability to speak at a prayer meeting, one can imagine the anxiety that accompanied speaking and/or being baptized in front of the entire church.

However, once the initial awkwardness of declaring church membership was over, girls who were approaching womanhood in the 1870s and 1880s would have found plenty of scope for their talents and ambitions in various local and national religious organizations. Sunday School, prayer meetings, and church benevolence societies were all places where girls might be both useful and religiously persuasive. Benevolence organizations continued after the war on a larger scale, working to relieve poverty and provide services on a local level and gradually evolving into organizations like the Chautauqua movement and the Woman's Christian Temperance Union, as well as many secular aid organizations. Historians Dorothy and Carl Schneider point out that the formation of the WCTU and the beginnings of the woman's rights movement were both, at least in part, a response to the refusal of churches to allow women to speak or preach, even if their desire to do so was based in the desire to speak about pressing social and moral questions:

> Both of these movements originated in part because of men's refusal to let women speak in the causes of temperance and abolition; both movements at least at first understood themselves as promoting religious values. Women's [sic] Christian Temperance Union president Frances Willard and temperance hatchet woman Carrie Nation saw their work as Christian ministry. And both afforded women experiences helpful in the pulpit [through public speaking] [Schneider and Schneider, *In Their Own Right* 59].

In other words, women formed their own organizations outside the church (and sometimes within it) because they were denied the option of speaking to the congregation on moral questions within the church, either as a preacher or as a layperson.

In *Learning to Stand and Speak: Women, Education, and Public Life in America's Republic*, Mary Kelley argues that antebellum women's seminaries and reading circles, along with benevolence organizations, were forums in which women learned to speak on contemporary political and social questions. Within the many women's academies and seminaries that opened in the first part of the nineteenth century, girls were taught the basics of rhetoric, composition, and debate along with many other subjects, including Latin and Greek. The original intent of school founders like Mary Lyon and Emma Willard was to educate women for "usefulness" in a variety of ways. While wealthier girls might pursue education in order to be a suitable "gentleman's companion," expected to talk intelligently on any number of subjects in drawing rooms and salons, other girls might teach, become missionaries, or organize voluntary associations. Writing and editing were also occupations that were increasingly open to women. In addition, women who married and became mothers claimed a responsibility for educating their husbands and sons in republican virtue and proper citizenship.

During their time at school, girls would often recite essays that they had prepared for class in front of their teacher and their peers. They would demonstrate their newly acquired knowledge in public examinations at the end of the year, in which they were compelled to stand and recite on any number of subjects for faculty, friends, community members, and sometimes important guests (Kelley, *Stand and Speak* 37–99). Students would also deliver essays during graduation exercises. In all of these ways, young women gained experience in speaking before an audience and presenting arguments on philosophical, moral, religious, and political questions.

Reading circles and literary societies were another way for girls to engage in debate. Adult women began organizing community reading circles just after the Revolution, well before the establishment of academies and seminaries. Such groups encouraged extensive reading, the formation of educated opinions, and literary creativity and production (Kelley, *Stand and Speak* 115–117). Similar organizations were created within new female academies and seminaries, either sponsored by teachers or organized by the students themselves. Often these groups produced their own fiction, poetry, and literary magazines. Some groups required that members present and/or debate on the weekly reading material at each meeting. Girls also had their work published in newspapers and school promotional materials (Kelley, *Stand and Speak* 99; 117–122).

One of the most important effects of these societies were the networks they created between students and alumnae, since school literary societies frequently published the letters of former students who were engaged in benevolence, teaching, and missionary work. Girls therefore learned of new prospects for community and social service through the news sent by graduates. Literary societies sometimes reached beyond their original goals to participate in some form of benevolence; indeed, the organizational structure of such societies was often consciously modeled after benevolent associations (Kelley, *Stand and Speak* 126). In pursuing education, intellectual argument, and public speaking in a community setting, either during school or after graduation, women prepared themselves to move into benevolence and reform as well as teaching and missionary work.

The opportunities for community discussion of social problems only increased as the Civil War approached, with abolition societies embracing both male and female members and women's rights advocates beginning to organize meetings. While women were often prohibited from speaking in public meetings comprised of both sexes, they made their voices heard in mixed private meetings, all-female meetings, and in print. After the war, the closely intertwined Chautauqua Institute and WCTU, particularly, provided occasions for public speaking, as well as additional education, that gave women confidence in their own abilities and allowed them to practice moral persuasion on a large scale.

The Chautauqua Institute and the Woman's Christian Temperance Union

The temperance movement really began in antebellum temperance organizations primarily made up of men who were church members and who already refused to drink alcohol. Women were originally excluded from these societies; they were simply encouraged by the male members to train their sons not to drink and discourage their husbands from doing so. In the 1840s, the secular Washington Society began to invite drinking men who wished to renounce alcohol to join their membership lists. This male organization also created the first women's auxiliary group, the Martha Washington Society. Eventually, the "Washington" groups died out and were replaced by the Sons and Daughters of Temperance, which were the primary temperance organizations in the U.S. for the twenty years preceding the Civil War (Epstein 91–93).

The impetus for women's extensive involvement in the temperance crusade, however, came with the Woman's Crusade of 1873–74. Dio Lewis, a man who made a living on the lecture circuit by talking about women's health, delivered a talk in Hillsboro, Ohio, in December of 1873 that encouraged the town's women to stand up against local saloons. At the conclusion of his lecture, a committee was formed to accomplish that objective, and the next morning eighty women gathered and began to invade the saloons with temperance pledges and prayers (Epstein 95).

The crusade quickly spread to surrounding towns and other Midwestern states, including Ohio, Michigan, Indiana, and seventeen other states. Ultimately, over one thousand saloons were at least temporarily closed as a result of women's efforts. While the effects of the Crusade were not permanent (most of the saloons eventually reopened), the women who had participated were profoundly affected by the experience. A good number of those women would find their way to the inaugural meeting of another important nineteenth-century organization: the Chautauqua Institute.

Chautauqua was originally an organized summer retreat for Sunday School teachers, ministers, and other church workers. It was meant to be "the national headquarters for progressive forces in the Sunday School Movement" (Rieser 37), and it fulfilled that function by offering two weeks' worth of lectures on pedagogy, Bible history and geography, and other subjects. It quickly expanded to include speeches and debates by famous scholars and speakers as well as a correspondence school, the Chautauqua Literary and Scientific Circle.[7] The first Chautauqua meeting took place in the summer of 1874 at Chautauqua Lake, New York, and included Presbyterians, Baptists, and Congregationalists as well as Protestants from other denominations. This institute would become the "mother" of all Chautauquas, spawning satellite organizations all over the country.

While the male leaders of Chautauqua were the public face of the organization, Chautauqua women were a key part of its social power and extensive outreach. As the organization grew, more and more women began to participate. Like their antebellum predecessors and many of their contemporaries, Chautauqua women used the safety of the home and family as their primary argument for involvement in reform: "[F]or public women to win acceptance, they would strike a Faustian bargain with tradition. In exchange for the unusual level of moral authority they held within the assembly, women rarely challenged patriarchal assumptions directly. Instead, they used the metaphors of domesticity to justify greater involvement in civic affairs" (Rieser 196–197). Chautauqua women did their best to reorganize and revolutionize their homes and churches from within, directing all kinds of church organizations, charities, Sunday Schools, soup kitchens, and health clinics. Their greatest contribution to national reform, however, was the formation and support of the WCTU.

The initial idea for the national Woman's Christian Temperance Union originated at the first Chautauqua meeting in 1874. Veterans of the Woman's Crusade gathered together to share stories about their temperance protests, and it was suggested that there should be a central organization to help coordinate temperance efforts. The women approached Chautauqua founder John Heyl Vincent with the idea, and he agreed to endorse it, after which the planning for a national convention in Cleveland was quickly carried out. The first national convention of the WCTU was held in November of 1874 (Rieser 180–181; Bordin 34–36), and there was a great deal of crossover between Chautauqua participants and WCTU members for forty years after that (Rieser 180–181).

Historian Andrew Rieser argues that Chautauqua was the most successful of the postbellum summer resorts and camp meeting institutes because it accomplished several important cultural moves simultaneously. First, it embraced ecumenical Protestantism and social Christianity, ideas which had already gained a firm foothold in the middle class thanks to antebellum benevolence organizations (Rieser 8–13; 163–165). Second, it attempted to make all activities spiritually enriching, both in the church and outside of it: "If Chautauquans had their way, no longer would the sacred be experienced in places far removed from the prosaic workings of community life — rather, all social activities, including leisure and education, were sacred" (Rieser 46). Third, in line with these principles, it offered a summer institute that was both educational and spiritual, a place that allowed the middle class to come and vacation with a higher purpose. Chautauqua thus helped make summer vacation an acceptable middle-class institution by gaining support from clerics and churches. Time away from the daily routines of home and work could be used for spiritual growth and encourage lay ministry once participants returned home (47–50). Ultimately, Rieser says, Chautauqua helped to solidify the middle class precisely because it encouraged its adherents to extend their religious beliefs and their hopes for social change into many areas of civic life (84–85).

Is it any wonder, then, that the women who participated in the Woman's Crusade for temperance in 1874 had no trouble conceiving of and organizing a national temperance organization, or that they found a ready ally in Chautauqua founder John Heyl Vincent? Trying to change the moral standards and behavior of communities through organized teaching was precisely what Chautauqua had been founded for; its beginning as an institute for Sunday School teachers contained the same basic mission as all of its later endeavors, including its correspondence school. Vincent fully believed in temperance as a cause and so could hardly refuse to support the idea of a national organization, particularly when it was being sponsored by women who also worked tirelessly for the Chautauqua program. What he could not foresee, however, were the ways in which women's activities for temperance and other causes would increasingly bring the political into the domestic and sacred sphere.

The WCTU perhaps best exemplifies the ways in which True Womanhood ideology expanded and shifted after the war. Ruth Bordin points out that in the antebellum years temperance women were expected to use their "moral suasion" and "influence at home" (8) to reform their male relatives. The male relatives would then, hopefully, wield their influence in politics to make laws regarding the drinking and selling of alcohol. While local and state legislation passed in the 1850s did reduce overall alcohol consumption, "production and use rose again rapidly during the Civil War, and the number of saloons grew quickly in the generally prosperous postwar period" (Bordin 6).

It was at this point that female temperance activists began to look to legal solutions at all levels, but postbellum women's desire to push the issues of temperance into the public sphere of government needed some justification:

> [T]he old concept [of woman as the protector of the home] provided the rationale for this leap into the outer world. If the saloon was a threat to home and hearth, was it not a woman's duty to invade the public sphere to defend what was universally acceded to be her special area of responsibility? To many temperance women, therefore, participation in the post–Civil War movement took place on a basis that *did not fundamentally alter* the ideology that held women responsible for the home [Bordin 8; my emphasis].

Woman's duty to protect the home and nurture the family, to fulfill her obligations as a True Woman, had not changed for those involved in temperance agitation. Their move into the public sphere was precipitated by a public threat to their homes and families: the saloon. It was as mothers, wives, and sisters that they stepped out into the public sphere to face that threat and hopefully eradicate it.

This does not mean, however, that WCTU women failed to learn about political agitation and lobbying. Far from it; they learned every political trick in the book: "[The WCTU] effectively used political influence and developed a range of sophisticated political weapons — testifying before Congressional committees, lobbying the members of legislative bodies, writing legislation, or hiring a professional paid lobbyist in Washington — to achieve political, primarily legislative, aims" (Bordin xiv). The women of the WCTU had entered public politics with the rhetoric of domesticity and the morality of wives and mothers to back them up. To effect real change, they had to become political strategists and learn the inner workings of state and national legislatures. Using their cultural mandate as the guardians of morality to enter the political arena was precisely what made WCTU women "radical"; the temperance organization was exactly the "radical kind of women's activism" (Brekus 278) that antebellum male preachers had feared would eventually emerge from female preaching. The fervent activity of Chautauqua women on behalf of temperance eventually led most of them to join the suffrage movement, despite Vincent's firm opposition to women's suffrage. Even Vincent himself came to acknowledge that the wish for suffrage was rational, since Chautauqua women were so dedicated to expanding the various social missions that the Institute had helped set in motion (Rieser 166; 180–184).

Although the WCTU's work culminated with Prohibition, passed in 1919 as the Eighteenth Amendment to the Constitution, temperance was not its only goal or the only area in which it had lasting legal effects. Beginning in the 1890s, WCTU workers managed to get many local and state bills passed that raised the sexual age of consent, established required educational curriculum on temperance, appointed women police officers to deal with women offenders, and created rehabilitation institutions for women and children who were disabled or delinquent (Bordin xiv; see also Odem 8–37).

The gains that the WCTU made over seventy years, however, could not have happened without an influx of new members, new young women to take up the projects and legislation and move them forward. One of the best ways to recruit a new generation of women into the work of organizations like Chautauqua and the WCTU was through a widely encouraged pastime for girls: reading.

Girls and Reading

Over the course of the nineteenth century, reading became an increasingly important leisure activity for middle- and upper-class women. Reading was an important method of self-cultivation and education; as literacy and schooling became more valued for both women and men, the demand for reading material also increased.

There were several groups that had a vested interest in reading as a skill and printed materials as a business. A large coalition of educators, reformers, and professionals supported the idea of increased literacy from motives of both moral conviction and profit. School reformers argued for a longer school year and more frequent average attendance for each student, believing that the erratic schooling that took place around farm planting and harvesting made for an undereducated populace. Teachers, school committee members, superintendents, book publishers and tradesmen, and textbook writers all stood to benefit from a longer school year (Kaestle 110–111; Soltow and Stevens 74–80). More schooling per student meant more readers, more textbooks, and a larger staff of teachers. As the reformers utilized the pages of new, rapidly expanding newspapers and found editors who were willing to be their allies on the editorial pages, they slowly won their points and school districts changed their policies. Local governments did not use uniform tactics to accomplish the twin goals of more school days and more frequent attendance, but districts and states achieved both: "[A]pproximately 90 percent of the adult white population, men and women, entered the literate category during the first part of the nineteenth century. By the 1840s America had the largest reading audience ever produced" (Kelley, *Private Woman* 10).

Women had a particular set of investments in spreading literacy, as Sarah Robbins shows in *Managing Literacy, Mothering America*. In the antebellum period, advocating literacy for both themselves and their children allowed women to expand the duties of republican motherhood while at the same time increasing their own access to education. Raising their sons as proper moral citizens meant that they needed to oversee learning at home until their sons went to school. At the same time, teaching their children how and what to read, and holding conversations about the lessons conveyed in schoolbooks, allowed women to raise responsible citizens for the nation as well as transmit a specific set of middle-class values to those children. As the nineteenth century progressed, "domestic literary management," as Robbins calls it, was performed not only by mothers, but by single female teachers, women writers, and women editors, as well as women who filled several of those roles simultaneously. The management of literacy opened up career opportunities for women by reinforcing an ideology that painted *all* women as mothers and teachers for the nation, regardless of their actual marital or maternal status. At the same time, the increasing assumption that women were the *only* fit teachers for children, especially young children, made room for expanded education curriculums and an increased number of seminaries for young women seeking to be teachers.

In the postbellum period, mothers, female teachers, and women writers became the primary transmitters of middle-class Protestant values, using their status as moral guardians to extend their influence through periodicals and novels. Women authors often emphasized women's religious and moral role in their writings for adults and children, and utilizing the Bible as an instrument of literacy helped reinforce women's position as moral teachers: "Repeated references to the Bible as the primary literature for literacy development helped situate women's domestic teaching in a tradition affirming believers' ability to access the Word directly. Such patterns aligned this feminized teaching with a potentially empowering version of spiritual life for women..." (Robbins 72). In other words, because the Bible was so often used as a tool for literacy and women were already seen as the primary moral teachers for the nation, their teaching of literacy both at home and in the schoolroom also added to their religious influence.

The increase in literacy had specific consequences for young women. More young women than ever before could read, and they had access to an unprecedented range of periodicals and books. Both public libraries and Sunday School libraries acted as free or inexpensive sources of reading material.[8] Those institutions did their best to stock books that were considered "suitable" for young women, although public librarians eventually had to compromise their belief in "genteel" reading for young women with girls' obvious desire for sensational romance. Middle- and upper-class girls were encouraged to read religious writing, history, philosophy, biography, travel writing, and science as part of a proper and thorough education. Parents, advice writers, and librarians considered novels a dubious form of reading. It was up to them to make sure that their daughters read the "right" kinds of stories, novels that would demonstrate a woman's place within the home and family. "Proper" novels for girls generally included Scott, Austen, Dickens, and Alcott (J. Hunter 57–62).

"Sensation" literature, or the literature of story papers and dime novels, was almost always considered unacceptable for middle-class girls, although some girls (like Alice Stone Blackwell, daughter of abolitionists and suffragists Lucy Stone and Henry Blackwell) fought with their parents over the right to read the story papers. While the production of this literature is discussed more fully in Chapter Three, its appeal for girls was in the romances that often depicted dangerous and thrilling experiences. Parents worried about the evil effects of heightened emotions and exposure to unwholesome behavior and sexuality (J. Hunter 66–68 and 78–80).

Another problem for middle-class parents may have been that story papers were highly popular among the working classes. Middle-class parents did not want girls to be exposed to the vulgar manners and lower morality of the working class, even if that exposure was only on the printed page. The readers of story papers and dime novels included members of the working class, of both sexes, as well as members of the middle class who read "cheap" literature on the sly. It is difficult to know for certain what postbellum workers read, but we do have evidence that the later story papers and dime novels played an important role in workplace culture. Unfortunately, there are very few accounts of working men's reading that include specific titles of dime novels or specific instances of reading. Working men and boys were avid readers of dime novels, including those who worked in factories, as farmers and mechanics, and as hotel employees. There is also anecdotal evidence that middle- and upper-class men would occasionally read dime novels (Denning 29). Public libraries run by the middle class, for the most part, chose to exclude dime novels and story papers from their inventory in favor of "good" reading that might improve the culture of the working classes. However, union libraries responded to the wishes of their workers and "bought only those books that would be widely read—novels, romances, travels, and elementary texts on mechanics and physics" (Denning 50). The sales of dime novels were enormous and made a pretty penny for their publishers, but neither the publishers nor the booksellers seem to have kept any consistent records concerning the class or age groups that bought them. This makes it difficult to determine how far dime novels penetrated into the middle and upper class (Denning 29; 27–46).

Perhaps counterintuitively, there seems to be more solid evidence and specific facts concerning what women workers read in the postbellum period. Nan Enstad and Michael Denning have demonstrated that some lower-class women found time to read during their workdays. Women in sweatshops, when they were left to themselves, read aloud dime novels or story papers that printed novels in installments (Enstad 51–60; Denning 197–200):

> Working women's act of reading at work, during their thirty- to forty-minute lunch hours, was a rejection of the relentless tedium of the workplace.... Women literally changed the shop itself during the lunch hour to a place that could provide relief from labor. In addition, by reading women refused to act like machines. They engaged their minds with thrilling adventures, and some simultaneously practiced their English literacy skills [Enstad 57–58].

Those workers who were literate could read to themselves, and those who were not might learn to read from others or listen to new stories being read. In addition to giving women workers some much-needed relief in their workday, Enstad points out that reading dime novels in English was part of the process of Americanization for immigrant workers (Enstad 55) and also allowed women to create "collective meanings and experiences in relation to their commodity consumption" (Enstad 57). Their shared reading was a crucial element in helping them to create a community of friends and allies in the workplace.

However, the widespread consumption of story paper and dime novels by working men and women would have set off alarm bells in the newly-forming middle class. Reading was supposed to be for self-culture and intellectual enjoyment rather than emotional stimulation. It therefore became something of a double-edged sword for Victorian girls: "On the one hand ... reading could be a way of demonstrating rectitude and diligence; on the other, it could be a route to indolence and the shirking of responsibilities.... Reading good books was of course a way of demonstrating virtue" (J. Hunter 71). Hunter argues that part of the importance of reading for middle-class postbellum girls was that reading gave them the opportunity to develop personalities and tastes outside of what was expected of them by their parents and social groups:

> Restrained from having too many real experiences, they drew on their surrogate reading lives to develop the sensibility and selves they would offer to the world.... In their judgment of their reading matter, carefully documented in diaries and journals, they developed fictive personalities, which coexisted with and sometimes trumped the dutiful daughter who lived at home [J. Hunter 57].

Reading allowed women to experience the outside world while still at home and understand the risks of failing to "be good" as well as the potential rewards for correct social behavior. Novel heroines, especially heroines of the more "thrilling" types of novels, often experienced situations where they almost lost their virtue or their moral authority. Often, virtue and moral authority were written as one and the same quality; to lose one was to lose the other. Some heroines almost became engaged to the wrong (read: immoral) man, or almost lost their virginity to a criminal, or almost lost their faith in God, or almost fell into prostitution. Reading girls could experience the thrill of nearly being "bad" even while they were on their way to being "good." For example, a girl who read Jane Austen's *Mansfield Park* could shiver with both delight and repulsion while Fanny Price considered marrying the rake Henry Crawford. Reading allowed imaginative access to dangerous and thrilling situations that could be highly damaging in real life, but on the page served to reinforce lessons about correct behavior. Girl readers could vicariously brush elbows with danger while outwardly demonstrating their "goodness" by reading acceptable literature.

Another worry for parents may have been the sheer *volume* of reading material that was available, particularly in spaces outside the home. Even by the Civil War, print of all kinds was pervasive in U.S. cities, and could be used for everything from advertisements, street signs, and handbills to currency, newspapers, and magazines. In his extensive study of print culture in antebellum New York City, David Henkin asserts that reading was a constant, public activity that both disseminated knowledge and encouraged anonymity, two trends that only increased once the Civil War began: "Public spaces marked with signs and littered with paper made it possible to find one's way, pursue a livelihood, negotiate a range of private and public pleasures, and forge a new identity without having a long history in the community and without relying on traditional institutions of social control" (Henkin 175). While New York had the largest population and the greatest amount of print culture in the U.S. in the nineteenth century, girls who lived in other cities like Boston and Philadelphia may also have had chances to read papers, novels, and other forms of text that were not pre-approved by their parents. Simply by walking the city streets, they could skim signs, posters, handbills, sandwich boards, and purchase the day's newspaper or the latest story paper from a vendor. Girls who were a little more daring might have circumvented parental authority in this way, making at least *some* of their reading a public and potentially anonymous activity.

Religious, moral, and social behaviors were not the only issues discussed in postbellum novels. As will be demonstrated in this chapter and the next, books that openly promoted Evangelical Protestantism often contained discussions of race relations, temperance, and suffrage in addition to religious instruction, since a great many of the arguments of each movement were based at least in part on Biblical scripture. Books that took on such openly political topics as part of educating girls into a particular religious worldview may have pushed girls to assess the arguments made and either accept or reject them. Parents could encourage their female children to read books that promoted either conservative or liberal religious and social behavior, and even encourage them to internalize the viewpoint that such books presented, but they could not force girls' mental compliance. Nevertheless, girls who read postbellum series were quickly exposed to religious and political arguments. Reading novels presented opportunities for girls to develop opinions about contemporary social questions. Therefore, for some young women, their reading may have influenced them to act on reform issues.

Plenty of American women were willing to provide reading material to girls in the postbellum period. As noted earlier, the Chautauqua meetings provided women with the perfect opening to write novels, articles, pamphlets, and stories about the summer institute. Their writing extolled Chautauqua's version of liberal Protestantism as well as the virtues of active, religious young women. Such novels would have been an easy way to recruit young women into the Chautauqua Institute and increase membership. The *Chautauqua Girls* novels discussed in the next chapter are only a few of the many volumes, both fictional and nonfictional, that were written by women to promote Chautauqua's program. Author Isabella Alden (who used the pseudonym "Pansy") frequently attended Chautauqua and became well known for books about Christian womanhood, including the *Chautauqua Girls* and the *Esther Reid* series. The *Chautauqua Girls* series was originally published between 1876 and 1913. Alden also was the editor or one of the editors for at least four Christian periodicals in the second half of the nineteenth century and an active member and teacher of the Chautauqua meetings. Alden and her husband even owned a summer home in Chautauqua Lake, no doubt to make Alden's activities with the Institute as easy as possible (Johnson, "Isabella MacDonald Alden").

Martha Finley was another woman who made a name for herself by writing the twenty-eight volumes of the *Elsie Dinsmore* series. The books tell the story of a religious little girl from a Southern plantation family who reforms her spiritually misguided father and other members of her family and community. While the *Elsie* series will be discussed more thoroughly in the next chapter, it is important to note that Finley (and Elsie) was amazingly popular with the public from the beginning. The series initially ran from 1867 to 1905, and remained in print throughout the first half of the twentieth century as well. By 1945, five million copies of the books had been sold (Johnson,

"Martha Finley"). Despite her popularity, however, Finley's writing stirred controversy, even among her contemporaries. Agnes Repplier, in an 1896 article for *Scribner's Magazine*, wrote that Elsie has "the precocious melancholy of a prig" and that Finley's tales "exhibit an abundance of ignorance and a lack of charity that are equally hurtful to a child." She roundly abuses Elsie for her self-righteousness and the father figures in the books for their harsh and excessive discipline. Both the controversy and popularity of the *Elsie* series continues up to the present. Literary critics still scorn Elsie, even while there has been a renewed popular interest in the books thanks to edited and revised reprints.

There is very little reliable biographical information on Finley; a good many of the sources about her do not agree with each other. As Deidre Johnson states: "Biographical sketches on Martha Finley agree that she was born in Chillicothe, Ohio, in April, 1828, the daughter of Dr. James Brown Finley and his wife and first cousin, Maria Theresa Brown Finley, and that she lived a quiet life. In spite of this — or perhaps because of it — her biographers seem to have considerable trouble agreeing on much else about her life" (Johnson, "Martha Finley"). Johnson's short biography of Finley is filled with "either/or" possibilities, the only certain information being that Finley eventually settled in Maryland and, in addition to her novels, wrote pamphlets for children that were published by the Presbyterian Board of Publication. Unfortunately, as far as I have been able to discover, Finley's papers were not saved or archived. There is nothing to tell us how Finley came to her religious convictions, or how she might have been acting within or against her upbringing. That she was highly active in writing didactic literature for the Presbyterian Church is indisputable, and the *Elsie Dinsmore* series (along with its companion series *Mildred Keith*) is clearly a statement of Evangelical Protestant faith in a larger form.

Many literary critics have discussed Finley's *Elsie Dinsmore* books because the books are, at this point, well-known and rather infamous. In contrast, Alden has been almost entirely overlooked, probably for several interrelated reasons. She wasn't as popular or controversial as Finley, although she did very well both in terms of sales and financially. While the sales estimates of her one hundred and ten books were estimated at 100,000 copies a year in 1900, her books were not reprinted into the twentieth century like Finley's; original copies of Alden's work are very hard to come by.[9] It did not help that Chautauqua as an institution eventually went out of fashion and lost the cultural capital it originally had; books about an institution and a place that no longer exist in their old forms are not very marketable and probably did not seem very relevant to the reading public after a few decades. In addition, Alden was more moderate in terms of her characters and her religious convictions. While she was very devoted to Evangelical Protestantism, she made allowances for human failings and even poked fun at them. She is quite possibly a better writer than Finley in some ways, creating more believable characters who struggle with their faith as they try to live in a world preoccupied with class status and social advancement. Her plots and characters are not overflowing in melodrama. Finley, however, is certainly not lacking in food for thought, whatever the merits or faults of her actual writing. Alden has been lost both because of her more moderate positions and because of her particular associations with the Chautauqua Institute, which by the early twentieth century only existed in a greatly altered and reduced form. However, her fictional books about Chautauqua are highly revealing about the expectations surrounding women and Evangelical Protestantism, particularly when it comes to how the girl heroines find their faith.

The WCTU also took advantage of the new demand for reading; Karen Sanchez-Eppler says in her study of temperance fiction that "by the 1850s fiction had clearly become the favored form for temperance propaganda" (7, footnote 2). The WCTU had their own publication organization, the Woman's Temperance Publishing Association, and the Association put out the *Union Signal*, the WCTU's temperance journal, which went from about 14,000 subscribers in 1884 to 100,000 subscribers in 1890. It was the largest women's paper in the world. The Publishing Association also turned out "two periodicals for children, one German-language temperance paper, and an average of a dozen books and two million leaflets a year" (Bordin 90). Carol Mattingly cites at least twenty temperance novels in her chapters on women temperance novelists, and laments the number of texts and the amount of historical information that has been lost over time. One example she gives is that of Mary Dwinell Chellis, who wrote at least forty-two novels as well as other tracts and pamphlets, and yet we know nothing at all about her life. Although the majority of temperance literature is no longer read or studied extensively, in the postbellum U.S. temperance fiction was everywhere and easy to come by, and it seems more than likely that girls would have been exposed to it, perhaps even encouraged to read it. Through such literature, more young women could be brought into the WCTU national organization.

Reading, then, may have helped girls to internalize not only the social expectations around Christian wifehood and motherhood, but also the social possibilities of their position, the ability to be a part of a large movement (or several large movements) that was seeking to effect social change. While parents relied on reading to ensure the proper religious and moral behavior of their daughters, that same reading also allowed girls to glimpse a means for personal agency — the religious social reform organizations that gave women an outlet for meaningful, if often unpaid, work. Once young women were old enough to become teachers, they could pass on that same social literacy to their students and eventually their own children. They could, if they wished, combine Protestant social activism with the "domestic literary management" of teaching and motherhood.

In short, reading had the potential to attune postbellum girls to a wide range of possibilities for their lives, even if those possibilities were not as numerous as they would become for women of the Progressive Era. Women's colleges were just coming into existence in the 1870s, and they were only an option for a very few in the upper class. Full-fledged careers in something other than education were rarely possible. However, benevolence societies allowed young women contact with people of other races, ethnicities, and classes, people who desperately needed economic help and material comfort. While such people and their living conditions might have seemed like something out of a novel initially, plenty of benevolent women quickly found reason to identify with the working-class women they were trying to help. The larger national organizations that emerged in the postbellum period, like Chautauqua, the WCTU, and the expanding suffrage movement, gave women the skills to organize politically, to fight for legislative change and improve their own circumstances as well as the circumstances of other women.

I am not claiming that every girl who read her way through Alcott, Finley, or Alden's series subsequently went out and joined their local benevolence organizations, the Chautauqua Institute, or the WCTU, but some of them certainly did. These books were intended to promote a certain religious and social outlook, and in many cases they were intended as recruiting tools as well as pleasurable fictions. The fact that Chautauqua and the WCTU both sustained themselves for three-quarters of a century is another indicator of their ability to recruit through multiple generations of women. As the next chapter will show, postbellum series fiction offered young women an introduction to a unique sort of social and moral empowerment, focused on national "housekeeping" and religious and moral teaching — teaching that (not always comfortably or easily) extended white, middle-class Protestant values to the lower classes and African Americans.

One example of the persistence of these values in series fiction can be found in the opening volume of the *Witch Winnie* series by Elizabeth Champney, which was published in 1889. Adelaide, Nellie, Emma, Milly, and Winnie, who all attend a boarding school known simply as "Madame's," decide that they would like to form a benevolent society to help city children. They encounter a child named Jim Halsey whose mother works as a seamstress and domestic. Mrs. Halsey has no spouse, and she knows many other families that have either one working parent or two. The parents cannot look after their children and earn money at the same time, so the children are often sent to "baby farmers" who provide mediocre childcare and charge exorbitant rates.[10]

The five schoolgirls recruit other girls in their class to help them and organize a fair, the proceeds of which allow them to rent several floors of a nearby building for a year. They take donations of furniture and other items from the community and open the Home of the Elder Brother. The children of working parents are boarded, fed, sent to school, and taught basic trade skills. The parents contribute to their children's board according to their income. The King's Daughters, as the boarding school girls christen their group, thus create a home where children can be safely cared for while their parents are earning money. Parents can see their children if they wish and still contribute to their child's welfare without going beyond their means.

In an interesting introductory note, Champney says that the idea for the Home of the Elder Brother and the King's Daughters society depicted in her book was inspired by a group of real children in New York City who raised money for the Messiah Home for Little Children, an actual home that functioned much like its fictional counterpart. She says that she hopes similar kinds of homes will emerge all over the country. This introduction reveals the extent to which fictional series mirrored actual charities and organizations that were often sponsored and/or run by women. By re-creating the Messiah Home for Little Children in her book, Champney not only extends knowledge of the Home and its operational methods to (presumably female) readers, but also encourages them to sponsor similar Homes wherever they happen to live. She takes a real institution, translates it into a fictional medium, and, via her introduction, asks other women to duplicate the real institution as a service to society. With such open and acknowledged interplay between the real and the fictional, and authors like Champney, Finley, and Alden who attempted to persuade their postbellum female readers to engage in social activism, series fiction helped promote a more active and political True Womanhood in the postbellum period.

Notes

1. Establishing the ways that non–Protestant girls might have read these books is something that should be explored. A great deal of the historical scholarship on postbellum girls and reading focuses on Northeastern Protestant girls. Not only were Protestants the majority of the middle- and upper-class population, but Protestant

young women left extensive records of their religious and reading experiences in diaries and letters. Jews and Catholics were still immigrant minorities in the postbellum period, although their numbers rose drastically after the turn of the century. Very little research has been done on the religious and reading experiences of Jewish or Catholic girls, so one can only guess how they might have reacted to reading series books that were so hostile to their respective faiths. More research into the adolescent experiences of girls who were part of religious minorities would certainly be useful in understanding how faith shaped their expectations for adulthood and how reading was included or excluded from their daily lives.

Mary Ewans' exploration of the work of Catholic nuns among the nineteenth century immigrant population offers tantalizing suggestions about the experiences of Catholic female adolescents. Ewans asserts that the number of Catholic nuns in the U.S. increased "from under forty to more than forty thousand" over the nineteenth century (101). There were many nuns who came straight from Europe to the shores of the U.S., looking to spread Catholicism in a new country: "Ninety-one of the 119 communities of sisters established in American in the nineteenth century had European or Canadian origins" (103). However, for twenty-eight other convent communities, presumably made up of U.S. citizens, to flourish during the 1800s, some native-born or immigrant women had to choose the convent life. How did young women learn about the Catholic faith?

Ewans' answer seems to be schooling. Catholic sisters ran every kind of school in the nineteenth century, including 663 academies for girls. They also ran day-care centers, homes for working women, homes for delinquent girls, and homes for unwed mothers. All of these places would have allowed young women, many of them immigrants, to be exposed to Catholic theology and the kindness of Catholic nuns. Many Catholic immigrants sent their children to convent schools, and the Catholic sisters put great effort into maintaining their religion in the immigrant population. Even some native-born girls might have seen more possibility for themselves in the life of a nun. With so many schools and charitable organizations to run, a young woman who became part of a convent would have plenty of opportunity to exercise talents and lead a useful life: "Indeed, there were complaints in some places that the convents were removing too many of the marriageable girls from the countryside" (Ewans 103). Clearly Catholicism offered certain freedoms to young women who did not care to be married and have a family. However, Ewans offers little insight into the *process* of their conversion to Catholicism.

The dearth of information on young women's experiences outside of Protestantism extends to Jewish young women as well, whether German or Russian. Joyce Antler has done the most extensive study of Jewish women's upbringing in the United States, and she finds that most Jewish immigrant women struggled to reconcile their Jewish religion with American culture. Jewish women writers like Mary Antin and Anzia Yezierska often rejected their Judaism in favor of secular Americanism, but at the same time felt guilty and saddened by their own loss of faith (33–34). However, Jewish women at the turn of the century also actively sought to increase their own visibility in civic affairs and benevolence organizations, feeling that they were not equaling Protestant women's efforts for reform (Antler 1–5). They wished to be just as involved in their own communities as Protestant women were, and they attempted to extend their traditional domestic skills outside the home and into social reform.

Ann Braude asserts that Jewish women gained much more equality within the United States due to the fear that women would leave the Jewish religion for Protestantism if Judaism did not offer some of the same privileges for women. The Reform Synod of 1846 specifically made women the equals of Jewish laymen, although not the equals of rabbis (153). As a result, women were allowed much greater participation within synagogues, including Sunday schools and confirmation classes. Even orthodox Jewish women who had come to America, despite their overall adherence to traditional roles for Jewish women, increasingly vocalized their opposition to reform in church periodicals. Again, however, this tells us little about any religious rites of passage (or lack thereof) that Jewish girls might have been expected to observe.

In short, there is an abundance of research that still needs to be conducted on postbellum girls and their religious and reading practices, particularly when it comes to girls who are part of racial, ethnic, or religious minorities. The institutionalized racism in series books published after the Civil War up to the Great Depression needs to be meaningfully addressed without being simply dismissed as cultural ignorance. The anti–Catholicism and anti–Mormonism that is so evident in the pages of the *Elsie Dinsmore* books should be thoroughly contextualized and placed in historical perspective, and the *Elsie* texts should be examined for the relationship between Finley's religious stance and larger contemporary groups and trends.

2. In her history of anorexia nervosa, *Fasting Girls*, Joan Jacobs Brumberg also identifies some late-nineteenth century women, both young and old, who gained a reputation for being pious and/or connected to the spirit world by refusing food. Often they gained notoriety and were ridiculed in the popular press, but in some religious denominations, particularly Catholicism and Spiritualism, they were regarded as holy. Brumberg places these women as part of a tradition of fasting religious women going back to medieval times. While their refusal of food would have prevented the kinds of physical and social activity enjoyed by other female church members, fasting women did gain a place of importance in some churches.

3. Nancy Hardesty's works on Charles Finney and the women who followed him (who were influenced by his theology and politics) is incredibly helpful for tracing the ways in which evangelical women often moved from revivalism and religious activism to political work in abolition and temperance. See *Your Daughters Shall Prophesy: Revivalism and Feminism in the Age of Finney* and *Women Called to Witness: Evangelical Feminism in the Nineteenth Century*. Taken together, the two books paint a clear picture of the ways that early feminists like Frances Willard, Angelina and Sarah Grimke, Lucy Stone, and Antoinette Brown Blackwell were influenced by Finney's theology and the active place he gave to women in the church. *Your Daughters* is also highly helpful for understanding precisely how Finney's theology was a revision of his Presbyterian, Congregationalist, and Methodist predecessors.

4. Catherine Brekus has written the definitive work on women preaching in the United States from the colonial period through the mid-nineteenth century, titled *Strangers and Pilgrims: Female Preaching in America 1740–1845*. She includes an extensive section on the backlash against female preaching; see 267–335.

5. The ministerial anxiety detailed by Douglas was only one facet of a more general cultural concern about American masculinity. E. Anthony Rotundo has done extensive work on the changing ideals of masculinity in the nineteenth-century U.S., and he claims that the widening of women's sphere both in the church and outside of it caused alarm about the "feminine" nature of civilization. If ministers were concerned about the lack of men in the pews and the high number of women running church organizations, other men were worried about the encroachment of women into public space. Through childrearing, teaching, office work, religion, literature,

social events, and reform movements, women were setting the standard for public as well as private moral behavior. The emergence of the Woman's Christian Temperance Union and related social purity organizations led men to reexamine the meanings of masculinity and move toward "muscular Christianity" and Roosevelt's "Strenuous Life" by the turn of the twentieth century. "Men had endorsed women's moral stewardship as long as it did not extend to their public sources of power and pleasure, but they began to balk when women attacked taverns, [fraternal] lodges, and brothels" (Rotundo 253; see also 222–283). Male resistance to female moral reform organizations was really an attempt to defend their sphere of influence. Mark C. Carnes has also documented the ways in which fraternal lodges and their rituals were a reaction against liberal Protestant theology and women's moral authority within and outside of churches: "The rituals' exclusion of references to Christ and their implicit refutation of liberal theology can best be understood as an indirect assault upon women and women's role in the church" (*Secret Ritual and Manhood*, 79).

6. Most of the young women Hunter studies appear to have been Protestants, Evangelical or otherwise; as discussed in my introduction, there has been very little work done on either the religious or reading experiences of Catholic and Jewish girls growing up in the postbellum and turn of the century U.S.

7. I rely heavily on Rieser's study of Chautauqua in this chapter because, although there have been many articles and theses written about various segments of the Chautauqua movement and its offshoots, his is the only comprehensive history of the movement to have been published. Rieser gives a thorough bibliography of these sources in his book, and many of them trace Chautauqua assemblies in specific states, or trace the history of Chautauqua's correspondence school, without attempting to analyze the organization as a whole.

8. Sunday School libraries were actually established much earlier than free public libraries, which did not come into existence until the last quarter of the nineteenth century. Subscription libraries were more common, where members would pay for access to a shared collection of books. As Carol Mattingly points out in her study of women's temperance literature, "Sunday school distribution was of supreme importance because, for most of the nineteenth century, Sunday school libraries provided the only publicly accessible books for the majority of Americans" (125).

9. If one divides the sales of Alden's books up evenly, each book would have sold about 909 copies per year, although some were surely more popular than others. While Alden's sales are impressive for her time, they do not come close to the wild popularity of Elsie. First and second editions of the *Elsie* books can still be found, while early editions of Alden's books are rare. Living Books, a division of Tyndale House, reprinted all of the *Chautauqua Girls* novels save one in the late 1990s, and slightly edited reprints of all the *Chautauqua* books are still available from Keepers of the Faith publishers.

10. Actual nineteenth-century baby farms like the ones Champney describes also had notoriously high infant mortality rates; see Regina Kunzel, *Fallen Women, Problem Girls*, 69–70.

Two

Angels in the House
Christian Womanhood and Community Power in Postbellum Girls' Series

Series books produced in the last half of the nineteenth century tell stories about young women who undergo various types of discipline to attain Christian True Womanhood and become Christian wives and mothers. Some, like Elsie Dinsmore, come to the Christian faith from childhood but encounter conflict with an atheistic and/or harshly disciplinarian parent. Some, like Jo and Amy March of *Little Women*, struggle not only with faith but also with "being good" and ladylike. These books were intended to teach girls how to be True Women, which meant not only how to "be good," but also how to be Christian. Religious faith and good behavior are entwined in these books as the two essential components of True Womanhood that every girl must achieve, so much so that they can hardly be separated out in the narratives. On the other hand, religious faith and church community offer the women of these books considerable amounts of moral and social power along with a support network of other women. The *Chautauqua Girls* series by Isabella Alden illustrates such a network, giving a detailed account of young women who immerse themselves in benevolence, temperance, and social reform, aided by the faith community at the Chautauqua Institute.

In her analysis of women's antebellum benevolence organizations, Lori Ginzberg identifies the contradictions inherent in this vision of womanhood:

> [A]n analysis that conflated femininity and morality contained within it both conservative and radical implications for the work of female activists themselves ... the insistence on women's shared characteristics and experience could constitute a conservative defense of existing sexual inequality but it could also provide the basis for women's organizing on their own behalf. These radical and conservative possibilities were always in tension: the very assertion of an identity based

on female morality carried within it both the conservative imperative to conform and a more radical call to define and act upon women's needs [18].

Although Ginzberg is looking at women's benevolent organizations in the antebellum era, the series books written after the Civil War allow us to see that this conflicted conception of female morality lasted well into the late nineteenth century. These same-sex organizations that promoted moral and charitable works allowed women to engage in an *active* True Womanhood, rather than being passive domestic beings confined to the home. By the time Isabella Alden's Chautauqua Girls reach their fourth book in 1888, her heroines have become active workers in the Woman's Christian Temperance Union, the city slums, and various church organizations. Their activism, along with the earlier benevolence of Elsie Dinsmore and the March girls, provides a prototype for the New Woman that would emerge in full force during the Progressive Era. While the True Women in these texts restrict their activism primarily to work in the church, charity, and temperance, the church is in some ways part of the public sphere, particularly when religious views are used to influence public morality. New Women move away from the church and into full-blown public activism, including public health and sanitation, child care, medical care, education for immigrants and working women, and myriad other projects. The earlier activism of True Women provides a model for these shifts, as do the series books where True Women are the heroines.

Unfortunately, many of these postbellum series books have either been ignored by scholars or studied primarily for the purpose of criticizing their failings, rather than to tell us what they accomplish socially and historically. Martha Finley's *Elsie Dinsmore* series is usually looked at with scorn for its melodrama and emotionalism, incredulousness for its overly stern child disciplinary practices, or anger for its overt religious didacticism and intolerance of other religious beliefs.[1] With the exception of historian Andrew Reiser, there has been no critical examination at all of Isabella Alden's *Chautauqua Girls* series. It is crucial to realize that Alcott and her contemporaries Finley and Alden were *continuing* a tradition of True Womanhood in their texts, not just dismantling it. All three series tell us a great deal about what "True Womanhood" looked like in the decades following the Civil War, and how these socially and politically active "angels" were the forerunners for the emerging phenomenon of the "New Woman."

Postbellum True Womanhood *in* Little Women

Little Women and the other two books that Alcott wrote about the Marches are exceptions to the dearth of scholarly writing on postbellum girls' series. The trilogy of *Little Women*, *Little Men*, and *Jo's Boys* has been studied extensively for everything from clues to Alcott's life to the queer genders and sexualities of the main characters.² However, scholars have tended to disregard the religious aspects of her novels, perhaps for fear that they would be relegated to the same obscurity as the other series examined in this chapter. Alcott herself called her books "moral pap," but scholars have tried, for the most part, to avoid using that label and have valorized Alcott as one of the first successful female authors in America.

In Madeleine Sterns' collection *Critical Essays on Louisa May Alcott*, there are twenty-six selections concerning *Little Women*, with five contemporary reviews included, followed by twenty-one essays that span the twentieth century. In the entire group, only nine of the essays mention religion at all. Most of those are casual mentions of "preaching" or references to Alcott's use of *Pilgrim's Progress*. Even the authors who discuss Bunyan see the analogy between the stories as a moral journey rather than a religious lesson. The most vitriolic criticism is directed toward Alcott's "sentimentality," that tear-inducing quality that critics both then and now have castigated as the besetting sin of nineteenth-century women novelists. Her supposedly stereotypical delineation of sex roles comes in for a close second as the most unfortunate characteristic of her books. Jo's characterization as a short-tempered, ambitious tomboy who is allowed to fulfill some of her professional ambitions as a writer makes her the exceptional female in *Little Women*, a contrast to her sister Beth's "Angel in the House," Meg's contented domestic motherhood, and Amy's glamorous marriage to wealthy Laurie. Some critics even fail to concede Jo's uniqueness, seeing her marriage to Professor Bhaer as a capitulation to patriarchy and women's oppression.

Contemporary critics of Alcott also had mixed reactions to the morality of her books. While the *Springfield Daily Union* praised the first part of *Little Women* as a "charming book" that taught "in a pleasant, cheerful way lessons which the young need to learn, to make home happy" and portrayed "just what every christian [sic] home under judicious training should and may be," the *Zion's Herald* commented that although the book was a "vivacious story," it was "without Christ, and hence perilous in proportion to its assimilation to Christian forms" (Clark, *Contemporary Reviews* 62–64). The *Herald* objected strongly to Alcott's "disspiritualizing" of *Pilgrim's Progress*, and wound up with the verdict "Don't put it in the Sunday School library" (Clark, *Contemporary Reviews* 64). The *Eclectic Magazine* apparently appreciated Alcott's non-evangelical morality, saying, "Miss Alcott ... is too appreciative of the truly beautiful in childhood to attempt to preach [children] into stiff-backed, spiritless propriety" (Clark 64). *The Ladies Repository*, however, echoed the concerns of the *Zion's Herald*: "[I]t is not a Christian book. It is religion without spirituality, and salvation without Christ. It is not a good book for the Sunday school library" (Clark 65).[3]

Critics, then, have moved from arguing about the religious nature of Alcott's work to ignoring it almost entirely, instead choosing to focus on Jo's liberating personality and difficult maturation, on the contradictory messages about gender roles in the novel, on Alcott's place in the canon of women's "sentimental" writing, and on the glimmers of Alcott's feminism that are revealed at various points in the narrative.

However, simply because Alcott had other aims in view besides, or in addition to, convincing her readers to live religiously does not mean that the religious project in her books should be ignored. Alcott's *Little Women* books portray learning the Christian life as learning to walk on the right path, learning to conquer one's desires and selfish wants, learning to live for others, and learning to be kind and charitable both within one's family and outside of it. For example, in one of the early scenes of *Little Women*, the four March girls each receive a little New Testament for their Christmas present. Their mother, Marmee, has been talking to them about beginning their journey of "Pilgrim's Progress" (referring, of course, to John Bunyan's tale) as a life journey, rather than as the game they used to play when they were little girls:

> Do you remember how you used to play Pilgrim's Progress when you were little things? ... We are never too old for this ... because it is a play we are playing all the time in one way or another. Our burdens are here, the road is before us, and the longing for goodness and happiness is the guide that leads us through many troubles and mistakes to the peace which is a true Celestial City. Now, my little pilgrims, suppose you begin again, not in play, but in earnest, and see how far on you can get before father comes home [15].

The girls must learn to conquer their faults and become young Christian women that their parents can be proud of. This includes giving assistance to their poorer neighbors, learning to smother any petty or selfish emotions, and sometimes giving up greater ambitions for the sake of home and marriage.

What is so interesting about this discussion is that Meg, the eldest sister, connects the idea of playing pilgrims explicitly to "being good," not to being Christian, although the Bunyan story is a Christian allegory. Meg says, "It is only another name for trying to be good, and the story may help us..." (15). A method for living a Christian life is precisely what Bunyan's story provides, and "trying to be good" is so connected to trying to be Christian that the one is implicated in the other. Neither Meg nor Marmee separate the two concepts. It is after this conversation, on Christmas morning, that the girls receive New Testaments as Marmee's Christmas present.[4] They read some of their new books every morning, and Alcott continues the "pilgrim" theme throughout the first half of the novel. She refers to the girls as "pilgrims" frequently, and some of her chapter titles mirror, reference, or parody Bunyan's story, including "Playing Pilgrims," "Burdens," "Beth Finds the Palace Beautiful," "Amy's Valley of Humiliation," "Jo Meets Apollyon," and "Meg Goes to Vanity Fair."

On the surface, the pilgrimage the girls undertake to become good, unselfish Christians sounds fearfully repressive, and indeed it is, in some ways. Jo March, for example, has a temper that she has inherited from her mother, but Marmee has learned to control herself and always be calm and mild-mannered.[5] Martha Saxton links this repression of emotions and the learning of internal self-control to the rise of republican motherhood in the post–Revolutionary era. When mothers became primarily responsible for their children's characters and well-being, for forming their children into proper citizens, they had to adjust their own behavior so their children would not be harmed:

> For the new nation to maintain its purity it needed citizens who, in the absence of many institutions or other restraints, could pursue virtuous lives. Self-control and decorous behavior were primary among the qualities children needed to learn to join the growing middle-class. Because every impression was of great impact on a tiny child, mothers had to adjust their own comportment to show only tranquility and love.... Mothers' love was to exemplify self-control within heroic self-suppression, not only restraining mothers' desires but measuring and controlling their emotions so as to display only mildness, care, and pleasure in their children's progress. Such behavior would lead not only to a child's salvation, the ultimate goal of a mother's instruction, but also the mother's salvation [Saxton 269–270].

Marmee is always full of tranquility and love, and only Jo, who shares her temper, catches the small moments where Marmee has to control herself. The necessity for the March girls to develop "self-control and decorous behavior" is even more imperative because they are always on the verge of falling out of the middle class, always on the edge of becoming part of the lower working class and losing their gentility. If the girls do not absorb the social graces, mild temper, and Christian goodness that Marmee models for them, they are in danger of not marrying and losing their social position entirely.

However, John Matteson points to another, more liberating interpretation of the self-sacrifice that the March girls learn so well. By turning their willingness to be good into acts of community benevolence, the girls simultaneously improve their community and open up spaces for women to use their talents and energies. Examples abound: Marmee's endless work for the soldiers who are fighting; the girls taking their Christmas breakfast to the poor Hummel family; Beth's careful watching of that same family of children; Amy donating her art to a charity fair and manning a table herself; Beth's creation of mufflers, mittens, and other handy items for the neighborhood children, even when she herself is ill; and, eventually, the Bhaers's school at Plumfield and the Laurences's charities. Women are instrumental in all of these endeavors, and Mattheson argues that this was intentional on Alcott's part:

> Women's rights, for Alcott, was never an end in itself. Rather, expanding opportunities for women was the great and necessary means by which previously neglected talents and energies might be made available to benefit the entire societal family. Jo learns that abilities used to benefit only oneself are thrown away.... Only when one gives freely to all do talent and effort attain their highest value [Matteson 460].

Jo gives first to her family, and then to her school and her boys, while Amy and Laurie manage to help struggling artists, homeless children, and genteel but poor young men. Beth, during her short life, gives assistance and love to everyone she can; while she sometimes seems to be nothing more than the resident angel in the house, she learns the lesson of selfless community giving much faster than any of her sisters. Meg is the exception of the four; in *Good Wives* she is mostly absorbed with her husband and two young children. However, once John Brooke passes away in *Little Men*, even Meg resolves to take a greater part in the rest of the world, "feeling that her best help would be to live for others, as her John had done" (*Little Men* 285). Meg becomes a mother and counselor to the girls of Jo's school and takes up her part in the communal family effort to make Plumfield and Laurence College successful (*Jo's Boys* 1–17). Alcott's development of women through community benevolence falls in line with Lori Ginzberg's observations. In series postbellum fiction, at least, women who spend time caring for members of their community garner a great amount of respect both within the church and outside of it. Certainly the Christian male figures in the novels do not object to their activities; the unconverted men are often the ones who complain.

An important difference between the historical world that Berg and Ginzberg analyze and the fictional one that Alcott creates is that Alcott demands the participation of men as well as women. Historically, women dominated the charitable societies almost entirely, with only a few supportive men also assisting in the work. Sometimes men would serve on a governing board for the sake of appearances; sometimes they would serve as chaperones; occasionally they would participate in the work themselves. In Alcott's world, on the other hand, women run the community but at the same time insist that "their boys," including Laurie and all of Jo's boys, learn to give charity, help when necessary, and not be tight-fisted with their wealth. Laurie learns his lessons admirably and is an example for all the others; in *Jo's Boys*, wild

Dan is determined to give a good portion of his money to someone who needs help, whether it is another boy or an oppressed group like the Montana Indians (*Jo's Boys* 62–64).

Some women who were involved in benevolent work saw men as the source of women's suffering and women as the primary losers in a system that was cruelest to the most vulnerable. Alcott seems to acknowledge all types of suffering regardless of sex. The March girls hover on the edge of poverty when we first meet them; Jo and Laurie help girls and boys alike who come from all sorts of varied backgrounds; Dan feels keenly the sufferings of the Native Americans as a group. Like the moral reformers who were her contemporaries, though, Alcott sought to end at least part of the double standard of morality by demanding the same behavior of women and men. Women held the upper hand in the moral equation, and men had to learn how to measure up: "Alcott expected the self-sacrifice of good men as well as good women. Her ideal of equality touched principally on opportunities to serve rather than any presumed right to seek one's individual happiness" (Matteson 460). She requires that every human being do their best for every other no matter how poor the parties involved are or how little of a material nature they have to give. It is our obligation as humans, Alcott seems to say, to take care of one another. Women fulfill their obligations as True Women not only by raising *all* of their children to be good citizens and Christians, but also through generous Christian deeds that sustain others in their communities.

Postbellum True Womanhood in Elsie Dinsmore

If the story of the March girls is, in part, a story about young women retaining their middle-class position through faith, benevolence, and "being good," Martha Finley's *Elsie Dinsmore* series is about a female child from a wealthy Southern family who uses her upper-class position to spread faith in her community and practice benevolence on a large scale. The series is also about a daughter who overcomes her father's stubborn resistance to Evangelical Protestantism. Eventually, she grows into a woman who happily uses all the power of "True Womanhood" to convert others to Christianity.

Elsie's first and greatest challenge is asserting her moral and religious authority over her own father, Horace Dinsmore. Dinsmore is a nominal Protestant who believes in going to church as a member of the community but not in manifesting his faith in his daily life. He does not see the need to follow the Bible (and therefore God) in all things; he trusts his own judgment to bring him to moral decisions. Those decisions ought to be enough to allow him to enter heaven. When Elsie tries to convince him that he should actively try to love Jesus and give up his own will, he either laughs at her or becomes angry with her. He does not know the Bible as well as his little daughter, and when her interpretations of what is morally and religiously correct conflict with his own, he resents her audacity in telling him how to behave.

In the first volume of the series, *Elsie Dinsmore*, Horace and Elsie's clashes over proper religious behavior culminate when Elsie is commanded to play a song on the piano for company. It is a Sunday, and Elsie does not consider it an appropriate song to play on the Sabbath, so she refuses. Her father, angry at her disobedience, orders her to sit on the piano stool until she is ready to obey him. After sitting there for several hours in the heat, Elsie faints away and strikes her head on the furniture. Mr. Dinsmore and his friend Mr. Travilla rush in to discover her unconscious and bleeding, and Mr. Travilla openly calls his friend "a brute" (Finley 290). Frightened for his child's life, Mr. Dinsmore forgives her the offense, and Elsie's troubles end temporarily.

However, the conflict only escalates in volume two, *Holidays at Roselands*, when Mr. Dinsmore becomes ill and Elsie refuses to read a novel to him on the Sabbath. Just as before, Elsie's disobedience angers Horace to such a degree that he commands her to read the book, but she will not. The immediate end to the altercation is that Horace banishes her from the room and ceases to acknowledge her as his daughter, refusing any affection or interaction but the most formal. When Horace goes away himself and threatens to send Elsie to a Catholic convent, Elsie becomes ill to the point of death.[6]

Barbara Epstein's observations on the different conversion experiences of nineteenth-century men and women are helpful when comparing Horace and Elsie's religious viewpoints. Epstein says that nineteenth-century men often rejected orthodox Calvinism because of its emphasis on emotional investment, the ever-present threat of hell, and the will of God in all earthly success and failure. While Finley does not specifically use Calvinism in her text, the conversion patterns that Epstein observes are still useful. Men often felt that the demands of orthodox Calvinism deprived them of agency and worth as humans. They turned to the Unitarian or Universality churches, which emphasized moral actions as the best way to live a Christian life. Epstein also suggests that some men found Calvinism incompatible with the way they had to behave in order to succeed in the workplace:

> Men who prided themselves on their work and who believed that whatever success and status they had achieved were the result of their own unaided effort and therefore well deserved were likely to be attracted to doctrines that placed more confidence in human efforts.... The rationality and emotional control that seemed most favorable to worldly success were more compatible with sects that

stressed good behavior than with Calvinism, which demanded soul-searching and the emotional crisis of conversion [50].

Horace Dinsmore is just such a man, one who prides himself on his ability to make moral decisions and resents interference in his life or anyone's attempt to control him (especially a God who would be all-controlling): "Horace Dinsmore was ... an upright, moral man, who paid an outward respect to the forms of religion, but cared nothing for the vital power of godliness; trusted entirely to his morality, and looked upon Christians as hypocrites and deceivers" (Finley, *Elsie Dinsmore* 72). Horace believes that emotional control and good behavior are the surest ways to social and financial success. Moreover, one of his first efforts in governing his daughter after his eight-year absence from her life is to try and force her to gain control of her emotions: "'You have been crying,' he said, in a slightly disapproving tone. 'I am afraid you do a great deal more of that than is good for you. It is a very babyish habit, and you much try to break yourself of it'" (Finley, *Elsie Dinsmore* 99–100).

In contrast to men, women embraced the emotional aspects of religious conversion and often found that their good behavior masked indifference, selfishness, or anger: "[W]omen were much more emotional and experienced God more intensely ... most felt real anguish over their estrangement from God" (Epstein 55). The ultimate extreme was for women to find that not only had they been hypocritical and indifferent to religion, but also that they actually harbored hatred for God. Elsie, like the young women that Epstein examines, is convinced that she is inherently wicked and is appalled by her rebellious feelings toward those who treat her badly: "[T]he little Elsie sat at her desk, striving to conquer the feelings of anger and indignation that were swelling in her breast; for Elsie ... often had a fierce contest with her naturally quick temper" (Finley, *Elsie Dinsmore* 15–16). Elsie never goes so far as to hate God (and indeed, Finley makes it nearly impossible for readers to even contemplate the possibility of such an emotion from Elsie), but she does worry about moving away from God and becoming too caught up in her earthly life.

Horace Dinsmore focuses most of his energy on his mortal existence and material success. He hopes to teach his daughter to do the same, and it is Elsie's resistance to his secular teachings that causes the emotional battle between them. In contrast to the traditional depiction of the nineteenth-century family patriarch, Elsie's biological father and her heavenly one are neither conflated nor collapsed. Horace Dinsmore is *not* Elsie's living substitute for God. In spite of the intensely emotional relationship between Horace and Elsie, and in spite of the God-like power that Horace Dinsmore tries to exercise over his daughter, Elsie refuses to concede that her father carries God's authority. This distinction between Horace Dinsmore and God is the crux upon which his entire relationship with Elsie turns. Elsie's refusal to recognize him over and above a heavenly God, her refusal to consider him the ultimate paterfamilias, is what causes all of the strife in their relationship for the first few volumes of the series. Elsie will not obey Horace if it means disobeying her Christian principles, even though he may try to convince her that his word and God's are one and the same. Helena Michie points to this struggle as the one that defines Elsie's life in her comparison of Elsie and Little Eva from *Uncle Tom's Cabin*:

> Eva struggles to change the law of the land by converting her father to Christianity and thus to abolition, while Elsie works to convert her authoritarian and secular father to the higher law of Christianity. Both seek desperately, through the pathos of their bodies and the power of their words, to align the laws of their earthly and heavenly fathers.... Each girl has two competing fathers who embody two competing laws; each comes to a sense of identity and power by constructing and manipulating the struggle between them for the daughter's love and obedience [Michie 190].

Elsie's struggle between the laws her father lays down and the ones that God has laid down is indeed the crucial fight. However much she tries to reconcile these two codes of obedience, she cannot accomplish it perfectly because her father resists the law of God. In fact, Horace Dinsmore is jealous of the devotion that Elsie gives to God and troubled by her spirituality because he cannot comprehend it. He does not truly believe in God himself: "He was ... not quite willing that she should love even her Saviour better than himself" (Finley, *Elsie Dinsmore* 293; see also 72 and 301–302).[7] While Mr. Dinsmore certainly strives to be the all-encompassing masculine presence in Elsie's life, Finley takes pains to say that Elsie is *more* devoted to her God than her father. While her father is precious to her, God is the guiding influence of her life. The two are not the same, no matter how much Horace himself would like that to be the case. Finley intentionally differentiates them and makes clear that Elsie's ultimate loyalty is to God and Christianity.

Only when Elsie becomes ill does Horace see how cruel he has been to the child. Through the worst days of her illness he turns to God for help. Love for his daughter and the realization that she has been correct in her religious convictions, while he has been the one to fail in both religion and parenting, are the two forces that bring him to profess Christianity. Mr. Dinsmore is ultimately converted to his daughter's faith after several days and nights of soul-searching during her illness. He sees the error of placing all his confidence in his own judgment and conflating worldly advancement with spiritual health:

> [H]e had been very proud of his morality and his upright life, unstained by any dishonorable act. He had always thought of himself as quite deserving of the prosperity with which he had been blessed in the affairs of this world, and just as likely as anyone to be happy in the next ... [as he thought of Elsie's behavior] and contrasted it with his own worldly-mindedness and self-righteousness, his utter neglect of the Saviour, and his determined efforts to make his child as worldly as himself, he shrank back appalled at the picture, and was constrained to cry out in bitterness of soul: "God be merciful to me, a sinner" [Finley, *Holidays at Roselands* 129].

Horace is "saved" through his love for his daughter and an emotional conversion experience that forces him to question all of his previously "rational" behavior. He surrenders his will to God, Elsie's wish that her father might "love Jesus" is fulfilled, and the two laws she has been working so hard to make compatible finally become one. She disciplines Horace through *both* her love for him and her love for God, through her illness, suffering, and self-sacrifice coupled with an ever-persistent love for him even in the face of his anger. Love and religion are the two key elements that allow Elsie to finally reform her father and bring him into the moral safety of the Evangelical Protestant church. She thus succeeds in reconciling the "two competing laws" of her "two competing fathers" (Michie 190). As a religious daughter, she not only has the power to reform Horace's behavior, but also to save his soul.

In a way, this feels like an incomplete sort of victory, since Elsie does not win a great deal of personal agency after her long ordeal. Horace promises never to ask her to do anything that interferes with her religious conscience but still expects absolute compliance when it comes to his wishes in everyday affairs. Elsie, however, has won the right to follow her own principles and has the pleasure of seeing her father brought into the Christian faith. Her father's conversion to Christianity also ends most of the strife between them and increases their love for one another. From then on, Elsie is able to exercise the religious benevolence of Christian True Womanhood even before she is fully grown.

When assessing the characterization of Horace Dinsmore and his conflicted relationship with Elsie, critics have overlooked the possible moral and religious lessons that may have motivated Finley's choices. Scholars and reviewers read the values and behavior of the irreligious Horace as something Finley condones, rather than reading her text as a carefully constructed critique of his behavior.[8] Elsie is mostly an obedient and submissive child; she resists her father's will when *and only when* she feels his directives countermand her duties as a Christian. Horace is a horrible character, initially, but he is supposed to be horrible so that we can see his transformation as his daughter teaches him about the proper beliefs and actions of a Christian adult. The development of Horace and Elsie as contrasting foils for one another, however exaggerated it seems to a modern reader, has a specific dramatic purpose in the narrative. Elsie is the being who changes her father's life, through her love for him, her love for God, and her carefully considered moral scruples. Horace Dinsmore has been a drifter since the death of Elsie's mother. He has neglected his child out of grief and anger and spent his life in travel and leisure that held little pleasure for him. Thanks to his neglect of his family life, he has also become a selfish being, one who expects to have his wishes fulfilled and who is none too generous in his assessment of other people. Elsie changes all of these things. Her father becomes a gentler and more Christian man who takes on his family responsibilities and makes sure everyone around him is provided for before himself.

Elsie brings other members of her family besides her father to the Christian faith. In the first volume, Elsie teaches her young aunt Lora, only five years older than Elsie herself, about Jesus and the Bible. Before and during her illness, in volume two, Elsie brings about the conversion of her Aunt Adelaide. Adelaide's fiancé dies and she is grief-stricken, whereupon Elsie tries to assuage her sadness by talking to her and reading to her from the Bible. The little girl's love, sympathy, and faith win over her aunt, and Elsie's illness completes Adelaide's devotion to God as she nurses her niece and prays for her recovery (Finley, *Elsie Dinsmore* 186–190; *Holidays at Roselands* 98–102 and 111–136).

In addition to encouraging her family and friends to truly believe in God, Elsie makes it part of her mission in life to comfort and aid others. Unlike the Marches, she is wealthy, possessed of a large fortune. Once Elsie is grown up, she uses her wealth to maintain her household and help those who are poor and in need. She does a great deal of good in her community by offering monetary and material help to those who are less well off than she. Elsie, her father, and eventually her husband and children freely make use of their money to better the situations of other people. Philanthropy and compassion are essential parts of leading the Christian life of a True Woman in these stories.

It should be clear at this point that one key difference between Elsie and the Marches is Finley's emphasis on Evangelical Protestantism. While the Marches perform good deeds and acts of charity as part of training themselves to be Christians, they do not openly proselytize. For them, good works and private faith are enough; for Elsie and her family, trying to convert those whom they assist are two sides of the same coin. To neglect either aspect of their benevolence would mean that they failed to do their duty as faithful Christians:

> "It is extremely kind in you to call on us — strangers and living in this poor and unpleasant locality" [said Mrs. Allen].
>
> "It is nothing — it is a privilege, if in so doing we bring succor to one of God's dear children," Grandma Elsie replied. "How glad I am to learn that you are one of his. I had heard only that you were ill and in want" [Finley, *Elsie and the Raymonds* 40].

In this particular case, Elsie does not have to save the poverty-stricken and ill Mrs. Allen; it is simply "a privilege" to be able to help her, one of "God's children." In other cases, however, Elsie is the active agent of conversion, as in *Elsie Yachting with the Raymonds*, when she proselytizes one of the male crew members of their boat and succeeds in persuading him to convert. The need for the Dinsmores to preach to their beneficiaries becomes especially crucial when the beneficiaries in question are from a different denomination; Finley repeatedly warns against Mormonism and Catholicism in her texts. In *Elsie's Children*, Elsie's Aunt Louise sends her daughter Isadore to a convent, and Isadore comes back home professing the Catholic faith. Once the family learns of her conversion, they do everything possible to bring her back to Protestant Evangelicalism, including setting up a family Bible study. Naturally, she eventually returns to her original faith (62–67 and 93–102). In *Elsie and the Raymonds*, volume fifteen, Finley denounces Mormons and their "new revelation" as a "base fabrication" (182), using Elsie's son-in-law Captain Raymond as a mouthpiece. In addition to providing material help, bringing more members of the lower classes into the Evangelical Protestant faith is clearly a vital part of being a True Woman. The newly prosperous converts thus come into the middle class with not only sufficient income, but also the "right" religious faith; they will conform to a white, Anglo-Saxon, Protestant ideology.

The other important difference between Elsie and the March girls is Elsie's economic class and some of her methods of giving. The March girls are only able to help a few poor families in their immediate community by giving what little extra they have. Such charitable giving allows them to both display their religious virtue and keep their shaky position in the middle-class. They are practicing benevolence from the bottom up, helping those who have the least with a few extra material goods of their own. Elsie, on the other hand, is not only able to help blacks and poor whites in her community, those that she knows personally, but she can also donate large sums to the church, missions, and charity, practicing philanthropy from the top down and assisting other organizations. She uses her wealth to help others prosper and become part of the middle class, while at the same time encouraging them to follow her religious example.

In a sense, the March women and Elsie are both operating from the idea that class is not defined by money, but by morality and faith. They all give what they can to others as part of their religious duty, and it is their benevolence that defines their status rather than the amount they are able to give away. Lori Ginzberg notes that this shift in attitudes regarding women, wealth, class, and morality was particularly meaningful for middle-class women:

> In noting the tenuous nature of economic well-being and in attributing its fluctuations to men, some benevolent women sought to redefine social status as a measure of virtue — a female trait — rather than of class. Class, they claimed, was an artificial condition imposed upon women by men. If women only fulfilled their "female destiny," and behaved more morally than men, they could dissolve class boundaries, at least for women. If they identified with "virtue," all but the poorest could achieve what has come to be labeled "middle-class respectability." The ideology obscured real class differences among women (not least the class interests of reformers themselves), but it also contributed to many women's sense of power and autonomy [24].

In other words, by the mid-nineteenth century middle-class reformers attempted to claim that class was not about money, it was about virtue. Whether you were a rich or poor woman, virtue consisted of loving your neighbors better than yourself and caring for your community as well as your family with acts of Christian benevolence. Both Alcott and Finley recognize the social power available to women if class respectability is based on morality and virtue rather than wealth, and both of them demonstrate it through their characters. The Marches are poor but still keep their middle-class status through their faith and their endless tending of others who need assistance. Elsie is wealthy and sustains much of her community through her charity; other women she meets are classified as respectable or not depending on whether they believe in Christ and act on Evangelical principles. If class status was based on virtue rather than on income, more women could transcend economic hardship and become part of the new middle class. Women of Elsie's status could assist other women and help better their economic conditions.

However, as much as women from all classes might have embraced the idea of "virtue-as-class" and used it to their advantage, the texts themselves belie the idea. Elsie's benevolence *is* about class; her entire objective is to help others attain a middle-class status and have them conform to an Evangelical Protestant faith. While a common faith and common goals undoubtedly helped some women to cross class lines and form friendships and working alliances, Ginzberg rightly points out that there were undoubtedly biases and conflicts as well. No matter how much Elsie improves the economic situation of those who she helps, the material difference between her and her beneficiaries cannot simply be erased. She is upper class, with more money at her disposal than the majority of people with whom she interacts. Even if she succeeds in comfortably placing a person or family in the middle-class, they will be one class lower than she:

> Grandma Elsie's sympathetic listening and questioning [drew] from Mrs. Allen the secret of her desire for outdoor employment of a kind not too laborious for her slender strength, and her idea that she might find it in bee-raising, had she the means to buy a hive, a swarm of the insects, and a book of instructions.
> "You shall have them all," Grandma Elsie said, "everything that is necessary to enable you to give the business a fair trial" [Finley, *Elsie and the Raymonds* 123–24].

Mrs. Allen insists on the advance being only a loan, so that she may pay Elsie back in the future. Elsie is perfectly willing to give Mrs. Allen all the "means" that she needs to start in beekeeping, and the two women find that their common faith is a strong bond of friendship, but the fact remains that Elsie herself would never have any need for a loan, or even a profession. Mrs. Allen and her daughter will be employed and comfortable, but they can never attain the class status of the Dinsmores.

It might appear to be a contradiction in terms that Elsie, a deeply devout Protestant, does not feel qualms about her wealth. William Leach, in his study of the development of department stores, points out that wealth and Christianity were often seen to go together in the nineteenth century, despite the clear problems of poverty that capitalism presented and the secular culture that was just beginning to make inroads into religious life. Department store mogul John Wanamaker was a primary example of this attitude:

> For his part, Wanamaker believed that religion and commerce were both in a healthy condition in the United States, not the one declining, the other rising, because he himself had worked so hard to give life to both worlds. And he was hardly alone in this conviction. It was probably the majority view, shared by many affluent evangelical and liberal Protestants in established denominations, as well as by many middle-class Catholics and Jews [191–192].

If wealth was bestowed on an individual or a country, it was seen as a sign of God's favor. Those who possessed wealth had an obligation to spend at least a part of it on the public good. Wanamaker built four churches and the Bethany Mission in Philadelphia, became one of the major benefactors and close friends of the evangelist Dwight Moody, and was the first paid secretary of the national YMCA. Wealth was a blessing from God, and as long as one willingly used the money to help others, there was no need to be ashamed of it.[9] Elsie and her entire family act on this philosophy throughout the stories. Despite the class differences that remain between the Dinsmores and their beneficiaries, Finley succeeds in creating a common ground based on religious virtue, and in this sense her views correspond with those of the benevolence workers. Elsie and her family are happy to interact with any Evangelical Protestants, no matter what their class. Virtue is a greater asset than wealth and useful work is always preferred over idleness. Young Elsie, Elsie's oldest child, marries a poor man by the name of Lester Leland. Her parents approve of the match because he is a faithful Christian and an industrious worker; they do not object to his poverty. Elsie does her best to teach her children that they must not depend on the wealth that their parents possess, but plan on learning a profession. An example of this is given when Elsie's son, little Herbert, expresses his opinion that he probably will not need a career since they are so wealthy already:

> "But mamma, it seems to me I shall not need to do much when I'm a man," [Herbert] remarked a little shamefacedly; "haven't you a great deal of money to give us all?"
> "It may all be gone before you are grown up," she said gravely. "I shall be glad to lose it if its possession is to be the ruin of my sons. But I do not intend to let any of you live in idleness, for that would be a sin, because our talents must be improved to the utmost and used in God's service, whether we have much or little money or none at all. Therefore each of my boys must study a profession or learn some handicraft by which he can earn his own living or make money to use in doing good" [*Elsie's Widowhood* 99].

Here, like Alcott, we see Finley advocating for a life of Christian usefulness over one of worldly-minded wealth. Herbert might be right in thinking that he will not have to work in order to maintain himself, but that is not the point. Being useful and helpful to others is directly related to living a commendable Christian life and being a good community member and citizen. If Herbert makes enough money that he does not need all of it, he can use it to improve the lives of others. Elsie directly references Matthew 25: 14–30, the Parable of the Talents, when she says "our talents must be improved to the utmost and used in God's service." That Finley's characters are wealthy and Alcott's are relatively poor matters not at all; what matters is what the characters do with their resources. Being a good citizen and a good Christian is about being charitable and sustaining the community in every way, no matter how much or how little one has to give. While men like John Wanamaker might have provided large sums of money for bigger projects, it was women who did much of the everyday community caretaking, church fundraising, nursing, and work of poverty relief.

It is to Finley's credit that Elsie is not only generous to the poorer whites that live in her community, but to the former slaves and their children. Like the class dynamics, the racial barriers never entirely fall away in the text, but Elsie does extend her generosity to the newly free men and women who still work for her family. In *Christmas with Grandma Elsie*, for example, Elsie and her children and grandchildren set up Christmas trees and gifts in two schoolhouses, one for the poor white children of the neighborhood and one for the African American families. Finley writes that the white children "received a suit of warm, comfortable clothes, a book, a bag of candy, a sandwich or two, some cakes and fruit. The tree was hung with rosy cheeked apples, oranges, bananas, bunches of grapes and strings of popcorn" (Finley, *Christmas* 39). At the schoolhouse for the African American children, "The exercises and the gifts to the children were very nearly the same, but there were older people — house servants and laborers on the estates — to whom were given more substantial gifts in money and provisions for the support of their families,"(Finley, *Christmas* 39).

It is ironic from our twenty-first century viewpoint that Elsie's family (at this point made up of Dinsmores, Travillas, and Raymonds) should hold such separate but equal celebrations for the poor whites and the African Americans in their neighborhood. One is forced to wonder how these two groups might have interacted had they all been invited to the same Christmas party. The Dinsmore clan, wittingly or unwittingly, is reinforcing not only class but also racial lines by separating their African American workers from their poor white neighbors and holding Christmas for the two groups in different locations.

Furthermore, there is the curious fact that only the white children and their teacher are present at the white schoolhouse, while parents and older family members are included in the gift giving at the African American schoolhouse. Why are the African American adults given "more substantial gifts in money and provisions" while the white adults are not? Why are the white adults not even present to see their children receive gifts? Finley may be making a subtle, perhaps unconscious, commentary on race and class: the African American adults have no choice but to accept "substantial gifts" from the Dinsmores if they want to survive economically, just as they have little choice in working for them.[10] The white adults have a choice: poor as they are, they can refuse outside assistance for the sake of pride, though they might allow the Dinsmores to make a happy Christmas for their children. By the same token, the Dinsmores might feel that they would offend the white adults by inviting them to the celebration and giving them gifts as though they were objects of charity. The African Americans, by virtue of their class and race, are automatically classified as in need of benevolence. Giving the adults gifts as well as the children renders the adults childlike, removing them one step further from the spiritually evolved, economically prosperous, and white Dinsmores. Although the Dinsmores might be trying to assert the *spiritual* equality of everyone, regardless of race or class, the presence of the African American adults reveals a dark side to the Dinsmores' altruism.

Elsie influences the community in other ways beyond her generosity to her neighbors. In *Elsie's Widowhood*, a male member of the church calls on her to ask her opinion of one of the church's ministerial candidates. Mr. Embury is surprised to find that Elsie does not approve of the candidate, a Mr. Jones, because his faith and his preaching alike are unacceptable. She argues:

> "[H]is preaching is far from satisfactory to me; he makes nothing of the work of the Spirit, or the danger of grieving him away forever; nothing of the danger of self-deception; instructing those who are in doubt about the genuineness of their conversion that they must not be discouraged, instead of advising them to go to Christ now and be saved, just as any other sinner must. I fear his teaching may lead some to be content with a false hope. Then he often speaks in a half hesitating way, which shows doubt and uncertainty, on his part, of truths which are taught most plainly and forcibly in scripture. In a word, his preaching leaves the impression upon me that he has no very thorough acquaintance with the Bible, and no very strong confidence in the infallibility of its teachings. Indeed so glaring are his contradictions of scripture, that even my young children have noticed them more than once or twice."
>
> "Really, Mrs. Travilla, you make out a strong case against him," remarked her interlocutor, after a moment's thoughtful silence, "and upon reflection I believe a true one. I am surprised at myself that I have listened with so little realization of the important defects in his system of theology. I was not ardently in favor of calling him before; now I am decidedly opposed to it" [135–36].

This passage is critical. Elsie does not interpret the Bible for Mr. Embury or the minister, but she is saying that the minister interprets Scripture badly and cannot put its messages together into a coherent sermon. Even her children — like Elsie herself as a child — can see the errors in the minister's reasoning. To make it even worse, the minister impedes the conversions of his congregation because he does not encourage them to go immediately to God with their doubts. He is not only weak in faith, he is weak in instructing others in faith. Elsie's reference to "the work of the Spirit" is also important; she echoes many nineteenth-century women evangelists who claimed that the Spirit was the religious authority with whom they had intimate contact and who guided their actions. By "mak[ing] nothing of the work of the Spirit," Mr. Jones may even be impeding Elsie's connection to the Spirit and God. As we know, this is something that she will not allow even her father to do, much less her minister. He is hindering her faith instead of helping it and doing the same to other members of the congregation. Elsie presents a case against Mr. Jones to a man who is her superior in the church hierarchy because it is her duty to God to try and prevent this minister from being called to her congregation.

Elsie's duty as a True Woman demands that she help to uphold the morality of her community. Community members cannot be good Christians if they do not have a strong leader, and Elsie's moral authority as a respected Christian woman gives her the power to pass judgment. Her persuasion is even more impressive in the text because Mr. Embury is brought to a realization of his own flawed assessment; he has failed to absorb the "important defects in [Jones's] system of theology." Elsie's argument convinces him that she is right. In this passage we see that not only does Elsie take charge of caring for her family, neighbors, and employees, looking after them body and soul, but she even has the ability to recommend that her church not accept a pastor who seems weak in faith. For a woman to demonstrate her intelligence in regard to moral and religious questions was seen as a natural part of the endowment of her sex, even though her mental abilities might be questioned in other areas. For Elsie, taking advantage of that assumption is another way of keeping the community together through the church and ensuring the spiritual well-being of the congregants.

Postbellum True Womanhood and the Chautauqua Girls

Despite all of her careful care of her family's spiritual needs, her active benevolence in the community, and her donations to missions and other benevolent societies, we do not see Elsie become involved in organized social reform or temperance. Isabella Alden's *Chautauqua Girls* series creates the final bridge, in some ways, between the antebellum and postbellum ideas of True Womanhood, benevolence, and Protestantism. Her four heroines take that final step, deliberately becoming active in managerial philanthropy and temperance, equal parts evangelists and political activists. They move one step closer to the New Women of the Progressive Era.

The first volume of Alden's Chautauqua series, *Four Girls at Chautauqua*, is based on the events of the 1875 meeting and was published in 1876 (Rieser 185–186).[11] Ruth Erskine and Flossy Shipley come from quite wealthy families, while Eureka "Eurie" Mitchell is a doctor's daughter, and Marion Wilbur is a single teacher with no family. Eurie's family is middle-class, although their income varies with the number of patients the doctor has to see. Marion makes enough to keep herself in a boarding house and dress very respectably, but she is the poorest of the four. The girls travel to Chautauqua for their summer vacation thinking it will be a "frolic" (Alden, *Four Girls* 2). What they find are their respective faiths and their callings as Christian women, although the effects of the vacation are not explained until the second volume of the series, *The Chautauqua Girls at Home*.

The Chautauqua Girls undergo conversion experiences while spending the summer at Chautauqua Lake. Each has a different personality and different shortcomings, and Alden makes clear from the beginning that the only thing they are all lacking is true religious faith. That lack is why they have failed to reach their potential as Christian women and community leaders. Christianity is not something that these girls feel at a young age the way Elsie Dinsmore does. They are churchgoers but indifferent Christians, going to church as a matter of social duty. In this sense they might be more analogous to Elsie's father; church is something to be endured for the sake of respectability. The experience of conversion for each of these four girls is portrayed as something profoundly emotional and spiritual, something felt with the heart and altering one's perception of the world. Also unlike Elsie, these girls occasionally fail at their attempts to be upright Christians; despite their best intentions, they sometimes do not behave in the way that they should, and they miss opportunities to bring others to their faith. They are refreshingly imperfect, not immediately realizing all of their potential influence over the lives of others, although they gradually learn to exercise it.

It is important to define precisely the kind of conversion these girls undergo. In some respects it is easier to define the conversions by what they are not. The Chautauqua Girls are not brought up as devoted Christians from day one, as Elsie is. They do not fall ill or have visions of God and Jesus, as so many of the female evangelists from the Second Great Awakening did. They do not feel called to preach. They do not come to Christ through the illness of a loved one, as Horace Dinsmore does, nor do they spend days and nights agonizing over their own sinfulness. Each girl spends several days of the meeting feeling restless and unhappy without quite knowing the cause. Over the course of their two weeks at Chautauqua, each girl has experiences that lead her to question her lack of faith. Slowly, they all begin participating in the different Chautauqua events instead of being passive listeners. Each has some unique, personal experience that shows her the love of God, either with other members of the meeting or in solitude. Each girl resolves in her own heart to be a Christian and makes a conscious effort to act as one from that moment forward. Like Finley, Alden is not advocating the doctrine of election in her books; one can choose to save oneself, but one still has to offer oneself to God as an instrument and be prepared to follow the will of God.

Flossy comes the closest to the Elsie Dinsmore model of Christian womanhood. Flossy is happy to ignore social position in the name of bringing souls to Christ; people who already profess the faith are important to her no matter what their class. When she is just beginning to learn about her faith at the Chautauqua meeting, she impulsively teaches a Sunday School lesson to two poor boys. She is a little afraid of their appearance, at first: "Had they been a little older, and been dressed well ... she would have known what to say to them. But boys who were not more than twelve or fourteen, and who were both ragged and dirty, were new phases of life to her" (Alden, *Four Girls* 178). Flossy must learn to overlook class; she has to see past the "ragged and dirty" bodies of the young boys before she can teach them. She is a quick learner, however, and successfully engages them in the Sunday School lesson.

From then on, religious faith for Flossy becomes the true way to judge a person's merit. Class does not matter in the least to her even when she becomes engaged. She meets a gentleman named Evan Roberts at Chautauqua who befriends her and helps her to find her faith. He reappears in *The Chautauqua Girls at Home* to ask for her hand. She delightedly accepts, realizing only belatedly that she knows nothing about his social position:

> [H]e might have some money or he might be very poor, she had not the least idea which it was; he might be of an old or honored family, or his father might have been a blacksmith and his mother, even now, a washerwoman. She admitted to herself that she knew nothing at all about it; and she was obliged also to admit that, so far as she herself was concerned, she did not care.
> But Mr. Shipley was very different. Most assuredly he would care [Alden, *At Home* 270–71].

Mr. Shipley does care. He is already upset with Flossy for refusing the proposal of a Col. Baker, an old friend of the family who is also quite wealthy. He regards her refusal as a rebellion against him, a passing phase to be blamed on her Chautauqua experience. He does not share or approve of her religious sentiments. In a discussion of the family pastor, Dr. Dennis, Mr. Shipley rejects the religious and community authority that the preacher is supposed to hold: "I never call them my spiritual guides, and I have not the least desire to have my daughter do so. I consider myself capable of guiding my own family, especially my own children, without any help" (Alden, *At Home* 112). Mr. Shipley is not unlike Mr. Dinsmore in his attitude toward the clergy and organized religion. Flossy's resistance to card playing, dancing, and playing secular songs on the Sabbath all irritate him exceedingly, although he does not physically punish her for refusing his requests as Horace Dinsmore might have done. Flossy succeeds in following her own conscience, but she fails to convert her father to Evangelical Protestantism. As far as we are told, she does not succeed in bringing either her mother or her father to a change of heart.

When Evan Roberts proposes to Flossy, we see exactly how susceptible Mr. Shipley is to wealth. Unbeknownst to Flossy, Mr. Roberts is a junior partner in one of the most prosperous mercantile firms in the country. He is highly respected and very wealthy. He approaches Mr. Shipley simultaneously with offers of business and a request for his daughter's hand. Both are granted almost without a murmur. Evan says after his interview with Mr. Shipley, "That man would actually sell her, if by that means he could be recognized in business by our house" (Alden, *At Home* 273). Thanks to the social prestige of her new engagement, Flossy's father allows her to do anything she likes: "She was free, now, to go to parties or to prayer meetings or to stay at home ... for was she not the promised wife of a partner of the firm Bostwick, Smythe, Roberts & Co.?" (Alden, *At Home* 274).

Flossy ignores her father's snobbery, however, and readers soon see how invulnerable she has become to considerations of class and social position. Evan takes her to the city slums, where he has been providing for a mother and daughter who are both very sick and living in a cellar:

> A dreadful pile of straw covered over by a tattered and horribly dirty rag that had once been a quilt; on this bed lay a child not yet ten years old whose pale face and glassy eyes told of hopeless sickness. No pillow on which to lay the poor little head with its tangled masses of yellow hair, nothing anywhere that told of care bestowed or necessary wants attended to. Over in another corner on another filthy heap of straw and rags lay the mother, sick, too, with the same absence of anything like decency in everything that pertained to her [Alden, *At Home* 276].

As in the *Elsie Dinsmore* stories, the picture of poverty presented in the text belies the idea that class can be erased through a common faith. The "filthy heaps of straw" and "horribly dirty rags" must be replaced by actual beds and clean linen, as well as washed bodies, problems which Flossy and Evan immediately solve. The sick woman and her daughter must be given the basics of respectability and "decency"— in other words, the basics of middle-class status — along with the basics of Evangelical faith.

Interestingly, in this particular scene we do not see any proselytizing; it is only implied in Flossy's resolution to come back and make sure the child is cured and the mother is comfortable. Flossy's exposure to such severe poverty and her graceful response to it are the key pieces of this scene. She is able to take poverty in stride and try to alleviate it, as a good Christian should. As she says to Evan, "I never knew there was anything like this in the world; I am bowed in the very dust with shame and dismay. There is very little that I know how to do, but I can wash this poor, neglected child's face" (Alden, *At Home* 278). She does not shrink from the filth and the illness surrounding her; she simply does the first job at hand, which happens to be washing a child's face. She turns her "shame and dismay" at the state of the little family into immediate actions.

Evan introduces her to "the great and systematic charities of the city" and Flossy takes a keen interest in them. She actively moves into organized charity and benevolence, learning very quickly "what wonderful things God's wealth could do, placed in the hands of careful and conscientious stewards" (Alden, *At Home* 274). She also realizes that, thanks to Evan's income, she may contribute generously to these charities in addition to doing hands-on work:

> She had thought at first that it made no difference at all to her whether Mr. Roberts had to work for his daily bread or whether he had means at his disposal; but very early in her acquaintance with him she learned to thank God that great wealth had been placed in his hands, and so, was to be at her disposal, and that she was learning how to use it [*At Home* 274].

The allusion to the Lord's Prayer with the phrase "his daily bread" is curious. Ordinarily, the prayer asks God to "give us this day our daily bread," implying that anything gotten through work is a gift from God. Flossy thanks God that "wealth has been placed in Evan's hands," implying again that it is a heavenly gift. By this logic, whether Evan has to work for his income or whether he is independently wealthy makes no difference; whatever income he attains comes from God. We know that Evan is a junior partner in a mercantile firm; the difference implied by "work" or "means at his disposal" seems to be a class difference. "Work" might mean that he attains a comfortable middle class income, but is never wealthy; "means at his disposal" indicates that he is comfortably upper class. Despite Flossy's conviction that the level of Evan's income does not matter to her, his wealth makes an important difference in her circumstances. Evan's income and his promise of marriage keep Flossy herself in an upper-class position and assure that she is not subjected to any of the miseries of poverty that she tries to alleviate. The Lord's Prayer allusion illustrates the same ideal which appears in *Elsie Dinsmore*, that wealth is a sign of God's favor and should be used to help others. By the end of the novel, after more excursions with Evan, Flossy says, "I do think there ought to be an organized system of charity in our church; something different from the haphazard way of doing things which we have. Mr. Roberts says that in New York, their church is perfectly organized to look after certain localities, and that no such thing as utter destitution can prevail in their section" (Alden, *At Home*, 296). We are left to assume that Flossy makes that thought an accomplished fact.

Flossy also has a great deal of skill in advocating for those who might not need monetary help but could use social polish and connections to make their lives smoother. Yet again, her blindness to class, her ability to see people as humans she can help, is part of what makes her a useful and successful Christian minister. When she takes over the Sunday School class of teenage boys at church, her one earnest desire is to teach them a little of what she knows about the Christian way of life. Simply by her example, she also teaches them manners and social courtesy: "She had not only helped her boys to be true to their convictions of right and dignity, not only to take on true manliness of decision in regard to the all-important question of personal religion, she had helped them to be gentlemen" (Alden, *At Home* 284). She has all of the boys to a party at her home, along with a very carefully chosen set of acquaintances who will be willing to help the boys along their way, whether by helping them to find jobs or giving them social opportunities. Flossy makes everyone, especially the boys, feel at home, and because she takes no notice of the fact that they are of a slightly lower class than herself, no one else does either. This is Flossy's gift, and she employs it all throughout her life. As in the *Elsie Dinsmore* series, overlooking class differences is part of what allows women to assert themselves and become activists for themselves and others. To reiterate Lori Ginzberg's point: "If women only fulfilled their 'female destiny,' and behaved more morally than men, they could dissolve class boundaries, at least for women. If they identified with 'virtue,' all but the poorest could achieve what has come to be labeled 'middle-class respectability'" (24). Flossy demonstrates that through her moral conduct as a Christian woman, she can also dissolve class differences between men.

The other wealthy girl of the quartet, Ruth Erskine, has less success than Flossy in putting the lessons learned at Chautauqua into practice. The four remaining volumes of Alden's six-volume series focus primarily on her. Ruth's father has even more money than the Shipleys, and Ruth has always been a social leader. After her experience at Chautauqua, Ruth considers herself a Christian, but she has a harder time learning how to live as one and makes many and frequent mistakes. Class snobbery is her primary problem, and it is a much more difficult one for her than Flossy. Ruth has a terrible tendency to look down on people who are not as wealthy or refined as herself. This is comically illustrated the first time she attempts to make a church call at the request of her pastor. She expects to call on the poor and distribute religious tracts; she is dismayed to find that she is actually calling on members of the middle class. She has no idea how to talk to them. She perceives them as her social inferiors, but they are not poor enough to need charity; therefore, she feels as though she cannot do anything for them: "Ruth had never made calls before when she had the least tinge of embarrassment. If she could have divested herself on [sic] the idea that she was a district visitor out distributing tracts, she would not have felt so now; but as it was, the feeling grew upon her every instant" (Alden, *At Home* 151). Not only does Ruth know almost nothing about charitable visits (Flossy is miles ahead of her in this respect), but she has not learned how to be sociable with anyone in the middle class. She has no idea how to be simply neighborly to anyone who is not in her economic bracket.

When her friend Marion Wilbur learns of her attempts at calling, she laughs heartily and points out the folly of Ruth's attitude, driving home yet again the idea that wealth should not be used to judge the character of others: "Do use your common sense; you have some, I am sure. Wherein are these people whom you went to see on a lower footing than yourself? Granting that they have less money than you do, or even, perhaps, less than I have, are you ready to admit that money is the question that settles positions in society?" (Alden, *At Home* 155). Ruth is not given a chance to answer; Marion's rhetorical question ends the chapter. Faith, not money, is what should "settle positions in society"; the fact that the families Ruth calls upon are members of her church and her faith should make them her equals. Class is a longstanding problem for Ruth, and it takes her a good portion of her adult life to conquer her prejudices. She must learn to overlook class as Flossy does and see the goodness in people without regard for their class standing.

Ruth's second obstacle to realizing her full potential as a Christian woman is her reluctance to share her faith with others and actively try to bring them into the church. She shrinks from personally witnessing to others throughout the first three books of the series. She refuses to discuss her faith with her father (Flossy succeeds in getting Mr. Erskine to a prayer meeting, which is the beginning of his faith), with her first fiancé Harold Wayne, who eventually dies from an illness, with her husband, Judge Burnham, who disapproves of evangelism, or with her two stepdaughters, who are determined social butterflies. Eventually, however, she is drawn into the Woman's Christian Temperance Union by one of the married ladies of her community. As a member of this organization she begins to make significant inroads on her own weaknesses.

Ruth's first task for the WCTU deals with a local hotel, the Shenandoah, which her husband owns. Judge Burnham must consent to any liquor being served on the premises, and Ruth tries to convince him that he should not allow alcohol at the hotel. He initially refuses her persistent requests, but after a long and bitter quarrel, the judge deeds the hotel to his son, with Ruth as the executor of the property until their son is of age. The Shenandoah becomes a dry hotel, Ruth's relationship with her husband heals to a certain extent, and the ladies of the WCTU embrace her as a member. Ruth gives her full support to the WCTU and becomes a constant at their prayer meetings.

The next step in Ruth's activism, and in overcoming her reticence about her faith, is leading a WCTU temperance meeting. She consents to it with great reluctance:

> You who were well acquainted with Ruth Erskine will remember that this would have been a startling innovation to her, even in her girlhood, and the matron had not developed in those directions ... [H]er conscience, being closely questioned, could give her no sufficient reason why she should refuse to share in a work whose object she approved [Alden, *Burnham's Daughters* 150].

Ruth has not "developed in those directions" because she has always refused to personally witness her faith to anyone. It is a momentous step for her to lead a public meeting and openly profess her religion in front of a roomful of strangers. Her courage is rewarded, however, in two ways. Her preaching in the crowded hall brings a young working man into the evangelical fold, and he also decides to take the temperance pledge: "And she had been the instrument! It was the first time in her life that she had ever been so distinctly chosen and used" (Alden, *Burnham's Daughters* 159). In addition, that same meeting acts as a turning point for Ruth's husband, Judge Burnham; he begins to seriously question his own ideas about faith from that point forward. Although at the time he is highly displeased with Ruth's decision to speak publicly, he tells her afterward that "I never forgot it ... I silenced you, but not my own conscience; I never got away from it" (Alden, *Burnham's Daughters* 276). Thus Ruth's willingness to finally witness to her community is rewarded by seeing her husband come to God.

Ruth slowly realizes that simply becoming a Christian at Chautauqua is not enough. She must learn to overlook class differences and speak of her faith to others if she wants to be more active in bringing souls to her faith and creating change. The WCTU allows her to do both of those things as well as promote the temperance platform. Alden's accomplishment in her writing is that she vividly depicts the personal struggles that Ruth, Flossy, and other women overcome in order to be advocates for their faith and their social beliefs. Flossy fights her parents and siblings (although not her husband) for the right to live by her own conscience and make her own moral choices; Ruth consistently fails to live up to her own standards of Christian behavior and encounters continual resistance to her faith from most of her family, including her husband and stepdaughters. It is not until she joins the WCTU that she finds a clear calling and truly learns how to be an Evangelical Protestant.

For the Chautauqua Girls, learning to live as Christian women means that they have to learn *both* the lessons of the Marches and of Elsie Dinsmore: They must learn to "be good," to begin with, to shed their class privilege, snobbery, and other faults, to think of others before themselves, and to help members of their community through charity and personal assistance. Like Jo and Amy March, they have to learn to control their character flaws. Then, like Elsie, they must learn to use their religious faith to bring others to the church. They must encourage other members of their families and towns to become active Christians. While Alden's religious beliefs are as prominent as Finley's, she makes her characters less perfect and more believable than Elsie, more prone to human faults and failures. Ruth's faith must be constantly worked at, consciously thought about, continually renewed, for her to live as a Christian woman, for otherwise she falls back into the lax non-religious lifestyle of the upper class. Flossy, too, though she is much less prone to class faults than Ruth, has to guard against her need to please people at the expense of her faith. It is very easy for her to say "yes" to her father, her mother, or her brother, and much harder for her to say "no," even when her "no" is in regard to a matter of religious principle. Finally, the Chautauqua Girls move several steps beyond the Marches and Elsie, becoming workers for organized benevolent associations and political activists with the WCTU.

The fictional series written by Alcott, Finley, and Alden reveal the ways in which True Womanhood slowly transitioned into New Womanhood. With their acceptance into their community church, the young women in these stories gain a new sort of influence that has been greatly overlooked and undervalued in critical assessments. To begin with, they become part of a spiritual community that supports them emotionally and gives them other people to lean on and look to for help when it is needed. They acquire the power to spiritually influence others and to literally alter the direction of individual lives. By ministering to family members, the poor, the ill, and sometimes even the criminal, these women gain the power, at least on paper, to bring others to Christianity and thereby give those others a chance to reform themselves. The heroines of these stories become the centers of communities that look to them for advice, wisdom, and spiritual leadership.

The Marches and Elsie Dinsmore represent the best efforts of individual women to help other people in need and create a supportive Christian community. With their embrace of Chautauqua, organized benevolence, and temperance, Alden's heroines take the next steps into public political activism. Organized benevolence and WCTU work give Flossy Shipley and Ruth Erskine opportunities to develop organizational and political skills. They find a sense of purpose, excitement, and fulfillment by aiding their church, creating aid programs for the poor, tending those in their community who are sick, teaching Sunday School for the children in their lives, campaigning for temperance, and encouraging others to turn their lives around and live cleanly by embracing God. While the values espoused in these series were more conservative than those that would appear at the beginning of the new century, they nevertheless give us a clear sense of changing political and personal ideals for young women.

Notes

1. For critical work on Elsie Dinsmore, see Agnes Repplier, "Little Pharisees in Fiction"; Janet E. Brown, "The Saga of Elsie Dinsmore"; Jacqueline Jackson and Philip Kendall, "What Makes a Bad Book Good: Elsie Dinsmore"; Pam Hardman, "The Steward of Her Soul"; Deidre Johnson, "Nancy Drew — A Modern Elsie Dinsmore?"; and Gwen Tarbox, "American Children's Narrative as Social Criticism, 1865–1914."

2. See Kent, *Girls Into Women*; Foote, "Resentful *Little Women*"; Parille, "'Wake up, and be a man'"; Quimby, "The Story of Jo"; Robinson, "How Katy Lied"; and Stern, *Critical Essays*.

3. All of the reviews cited in this paragraph were published between October and November of 1868.

4. There is disagreement over whether the books Marmee gives to the girls are New Testaments or copies of *Pilgrim's Progress*. I read the books as New Testaments because Alcott calls them "that beautiful old story of the best life ever lived" (17), which is usually a euphemism for the life of Jesus. In the notes to the Modern Library edition of *Little Women*, however, Shawn Shimpach writes, "Each sister receives a copy of the same book. Although it might seem here that the book is the New Testament, later references in *Little Women* make it clear that it was *The Pilgrim's Progress*" (478). It is true that Alcott makes many references to Bunyan, but her specific description of the books leads one to think of New Testaments.

5. Geraldine Brooks has created quite a different portrait of young Marmee in her recent novel *March*, which actually details the life of Mr. March both before and during the Civil War. The Marmee of Brooks' creation is opinionated, passionate, politically active, determined, and willful — someone who would, indeed, need to learn control in order to move in society without causing scandal. In Alcott's work, we get only a hint that Marmee was like Jo — when she is trying to help Jo control her own temper. See pages 78–82 of *Little Women*.

6. That Finley is definitely not writing for Catholics becomes clear here, since Elsie has an absolute horror of convents and begins to have delirious dreams about the tortures they will put her through at such a place: "much of Elsie's reading had been on the subject of Popery and Papal institutions; that she had pored over histories of the terrible tortures of the Inquisition and stories of martyrs and captive nuns, until she had imbibed an intense horror and dread of everything connected with that form of error and superstition" (*Holidays at Roselands* 110). Elsie is terrified of going to mass, or worshiping crucifixes; to her these things are more terrible than dying.

7. Various critics have speculated that the intensity of Horace and Elsie's relationship arises from the barely concealed erotic behavior between father and daughter. Pam Hardman calls it "latent eroticism" (74), Janet Brown notes that the relationship between father and daughter is "that of mistress and jealous lover" by the end of the series (quoted in Johnson, "Modern Elsie" 15), and Jackson and Kendall go so far as to name it "erotic passion" and "incest" (58). I am wary of using the final term because the relationship between Elsie and Horace does not necessarily correspond to actual experiences of incest or to its clinical definition. Nevertheless, their relationship is certainly erotically suggestive and emotionally symbiotic. Elsie and Horace tend to put each other before everyone else and seem completely dependent on each other's

approval and love. If Elsie's love and the threat of losing her are ultimately what brings Mr. Dinsmore to convert to Evangelical Protestantism, it is equally true that Elsie's continual need for her father's love and affection is what forces her (most of the time) into his definition of "good" behavior.

Karen Sanchez-Eppler uncovers a similar pattern of father-daughter behavior in temperance fiction, a pattern that moves several steps closer to actual incest. Temperance fiction often depicts a father literally crawling into his daughter's bed out of repentance for his intoxicated cruelty, a scene that never appears in the *Elsie* books. The picture of a father in his daughter's bed certainly carries an indication of sexual abuse, or at least the potential for it. However, despite the fact that nothing in the *Elsie* books carries such a dark connotation of incest, the erotic tones, emotionally dependent relationships, and reformative aims of the narratives can be seen as analogous. In both, the love of a child for a parent is instrumental in reforming the behavior of that parent. Sanchez-Eppler argues that scenes like these are not simply about the redemptive power of children, but about the specific combination of desire and moral authority that is part of the father-daughter relationship. The desire of the father for his daughter is partly why she carries the influence she does. Drawing on Richard Brodhead's ideas about nineteenth-century disciplinary intimacy, Sanchez-Eppler states, "I am suggesting not merely that the practice of disciplining through love has erotic content, but indeed that this eroticism is essential to its functioning" (88). While Sanchez-Eppler does not bring religion into her discussion, I see it as the other key component of this type of daughter-father teaching and discipline.

8. Most of the modern criticism of *Elsie Dinsmore* seems to come from several sources of discomfort that have nothing to do with the actual merits of the books or their social arguments, including the following: (1) The books are in a series and are intentionally didactic, two traits that serve as strikes against them in the world of literary criticism. In addition, they take religion as their central agenda and theme, something not likely to endear them to readers who may feel that the books are nothing better than sermons in disguise. (2) Horace Dinsmore's methods of child-rearing are so unacceptable by current standards that they can prove hard to read about. Most critics do not consider the fact that Finley is *intentionally* painting a portrait of a father who is erring in judgment and needs parental and religious reformation. (3) The aforementioned emotionally intense relationship between father and daughter is likely to create extreme discomfort in any post–Freud reader. Most critics have commented on it either with ridicule or displeasure. (4) Elsie's "priggishness," or her certainty about morality and religion even when she is so young, may be read as self-righteousness, reinforcing the feeling that these texts are nothing better than stories that spoon-feed religion to children. While they were no doubt meant to instruct, at least some contemporary readers would have seen in Elsie a precocious child who had rightly and beautifully absorbed her duty to God. She has more than the usual potential to grow up and be a model of Christian Womanhood, a pillar for her family and community to look to for guidance. (5) In a post–Second Wave world, it is very hard to read the situations of Finley's female characters as anything but oppressive and therefore repugnant. Elsie and her daughters are permitted education of a limited kind and scope (no college or profession allowed). They are kept at home with their fathers until they marry, they keep their sexuality under lock and key, and their sole aims in life seem to be domestic and family-oriented. They hardly seem to have individual tastes or interests, having subsumed them all to the care of their husbands and children. Allen Shepherd summed up the general objections when he said, "Finley offered, one

may say, an orgy of approved bathos, crude, didactic melodrama, genteel, sub-literary sentimentalism; one could easily hypothesize further dismissive judgments..." (59).

In short, the *Elsie Dinsmore* books have not been evaluated based on their historical context; the tradition of religious benevolence that they arise from has not been considered. Most of the time, critics fail to assess Finley's work on its own terms because her moral stance and religious beliefs do not meet our current social standards of what is right, nor do they include rights for women and children that we now take for granted. These nineteenth-century texts are dismissed for failing to live up to a twenty-first century code of ethics. It needs to be recognized that within her historical time and place, Finley raises serious points about the power of women to exert positive influence in the world, about women and benevolence, and about children and religious belief. She creates a world where children who have been raised with a love for Evangelical Protestantism have a profound effect on the morality of their families and friends. Female children, in particular, exert this power. In my assessment, give the expectations that surrounded nineteenth century girls and women about becoming moral exemplars and pious mothers, it is precisely Elsie's acquired knowledge of Christianity that makes her a powerful figure in her family and eventually in her community.

9. For a discussion of the ways in which turn-of-the- century Protestantism and capitalism accommodated one another, and in fact depended on each other, see William Leach, *Land of Desire*; Susan Curtis, *A Consuming Faith*; and Andrew Rieser, *The Chautauqua Moment*, especially pages 47–85. Curtis goes the furthest in arguing that by 1930, religion had become simply one more product available to consumers, and that churches contributed to the new consuming ethos by marketing themselves as commodities, while Leach agrees that "the reaction of established religions was finally so sympathetic to America's new culture and economy as to form yet another pillar upon which the new order rested and was sustained" (192).

10. This Christmas celebration that Finley creates is even more interesting because of the post–Reconstruction tensions that were rising between poor whites and free blacks by the end of the nineteenth century. Poor whites resented sharing their class status with free blacks; they used race as a way of asserting dominance over the free black population. Race was also a way of claiming jobs and education that were made inaccessible to African Americans. The African Americans in this Christmas scene don't have a choice about working for the Dinsmores or any other white family; they have a highly limited number of options when it comes to earning money, and most of those options involve service to whites. Serving whites recreates the power dynamics of slavery even if slavery is no longer legal. Poor whites, on the other hand, are not necessarily restricted to working in the houses or fields of wealthier whites; they have greater access to education and therefore a wider range of jobs to choose from.

The timeline of the *Elsie* series may also be part of why Finley wrote this passage the way she did. While *Elsie's Motherhood* (volume five), for example, was published in 1876, Finley says in her introduction that it is set during 1867–68, immediately following the Civil War. *Christmas With Grandma Elsie* was published in 1888, but the events of the story would take place in about 1879. Finley may have been trying to keep her picture of the Reconstruction South accurate, or she may have been painting a picture of the way Reconstruction was *supposed* to work in the South, rather than portraying the disintegration that eventually took place.

11. Alden also mentions the departure date of her fictitious characters, "August 2, 1875," on page 11 of *Four Girls at Chautauqua*.

Three

A Revolution in Series Production
Edward Stratemeyer and the Commodification of Series Books

During the nearly four decades spanned by the beginning and end of the *Elsie Dinsmore* and *Chautauqua Girls* series, the transition from True Womanhood to New Womanhood as a social ideal was not the only upheaval taking place. While upper- and upper-middle class young women were being trained by their mothers in the principles of benevolent Christianity and leading the fights for temperance reform and suffrage, and the radical changes of the Civil War and Reconstruction were altering race relations, a revolution was happening in the world of publishing that created permanent changes in a number of entwined areas. Better printing technology, mandatory schooling laws, and an increase in literacy rates all had effects on book publication. The development of dime novels and story papers as forms of reading was particularly significant for series books in particular. One man was able to use these developments to transform series books from the luxury items of the late nineteenth century to highly desired commodities in the early twentieth century: Edward Stratemeyer.

Edward Stratemeyer and Dime Novels

Stratemeyer was born in 1862 in Elizabeth, New Jersey, just as the dime novels that he would later write were coming into existence. He grew up reading dime novels and Horatio Alger, Jr., stories as well as the literature considered "suitable" for his education, and showed an early inclination for writing.

While he was still in school, he attempted several amateur story papers either alone or with friends, including "Our Friend" and "The Young American." He continued his attempts after graduating from high school, creating "Our American Boys," a two-issue, eight-page story paper. He also had several short stories and poems published in various periodicals (Keeline, "Author and Literary Agent" 1–5).[1]

Stratemeyer was hardly alone in reading dime novels as he grew up. The cheap little books were ferociously popular almost from the moment of their appearance in 1860. The story paper, the forerunner of the dime novel, had provided cheap reading to the working classes since the 1830s and expanded tremendously starting in the 1850s. Michael Denning, in his book *Mechanic Accents*, defines a story paper as "an eight-page weekly newspaper, which cost five or six cents, and contained anywhere from five to eight serialized stories, as well as correspondence, brief sermons, humor, fashion advice, and bits of arcane knowledge" (10).[2] As one example, Robert Bonner of New York City bought the *Merchant's Ledger* in 1851 and by 1856 had turned it from a business paper into a story paper. He paid lavish sums to famous authors to print their pieces and spent a fortune on advertising. His peak circulation with the refashioned *New York Ledger* was 350,000 copies weekly (Kelley, *Private Woman* 4). Other publishers soon followed suit: Street & Smith began the *New York Weekly* in 1859, and four other story papers appeared in the next fourteen years (Denning 10–11).

Dime novels came into being slightly later through the publishing firm Beadle and Adams, also known as Irwin P. Beadle and Co. (Johannsen). The firm brought out their first ten-cent book in 1860 and sold four million of them by 1865 (Denning 10–11). They hit upon the idea of running the books in a "series" or set that could be collected: "*Beadle's Dime Novels* (1860–1874) was a series of paper covered booklets, published at regular intervals, and numbered in sequence. For 14 years, a new title was issued by the publishers ... every two weeks or so, 321 in all. Each booklet was approximately 4 by 6 inches in cover size and was about 100 pages long" (Cox xii). Dime novels were easily transported, being much lighter and more compact than a more expensive printing would have been. Working-class men, boys, and young women all carried them to work, sometimes sharing the stories with their fellow workers and reading aloud in the factories or during their lunch hour (Enstad 56–58). The small size of dime novels was also a boon during the Civil War. Albert Johannsen writes, "The newly levied troops which afterwards made up the Army of Northern Virginia had a craving for print, and hundreds of thousands of the novels were sent to occupy their idle hours in the camp" (1: xxiv). Johannsen later indicates that the Northern Army also received dime novels from the firm (1: 39). Other ambitious publishers, including George Munro, his brother Norman Munro, Frank Tousey, Street & Smith, and Robert DeWitt, copied the form pioneered by Beadle and Adams (Cox xviii-xix; LeBlanc 15–18).

The four by six dime novel format changed as other firms put out dime novels and as competition pushed everyone to come up with new ideas that would capture the public. The next innovation was the "library," a series of new dime novels that was issued on a weekly basis. The name "library" eventually gave way to the name "weekly" due to the timing of each new novel.

> The term "library" ... did not originate with Beadle and Adams nor was it restricted to their publications... As applied to dime novels, it described publications which were 8 × 11 inches with at least 16 pages of double and triple-column fine print and which were issued in regular sequence. There were other sizes as well; smaller ones were 6 × 8 inches, with 32 pages, larger ones 9 × 12 inches with more than 60 pages [Cox xiv].

The term "dime novel" was a catch-all that included at least four different formats of a story, with a varying number of pages depending on the paper size of the publication. Nor were all dime novels ten cents; beginning in the 1870s, Beadle and Adams and other firms began issuing stories that were shorter and sold for five cents, hoping to appeal to poorer and younger boys that did not have as much money to spend (Cox xiv). In addition, once the dime novel libraries became "weeklies," the dime novels and story papers begin to overlap to a greater and greater extent. A story that appeared in installments in a weekly or a story paper would very often be issued again as a dime novel, capitalizing on the same story and the same market twice over.

Stratemeyer learned the tricks of the dime novel and story paper trade firsthand. As a twenty-seven year old, while working in his half-brother's tobacco shop, Stratemeyer submitted a story for boys to the Philadelphia youth magazine *Golden Days* which was accepted and brought him seventy-five dollars. The following year, in 1890, Stratemeyer began working for Street & Smith, the publisher of many dime novels as well as the *New York Weekly*. In 1892 alone Stratemeyer wrote fourteen dime novels for Street & Smith, and soon after that he became the editor of *Good News*, one of the publisher's story papers for boys. He wrote another twenty-eight dime novels for Street & Smith in 1893 (Johnson, *Stratemeyer Pseudonyms* xiv-xvi). By 1896 he had published several hardcover books for boys and started his own fiction magazine, *Bright Days*. Although the magazine only lasted about a year, Stratemeyer increased his story resume by publishing his own work (*Stratemeyer Pseudonyms* xvii). In 1899, Stratemeyer picked up work finishing an incomplete manuscript by Oliver Optic, the pen name of William Taylor Adams. The

Optic stories were some of the most popular and enduring dime novels. When Adams died in 1897, he left a first chapter and an overall outline for a book, which Stratemeyer completed. All of these experiences plunged Stratemeyer fully into the world of turn-of-the-century publishing and popular fiction.

Story papers and dime novels were successful for a number of reasons. The improvement of printing technology in the first half of the nineteenth century played a significant role in making reading material more accessible to the public. Perhaps the most significant improvements for the production of both story papers and dime novels were those related to the printing press.[3]

The need for fast and cheap periodical production drove the development of new printing technology throughout the nineteenth century. Book costs lowered gradually, but the development of national newspapers demanded presses that could handle large editions and massive amounts of type on a daily basis: "Serving both public purpose and private interest, newspapers proliferated at a dizzying pace up and down the coast and deep into the Western frontier.... Some 200 papers circulated in 1800; a quarter-century later, that figure had grown four-fold to 861, then swelled to 1,400 by 1840" (Gross 317). Better presses and binding machines were what allowed for the massive increase in newspapers, periodicals, and other types of printed material.

The success of the dime novel and story paper publishers was not only due to faster, more efficient printing and distribution.[4] Publishers created a "fiction factory" system that allowed stories to be created quickly, cheaply, and in massive numbers. Editors or their subordinates would create a basic plot outline for a story that would then be handed off to any number of writers employed by the firm. The average dime novel story was 30,000–40,000 words, and a writer would be paid $100-$250 for his or her work, no royalties attached (Denning 21–22; Johnson, *Stratemeyer Pseudonyms* xv-xvi.). Writing dime novels was often a way to supplement a low income: "[D]ime novel writers were able to support themselves by their writing for a time, but only the most prolific kept it up for an entire career and few seem to have made large sums of money.... Writing cheap stories was often combined with journalism, schoolteaching, and working for the popular theater" (Denning 20–21). Pay for one story would sustain a person for a few weeks, depending on how cheaply or expensively one lived, but not longer than that. Since dime novels were a strong market up until the economic panic of 1893, as long as one could keep writing, one could earn money.[5]

Formulaic plots and characters were another staple of the dime novel. This partly served to make the work faster for ghostwriters: "Stock characters, situations, and plots were played and replayed with minor variations, an almost unavoidable consequence of the pressure on writers to keep pace with production by turning out 25,000 to 50,000 words of frenetically paced story on a weekly, biweekly, or monthly schedule" (Johnson, *Edward Stratemeyer* 18). John Cawelti also points to this unavoidably practical aspect of formulaic stories: "For creators, the formula provides a means for the rapid and efficient production of new works" (9). It has been suggested that the popularity of these stories rests precisely on their repetitiveness and familiarity. In *Sensational Designs*, Jane Tompkins says:

> For a novel's impact on the culture at large depends not on its escape from the formulaic and derivative, but on its tapping into a storehouse of commonly held assumptions, reproducing what is already there in a typical and familiar form. The text that becomes exceptional in the sense of reaching an exceptionally large audience does not do so because of its departure from the ordinary and conventional, but through its embrace of what is most widely shared [xvi].

Domestic fiction, in other words, was popular precisely because it followed a formula, because it reflected assumptions held in the culture at large. The same was true for dime novels and series books, even though the former was marketed toward the working class and the latter toward the middle class. The formula changed depending on the class of reader, but within dime novels or series the plots and characters stayed very consistent and predictable. Dime novel heroes were slightly darker and more imperfect than their series book counterparts; although "They are courageous, generous, and physically fit, as well as resourceful, quick-witted, and prone to act while others stand agape" (Johnson, *Edward Stratemeyer* 23), they are also prone to vices like drinking, gambling, patronizing dance halls, and using slang. Series book heroes and heroines are unimpeachable. They posses all the qualities of dime novel heroes without any of their vices.

Cawelti astutely argues that children, adolescents, and adults all find comfort in formula fiction, although for different reasons. Children love hearing the same story over and over, both because it is happily familiar and because it allows their imagination to roam. While new stories and imaginary places make sure children "are prepared to deal with new situations and experiences" (1), the repeated stories allow retreat to a familiar and desired, if fantastical, place.

> Older children and adults continue to find a special delight in familiar stories, though in place of the child's pleasure in the identical tale, they substitute an interest in certain types of stories which have highly predictable structures that guarantee the fulfillment of conventional expectations: the western, the romance, the spy story, and many other such types [Cawelti 1].

Dime novels and series books were two other types of books that relied on conventions to attract their audience. Each new dime novel or volume of a series featured a common hero or heroine and a plot that contained expected elements, but the details and complexity of each story were different, thereby keeping the readers' interest and comfort in the stories ongoing.

Publishers were not above using the same story twice in a series, either. In addition to moving a story from the story paper installment to a complete dime novel, editors and publishers would sometimes have the same story reworked and issue it as a later number in a library series. Sometimes the same story would be reprinted in its entirety, with a new title or a new pseudonym affixed to it (Johannsen vii–viii). Publishers thus fed the voracious appetites of their readers even when they were short on finished copy.

The other important piece of dime novel production was the use of pseudonyms. Publishers kept all copyrights to themselves, and authors were required to sign away any rights to creation, copyright, or royalties. This gave publishers the rights to issue books under pseudonyms, thereby creating the illusion of one author when in reality there were several or perhaps many. This also meant that the publisher had complete control over their fictitious "author," even to the extent of being able to defend that "person" in court: "[T]he tendency of the industry was to shift from selling an 'author,' who was a free laborer, to selling a 'character,' a trademark whose stories could be written by a host of writers and whose celebrity could be protected in court" (Denning 20). A "character" author would never leave the company, even if individual authors came and went. "Oliver Optic," "Horatio Alger Jr.," "Carolyn Keene," "Franklin W. Dixon," and countless other "writers" could go on endlessly, no matter who was holding the pen.

Stratemeyer began writing formula fiction in earnest when he started the *Rover Boys* series in 1899, the same year that he completed William Adams' unfinished story. The books told the story of three brothers, their adventures at school, through college, and marriage and then continued with the story of their own sons. The series ran for thirty volumes and was an unqualified success. Stratemeyer put the books out under the name "Arthur M. Winfield," and the series established the template for other series that he would produce when he began his publishing syndicate seven years later. Stratemeyer took up the work of another famous author from 1900 to 1908, when he completed eleven manuscripts left behind by Horatio Alger, Jr., author of *Ragged Dick* and many other rags-to-riches stories. Alger had been a favorite author of Stratemeyer when he was a boy, and the two corresponded before Alger's death (Marilyn Greenwald 3).

In 1906, Stratemeyer took the step that would make him famous in the world of juvenile publishing. He formed the Stratemeyer Literary Syndicate, the company that would be behind such famous series as *Tom Swift, The*

Bobbsey Twins, *The Hardy Boys*, and *Nancy Drew* as well as series that are less familiar today, such as *The Happy Hollisters*, *The Outdoor Girls*, and *Dave Fearless*. The syndicate put out a total of about one thousand five hundred books under the management of Stratemeyer and his daughters Harriet and Edna; after Simon and Schuster bought the company in 1984 they issued another two hundred and ninety volumes in various Syndicate Series (Johnson, *Edward Stratemeyer* ix —17). Stratemeyer combined every trick he had learned in working for story papers and dime novel publishers with new marketing and publicity techniques in order to make the Syndicate successful. He oversaw everything, from ghostwriters to book prices, cover art to story outlines (when he wasn't writing the stories himself).

Stratemeyer imported the ghostwriter techniques from dime novel publishers. He created outlines for different series volumes himself, hired writers for a flat fee, had them sign away all rights to their manuscripts, and gave them the outlines with instructions to produce a finished manuscript. He bound the authors to secrecy in these contracts as well; they were not allowed to use the pseudonyms for their own work or acknowledge their work for the Syndicate. One might wonder why many of the authors were so willing to sign away their rights to their work. As in the case of dime novels, the answer was simple: money. It also helped that Stratemeyer paid writers as they finished their manuscripts, rather than waiting until the book was actually published.

> The amount paid to the Syndicate writers, often between $75 and $250, sounds small today but it was a significant sum in the first third of the twentieth century. A typical newspaper reporter job might pay $60-$70 per month. Also, when writers offered their own stories to publishers for outright payment, they would get no more but would have to wait until the book was published before they were paid. Stratemeyer's immediate payment upon the completion of the work was welcome [Keeline, "Syndicate 101" 2].

Stratemeyer wrote the entire text of many volumes himself, at least in the beginning. It appears from his correspondence that he made sure to write the full text of any volumes printed under his own name, as well as write all the manuscripts of *The Rover Boys* series. He contends in several letters that even books under his pseudonyms, Capt. Ralph Bonehill and Arthur M. Winfield, were sometimes collaborative productions. As the Syndicate became more prosperous, and more and more series were under production, Stratemeyer had to be in charge of simply keeping track of them all. At that point, *The Rover Boys* and the books published under his true name became his major literary efforts, although he still wrote all of the story outlines that were sent to other Syndicate authors.

Three. A Revolution in Series Production 91

Occasionally, Stratemeyer offended someone when he approached them about writing for the Syndicate. In 1906 he wrote to Mrs. Gabrielle E. Jackson, asking her to write a girls' series for the Syndicate. Stratemeyer had apparently been approached by a publishing company about a series for girls and was looking for a writer who could do a good job. According to his letters, he remembered receiving one of Mrs. Jackson's manuscripts when he was working for Street & Smith. However, Mrs. Jackson had achieved quite a bit of success as an author in the meantime and apparently was insulted at the idea of working for such a small fee (Stratemeyer to Jackson 18 Oct. 1906 and 26 Oct. 1906).[6] In Stratemeyer's second letter, he apologizes profusely and admits his lack of knowledge about girls' juvenile fiction:

> It all comes of my ignorance concerning girls' books and those who pen them, for I have devoted nearly fifteen years of my life to boys' books and boys' periodicals. When this new concern asked me to see what I could do about some girls' books I happened to remember that you had once offered to Messrs. Street & Smith, when I was doing some editorial work there, a clever manuscript of a girls' book for $150.— or perhaps it was $200.— certainly a low figure for such a production. I have not followed up your magnificent success, and if you can get a publisher to give you $1250.00 for a 40,000 word story you will certainly not want to write a tale for a fraction of that sum. And if you can get a good royalty, with an advance or a guarantee, I should not think you would care to sell outright at any price [Stratemeyer to Jackson 26 Oct. 1906].

Since his voice in other correspondence is highly confident (at times verging on arrogant and overbearing), it is surprising to find that Stratemeyer felt himself at all unequal to the task of providing a girls' series to a publisher, although it is perfectly true that he himself had, up to this point, devoted his entire career to writing for boys. He may well have had a few qualms about his ability to judge whether a manuscript for girls would be equally successful. However, one also has to wonder whether his comments to Mrs. Jackson were slightly disingenuous, meant to placate a highly-paid author who might also be a valuable ally. He approached another female author, Mrs. Evelyn Raymond, only eleven days after his written apology to Mrs. Jackson (Stratemeyer to Raymond 7 Nov. 1906). In that first letter and the subsequent one to Mrs. Raymond, Stratemeyer casually held up his own *Rover Boys* series as a model for the kind of girls' series he would like to have written:

> If you will look over the outlines of the "Rover Boys" I feel sure you will catch my idea for a girls' line. In that series the three Rover boys go first to school, then take a trip on the ocean, the go to Africa to look for their father, then go out west to establish a family claim to valuable mine, etc. In each book the main characters of all the books appear, and each book has a complete plot in itself, although all are somewhat united [Stratemeyer to Raymond 10 Nov. 1906].

He also included two titles and plot ideas for the first book of the series, and allowed Mrs. Raymond to choose whether the books would feature a pair of sisters or a single girl. The books eventually became the *Dorothy Chester* series. Mrs. Raymond accepted Stratemeyer's offer and wrote at least the first three volumes of the eleven-volume series (Stratemeyer to Raymond 17 Nov., 6 Dec., 10 Dec. 1906 and 5 Feb. 1907). Since her name appears on all the volumes, it is possible that she authored the entire series, something that would become a rare occurrence as the Syndicate grew.[7]

Another one of Stratemeyer's borrowings from the dime novel production factories was price. He wanted to produce quality books for the middle class, rather than cheap books for the working class, but he didn't want them to be too expensive. He was continually negotiating prices with his publishers; it is a misconception that all the books were "fifty-centers." In the early years of the Syndicate, they ranged in price from thirty-five cents to a dollar. By WWI, since there were paper shortages, the prices for the cheapest volumes (about forty or sixty cents) went up to fifty or seventy-five cents (Keeline, "Comments on Emily's Prospectus"). Stratemeyer counted on volume to make up his profits, and his strategy worked; the cheaper price put the books within the reach of eager young readers.

Also like the dime novels, Stratemeyer relied on formulas to please his readers. He moved into "cleaner" plots and characters for his series stories, creating main characters who were moral, middle-class, educated, and patriotic. Unlike dime novel heroes, series book characters did not use slang, did not gamble, drink, go to dance halls, or associate with other shady individuals. As Carol Billman points out in her analysis of Stratemeyer's methods:

> Leading characters in Stratemeyer's series are ... Übermenschen. They are exaggerated types, not perfect but indisputably extraordinary adolescents. They are, for instance, skilled at everything that comes their way, be the challenge a matter of commerce, science, the arts, or sports ... these characters may be flanked by assistants and/or well-wishers, but their achievement is singular, and their supporting casts are only foils that make this point plain [29].

Typecast characters endured from domestic novels to dime novels, and have carried right through to the series that are still being published today.

Series books as Edward Stratemeyer conceived them were a natural evolution of both the domestic novel and the dime novel. Middle-class publishers, authors, and readers generally maintained a careful distinction between dime novels and domestic fiction. They wanted their output to be viewed as literature of high quality, in no way associated with the "cheap" or "trashy" production of dime novels for the working class. Despite similarities in structure, middle-class women asserted that the difference between their fiction and dime novels lay in the former's moral value, conveyed to the reader through heavily religious and didactic plots (Enstad 41). The *Elsie Dinsmore* and *Chautauqua Girls* series discussed earlier are domestic fiction in series form, and it is highly probable, given their sales, that they were read by just as many full-grown women as adolescent girls. Despite the class distinctions, however, "domestic women's novels emerged from the same technological advances as dime novel fiction, and like dime novels became a highly successful series of commodities" (Enstad 41). Stratemeyer's innovation was to create a literature that not only combined new printing technology with the publishing techniques of dime novels, but also melded the working-class excitement and action of dime novels with the morals and patriotism of middle-class domestic fiction. The result was fiction that was distinctly geared to middle-class adolescents, stories that appealed to their sense of adventure and fun and channeled most of the morality into secular ideas of loyalty, bravery, justice, patriotism, and friendship. However, the secular nature of Stratemeyer's books as well as their dime novel origins put him on the offensive with one very important group: librarians.

Series Books, Librarians, and Morals

Despite the massive popularity of Stratemeyer's books, librarians were very unhappy with his success.[8] The Newark Library attempted to remove all books by Stratemeyer from its shelves in 1901, before Stratemeyer had even formed the Syndicate. Many libraries refused to carry any books produced by the Syndicate well into the twentieth century. As interest in the quality of childhood increased through the early part of the century, so did the criticism of the Syndicate's volumes, but it didn't hurt the sales. In fact, the controversy in libraries ultimately helped sales of the books. The boycott of the Newark Public Library prompted Stratemeyer to write to the Chairman of the Newark Library's Book Committee, "Personally, it does not matter much to me whether or not my books are not put back on the shelves of the juvenile department.... Taking them out of the Library has more than tripled the sales in Newark" (qtd. in Rehak 97–98).

The debate over series books was much like the earlier debate over story papers and dime novels, another indication of the similarity of their origins and their cultural capital. Librarians saw the books as trashy, poorly written, and a threat to the morals of young readers, much the same reaction they had to dime novels for working adults a few decades earlier. Louisa May Alcott, back in 1868 when Stratemeyer was six years old, denounced story papers in the second half of *Little Women*, and she went on to do it again in *Eight Cousins*, published in 1874. It is profoundly ironic that Alcott denounced the very work that kept her family solvent, for she herself wrote for the story papers under various pseudonyms, as does her heroine Jo March. When Jo wins her first check from a prize story sponsored by one of the papers, she is ecstatic and sends Marmee and Beth to the sea for a month. However, her father says, "'You can do better than this, Jo. Aim at the highest, and never mind the money'" (261). A little later in the story, it is her future husband Professor Bhaer who maker her realize the "evil" nature of the story papers:

> I wish these papers did not come in the house; they are not for children to see, not young people to read. It is not well; and I haf no patience with those who make this harm.... I do not like to think that good young girls should see such things. They are made pleasant to some, but I would more rather give my boys gunpowder to play with that this bad trash [343].

Jo promptly reads over her stories, finds them to be completely tasteless, condemns herself for going down a slippery slope to moral pollution, and burns them all in the stove. Alcott conveniently lets Jo keep the money "to pay for [her] time" (344) while condemning the act and having Jo cease her story paper writing. Thereafter Jo sticks to healthy, wholesome stories that win her eventual fame.

Damaged innocence and unwholesome reading were not the only objections of librarians and literary critics. Dime novel reading (and later, series reading), critics argued, led to other dangerous behaviors, including gambling, drinking, and criminal activity. Alcott also echoed this concern in her "wholesome" literature. In *Eight Cousins*, Alcott presents a small lecture about dime novels when two of Rose's boy cousins are reading them. The boys' mother, Aunt Jessie, tells them:

> [The books] give boys such wrong ideas of life and business; shows them so much evil and vulgarity that they need not know about, and makes the one success worth having a fortune, a lord's daughter, or some worldly honor, often not worth the time it takes to win. It does seem to me that some one might write stories that should be lively, natural, and helpful,—tales in which the English should be good, the morals pure, and the characters such as we can love in spite of the faults that all may have [189].

In other words, Alcott promotes works like her own, and simultaneously disavows her old type of writing and its legitimacy. Alcott wrote her "sensation" stories under a pseudonym for a reason, and after the phenomenal success of *Little Women* she did not have to write them anymore to make money. No one connected her to the "cheap" stories from the papers until Leona Rostenberg and Madeleine Stern unearthed Alcott's story paper pseudonym of A.M.

Barnard in the 1940s. Stern then published edited collections of Alcott's stories and dime novels in the 1970s and 1990s, respectively.[9] It is hard to know whether Alcott wrote her critiques of dime novels and story papers into *Little Women* and *Eight Cousins* merely to poke fun at herself, unbeknownst to her readers, or whether she actually regretted her involvement in the production of "cheap" literature. Since she regarded most of her later work as "moral pap" for young people, it seems quite possible that she did not share Aunt Jessie's moral scruples about "sensation" literature.

However, regardless of Alcott's actual feelings on the matter, whatever they were, cultural critics in the 1910s took up the thread of Alcott's protests and redirected them at the "fifty-centers" that Stratemeyer sold by the thousands. The most vitriolic and inflammatory was an oft-cited article by Franklin Mathiews, the chief librarian of the Boy Scouts of America. Titled "Blowing Out the Boys' Brains" and published in 1914, the article excoriated both the Syndicate's methods of production and the moral substance of the books it produced: "As some boys read such books, their imaginations are literally "blown-out,' and they go into life as terribly crippled as though by some material explosion they had lost a hand or foot," Mathiews wrote (qtd. in Johnson, *Edward Stratemeyer* 163).

The debates continued through the 1950s, but Stratemeyer's books showed enormous success for decades after his death in 1930, and while he was still living he could literally afford to ignore the criticism hurled at him.[10] It is important to note, however, that even though he was a practical man when it came to sales, as the above quote about the Newark Public Library shows, he still took offense at the critiques hurled at his volumes and combated the notion that they were little better than dime novels. Stratemeyer felt that he was producing books that were morally clean, patriotic, and gave good models for behavior. His books were everything that dime novels were not and had never been; he wanted young people to be reading books that were good for them and would not give them evil ideas or bad habits. In a letter to W.F. Gregory, a manager for Lothrop, Lee & Shepard of Boston who published Stratemeyer's writing under his own name, Stratemeyer conveyed his emphatic feelings about the quality of his books: "I do not claim everything for my books, but I do claim that they are clean and moral, written in good Anglo Saxon English, and that such works as have an historical and geographical background are historically and geographically correct. Boys and young men of to-day are full of vigor and action and demand stories which shall suit such tastes" (Stratemeyer to Gregory, 19 Feb. 1901). Stratemeyer's strong feelings about the morality of his books could be, he felt, backed by the many parents who happily bought his books for their children. It was always a small minority who condemned the works of the Syndicate, but since part of the minority contained people who decided what deserved the label of "good" literature, including librarians and literary critics, their voices had to be contended with.

Deidre Johnson hypothesizes that the real objection behind critics' moral posing was that the books gave young adults agency in a way that conventional literature for young people did not:

> Traditionally, in the more acceptable children's literature of the period, adults give children necessary advice and impose restraints on them. In series fiction, however, the adolescents make their own crucial decisions. They demonstrate the intelligence, capability, and freedom of adults, in violation of this tradition. Children, not adults, become the moral arbiters and shapers of their fate. They willingly enter the adult world and compete on an even footing — a fantasy, certainly, but one that appeals to almost every child [*Edward Stratemeyer* 165].

In the pages of fiction, children acted like adults, making responsible decisions under their own power, and had voices and opinions that were often ignored in real life. Series books gave young men and women a chance to make choices about who they wanted to be, what they wanted to do with their lives, outside the confines of adult authority. It did not hurt, either, that the Syndicate's books were in the price range of every child with a paper route or an allowance. Even girls could purchase an occasional book for themselves out of allowance money, provided their parents were not too strict about what they read. More resourceful young people might have hidden the books away or traded books with friends to get the most recent volume in a series.

Stratemeyer's correspondence suggests another possible reason for the war librarians waged against his books. Stratemeyer's strenuous defense of his books to Mr. Gregory at Lothrop, Lee & Shepard was in response to a report on fiction in the Boston Public Library, given to the trustees of that institution, in which Stratemeyer's books were apparently spoken of very badly. A woman named Elizabeth Parker chaired the committee that authored the report, and Stratemeyer was angered by her comments that his books were "'clean rubbish — very cheap and melodramatic.'" He went on:

> It seems to me, if such public statements hurt my books in sale I can hold her, or the committee, responsible. If the Public Library of Boston does not wish to handle my books they need not do so, so far as I am concerned. I have made the writing of books for boys a close study for twelve years, and I think I know more about what such books ought to be than does some person who has probably never written a juvenile in her life and who had never had any worldly experience.... [Stratemeyer to Gregory 19 Feb. 1901].

In his reply, Mr. Gregory recommended that Stratemeyer put some of his comments in a letter to the *Boston Transcript* and ask for a written defense in their pages (Gregory to Stratemeyer 21 Feb. 1901). While I have not yet been able to determine whether Stratemeyer did so, or whether any defense of him was published, his comments would hardly endear him to either the Boston Public Library or the American Library Association. His letter to Mr. Gregory implied little respect for either libraries or their employees. His willingness to hold the library responsible if his sales were reduced indicates that he did not see libraries as a particularly important venue for exposing young people to the Syndicate's literature. Nor did he seem to feel that library employees had any quantifiable knowledge of "good" literature; as a successful writer and producer of boys' books for a dozen years, he felt he was in a much better position of authority to educate librarians about quality reading for adolescents.

At the turn of the century, librarianship as a profession had finally attained a measure of stability. The American Library Association had been in existence for two and half decades; Andrew Carnegie had been donating money for library buildings for fifteen years, although the majority of his giving was yet to come (Bobinski 14). However, there was still a serious lack of professionally trained librarians: "By 1900, there were almost 5400 public, school, academic, and special libraries in the United States, but only some 377 graduates of all the library training schools were employed in them" (Bobinski 110). With such small numbers, it is possible that librarians felt their position was tenuous unless they could establish themselves as essential to the community. As professionals, librarians felt it was their duty to recommend "good" books to the public, and thereby influence the morality of their patrons. Wayne Wiegand points out that many of the services established by early libraries were both efforts to make libraries necessary community institutions and to fulfill what librarians felt was their professional obligation to distribute "better" reading.

> As a general rule they disapproved of popular works with mass appeal, preferring instead materials that had staying power and promised to uplift readers.... Work with children, immigrant's [sic], the physically handicapped, the functionally illiterate; the establishment of travelling libraries to rural areas, circulating collections to local schools, branch libraries whose collections were tailored (within acceptable limits) to local populations; ... all manifested the desire of turn-of-the-century public librarians to place the best reading into the hands of as many people as possible [Wiegand 3].

Of course, it was up to the librarians themselves, as well as the ALA, to determine what the "best reading" was, and often it did not include the books of Edward Stratemeyer or his Syndicate, as the report to the Boston Public Library makes clear.

However, it is also clear that Stratemeyer did not do much to ingratiate himself with librarians or their professional institutions. As his response to the Newark Public Library ban shows, it often improved his sales if libraries did not carry his books. In addition, he was not above telling librarians how to do their jobs. If it came to his attention that librarians were not classifying his books correctly, he did not hesitate to write them. There is a whole series of letters in his outgoing correspondence that are written to various librarians insisting that they correct their catalogs. He was determined that any books written under any of his pseudonyms were filed under those pseudonyms, rather than the name of Edward Stratemeyer. His crusade apparently began when he received a newspaper clipping of books most in demand at the New York Public Library, and found that one of the volumes issued under the pseudonym "Capt. Ralph Bonehill" was listed as being authored by himself. He subsequently wrote the New York Public Librarian, asking who had authorized him to list the book as a Stratemeyer book (Stratemeyer to Bostwick 21 Feb. 1905). The New York librarian, whose name was Arthur Bostwick, wrote back to Stratemeyer that his authority to list the book under Stratemeyer's name came from the Librarian of Congress (Stratemeyer to Bostwick 24 Feb. 1905). Stratemeyer then wrote the librarian at the Library of Congress, asking if it was required by law for them to list a book written under a pseudonym under the author's real name as well (Stratemeyer to the Librarian of Congress 25 Feb. and 14 Mar. 1905). Apparently the librarian answered that it was not, and promised to keep any mention of Stratemeyer out of the records of any of the books issued under his pen names (Stratemeyer to Bostwick 23 Mar. 1905).[11]

Although it is hard to tell how sincere Stratemeyer was, he framed his argument to the Librarian of Congress in terms of honesty to the reading public. He did not want readers to think that books issued under his pen names were solely his work, since he reserved the right to have other authors collaborate with him. Only the books issued under his own name, he claimed, were his work from beginning to end. It is also possible that Stratemeyer did not feel he was doing his best work under the pen names, so he did not want to be connected with them.

Stratemeyer followed up with the New York public librarian, Mr. Bostwick, and "positively forbid" the use of his name in connection with any of the pseudonyms he owned (Stratemeyer to Bostwick 23 Mar. 1905). He wrote letters to the librarians of Columbus, Ohio and Manchester, New Hampshire who had committed offenses similar to the New York Public Library. In short, Stratemeyer was so protective of his literary work and reputation that he was not at all worried about offending or alienating librarians by suggesting that they were incompetent. The hostility of librarians to the Syndicate's books may have been a direct result. However, discouragement from librarians did not stem the eagerness of adolescent readers for new Stratemeyer Syndicate volumes, and Stratemeyer willingly fed their appetite.

Publicity

Of course, the appetite of readers for new Stratemeyer books was helped along by catalogs, advertisements, store displays, and other new techniques of publicity that Stratemeyer either exploited or invented. As James Keeline has shown in his paper, "Booming the Books: Innovations in Book Promotion by Edward Stratemeyer," Stratemeyer was not only concerned with the drafting and writing of many of the Syndicate's books; he also oversaw the printing and publicity for them, coming up with new marketing schemes along the way. The first one was having the "author" give an introduction to the characters of the book and the series as a whole at the beginning of a volume. This happened frequently in his earlier series; by later books, he had managed to merge the introduction in the story itself.

> He ... engaged in promoting the prior volumes in the series by having the narrator break away from the action, often in the second chapter, to introduce the characters and mention past adventures that the reader should know about. When the next title was known at the time of publication, it would often be mentioned in the last few paragraphs of the story [Keeline, "Booming" 2].

Stratemeyer also wrote ads for particular series that were printed in the backs of the books, or ads that gave mini "biographies" of the various "authors" of his books, including "Frank V. Webster," "Annie Roe Carr," and "Spencer Davenport." Later, in the 1920s, lists of the books were printed on the inside of the book wrapper or dust jacket, to encourage readers to both buy the next volume in the series they had, and to purchase other series (Keeline, "Booming" 2–3). Other promotions for the books included mailed catalogs and postcards. Stratemeyer even made a board game prototype for his *Rover Boys* series, although the game was never mass-produced. He was also aware of the most current ideas about proper store display for books, and on at least one occasion he wrote a piece for *Grosset & Dunlap's Business Promoter,* a small magazine that "gave tips to booksellers about how they could better promote the books through effective advertising, window displays, contests, and cooperation with movie houses when a film based on a book was run" (Keeline, "Booming" 5). Stratemeyer did everything he could think of to make his books successful, at least anything that did not interfere with his sense of business ethics. Occasionally he would reject a publicity idea that he did not like, one that seemed overly self-interested or simply improper. Keeline cites one instance where Stratemeyer was asked to do a public book signing in a department store in Newark. He emphatically rejected the idea as a "cheap, clap-trap method of selling books" (Keeline, "Booming" 5–6).

Stratemeyer was not alone in his attempts to dominate the series books industry, however. Other publishers did their best to keep up with his tremendous output, and the book market was not the only place where young people were being bombarded with choices. By the turn of the twentieth century and Edward Stratemeyer's triumphant march into the world of juvenile publishing, consumption had taken hold as the new American creed. Series books were only one of many products designed to "hook" young people, especially young women, into making repeated and steady purchases of a particular item. Department store owners and managers, fashion houses, publishers, soap companies, makers of kitchen products, and myriads of other businesses looking to make a profit were all vying for the attention of married women and their daughters, and females all over the country responded eagerly.

Notes

1. Independent scholar James Keeline is currently working on the definitive biography of Edward Stratemeyer, and he has given me access to many of his unpublished conference papers, as well as the very few compiled sales figures for the Syndicate. His work and helpful criticism have been invaluable for the purposes of this chapter.

2. The history of dime novels is difficult to put together. The books were cheap, meant to be read once or twice and thrown away. There are several large collections of dime novels, including those at the Library of Congress, the University of Minnesota, and Northern Illinois University, but much of the day-to-day workings of dime novel publishers are hard to trace. Johannsen, Cox, and Denning are the major sources on dime novels and story papers, and they are the ones most used here.

3. The changes in the printing press were not the only ones that made cheap book production possible. One of the first and most important developments was new raw materials and processing techniques for paper. A mechanical paper-making machine was invented in France in the 1790s, by a Frenchman named Nicholas-Louis Robert. It was subsequently brought to London and manufactured by the brothers Henry and Sealy Fourdrinier and an engineer named Bryan Donkin. The machine was a huge success and could produce much more paper at once than any hand-operated machine. "By 1807, Fourdrinier papermaking machines had become commercially viable and were able to produce more paper in a day than a single vat for hand production could in a week" (Banham 274).

Additionally, by 1850, wood pulp had been discovered as a raw material for making paper. Initially, wood was simply ground up into pulp and used with purer fibers to make cheap newsprint and paper; by the 1860s it was found that if sulfite was added to wood chips, the sulfite would remove the natural lignin from the wood, and result in a stronger paper fiber that would not break down so easily. The result was a smooth, long-lasting paper that was less expensive than paper made from linen and cotton fibers (Gaskell 221–222; Banham 273–274).

While paper production was being mechanized, bookbinding was also becoming easier. Covers for books had traditionally been produced by hand, like everything else, separately from the books themselves. The actual paper portion of the book would have been folded and put together in sections, and the cover attached afterward. However, one of the first mechanizations to take place was the production of book covers. The key to this mechanization was the discovery that cloth could be used as a cover for the boards of a book, rather than making the cover out of leather. Cloth was much cheaper and required less care and handling than leather. Covers were created by machine entirely apart from the books and could be just as easily attached, saving time and labor (Gaskell 232). In addition, it was found that titles could be stamped directly onto cloth through use of a machine: "In 1830, [Charles] Pickering applied lettering to the spine of his cloth bindings using the new arming press—an iron printing press adapted for this purpose. The covers had to go into the arming press flat and this meant that they had to be made separately, so the lettering could be stamped on, before being glued to the book" (Banham 281).

Specific machines for each step of the binding process were invented throughout the early part of the nineteenth century, speeding up production of books of all kinds. Most of the large binderies had converted to using the machinery that was available by the 1850s, but there were still many processes that were not mechanized until the second half of the nineteenth century, including folding, sewing, rounding and backing, gathering, and casing, all steps that were necessary to complete each book. Therefore, binding gradually became faster throughout the nineteenth century, until by the fin-de-siècle it was entirely mechanized (Gaskell 236–27).

4. The Stanhope Press, introduced in 1803, was still hand operated but made of iron rather than wood and capable of applying a much more even pressure all over each page, in order to transfer the ink properly and produce clean impressions (Gaskell 198). According to Rob Banham, the real advantage of the Stanhope Press was not so much that it gave added power to impressions, but that it required less physical strength to operate it. That made it easier to create illustrations: "[T]he added power of the iron press did mean that it was better suited to printing wood-engraved illustrations ... they could be printed together with the type and quickly became a popular means of illustrating books, newspapers, and magazines" (Banham 276).

Although there were experiments in mechanizing printing in the late eighteenth century, a fully operating printing machine was not created until 1806. A German inventor named Friedrich Koenig moved to London and created a steam-powered flatbed printer that was capable of printing much larger sheets of paper than a typical hand press. Koenig's next invention was a cylinder press, of the kind that is still used for newspapers today. He refined it in 1816 so that it would print two sides of a sheet at one time (Gaskell 251–252).

Book printers were not so quick to change to the new technology; quality rather than speed was their overriding concern. Flatbed book printing machines, powered by steam, were in wide use from the 1830s to the 1860s in the United States. Book printers preferred them to the cylinder machines used by newspapers because the printing was more accurate, the ink had less of a tendency to blur, and the flatbed machines did not wear the type down so quickly. The cylinder machines were gradually improved during the same years so that they became more accurate and precise. By 1900, they had become just as good as the flatbed printers and were faster. They became the dominant type of machinery for both books and newspapers (Gaskell 253–262).

In other words, newspapers traded quality for quantity, while book printers looked for quality above all else. Speed was the name of the game in newspaper work because more volume meant more profits. The newer and faster printing machines led to the production of more newspapers and cheap periodical literature, including story papers and dime novels. Booksellers wanted volume as well but not at the expense of quality. Until accuracy improved in cylinder presses, book printers stayed with the flatbed presses that produced a better quality of text. High-quality bound books were therefore still out of the reach of most working people. Story paper and dime novel publishers capitalized on this untapped market of readers with minimal leisure time or expendable income.

5. Dime novels went into a precipitous decline after 1893 for a number of reasons related to the new international copyright laws and the economic depression; see Denning, Chapter 2, Note 3, pages 214–215.

6. I am not personally familiar with Gabrielle Jackson's novels, but the Library of Congress lists thirty-eight titles under her name, including seventeen published before 1906 and several more published in that year.

7. It is unclear whether Evelyn Raymond wrote all of the *Dorothy Chester* series or not. Stratemeyer commissioned Raymond to write the first two volumes, and he outlined the first two stories as he did with all other series. Ultimately, however, he sold the printing plates for the first two *Dorothy Chester* books, along with another Raymond manuscript. The publishing firm Chatterton-Peck asked Raymond to continue writing stories for the series, and she wrote at least some of the later volumes, but it's not clear whether she wrote them all. Once Stratemeyer no longer controlled the series, the "Dorothy Chester" books became just the "Dorothy" books; her last name was dropped from the titles of the series (Keeline, "Comments on Emily's Prospectus").

8. I talk more extensively about librarians' disapproval of Stratemeyer's work, and series fiction in general, in my recent article "Guardians of Morality: Librarians and American Girls' Series Fiction, 1890–1950." *Library Trends* 60.4 (Spring 2012).

9. For further information about this discovery, see Leona Rostenberg, "The Discovery of Louisa May Alcott's Pseudonym" and Madeleine B. Stern, "Dime Novels by 'The Children's Friend,'" both in *Pioneers, Passionate Ladies, and Private Eyes: Dime Novels Series Books, and Paperbacks*, ed. Larry E. Sullivan and Lydia Cushman Schurman.

10. Some clarification is required here. Stratemeyer could afford to ignore the criticisms of librarians because even if a library had his books on their shelves, they did not generate any income for him or the Syndicate. Those libraries that did carry his books only bought them once, and after that they were free to library members. If a library refused to carry Syndicate series, youth or their parents would have to buy the books in order to read them, thus increasing Stratemeyer's sales. Stratemeyer *did* worry about his sales in general; he monitored royalty statements, complained to his publishers when he felt they were not doing enough to sell his books, and sometimes would even pull the publication rights for his books from one publisher and give them to another firm. James Keeline writes, "He had a significant investment in each story, both in terms of his time, ghostwriter pay (equivalent to about two months'

Three. A Revolution in Series Production   103

wages a newspaper reporter), and sometimes artwork, printing plates, and shared advertising expenses. Consider that the manuscript alone might cost $125 but the per-copy royalty was about 2.5c for a 50c book (5 percent) and this required that 5,000 copies of a title sell before he earned back his investment. Some books made this back quickly but others did not" ("Comments on Emily's Prospectus").

11. It is important to note here that I am working almost entirely from Stratemeyer's outgoing correspondence and not the actual replies of the librarians themselves. Stratemeyer is quite clear in summarizing the responses he received from the Librarian of Congress and from Mr. Bostwick of the New York Public Library. Stratemeyer's correspondence is voluminous, and since I had a very limited amount of time at the New York Public Library archives, I chose to take him at his word about the contents of the librarians' letters.

Four
Communities of Friends
Series Heroines as Consumers, 1901–1930

In the twentieth century, consumption exploded both in life and in print as the new method of personal fulfillment. Home décor, ready-made fashions, prepared foods, motor cars, and motion pictures are just some examples of the many enticing new items that could be paid for and enjoyed. Within the fictional world of series, the moral life that would have been familiar to the March girls and Elsie Dinsmore disappeared almost completely within a decade and a half, eclipsed by the novelty of a consumer society and a massive marketing machine that appealed to both readers and consumers.

Like Stratemeyer and other magazine and book publishers, businesses were learning to take advantage of new marketing strategies. Department stores like Wanamaker's, Marshall Field's, and Macy's were building chains and had harnessed advertising to appeal to the middle and upper classes. Precisely *what* and *how much* one could consume became a marker of class and status. The *quality* of the goods one bought was just as important in distinguishing class as the *quantity*; manufacturers created cheaper lines of clothing, furniture, and other goods for those individuals and families that could not afford their higher-priced items.[1] Warren Susman asserts that American culture at the turn of the century was shifting from a culture of character — a culture focused on developing self-control and a moral social order — to a culture of personality where individuality and personal desires trumped group needs and morals. The development of both "character" and "personality" demand self-control and a particular kind of self-development, but the culture of personality was particularly suited for a country where consumption was becoming the focal point of the economy:

> The new personality literature stressed items that could be best developed in leisure time and that represented in themselves an emphasis on consumption ...

exercise, proper breathing, sound eating habits, a good complexion, and grooming and beauty aids were all stressed. At the same time, clothing, personal appearance, and "good manners" were important, but there was little interesting in morals [Susman 280].

Susman does not overtly examine the role of gender in this shift from character to personality, but gender was in fact a crucial part of the cultural transformation that took place at the turn of the century.[2] Women, much more than men, were seen as the primary consumers for households, and made consumption decisions not only for themselves but for their husbands and children. As department stores and other commercial leisure venues appeared in public spaces, women became the primary targets for advertising, store services, and lavish entertainments intended to entice customers into buying (Benson 4–7; Leach 91–111). Women made these new venues their own, socializing together in buildings filled with items that would help them define their personality. Saleswomen dominated the selling floor of department stories by 1900 and were also hired as buyers for some departments, although store managers continued to be mostly men (Benson 23–26).

Department stores developed slowly during the last half of the nineteenth century, but by 1890 they had taken a firm hold in major cities and were making massive profits by selling anything and everything to their customers. They were also aesthetically elegant and technologically modern. Marble, carpet, and carved hardwoods were generally standard features of the décor, and the three major chains of Macy's, Wannamaker's, and Marshall Field's had air ventilation systems, electric lights, and in-store telephones between the various departments. Lounges and restaurants provided spots where women could pause in their shopping, and all three chains continually enlarged the amount and types of goods they offered, so women could conceivably spend an entire day browsing and buying (Benson 17–21).

In his extensive study of American advertising and consumption from 1890–1945, Charles McGovern argues that male advertisers painted women as the quintessential consumers, encouraging them to participate in the capitalist market as a means of asserting their own rights as American citizens:

> Nowhere were independence and consumption joined more explicitly than in advertisers' treatment of women as sovereigns of the marketplace. Advertisers depicted consumption as the best means for women to achieve both their individual freedom and their full public power as citizens.... By treating women as natural consumers, advertisers "naturalized" them as citizens — spending was women's ritual of citizenship [79].

While McGovern's analysis initially seems to position American women as the pawns of ad men, the placement of women in advertising as the primary consumers for themselves and their families also had the effect of alerting women to their own purchasing power. A good many advertisement writers and agencies held that women were less intelligent than men (hence the need for informative ads to help them "correctly" choose brand name products), yet, like department stores, their industry was dependent on the choices of women consumers who turned the goods of their clients into successful economic products (McGovern 36–48). They recognized, despite their disdain, the power that women wielded in the expanding economy.

Series books published at the turn of the century were complicit in this newly emerging culture of consumption; after all, publishers wanted their readers to consume as many of their books as possible. Since girls in particular were encouraged to read as part of their self-development, series books were a sensible place in which to promote the idea that consumerism was the new, modern road to self-fulfillment and happiness. Women and girls could pick and choose goods that suited their tastes, openly display their personality through the clothes they wore and their home furnishings, venture into public places of business and exercise power as customers, and fulfill their citizenship obligations all at the same time. In equating women's spending and consuming with citizenship and turning it into a cultural truism, advertisers may not have realized that they were enabling women to assert a new kind of independence. Thanks to the rapidly expanding consumer economy, girls and women no longer needed a reason to be in "male" public spaces; they had a right and even an obligation to be there as responsible citizens.

Of course, the independence of actual women and fictional heroines was not always complete; their purchasing power often depended on money provided by fathers or spouses. Series books from this period reveal a great deal of anxiety surrounding the new capitalist market in general and female consumers in particular. Disproportionate buying and spending could lead to moral corruption by fostering greed, materialism, self-indulgence, and selfishness. If women succumbed to the allure of consuming for its own sake, then the moral standard bearers of the country would be permanently tainted. Finding a balance between too much and too little and developing the liberating possibilities of consumption while minimizing its drawbacks became a central cultural concern. Series authors spent a great deal of time demonstrating responsible, balanced consumption and warning against the excesses that led to moral decay.

Literary critic Peter Stoneley has extensively studied consumerism in girls' literature, and while my argument mirrors his in suggesting that girls' fiction produced at the turn of the century presents consumption as the means through which young women could achieve social and cultural power and independence, we diverge when he suggests that the narratives ultimately shut down the possibility of independence by marrying heroines off to older, well-to-do businessmen:

> [C]onsumerism was and is an especially effective means of discipline and control precisely because it seems to liberate and empower. The world of consumerism can create a misleading aura of female agency, in which the girl's powers are ambiguous.... The process of buying into womanhood not only provides the ideological foundation for the girl's identity, but it also transforms her into something to be bought. Her education in consumerism, in other words, produces her as a commodity to be consumed [Stoneley 5].

Stoneley contends that consumerism traps young women with false promises. By embracing the world of consumerism and the agency it offers, girls allow themselves to be made over into yet another commodity, something to be bought and sold on the marriage market.

However, his analysis of girls' literature produced at the turn of the century focuses primarily on single-volume narratives, like *Daddy Long Legs* and *Rebecca of Sunnybrook Farm*, about heroines that come from a working-class or lower-middle-class background and who are subsequently made over into upper-middle-class wives through education and the presence of a wealthy benefactor. Their ability to exercise agency through choice in the marketplace, Stoneley says, is ultimately negated by their conformity to the demands of middle-class respectability; they enter marriages that provide permanent economic security and bow to the patriarchal wishes of their husbands. He does *not* consider series fiction of the Progressive Era, which almost always features heroines who are middle- or upper-middle class to begin with. They do not have to be transformed to suit anyone; they stand on an equal class and social footing with their male peers. While girls' ability to consume is often enabled through family finances, fictional parents for the most part indulge their daughters and encourage the unification of friend groups (both all-female and mixed) through shared meals, parties, and shopping. Such activities become lessons in responsible consumption as well as opportunities for pleasurable socializing and sensory pleasure.

Consumption, Personality, and Domesticity in the Patty Fairfield *Series*

Patty Fairfield, the heroine of a series that began appearing in 1901, is consistently described by her ability to purchase the highest quality goods of all kinds. She is constantly throwing parties with fine linen and china and has multiple dresses for each day of the week and each time of the day. Patty reflects the early and enthusiastic belief that a greater choice of goods and specific consumption choices could help define a person's identity and could help make one happy by allowing one to develop preferences that were all one's own. She enjoys both her friends and her consumption of goods without having to earn the family wealth that maintains her. Instead of focusing on using that money to alleviate social ills and spread the Christian gospel, Patty is allowed (encouraged, in fact) to spend it on herself and her close friends, as well as to use it to maintain the family home and to pay for travel both within the U.S. and abroad.

It should be noted that the *Patty Fairfield* series was not a Stratemeyer creation; however, it was published by Grosset and Dunlap, a firm that Stratemeyer frequently used for his Syndicate series. The author of the *Patty* books, Carolyn Wells, wrote a number of series and individual books for young women along with poetry and mystery novels.[3] The seventeen stories that make up Patty's life lay out a great many of the pros and cons of the emerging consumer culture, and ultimately endorse consuming as a pleasurable and empowering activity for women.

A major part of Patty's education early in the series is learning how to be a responsible consumer and housekeeper. In *Patty Fairfield*, the first book of the series, Patty is sent to the houses of her four aunts, staying with each of them and their families for three months, to learn proper housekeeping and management techniques, though while there she learns as much about *incorrect* housekeeping as she does about housekeeping in its correct form. Correct housekeeping turns out to be a matter of consuming goods in the right "proportion," as Patty's father puts it, and understanding the kinds of goods that are both serviceable and pleasing to look at. Consumption run amok can make for an unbalanced, frivolous home where vanity rules.

For example, when Patty stays with her Aunt Isabel and Uncle Robert St. Clair, she finds out rather quickly what it means to consume too much and buy goods that are too costly. She writes to her father:

> In this house, money, and fine clothes, and making a great show, are out of all proportion to everything else. They never think of reading books, or doing charity work, or anything but showing off. And if a thing costs a lot, it's all right, but if it's simple and not expensive, it's no good at all. I can tell you, Mr. Papa, that when we have our home, we'll have less fuss and feathers, and more comfort and common sense. And it isn't only that the things cost so much, but they're always talking about it, and telling how expensive they are [Wells, *Patty Fairfield* 58].

What Patty (and Wells) implies here is that consumption can, and does, make a comfortable home when it is done judiciously. "Comfort and common sense" are the crucial aspects of sensible consumption; items must be useful as well as aesthetically pleasing. Buying for the sake of "making a great show" is misguided and socially unacceptable; the St. Clairs make themselves look ridiculous and embarrass Patty with their "fuss and feathers" and their open remarks about the cost of their purchases. She recognizes that the St. Clairs have lost some of the traits of moral character that she has been taught to value. Like her predecessors Elsie Dinsmore and the Chautauqua Girls, Patty still sees the need for charity and self-education.

In addition, Wells uses the St. Clairs to demonstrate that excessive consumption can also lead to morally flawed behavior. Patty's cousin Ethelyn is essentially a kind girl, but she is spoiled, casually disobeys her parents, and quarrels with her brother Reginald. Ethelyn is so used to being given whatever she wants, whether a new dress or a trip to New York, that she simply demands that her desires be fulfilled. Her younger sister Florelle, who is too young to assert herself the way Ethelyn does, nevertheless mimics her sister's behavior, beginning to cry every time she does not get her own way.

Even the names of the St. Clairs exemplify excess. Patty's Aunt Isabel declares that she "can't abide nicknames" (Wells, *Patty Fairfield* 32) and insists on calling Patty by her full name of Patricia. Ethelyn agrees with her mother at once that the longer name "Patricia" is better, and seems to think that Patty's new name and image will only add to the social stature of herself and Florelle: "'Oh,' she said, 'now your name is as pretty as mine and Florelle's, and we have the prettiest names in Elmbridge'" (Wells, *Patty Fairfield* 33). Ethelyn is a social climber; she wants to be at the top of her social circle, and she is willing to spend anything, and perhaps do anything, to attain that goal. Clearly, she and her mother are not above making over Patty to suit their mold, altering Patty's name for the duration of her stay and putting her in clothes that are far too elaborate and expensive. Patty sees the clothes as "befrilled and beflounced" with "conspicuous patterns," but her aunt insists that she wear the new dresses bought for her: "You are the guest of the St. Clairs, and your appearance must do us credit.... While you are with us you must be suitably dressed, else I shall feel ashamed of your appearance" (Wells, *Patty Fairfield* 56–57). Patty is expected to live up to her aunt's standards, whether or not they suit her own ideas of what is right. Aunt Isabel is constantly trying to meet the demands of society by spending more and more money on clothes, food, parties, and household items.

The St. Clairs treat Patty as their own Pygmalion, making over her appearance until she is scarcely recognizable. New clothes that are too gaudy, a new name that is just as elaborate, jewelry that Ethelyn takes from her mother's bureau and showers on her cousin, all threaten to change Patty into an affected, spoiled girl of society. Luckily, she is too sensible to let the practices of her relatives overwhelm her and generally takes note of the more absurd parts of their behavior. At a Christmas party for all of the town young people, Patty thinks "they all seemed like overdressed and artificial little puppets" (Wells, *Patty Fairfield* 63), and the consuming excesses of the St. Clairs imprint themselves on her brain in the same way. In a one-sided conversation with her mother's portrait, Patty says, "The grown-upness of [the party] was all out of proportion for children, I think, and,—as usual in this house, the expense was out of proportion to everything else" (Wells, *Patty Fairfield* 66). Patty acts as a mouthpiece for Wells' commentary on the dangers of being too extravagant and growing up too quickly.

The next family that Patty goes to visit is the Flemings, her Boston cousins, and here the new emphasis on consuming becomes explicit in an amusing scene. Patty's cousin, Tom Fleming, chaperones her to Boston, but when they arrive he meets a friend with some business news. Instead of escorting Patty home himself, Tom Fleming sends her home by messenger so that he can attend to his business at once. Patty thus becomes a package that must be delivered to its proper destination: "As Patty wrote to her father afterwards, she felt like a package sent from a department store, and she looked down, almost expecting to find herself wrapped in paper and tied with a string" (Wells, *Patty Fairfield* 91). Patty connects the odd method of arriving at her relatives' home via messenger with the new delivery services of department stores. She thus becomes a commodity, a parcel to be delivered and consumed by her Fleming cousins.

Wells' move from teaching Patty how to consume properly to turning her into an item to be consumed seems jarring, but it does serve to underscore the dark side of capitalism. Patty has avoided being spoiled by the overindulgence of the St. Clairs; their need to continuously buy new goods has not overwhelmed her. However, Tom Fleming's neglect of his cousin for his business signals a different kind of warning. Tom puts all of his time and energy into his business and his writing; he does not stop for any kind of familial or leisure activity. Patty quickly discovers that the rest of the Flemings share this particular personality quirk. Cousin Tom is writing a book, Cousin Elizabeth is already a successful novelist, and her Aunt Hester and Cousin Barbara spend almost all their time with various civic, political, and self-improvement organizations. They are all fervently devoted to improvement societies, charitable endeavors, and arts patronage; their activities literally consume all of their time and attention. Interactions with others are too frequently reduced to simple business transactions that succeed in accomplishing work but fail to foster emotional connections. Cousin Tom's preference for business over getting to know his young cousin and seeing her safely home ultimately reduces Patty to just another transaction, a parcel to be delivered.

Despite the serious social critique behind Wells' depiction of the Flemings, however, their obsession with charitable associations is meant to be funny, and Wells succeeds in making it so. She is satirizing both the myriad organizations that were springing up as part of Progressive Era politics and social life and the benevolence societies and charities that were so popular a generation earlier. Within the first few minutes of her arrival, Patty finds out that Hester, Elizabeth, and Barbara Fleming belong to the Current Events Club, a sewing class, the Town Improvement Association, a charity for bootblacks, a Greek pantomime, a Statue Fund, an Authors' Society, and a Dorcas Aid Society, among others. However, Wells' lesson still exists underneath the humor: Work, whether performed for wages or for charity, can be just as absorbing an occupation as spending, and while it might not lead to the same moral defects as financial profligacy, it still creates an unbalanced home and unbalanced people. The Fleming women are continuously running off to meetings, and Patty rapidly gets caught up in their busy ways: "[T]he Fleming family seemed fairly to push [time] along, they hurried so. At any rate they wasted none of it, and after a few weeks, Patty fell into the ways of the household, and hurried along with the rest" (Wells, *Patty Fairfield* 107).

As she did during her stay at the St. Clairs, Patty adopts the lifestyle of her cousins, but is able to remain objective enough to see the one major flaw in their lives: "So serious were they in their aims and purposes, that all fun was crowded out, and to fun-loving Patty this was a sad state of affairs indeed" (Wells, *Patty Fairfield* 114). Patty does get caught up and nearly consumed by the constant work of her cousins, but her place as a visiting observer lends her some objectivity about their lives. While the Flemings do not spend too much money on needless goods, they *do* spend too much time and mental energy on work and reform and not enough on enjoyment.

Wells has thus begun to build a list of negative attributes for a household using Patty's relatives as exemplars. Wealth should not be ostentatiously displayed, and obtaining expensive material goods should not be the sole aim of life. On the other hand, constantly working, even for worthy causes, is also unhealthy. The Barlows, Patty's third set of cousins, prove that all play is a harmful system as well. When Patty goes to their home on Long Island, she finds that they are fun-loving but completely unorganized and forgetful. Even the rate and method of consuming goods is up and down in the Barlows' house. Things that are bought may be forgotten about or never put away. The first night Patty is at the Barlows' she is amazed to realize that there is no bed in her room. The next morning, her Aunt Grace reveals that a brass bed was ordered from Philadelphia, but by some mistake, it was never set up and made. Mistakes like this happen on a daily basis in the cousins' lives:

> Nothing was ever to be found in its place; meals were served at any hour when old Hopalong got them ready. Sometimes the market orders were neglected and there was almost nothing to eat, and then again there was such an overstock that much had to be wasted.... Patty had not been at the Hurly-Burly [house] many days before she discovered that its proportion of order and regularity was entirely too small [Wells, *Patty Fairfield* 158–59].

Responsible consumption of goods, Patty discovers, is not simply a matter of choosing goods that are both useful and reasonably priced (her first lesson at the St. Clairs), but also is a process that needs regulation and order. Goods for the home must have specific places in the house and be put away when not in use; food in particular must be monitored carefully and be ordered and cooked in the right amounts, so nothing goes to waste. Consumption of goods becomes not just about individual taste, but about management of the goods one buys and uses.

The last home that Patty visits is the home of her Aunt Alice and Uncle Charlie Elliott, and Patty immediately senses that she has come into a different sort of environment. The Elliotts' house provides the first major contrast to the other homes where she has stayed: "[A]s they went through the halls, Patty thought she had never seen such a beautiful house in her life. It was as large as the St. Clairs' house, but the decorations and furnishings were in subdued tints and quiet effects and there was no loud or garish ornamentation" (Wells, *Patty Fairfield* 205). The implication of this passage is clear: the Elliotts have their consuming habits in firm order, particularly Patty's Aunt Alice, who oversees every aspect of the house. While the Elliotts are clearly wealthy, since their house is "as large as the St. Clairs,'" their home is not a showcase for their wealth. Everything is quietly and tastefully done, and the Elliotts do not brag about the cost of things as the St. Clairs do.

The Elliotts provide a contrast to the Barlows as well, for they have a time for every activity in the day, including meals, mending, and playtime. Everything also goes into its own place in the house; Patty sees this after her first morning of sewing with her cousin Marion. Marion organizes her workbasket and puts it away, and so Patty follows suit, realizing that none of the Barlows would have thought to clear up their work (Wells, *Patty Fairfield* 220).

Patty's Aunt Alice Elliott is an important character for several reasons. Patty's own mother is dead, and Aunt Alice really serves as a surrogate mother and teacher for Patty. Aunt Alice's efficient management of food, home decoration, and her family's work and leisure obligations marks her as the model responsible consumer. She knows how to balance work and leisure, useful accomplishments and pleasurable consumption, and she helps her family to do the same. She makes her family physically comfortable and mentally cheerful through judicious and tasteful purchasing of food and decoration as well as careful time management. As Patty tells her father at the end of the first volume, "'[A]unt Alice has everything in her life, and not too much of anything either. We children have lots of fun and good times, but we have to work some, too. And Aunt Alice teaches us to be kind and polite without making any fuss about it. And she does beautiful charity work, and she's so happy and sweet that everybody loves her'" (Wells, *Patty Fairfield* 246). Alice's character establishes important links of continuity between the postbellum private sphere and the new world of female consumption. Carroll Smith-Rosenberg's well-known essay "The Female World of Love and Ritual" documents the ways that nineteenth-century women carefully passed on their domestic skills to their daughters and asserts that cross-generational teaching tied women together by strengthening emotional bonds and creating common skill sets (64–66).[4] Since Alice serves as Patty's surrogate mother in the first few stories, she takes it upon herself to teach Patty her own store of knowledge about housekeeping and consumption. She instructs Patty in sewing, cooking, baking, and other rudiments of housekeeping. She easily navigates her way through the new department stores to buy furnishings and decorations for her own home and to help Patty and Mr. Fairfield pick out linens, dishes, kitchen utensils, and laundry tools for theirs (Wells, *Patty At Home* 61–63). At the same time, Alice performs charity work in the community, linking her to the older tradition of Christian charity represented by the Marches, Dinsmores, and Chautauqua girls. Aunt Alice teaches Patty to be simultaneously an old-fashioned household manager and a conscientious female consumer.

Even after learning her aunt's lessons, Patty is still more than happy to indulge her love of pretty things and her personal taste while purchasing consumer goods. In *Patty at Home*, the second volume of the series, father and daughter have taken up residence near the Elliotts in fictional Vernondale, a suburb of New York. When Patty is helping to pick out the furnishings for their new home, she has very particular preferences:

> [She chose] green as the predominant color, and the couch and easy-chairs were upholstered in a lovely design of green and white. The rug was green and white, and for the brass bedstead with its white fittings, a down comfortable with a pale green cover was found. The dainty dressing table was of bird's-eye maple; and for this Mr. Fairfield ordered a bewildering array of fittings, all in ivory, with Patty's monogram on them [Wells, *Patty at Home* 58].

This detailed description of Patty's room (and there are many other such descriptions throughout the series) indicates that Patty has very precise ideas about the kinds of goods she enjoys consuming, right down to the colors of each item. In addition, her choices are a clear demonstration that Patty has absorbed Aunt Alice's teachings about aesthetics; everything she chooses is in complimentary colors and harmonious styles. Finally, this scene is just one of many where Patty ventures into the public space of a department store or a clothier in order to choose items for her home and herself. On this particular occasion she is chaperoned by her father, but as she grows older she frequently shops with friends or alone.

The idea of consumption as a means of cultivating personal taste is constantly present in the *Patty Fairfield* series, and it is not only focalized through Patty herself. For example, when Patty travels to Paris in volume five of the series, her cousin Marian Elliott gives Patty a list of souvenirs that she would like to have, but she is so particular about them that Patty laughs at her demands. Marian asks for precise photographs of artwork ("There are several Madonnas that I want, and several more that I *don't* want"), tortoise-shell hair curlers, a beaded bag with a rose or hibiscus pattern ("not on any account the tulip pattern, because I hate it"), a long, cream-colored scarf ("with a Persian border in blues and greys"), "a lot of Napoleon things" ("things" eventually translates in the text to busts, paperweights, and pictures), and several other items (Wells, *Patty in Paris* 35–39). In one sense, Marian's list of gifts makes for a highly humorous scene, because not only is she requesting gifts for herself, but she is requesting such distinct items that it may well be impossible to fulfill her wishes. In another sense, however, Marian's highly specific gifts show a sharply honed sense of taste. She knows what she likes, and while some of her tastes are shared by large numbers of people, like photographs of Parisian monuments, other things are not nearly so generic. Wanting a "long [scarf], cream-coloured ground, with a Persian border in blues and greys" shows that Marian wants something distinctive, not a scarf that is sold on every Paris street corner. She can develop a unique personality through her careful selection and consumption of items, and since Patty is able to bring her items that are from Paris, it adds one more layer of sophistication to Marian's taste.

Kristin Hoganson argues in *Consumers' Imperium: The Global Production of American Domesticity, 1865–1920* that the trend for Parisian fashion among American women at the turn of the century had as much to do with imperialism and global distinction as it did with racial and class standing at home. American women who followed Paris fashions season after season were sending several kinds of messages. First, Parisian clothing signified their membership in an exclusive community of transatlantic female consumers, women who could afford to travel abroad and purchase their clothing from the world capitol of fashion (67). Since Paris designers borrowed from everywhere in the world, including China, Japan, and Turkey among other countries, wearing their clothing also suggested a certain level of familiarity with other cultures. Second, the elaborateness and expense of maintaining designer clothes signaled that the woman who owned them had both leisure and the ability to pay others to take care of her wardrobe (72). Third, Paris fashion suggested associations with European aristocracy and distanced women from classes and races lower on the social scale: "To buy into the fashion system centered in Paris thus meant to distinguish oneself from penurious, colored, and colonized people" (81). Parisian clothes and goods, then, became for women a way to assert Western whiteness, refined consumer tastes, and educated cosmopolitanism all at once.

I am not suggesting that Wells is deliberately or consciously promoting all of these ideas through her depiction of Marian's gift list, but the implications of Hoganson's analysis are worth considering. Marian clearly knows her own likes and dislikes; she has no difficulty in expressing her personality through selective consuming. Just as clearly, she knows which Parisian items are popular and/or common within her peer group; hence her request for a rose- or hibiscus-patterned bag, *not* ("on any account") a tulip-patterned one. To know that she hates tulip-patterned beaded bags from Paris, Marian must have seen them among her peer group or among the fashionable ladies of Vernondale. Not only does choosing a different pattern help her avoid the one she dislikes, but it will mark her beaded bag (and thus, her personality) as different and unique from those of her peers. Likewise, the scarf she requests, with its "Persian border in blues and greys," will not only assure others at a glance that she can afford Parisian fashion accessories, but also that she appreciates the beauty of Persian art that Paris designers have imported. Patty's trip to Paris enables Marian to fulfill the ultimate goal of upper-class American females: "Through fashion, American women affiliated themselves with the entitled and the trendy, the civilized and modern, from around the world" (Hoganson 71). Through Patty's travel and gifts, Marian will become a model of cultured taste among the Vernondale young people.

Patty's departure also illustrates the way in which gifts and other items of consumption could serve to solidify emotional bonds. Patty receives all kinds of gifts from her closest friends before she sails for France, and each item serves as a reminder of the girl who gave it, so that the gifts become stand-ins for the actual presence of each girl. The gifts include a flannel nightgown, a wrap for Patty's best hat, a cabin bag with pockets for toiletries, a postcard album, a French phrase book, and a large teddy bear. Patty, in return, gets her photograph taken so that she may leave photos with all of her friends before she sails. The images of her, like the gifts received from her friends, are a substitute for Patty's actual presence, a physical reminder of her that can be touched and looked at while she is on the other side of the ocean (Wells, *Patty in Paris* 41–45).

Patty travels to Paris with her friend Elise Farrington and Elise's parents, who are considerably wealthier than the Fairfields. Despite the orgy of gift-giving that heralds Patty's departure, Mr. Fairfield is careful to warn his daughter against over-spending while she is away:

> It will be somewhat expensive, my dear, but I can afford it, for as I told you, my finances are looking up. And, too, I consider this part of your education, and so look upon it as a necessary outlay. But you must remember that the Farringtons are far more wealthy people than we, and though you can afford the necessary travelling expenses, you probably cannot be as extravagant in the matter of personal expenditure as they [Wells, *Patty in Paris* 27].

Mr. Fairfield's warning to his daughter is, at its most basic, a warning about class. The Fairfields, like the Dinsmores and the Chautauqua Girls before them, are wealthy enough that they are in no danger of losing their class position, but a culture of consumption presents its own dangers of class. It is quite possible for Patty to consume too much on her Paris trip, to overspend her allowance, to overindulge in the wares that Paris offers. This danger is increased because she is with the Farringtons, who are sensible people but affluent enough to buy anything that they choose. Should Patty fall into their patterns of spending, as she falls into the various lifestyles of her cousins in volume one, she could easily spend far more than her father can afford. Patty does not do this; the seventeen-year-old traveler is very careful about her money and the items she decides to buy. However, Mr. Fairfield's warning reminds readers yet again that consuming has its downfalls as well as benefits. While money promotes independence and exploration for Patty, it is not to be misused abroad any more than she would misuse it at home.

While the primary concern of the first few volumes in the *Patty Fairfield* series is to emphasize the necessity of responsible consuming and the balance of work and leisure, the *Grace Harlowe* series reveals cultural concern about the permeability of class boundaries in the new world of consumer capitalism. If sheer income is the new standard of membership in the middle and upper classes, then the door is open for those who would lie and steal their way into a luxurious lifestyle. A great deal of tension thus exists between those who would claim a place in the middle or upper class through virtue and industry and those who see money as an end in itself. Grace and her friends, of course, stand on the side of virtue, and either oppose or educate anyone who declares that they are superior simply because of their fortune.

Consuming and Class Anxiety in the Grace Harlowe Series

Grace Harlowe was the heroine of a twenty-seven volume series published by the Henry Altemus Company between 1910 and 1924.[5] Similar to the *Patty Fairfield* series, the *Grace Harlowe* books are full of anxieties about class and consumption, but in this case there are more struggles over the permeability of class boundaries. Grace and her friends Jessica Bright, Nora O'Malley, and Anne Pierson comprise one crowd of the high school, and they refuse to pick and choose their friends on the basis of class. They are akin to Chautauqua Girl Marion Wilbur before them because they are not "willing to admit that money is the question that settles positions in society" (Alden, *At Home* 155). Although the power of consuming has taken the lead in American life, the old idea that virtue determines one's class respectability has not entirely disappeared for Grace and her friends. Another high school group, led by Miriam Nesbit, is composed of girls from the wealthiest families in school. These girls firmly believe that money *does* settle society position; having the most money to spend makes a person more worthwhile and important.

The opening of the first volume of the series, *Grace Harlowe's Plebe Year at High School*, sees Grace reaching out to Anne Pierson, who is new at their high school and clearly poor. Her clothing is described as "shabby," and Grace and her friends are shocked to discover that Anne lives on the poorest street in their hometown of Oakdale: "[W]hen little Miss Pierson stopped in front of one of the smallest and meanest cottages on River Street, the girls knew she must, indeed, be very poor. The house, small and forlorn, presented a sad countenance streaked with tear stains from a leaky gutter" (Flower, *Plebe Year* 11). The "sad countenance" of the house mirrors Anne's reaction when she hears the derogatory comments of Miriam Nesbit and her cohort. Miriam calls her "the shabbiest girl in school," "ha[s] a suspicion that her mother takes in washing or something" and says that socializing with her "would disgrace us" (Flower, *Plebe Year* 8). Anne's poverty marks her as unworthy and different, at least in the eyes of Miriam's crowd. Grace and her friends discover that Anne and her older sister must take in sewing in order to support their invalid mother, and while Miriam and her friends scorn and ridicule Anne for her destitution, Grace's group decides to befriend her. Grace invites Anne to a tea for the freshman class, asking her to help receive guests. From then on, Grace, Jessica, and Nora are Anne's staunchest allies.

Anne fits into the postbellum model of the worthy poor, but the rules that guide her benefactors have changed somewhat. Most importantly, Anne is not required to be Protestant. In fact, she does not have to belong to any religious denomination, and neither do any of her friends or the adults who take an interest in her. Considering the prominent place that religion held in girls' series fiction just a few years before, the *lack* of any kind of faith in these texts is stunning, particularly because Anne is otherwise presented as someone who is in need of benevolence. The only mention of religion in the first volume of the series is toward the end, when it is mentioned that Grace and Jessica pray in their rooms, while Nora, "good little Catholic that she was, went straight to her church and burned two candles..." (Flower, *Plebe Year* 243). Ecumenicalism has become the rule rather than the exception; as long as one follows *some* kind of faith, one is to be commended.

Grace and her friends do not befriend Anne out of any sense of Christian mission; they do so because they want to make her life happier. The girls feel that her poverty should not prevent her from having friends or exclude her from the pleasant social life of high school. Grace manages to couch her invitation to Anne in terms of equality by invoking student unity and achievement: "I am very ambitious for our class. I want it to be the best that ever graduated from Oakdale High School, and for that reason I think all the girls in it should try to be friends and work together to advance the cause..." (Flower, *Plebe Year* 12). Secular American ideas of democracy and economic mobility have replaced the old ideas of religious benevolence. Protestant Christianity is no longer the driving force of individuals and organizations that alleviate social inequality; equal opportunity for all is the motivation behind Grace's kindness.

There are still echoes of the older system, however. One of Elsie Dinsmore's beneficiaries mentioned in Chapter Two, Mrs. Allen, wishes to start a small beekeeping business that will allow her to work outside and slowly improve her health while simultaneously earning money to keep herself and her daughter. Elsie immediately offers to procure her the necessary insects, hives, and tools, and while Mrs. Allen gratefully accepts, she insists that the money Elsie spends must be a loan. She wishes to be as independent as she can be given her small income (Finley, *Elsie and the Raymonds* 122–124).

Like Mrs. Allen, Anne Pierson and her sisters work to support themselves, and Anne wants to exercise her talents and her intelligence to make more money for her family. She shares the same wish for independence as Mrs. Allen and will accept assistance only if she can render a service in return. For example, Mrs. Gray, a wealthy widow who is the sponsor of the high school freshman class, learns of Anne's poverty when she meets the girl at Grace's tea. She hires Anne as her new secretary to help alleviate Anne's financial difficulties and give her some independence (Flower, *Plebe Year* 37–38).

Along with the elimination of religious affiliation, intelligence and schooling are newly emphasized as a means of class mobility and increasing one's income. Anne manages to win the two freshman prizes that are offered by the high school. One prize of twenty-five dollars is awarded for the highest-averaging set of exams, and a second prize of one hundred dollars is given for a set of perfect exams. Anne, through continual hard study over the course of the year, wins both prizes, making her the first freshman ever to achieve perfect exams (Flower, *Plebe Year* 248–250).[6] In this case, Anne's zealous studying brings her and her family some economic security, and her continuing position as secretary to Mrs. Gray allows her to have a little spending money of her own.

Anne's experience as a successful student who receives monetary reward for her work is important because it showcases the possibilities and rewards of high school education for women. As an award-winning high school graduate, Anne has established herself as a member of the middle class through her industry, even if her family's income does not yet match the family income of her schoolmates. She may teach or go on to college if she desires to, opportunities that she probably would not have had if she had not received her diploma. Through a combination of genteel employment and study skills, Anne can help lift her family out of their poverty. College and seminary education of the postbellum period was generally attainable only by those who were *already* middle or upper class; the postbellum *Witch Winnie* and *Three Vassar Girls* series explore this older kind of education in detail. Anne, on the other hand, is a member of the lower class who belongs to the middle class by virtue, but not by income. Through her education as well as part-time employment, she can increase that income and her standard of living.

While Anne Pierson serves as the exemplar for the positive side of class mobility, Grace's friend Marian Barber becomes the poster child for the negative aspects of consumer capitalism, allowing her desire for money and social status to override her honesty and common sense.[7] In *Grace Harlowe's Senior Year at High School*, Marian befriends a man named Henry Hammond who supposedly works in real estate and investing. Marian gives him her savings of fifty dollars, which he promptly doubles for her. She combines the money with fifty dollars from her mother, and spends all of it on three new gowns and elaborate Christmas gifts for her friends. The gifts consist mostly of jewelry for the other members of Grace's crowd, and they are somewhat embarrassed by the costliness of Marian's gifts. The simple gifts the girls and boys have given Marian for Christmas are not nearly so expensive, and so Marian's gifts cause embarrassment as well as happiness (Flower, *Senior Year* 106). Grace observes afterward that "in the minds of her friends there lurked a secret disapproval of Marian's extravagance in the matter of gifts" (Flower, *Senior Year*

108). Not only have Marian's gifts discomfited the girls, but they disapprove of her spending so much money.

The gowns that Marian buys with her money are also inappropriate. The description given of one of them indicates that Marian has made herself over into someone else:

> Was this fashionably attired person plain every-day Marian Barber? Her hair was drawn high upon her head, and topped with a huge cluster of false puffs, which made her look several years older than she had appeared in the afternoon, while her gown of blue satin was cut rather too low for a young girl, and had mere excuses in the way of sleeves. To cap the climax, however, it had a real train that persisted in getting in her way every time she attempted to move [Flower, *Senior Year* 88].

This stylishly clothed, grown-up Marian has nothing in common with the schoolgirl who belongs to Grace's group. She has made herself look older than she is by wearing an outfit that is excessive in the extreme, from the false hair of her hairdo to the extra cloth of her train. In addition, the passage hints at sexual promiscuity by mentioning that the dress is "cut too low for a young girl" and has "mere excuses in the way of sleeves." Marian's dress is too costly and too immodest all at once. Mr. Hammond, as the agent who manages to double Marian's money, is perceived as a suspicious and predatory character by Grace and her friends; he is the unhealthy influence which has caused Marian to change so drastically.

Simple extravagance is not the only problem caused by Marian's association with Mr. Hammond, although her careless expenditures on clothes and gifts are enough to cause alarm. She could potentially become an irresponsible consumer, buying unnecessary items simply because they are expensive and spending far beyond her income. In addition, the clothes she buys allow her to create a false representation of herself: an older, wealthier, sexually mature Marian who belongs in a higher social circle than her school friends. Her purchasing power enables her to create a new persona that bears little relation to the person she actually is. Author Jessie Flower (one pen name of Josephine Chase) clearly shares Carolyn Wells' worries about too much consumption leading to moral corruption, but she also stresses personal and class vulnerability. When everyone can potentially buy his or her way into social respectability, discerning who truly is and is not socially respectable becomes very difficult.

Henry Hammond is a perfect example of the kind of charade that Flower warns against. Although he appears at first glance to be a reputable businessman, he is eventually exposed as a crook and a swindler. He persuades people to give him money to invest, then uses the money for his own benefit, and he is implicated in a number of outright thefts as well as a high-priced investment scheme. Grace discovers the truth of Hammond's identity when Marian foolishly gives him the five hundred dollars that the senior class has raised for a new gymnasium. She wants to best the fundraising of the seniors out of pride, and Mr. Hammond promises that he can triple the money for her. He loses it all in his speculation, and Marian confesses her wrongdoings to Grace. Grace, with the help of classmate Eleanor Savell, manages to expose Mr. Hammond's partner in swindling. She forces Mr. Hammond himself to write a check for the money he took from Marian, letting him leave town in exchange. Marian is never exposed, for Grace and Eleanor keep her secret, and all of the money raised for the gymnasium is recovered.

The point of this dramatic plot is that Marian allows her cravings for wealth, material goods, and social rank to intensify until she is willing to perform highly unethical actions to obtain them. She foolishly gives her own money into the hands of a speculator and swindler, spends the earnings on clothing and gifts that are too extravagant, then commits the ultimate crime of speculating with money that is not her own to surpass the achievements of girls who are her friends. She becomes selfish, self-centered, and reckless in her quest for social position. Flower delivers a heavy-handed warning in this volume about the personal ruin that can ensue when money and social status become one's only goals in life. Marian is redeemed by Grace and Eleanor's quick thinking; without it, Marian could have been charged with some very serious crimes that may have even led to a prison sentence. Mr. Hammond also exemplifies the idea that capitalism breeds criminals, that the desire for wealth can corrupt individuals and lead to moral degradation. It seems like an odd anomaly that both he and Marian escape penalty for their deeds when so much of series fiction is concerned with correct social behavior, but Marian's freedom is the price of Mr. Hammond's escape. Because Grace allows Hammond to go free, Marian's crime remains unknown. She can atone for her mistakes and go on with her life without any kind of social blemish on her character.

Despite Flower's textual warnings about the potential for blurred class lines and morally reprehensible behavior in a consumer society, she is by no means completely against consumption. She recognizes, as did Wells, that buying things for oneself or receiving new possessions as gifts can be an empowering and satisfying experience. Once again, Anne Pierson is the key character who illustrates this point. In Grace's freshman year of high school, Mrs. Gray holds a grand Christmas party that includes the four girls, three of their male friends from high school, and Mrs. Gray's great-nephew, Tom Gray, along with some of the other students. Having become particularly fond of Anne over the course of the year, Mrs. Gray gives her a pink silk party dress as a Christmas gift:

> Mrs. Gray and the girls had stolen out so as not to embarrass the young girl who, for the first time, saw herself in a beautiful new silk dress exactly the color of pink rose petals.... "We mustn't be too enthusiastic about the difference [whispered Mrs. Gray]. It might hurt her tender little feelings. But she does look sweet, doesn't she?" [Flower, *Plebe Year* 166–67].

Anne is awed by her beautiful dress, the first one she has ever owned, while Mrs. Gray and the other girls are well aware of the "difference" it makes in her appearance. The "difference" on the outside, of course, is that she does not look poor, but her friends realize that the change is also on an emotional level. Anne's dress makes her feel beautiful; it gives her confidence in herself and her looks that she did not have before. The dress is a luxury item that hides Anne's lower income from others and also boosts her self-esteem and confidence. One gift from a woman who has become her mentor helps change Anne's perception of herself in a positive way, and the kindness and love of Mrs. Gray and her school friends only makes the gift more special to Anne.

Another instance in which Flower demonstrates the positive effects of consumption for girls takes place in *Grace Harlowe's Sophomore Year at High School*, when the girls impulsively decide to get hot chocolate:

> "Oh girls," cried Nora suddenly. "I have a half a dollar."
> "Really?" said Jessica. "I didn't suppose there was that much money in Oakdale."
> "My sister gave it to me this morning," Nora went on, ignoring Jessica's remark. "I am supposed to buy a new collar with it, but if you are thirsty–"
> "I am simply perishing with thirst," murmured Grace.
> Five minutes later the four girls were seated in the nearest drug store busily engaged with hot chocolate, while they congratulated Nora on having spent her money in a good cause [Flower, *Sophomore Year* 169].

In this case, Nora makes a choice about her consumption priorities. Although she is "supposed to buy a new collar" with her fifty cents, she chooses instead to treat her friends and enable them to spend the afternoon together over cups of hot chocolate. While her sister will probably scold her for failing to bring home the collar, Nora sees the opportunity to socialize with her friends as more important than an item for her wardrobe.[8] Much like women who spend whole days in department stores, Nora appropriates some public space for her group by purchasing some of the wares offered by the drug store. Her "good cause" is providing the means for food to eat and space in which to talk, laugh, and expand the girls' friendships.

Consumer goods in these texts create positive changes in individual characters like Anne, but they can also facilitate group activities and encourage bonding between groups of friends. The ability to purchase luxury goods, from small things like hot chocolate to larger things like the fittings for Patty's bedroom, not only allows series heroines wider access to the public realm, but also allowed them to enjoy modern inventions. One luxury item in particular promised girls more freedom than ever before: the motor car.

Going Mobile with Patty Fairfield and the Outdoor Girls

Patty Fairfield is the earliest series where motor cars are in wide use, and the freedom enabled by them is extolled and commended. Undeniably meant, at least in stories, for the upper-middle and upper classes, motor cars or automobiles embody both modernity and prosperity, making them a perfect sign of class status. Nancy Romalov contends that series books involving automobiles are heavily biased against the working classes and non-whites, even while they promote gender equality and freedom among white young people of the upper classes:

> While these stories appear to carry the overt message of gender solidarity and equality, these fictions rest heavily on white supremacist assumptions. As these young girls match wits with and triumph over the highway men, gypsies tramps, anarchists, and foreigners they meet on their travels, they continue to establish and reassert their position as genteel American women, well-bred capitalists, and emissaries of leisure [83].

Romalov is right to take the books to task for their racist and classist assumptions; according to the texts, only white people from the middle and upper class own automobiles. They are a luxury item, meant to be used and enjoyed by those who can afford them. Where she and I differ, however, is over the role that men play in these series. She argues that female solidarity and mobility frequently take a backseat to relationships and marriage by the end of the series, making all of the girls' adventures "a passing phase, a necessary prerequisite perhaps to a companionate marriage" (Romalov 83). However, in her article she concentrates primarily on the appearance of boyfriends, never mentioning how fathers function in the narratives. She also does not comment on the frequent mixed-sex socializing that takes place within and because of motor cars.[9] When it comes to girl heroines owning and using automobiles and other motorized vehicles, male guardians are often the agents for their freedom. The driving skills and mechanical knowledge of girl heroines puts them on an even footing with their male peers, and so motoring becomes a democratic pastime that removes social barriers of sex and age.

Patty first encounters a motor car in volume four, *Patty's Summer Days*, when she spends the summer after her high-school graduation traveling with her friends the Farringtons. Mr. Farrington and his son, Roger, are the two primary operators of their family vehicle, but in this volume Patty is happy to simply enjoy motoring as a social activity. She falls in love with motoring, for it makes her feel as though she has entered some other world:

> The wonderful exhilaration of the swift motion through the soft June air, the delightful sensation of the breeze which was caused by the motion of the car, and the ever-changing natural panorama on either side of her, gave Patter the sensation of having suddenly been transported to some other country than that in which she had been living the past few weeks [Wells, *Patty's Summer Days* 121].

Patty has left behind her routine of schoolwork and domesticity, the rounds of calling and shopping, homework and Tea Club meetings that make up her everyday life. The motor car, which the Farringtons can easily afford to buy, allows Patty to enter "some other country" and freely travel to places that she has never seen. In doing so, she and her companions blur the lines between "private" space for women and "public" space for men. Not only are they all traveling together, in a heterogeneous group, but the women, in their contemporary motoring clothes, present just as much of a spectacle as the men:

> [As Patty] looked at the rather shapeless figure in the long pongee coat, and the queer shirred hood of the same material, and as she noted the voluminous chiffon veil with its funny little front window of mica, she concluded that she looked more like a goblin in a fairy play than a human being [Wells, *Patty's Summer Days* 128].

Patty's clothes, and the clothes of her party, change her into an alien being that she does not recognize. She becomes something otherworldly, suitable for the new world she is traveling in. While she does not become "masculine" per se (at least not yet), she is no longer human (or female) either. The clothing necessary for proper motoring creates even more distance from the world of home and school she is accustomed to by taking away her human and/or female attributes, leaving her androgynous or "like a goblin in a fairy play." As a passenger in the car piloted by the two males of their party, Mr. Farrington and his son Roger, Patty inhabits a no man's land between public and private, male and female, that is liberating as well as a little disconcerting.

However, the motor car is not a perfect vehicle for adventure. It breaks down several times over the course of the Farrington's travels, causing their party to be both delayed and frustrated. Wells may have been commenting on the unreliability of modern inventions as well as their positive possibilities; even something as liberating as a car has its flaws. Still, Patty enjoys motoring enough that when a chance comes for her to own a car, she jumps at it and proves the power of consumption again in the process.

In *Patty's Motor Car*, volume nine, the Rhodes and Geer car company issues a book of one hundred word puzzles for anyone to solve, and the prize is a luxury runabout known as a Stanhope. Men presumably run the automobile company, and since there are no gender limits on who can enter the contest, Patty is free to take advantage of the male executives' challenge. She is determined to win the prize, but her father expresses skepticism, saying, "Those contests are just planned for an advertisement. The prize goes to the daughter of the chief director" (30). Fred Fairfield has apparently learned enough about the persuasive power of advertising to be a little wary of the motor company's motives. While Patty sees the contest as a game, Mr. Fairfield sees it as a potential scam against participating consumers, run solely for the purpose of increasing revenues.

Patty, however, is determined to complete the puzzle book and enter the contest, and she enlists the help of her friends and acquaintances, as well as reference books, to do so. When she eventually wins the car, she is staggered when her father informs her that it is worth about three thousand dollars because it comes with all of the latest equipment and luxuries. When Mr. Fairfield suggests, however, that Patty should repay the company by praising the car to her friends and family, she disagrees:

> Oh, I don't feel under any obligation to the company. It was a business enterprise on their part. They offered a prize and I won it. Now we're quits. Of course, I shall praise the car to my friends, but only because it's such a beauty, and not because I feel that I owe anything to the company [Wells, *Patty's Motor Car* 99].

Patty's logic is interesting, here, because the motor company's contest was expressly meant to encourage consumer interest in their cars and inspire loyalty in their contest winner. Patty feels no gratitude or loyalty to the company; she sees it as a simple transaction that is now over. Had Patty been a real person, advertisers and department store executives would have despaired. Advertisers wanted to create brand loyalty, and department stores offered so many services (like home delivery, post offices, telephones, clothing alterations, etc.) because managers wanted women to keep shopping in their stores and encourage their friends to do likewise. If women see the buying of goods only as an exchange and not a pleasurable pastime, a sensory experience to be indulged in, then it becomes that much harder to ensure that they will return to the same brand or the same store. They can shop where they like, buy what they like, and they are under no obligation to the department stores that serve them or the companies that make their household goods. It is a one-sided economic contract in which the woman customer pays and the store or company provides what she paid for. In Patty's case, she "paid" with the book of puzzles put out by the motor company, and they gave her the promised car. Patty's declaration that she is "quits" with the motor car company emphasizes her power as a consumer. She owes them nothing. If she eventually decides that she would like a different car, there is no reason that she *has* to buy another Stanhope; she may, but she is not required to. In short, female customers hold all the cards. Far from being excluded from the public world of capitalism, Patty ventures into it and uses it to her own advantage, securing an expensive motor car of her very own with a few weeks of mental effort and no money at all. While this is hardly a realistic scenario, it does serve to illustrate the way that women consumers could make the most of sales and promotions, securing more goods for themselves with less money.

Once the car is actually in her possession, Patty gains even more freedom than she has previously had. Her car is not as large as the Farringtons' vehicle, making it easier to operate and store. Patty learns to drive the car herself by taking lessons from the Fairfields' chauffeur and from Mr. Fairfield himself. Although her father lays out some specific ground rules about her driving (she cannot drive after dark and must have an adult with her if she is driving in the city), she is otherwise free to use the car when she wants to and drive where she pleases. Just as Patty's ownership of the car is achieved through a male-run company, her ability to drive and repair her own vehicle is learned with the assistance of two men, her father and the family chauffeur (Wells, *Patty's Motor Car* 94 and 110–113). Seeing male figures encouraging young women in their use of new, motorized inventions seems unexpected given the amount of freedom that came with that encouragement, and given the resistance that male figures in some earlier series (Mr. Dinsmore before his reformation, for example) showed to any kind of female emancipation. Mr. Fairfield has to be convinced that Patty actually *wants* the vehicle when she decides to enter the contest, but he gladly takes her out for a driving lesson when the car arrives. On the page, at least, driving becomes a pleasurable activity for characters of all ages and both genders. The use of any kind of motorized vehicle encourages friendship and bonding across the lines of sex and age.

Patty's male friends from Vernondale, for example, are great admirers of her Stanhope. Roger Farrington declares that the car is "beautiful" and has "perfect mechanism" (Wells, *Patty's Motor Car* 161), while Philip Van Reypen admires the "perfection of detail" and "beautiful finish" of the car and calls it "a daisy" (Wells, *Patty's Motor Car* 171–72). Roger allows Patty to take him for a drive and show off her driving skills, and Philip decides to drive Patty so that he can size up her car for himself. Patty's girlfriends are not to be left out of the fun, either; both her Spring Beach neighbor Mona Gailbraith and her Vernondale chum Elise Farrington declare that they want cars exactly like Patty's (Wells, *Patty's Motor Car* 145 and 158). Fortunately for them, they both have indulgent fathers who can afford the expensive vehicles. Mr. Fairfield's initial reluctance aside, male friends and relatives seem perfectly happy to encourage Patty in her love for driving and motoring.

If one was not lucky enough to own or be able to borrow a car, there was a much simpler way to leave home and explore: walking. In the *Outdoor Girls* series, a Stratemeyer production that ran from 1913 to 1933 and reached twenty-three volumes, four girlfriends decide to form a camping and tramping club in order to travel to nearby towns and familiarize themselves with the area outside of their hometown of Deepdale. The original Outdoor Girls were Mollie Billette, Amy Blackford, Grace Ford, and Betty Nelson. Later volumes of the series gradually introduced new members of the group, with frequent appearances by the original quartet (all of whom had married by the end of the series).

Betty has the original idea for a three-week vacation at the beginning of summer in which the girls will cover about two hundred miles. On the first trip, the girls stay with relatives and friends each night after their walking, carrying with them a few changes of clothes each and basic foodstuffs. In the course of their hiking, the girls pass through eight nearby towns. They walk as a group, but they are unaccompanied, with no adults and no male members of their group. They are, in a word, unchaperoned, an abnormal enough occurrence in 1913 that those who observe the quartet are frequently astonished:

> They passed farm houses, in the kitchen doors of which appeared the women and girls of the household, standing with rolled-up sleeves, arms akimbo, looking with no small wonder at the four travelers.
> There were comments, too, not always inaudible.
> "I wonder what they're selling?" one woman asked her daughter.... A little later, a small boy ... scuttled back toward the kitchen, crying out, "Ma-ma! Come an' see the suffragists!" [Hope, *Of Deepdale* 99].

The girls are simply an unusual sight in the beginning of this passage. The juxtaposition of the Outdoor Girls with the working farm women indicates that the ability to walk and camp as part of a vacation is a luxury, something that one does for exercise when there is no manual work to be done. It is a vivid reminder that the activities of the Outdoor Girls are the provenance of the middle and upper classes; working-class people do not have the leisure for a vacation.

On the other hand, one woman assumes that the girls are selling something, though she doesn't speculate aloud about what that "something" is. This assumption obliquely equates them with salesmen, who are usually traveling *male* workers regarded with suspicion. The little boy who speaks last thinks the girls are suffragists, who were excoriated in the press for being mannish and unwomanly, stepping outside of their appointed place in the home and into the male-controlled world of politics. All of these comparisons render the Outdoor Girls unsexed. Being on foot in public space without any escorts, the girls have laid aside the normal rules of propriety that govern their behavior.[10] Like Patty Fairfield in her motoring clothes, they have become androgynous beings occupying a liminal space where both sexual distinctions and girls' mental and physical capabilities can be questioned, reevaluated, and expanded.

The Outdoor Girls' walking outfits also play a key role in disrupting observers' assumptions about their gender:

> Clad in their new suits of olive drab, purposely designed for walking, with sensible blouses, containing pockets, with skirts sufficiently short, stout boots, and natty little caps, the outdoor girls looked their name. Already there was the hint of tan on their faces, for they had been much in the open of late [Hope, *Of Deepdale* 90].

While "olive drab" as a general term refers to a color of brown-green generally used in cloth, it is also a reference to army uniforms, which were made with cotton or wool olive drab cloth. The cloth was also known as khaki. The U.S. Army began issuing khaki field service uniforms to all troops in 1902, replacing a highly mixed assortment of cloth and colors that varied by regiment and location (Mollo 218–223). Women were not allowed to enlist in the military in 1913, yet the Outdoor Girls wear olive drab suits as a uniform for their club. Their skirts are shorter than average, so that they may walk and climb unrestrained, and the girls wear boots instead of heels. Finally, the tan on their faces violates the unspoken fashion rule that ladies generally have white skin; in an earlier period being tan was indicative of membership in the working class, since it meant that one had to be outside for extended periods.

Strangely, being called suffragists makes the Outdoor Girls uneasy. After the incident with the little boy recounted above, the girls stop at a farmhouse for dinner, and the farmer's wife asks them if they are suffragists. Betty is disturbed by it: "'That's the second time we've been taken for them to-day,' Betty murmured. 'Do we look so militant?'" (Hope, *Of Deepdale* 117). One is almost tempted to laugh at her question. Of course they look militant; they are wearing walking outfits that deliberately mimic military uniforms both in form and function. That they are repeatedly taken for suffragists shows how prevalent the stereotypes about suffrage were; ghostwriter Howard Garis reproduced them here, although it is impossible to know whether he was actually opposed to suffrage or simply using the stereotypes to create humor. Romalov sees the girls' repeated denial of being suffragists and their denial of being political at all, which is Betty's response the third time someone asks them if they are a "Votes for Women crowd" (Hope, *Of Deepdale* 169), as yet another way of reinforcing conservative values over liberal feminism:

> For all their boasting of being modern American women who can compete with men ... the series heroines are quick to disassociate their activities from any political intent.... Having set their heroines up with the ability, courage, independence, and athleticism required to enact the heroic adventures that the genre calls for, the authors then set about negating, disrupting, or dismissing the radical possibilities that might have been realized [Romalov 81].

While Romalov is assessing several series at once here, not just the *Outdoor Girls*, I believe that her evaluation in this case is a little too cautious. Despite the explicit disavowal of feminist politics in the text, it cannot be denied that what the Outdoor Girls *do*—hiking together over long distances without adults or males—is new and exciting and very much public. All of the girls' "masculine" traits of dress and daring are indicators of several contemporary cultural trends *besides* suffrage that were emerging around young women. Some of those trends were certainly more traditional than suffrage, but others were right in step with the New Women of this period. Martha Banta asserts that the Outdoors Girl, which she identifies as a prominent cultural type in advertising, art, and storytelling from the 1890s through the 1910s (Banta 48), could serve several different cultural purposes simultaneously:

> By 1900 many women expressed genuine interest in athletics.... Publicity persuaded many women that such activities were the surest way to acquire the free-spirited look now expected of lively American Girls. The type of the Outdoors Girl could image a revolutionary process that promised the self and society would never be the same again. The type also supported the views of conservatives who reasoned that their daughters should cultivate an excellent physique as insurance for a stable society founded on sound motherhood. Or the type could be used to promote beauty products in an avidly consumer society [Banta 88].

The fictional Outdoor Girls serve all of these purposes except the last (cosmetics are almost never mentioned in the series). Betty, Grace, Mollie, and Amy are "free-spirited" by definition; they have the freedom to go camping unaccompanied and the spirit to accomplish their goal of two hundred miles. They wear uniforms that are reminiscent of men's army gear but are appropriately modified for women; they are obviously physically healthy, as indicated by their tan and their ability to walk twenty miles a day. The four girls from Deepdale are continually solving their own problems, from finding shelter during thunderstorms to fixing their automobiles.[11] Clearly, they are self-reliant, athletic, determined, and resourceful, characteristics that are the antithesis of the passive, dependent, physically weak young women whom traditionalists (like Stanley Hall and Edward Clarke) were so worried about protecting. Whether those new "masculine" skills are put to use as a mother or in a career, giving the Outdoor Girls a chance to develop them in the first place is a signal that cultural ideas about girlhood were changing and gender boundaries were being challenged, even when more traditional messages about marriage and family also found their way into the narratives.

The purpose of the Outdoor Girls' walking club quickly expands to include almost any kind of outdoor activity, including motoring and boating; they are not left out of the motoring craze for long. Mollie Billette is the first one of the foursome to get her own car. Book three, *The Outdoor Girls in a Motor Car*, opens with Mollie displaying her new touring car to her friends. The car is big enough to accommodate the four girls, and, like Patty Fairfield, Mollie has taken lessons so she can run it herself. She buys the vehicle with money that her father left her in his will, so the car is hers outright. Mr. Billette's original suggestion was for Mollie to take a trip to Europe; he is another male guardian figure who encourages his daughter's forays into public space. In this case, he even manages to do so posthumously! Mollie, however, convinces her mother that a car would be more useful for herself and the rest of the family in the short-term, and so her father's legacy provides the Outdoor Girls with transportation. Having a vehicle allows the girls to extend their camping and tramping to a wider geographical area, one that extends far beyond the boundaries of their hometown and the distance they could be expected to walk on foot.

Mollie's car is not the only type of motorized vehicle that helps the Outdoor Girls extend their reach. In the second volume of the series, *The Outdoor Girls at Rainbow Lake*, Betty receives a motorboat named the *Gem* as a gift from her uncle, Amos Marlin. Uncle Amos is a retired sea captain and "quite rich" according to Betty (*Rainbow Lake* 10). He buys the boat as a gift for Betty, since she loved sailing with him as a little girl. The girls take their initial boating trip to Rainbow Like, a few miles away from Deepdale, but when the girls go to Florida in volume five, Betty has the *Gem* shipped down so that they can use it on their vacation. Finally, in *The Outdoor Girls in the Air*, the penultimate volume in the series, the second generation of Outdoor Girls discovers the joys of flying in airplanes. The new leader of the group,

Stella Sibley, takes lessons from a male aviator named Bill Dunning so that she can fly planes by herself. Daniel Tower, uncle to Outdoor Girls Meg and Lota Bronson, takes the whole club with him on a business trip to Canada, chartering a plane to carry their whole party. Yet again, we see that male characters are more than happy to encourage girls in their love of driving, boating, and flying.

Mechanical inventions like the automobile and airplane provide girl heroines with an expanded worldview, allow them to explore communities outside their own, make decisions for themselves, learn the skills of driving and car repair (which are traditionally masculine pursuits), and form close bonds with each other in the process. Just as important is the fact that series heroines stand on an equal footing with men when it comes to driving and flying. As Patty's driving clothes and the Outdoor Girls' uniforms show, conventional markers of gender identity don't apply in a motor car, and a neutral space is created that allows for cross-generational and heterosexual friendships to develop.

Perhaps the most important motivator for series heroines who patronize department stores, indulge in consuming new goods, and eagerly learn to drive cars, however, is simply the excitement of experiencing new places and new ways of defining oneself. Betty Nelson says it perfectly when she remarks that doing so much outdoors "has unfitted us for the hum-drum sort of existence that used to satisfy us. We seem to want some excitement all the while now" (Hope, *In Florida* 25). The "hum-drum" existence is staying at home, while shopping in department stores, hiking in the outdoors, and traveling in cars and planes provides independence and the ability to make one's own choices. Patty Fairfield learns the rules of responsible consuming, but at the same time is happy to indulge herself in beautiful clothes and tastefully decorated rooms. Her cousin Marian Elliott consciously takes advantage of Parisian goods in order to create a sophisticated and unique persona among her peers. Grace Harlowe and her friends learn about both the benefits and drawbacks of class mobility and consumerism. Education gives Anne Pierson and her family more disposable income and self-respect, while Marian Barber almost loses everything in her attempts to generate more money than she has and consume more than she can afford. Finally, Patty and the Outdoor Girls discover the freedom of movement that comes with motor cars, boats, and planes. Grace, too, eventually learns to drive. They create solid friendships with both their male peers and older male relatives and acquaintances through their shared love of travel. Far from being opposed to girl heroines' ventures into public space, male relatives and friends encourage the girls in their exploration. New machines are the ultimate luxury goods that provide female autonomy and freedom. Nor would the "excitement" attached to new modes of transportation go away; in fact, some series heroines would use their driving skills to participate in the next big adventure: the Great War.

Notes

1. See William Leach, *Land of Desire*; Susan Benson, *Counter Cultures*; T. Jackson Lears, *Fables of Abundance*; Warren Susman, "'Personality' and the Making of Twentieth Century Culture" in *Culture as History: The Transformation of American Society in the Twentieth Century*.

2. Scholarly works on American women and the transition to consumer culture at the turn of the century include Elaine Abelson, *When Ladies Go A-Thieving*; Susan Benson, *Counter Cultures*; Nan Enstad, *Ladies of Labor and Girls of Adventure*; Margaret Finnegan, *Selling Suffrage*; Ellen Gruber Garvey, *The Adman in the Parlor*; Kristin L. Hoganson, *Consumers' Imperium*; William Leach, *Land of Desire*; T. Jackson Lears, *Fables of Abundance*; Charles F. McGovern, *Sold American*; and Kathy Peiss, *Cheap Amusements*. Scholarship on women and Progressive Era reform includes Sandra Adickes, *To Be Young Was Very Heaven*; Eric Rauchway, *The Refuge of Affections*; Dorothy and Carl J. Schneider, *American Women in the Progressive Era, 1900–1920*; Judith Schwarz, *Radical Feminists of Heterodoxy*; and Christine Stansell, *American Moderns*.

3. According to her 1942 obituary in *The New York Times*, Wells wrote juvenile books primarily in the first decade or so of her career, becoming better known in the teens and twenties for her mystery novels. She also was at least partly deaf; the Times says that she "had been afflicted with deafness since girlhood," but the article does not record the extent of her handicap or whether she spoke or used sign language ("Carolyn Wells, Novelist, Dead.").

4. "The Female World of Love and Ritual: Relations Between Women in Nineteenth-Century America" originally appeared in *Signs: Journal of Women in Culture and Society*, 1.1 (1975): 1–29. The version cited here was reprinted in Smith-Rosenberg's *Disorderly Conduct: Visions of Gender in Victorian America*.

5. Grace, like Patty, was not an Edward Stratemeyer creation. Josephine Chase wrote the first eleven *Grace Harlowe* books under the pen name of "Jessie Graham Flower" (James Keeline, "Comments on Emily's Prospectus"). Chase penned multiple series under several pseudonyms, including the *Marjorie Dean* and *Patsy Carroll* series ("Youth's Author Dies"). It would be interesting to do a detailed analysis of Stratemeyer series and non–Stratemeyer series in this period and see how they deal similarly or differently with issues of consumption and class, although such a comprehensive investigation is beyond the scope of this chapter. It is also worth noting that the *Grace Harlowe* series is often classified as four separate series: her high school years (four books), her college years (seven books), the *Grace Harlowe Overseas* series, which takes place during World War I (six books), and the *Grace Harlowe's Overland Riders* series, which finds Grace and her friends traveling to various parts of the United States (ten books). The books in the *Overseas* and *Overland Riders* series have been attributed to Frank G. Patchin (James Keeline, "Comments on Emily's Prospectus"). I have not been able to discover when this "splitting" of the series began. There is no reason that the books cannot be read as one series; the internal chronology remains consistent

throughout all the books and all books consistently feature the same set of main characters. Altemus may have originally marketed each set of books separately, but I have not yet been able to confirm that theory.

6. Anne does pay a physical price for her hard studying; she faints at the graduation and awards ceremony and has to be taken to Mrs. Gray's for food and sleep. Why Chase (who had a master's degree if the "A.M." after her pseudonym is anything to go by) would include this moment of collapse in her narrative is hard to know, unless it was purely for dramatic effect. This scene of physical weakness is particularly puzzling because it seems to confirm the warnings of Edward Clarke and Stanley Hall and go against everything else that Chase openly advocates in the series: an equal chance at a high school education for all girls, girls' high school sports teams (basketball in particular), college education for women, and women's careers. A similar occurrence appears in *Patty's Summer Days*, when Patty works herself to exhaustion through her senior exams, the commencement exercises, and the senior play. Right at the end of the play, she faints just as the curtain falls. Much like Anne, she is rushed home and put to bed, and she sleeps through until the next afternoon.

7. Marian Barber is a minor member of Grace's school crowd until she and Grace become friends in the second volume of the series, *Grace Harlowe's Sophomore Year at High School*. She is not to be confused with Miriam Nesbit, mentioned earlier in this chapter, who is a major character and one of Grace's enemies for the first few books of the series.

8. Historian Jane Hunter contends that the new ethic of consumption gave young women more opportunities to socialize and be seen in public space without being censured by their families or acquaintances. Once compulsory education laws were put into place, requiring girls to spend a specific number of hours per day in school, young women had more time to socialize with each other and develop friendships away from the oversight of their parents. Consumption of goods was another activity that united female schoolmates; by walking together and shopping after school hours were over, they could obtain both the health benefits of walking and the mental benefits of friendship: "[M]iddle-class girls' walking increasingly was tied up with shopping. Aside from going to school, the most common destination was 'downtown,' where girls got drinks at soda fountains, bought treats at a bake shop, and did errands for themselves and their mothers" (274; see also 169–192).

9. My reading of Nancy Romalov is incomplete here; while I am working from one of her anthologized articles, she also wrote a dissertation on girls' "mobile" series from the turn of the century. Unfortunately, it is currently loaned out from the University of Iowa library and unavailable for interlibrary loan. Romalov never published it in book form.

10. Peiss, Chinn, and Hunter in particular have shown that by the time *The Outdoor Girls of Deepdale* was published in 1913, seeing girls walking together in pairs or in groups in the city would have become commonplace. Middle-class girls were encouraged to walk as much as possible for their health, and working-class girls frequented city dance halls and amusement parks in groups. Deepdale is said to have about fifteen thousand residents, so it is not very large, but it also has a railroad and steamer line (Hope, *Of Deepdale* 25–27). Perhaps Howard Garis, the ghostwriter, or Stratemeyer himself felt that in a rural town with so few residents, new rules of etiquette for girls would not be as prevalent, and so the Outdoor Girls' club would have been a novelty — or perhaps they simply wanted the opportunity to poke fun at suffragists.

11. The *Outdoor Girls* series may well have been a response to the emergence of the Campfire Girls and Girl Scouts in the United States, founded in 1911 and 1912, respectively (Miller 14 and 25). The two competing organizations had different ideas about why camping and woodcraft were important to girls. The Campfire Girls organization focused on reclaiming a primitive domesticity for girls, helping them to reconnect to their primitive domestic selves that had been lost in the modern world (Miller 5). The Girl Scouts, on the other hand, connected outdoor life and crafts to the patriotism and self-reliance of early settlers: "Girls were taught that their camping experiences would allow them to channel the can-do spirit of early settlers . . . girls willing to venture into the American landscape could tap into hidden reservoirs of self-reliance and fortitude that had been bequeathed to ensuing generations" (Miller 6). The latter set of ideas appears again and again in the *Outdoor Girls*, linking the books in principle to both the Girl Scouts organization and Teddy Roosevelt's "Strenuous Life."

FIVE

Two Miles Forward, One Mile Back
Gender Battles During the Great War

The story of American women in the Great War is one of both progress and frustration. Although the United States did not enter the war until 1917, American women found many ways to be a part of the war effort long before the U.S. was officially involved in the fighting. Once the U.S. armed forces mobilized and sent men overseas, women served in ever-expanding ways and more and more industries, replacing and assisting men in the Army, Navy, Marine Corps, on farms, in the railroad yards, in the munitions factories, in the aviation hangars, and on the trolley cars. Women also formed their own small army of nurses, doctors, physical therapists (a brand new profession in World War I), and caretakers.

While American women found ingenious ways of working around military bureaucracy and civilian contempt, their ingenuity could only get them so far. Secretary of War Newton Baker was adamantly against women in the armed forces and made it nearly impossible for women to join the army. He refused to authorize the formation of a women's army unit that would have been analogous to the British Women's Army Auxiliary Corps. He was a key player in dismantling the Women's Land Army of America near the end of the war, through a series of bureaucratic maneuvers that starved the organization of resources and manpower. Congress also did its best to interfere with women war workers, refusing to grant army nurses military rank and denying benefits to female veterans of the Army Signal Corps.

On the other hand, women found powerful male allies in Secretary of the Navy Josephus Daniels, who authorized women to be enrolled in the Navy and prompted the Marine Corps to follow suit, and General John J. Pershing, who outright demanded the appointment of bilingual female telephone operators to the Army Signal Corps and American Expeditionary Forces (AEF). While women's work in the war was most often circumscribed and controlled by men, men like Pershing and Daniels actively worked to give women a place in the war. In addition, war meant that social constraints were lessened and relaxed across the board; desperate times allowed unorthodox behavior to be overlooked and sometimes even sanctioned. Women took whatever measures they deemed necessary to participate in the war. When the American Army would not accept female ambulance drivers, the female ambulance drivers enlisted with the French Army. When the Red Cross nurses and the YMCA canteen workers were not allowed near the front with their designated units, the women often went anyway, knowing that their presence would be conveniently overlooked by the commanding officers and thoroughly embraced by the soldiers. There was continuous tension between what women *actually* managed to achieve and what their male supervisors (Congressmen, commanders, male physicians, yardmasters, etc.) *thought* they could or should achieve. Women made gains for themselves often in spite of those who exercised authority over them, and discovered that their opportunities were immeasurably expanded in a nation and world at war — but like women before and after them, they also found that freedom was much more circumscribed once peace was declared. Nevertheless, the war created lasting changes in women's opportunities, and individual women were profoundly affected by the new careers and freedoms the war offered. The push-and pull, advance-and-retreat nature of women's gains in the Great War would spill over into the plots of series fiction on the home front. Whether recreating the adventures of female Red Cross workers or depicting the experiences of female ambulance drivers, series fiction both romanticized war work and disseminated ideas about women's freedom to a wider audience.

American Women as Wartime Adventurers

When the war in Europe began, American women had to find their own ways of helping the cause. In 1914, at the beginning of the conflict, Americans were not directly involved in the war and few citizens felt the need to support a war that they viewed as Europe's problem. Two years later, in 1916, Woodrow Wilson would be re-elected with the slogan "He Kept Us Out of War." Those Americans who believed it their duty to help European soldiers and civilians had to use their own initiative and finances to do so, sometimes creating and sometimes joining larger organizations that would give them credibility. "From 1914 on [women] formed literally hundreds of organizations like the Woman's

Committee of the Commission for Belgian Relief, the Vacation War Relief Committee, the Surgical Dressings Committee, the National Patriotic Relief Society, and the National League for Woman's Service" (Schneider and Schneider, *Into the Breach* 8). There were also the American Fund for French Wounded, the American Woman's War Relief Fund, the American Relief Clearing House, and many British and French organizations and private American charities. Other alternatives included the Women's Land Army of America, the Red Cross, the YMCA, the YWCA, the Salvation Army, the Navy, or the Marine Corps. The Red Cross, YMCA, YWCA, and the Salvation Army all fell under the aegis of the American Expeditionary Forces, while the Women's Land Army was an independent organization run entirely by women. Women were eager to serve, and while absolute numbers are hard to come by, 25,000 is a low estimate for the number of American women overseas, and tens of thousands more worked in wartime industries at home.[1]

While it might seem tactless or heartless to characterize women's war work as adventure, in reality adventure, danger, happiness, and sorrow blended in the lives of war workers to an astonishing degree. Women who participated in war work found an outlet for their desire to be useful and felt a profound sense of accomplishment in contributing to the war effort of the United States or the Allied countries. Many of them had never been away from home for extended periods, and even those who were self-supporting found new challenges away from the shop, factory, or office floor. On the other hand, women also made very deliberate choices about enlisting, going overseas, or working in the U.S. for an industry or one of the many auxiliary organizations that needed workers. Their concerns with wages, opportunity, and job experience reflect women who were shrewdly cognizant of their own economic situations and well aware of the professional and financial advances that war could provide for them.

Women war workers were, for the most part, white and native-born. They were also overwhelmingly Protestant. Official organizations shied away from women of other races or faiths, particularly excluding African Americans, Jewish, and Irish Catholic women. The one exception was French-Canadian immigrants or Catholic women of French descent, as organizations sought out women who spoke French fluently. Of course, such prejudices and exclusions did not necessarily hold true in private charities, where organizers could accept whomever they deemed competent. For any woman joining a branch of the service or an auxiliary federal organization, however, such discrimination was all too common (Zeiger 28–32).

Surprisingly, however, the family situations of women war workers were significantly more complicated than their racial and religious origins might suggest. Although wealthy women ran many private war work endeavors, and although they were featured most prominently in publicity campaigns, the vast majority of women who joined any American Expeditionary Forces group were from the lower-middle class. Most were urban dwellers and already self-supporting; those who lived with family members were often helping to support a household:

> Substantial, although fragmentary, evidence suggests that many servicewomen came from households that did not represent the patriarchal families then considered to be the norm. Sisters living and working together in an independent household, a working daughter supporting a widowed mother, brothers and sisters supporting a disabled or unemployed father — all these are represented in the prewar experiences of nurses, auxiliary workers, and office workers.... Furthermore, many women who entered the service in 1917 were, either by choice or by necessity, already living independently from their families [Zeiger 32–33].

A good number of women also held a high school diploma, and some women had additional education in the form of trade school or college. Finally, the majority of women who served overseas were in their mid-twenties to early thirties, while stateside Navy and Marine Corps women could be a bit younger; the enlistment requirements only specified that a recruit should be between eighteen and thirty-five, and while the Navy preferred women who had graduated from high school, they did not require it (Gavin 3).

While there was a wide swath of educational and working background among women in the AEF, the Navy, and the Marine Corps, they were undeniably middle-class. Working-class white women who lacked nursing and clerical skills had a hard time enrolling in any of the auxiliaries open to women (Zeiger 40). More often, they chose to change jobs at home. As industrial production increased and men joined the armed forces, women were allowed into munitions factories, airplane hangars, trolley cars, and railroad yards. Wartime pay in these industries was significantly better than anything women had been offered before (C. Brown 48–49 & 66; Maurine Greenwald xxvi). "As the war induced demands for laboring men to serve in the military, on the one hand, and for increased domestic production, on the other hand, the practice of substituting one group of wage earners for another was vastly accelerated. In particular, white women took the places of white men, while black women filled the jobs left vacant by white women and black men" (Maurine Greenwald xxvi). In other words, the movement of white and black men and white women to the overseas fronts allowed for a shift in work occupations at home. Black women moved out of domestic service and into factories and food plants (jobs formerly done by white women) while white women filled the more lucrative industrial jobs of welding, munitions work, airplane construction, railroad work, and trolley conducting. Women who could not participate directly in war work on the front still found ways to contribute to the wartime economy and the armed forces that desperately needed the products they fashioned.

This is not to say that AEF and military women, overseas or at home, were not concerned about being paid. On the contrary, it was a pressing issue for many of the war workers. The YMCA, for example, discovered that it was not able to recruit enough women workers unless they offered pay for the services rendered. Attempting to staff their offices and overseas canteens with volunteers was a resounding failure. Female YMCA workers were paid at the same rate as men (one hundred dollars per month), and their uniforms were provided (Zeiger 41). Part of the appeal of Navy enlistment was also the pay; Secretary Daniels decreed that all the yeoman women be paid the same as men: $28.75 per month and $1.25 daily subsistence pay, plus a uniform allowance and medical care (Gavin 5). Roughly, their total per month would have been $66.25. In the Marine Corps, women were paid according to their rank on the same scale as men: "private, $15 per month; private first class, $18; corporal, $21; and sergeant, $30. An additional $83.40 per month was paid out for subsistence and quarters, because there were no barracks available for the women Marines" (Gavin 28). Nurses in the Army Nurse Corps were paid fifty dollars a month through July 1918; after that their pay increased to sixty dollars a month in the U.S. and seventy dollars a month for overseas service. An interesting difference emerged between Army nurses and other armed services and auxiliary women workers, however. Nurses could actually make more money in jobs outside of the Army Nurse Corps, whether at a hospital or as a home nurse. Civilian work was more lucrative for them, yet nursing leaders were hesitant to press for the increase in Army pay, perhaps fearing that nurses' motives for service would be questioned (Zeiger 41). Still, service pay was necessary and important to most of the women who were part of the war effort; working free of charge was not usually possible for them.

Sandbagging: Relief Organizations

Before the U.S. entered the war, helping with war relief was an ad hoc, piecemeal effort that was put together through many independent organizations. Despite its patchwork nature and occasionally overlapping purposes, however, war relief that came from the U.S. was surprisingly well-organized and effective, particularly once organizations were up and running. Flexibility was key; war organizations had to be able to adapt to the needs they found on the ground. Nurses, doctors, runners, drivers, secretaries, coordinators, cooks — every kind of worker was necessary in order for these groups to run efficiently. A few of the largest and most famous, particularly the American Fund for French Wounded, the American Relief Clearing House, and the American Ambulance Hospital at Neuilly, serve as good illustrations of the kinds of work that women were able to accomplish.

The American Fund for French Wounded (AFFW) was set up originally as a clearinghouse for hospital supplies that were sent from America to be distributed to French hospitals. The French medical system was completely unprepared to deal with the massive numbers of casualties caused by the war, and the AFFW provided an invaluable service for the French doctors, nurses, and volunteers who needed medical supplies simply to give their patients a chance of staying alive. However, the AFFW also found that soldier patients were often severely lacking in basic hygiene supplies and comfort materials, and that the many thousands of displaced civilian refugees had need of clothing and medical care. They set out to rectify both problems, in the process becoming a much larger and more extensive organization (Schneider and Schneider, *Into the Breach* 45, 52–53).

Among other things, the AFFW distributed comfort bags to soldiers, small cloth bags that could contain soap, a razor, cigarettes, writing paper, and other small valuables that soldiers might want to carry with them and keep out of the mud of the trenches, or things that they had managed to keep with them until their arrival at the hospital. Using women physicians, they also provided medical care to refugees, mostly women and children. Sometimes the doctors would travel between villages, carrying as many supplied with them as they could, often with the help of a motor car driver (Schneider and Schneider, *Into the Breach* 45, 52–53).

The American Relief Clearing House (ARCH) was created in Paris as an umbrella organization that coordinated many relief efforts started up by American women who were foreign residents or expatriates. In total, ARCH oversaw 5,000 smaller organizations run by communities, churches, and schools (Schneider and Schneider, *Into the Breach* 51).

The American Ambulance at Neuilly was a large hospital in Paris founded, run, and financed by Americans residents. "By 1916 it had 600 beds and three operating rooms, staffed by eighty-five American-trained nurses, and a corps of American, British, and French volunteers" (Schneider and Schneider, *Into the Breach* 88). Women nursed, served tea, rolled bandages, cut surgical dressings, disposed of bodily wastes, and cleaned any rags that could possibly be salvaged, since cloth of any kind was in desperately short supply. While the American Ambulance was only one of the many improvised hospitals, they were also one of the most well-known and well-staffed for the duration of the war.

Women's organizations like these did their best to fill the myriad of needs produced by the war, both in the Allied armies and the civilian population. Disease was almost as deadly a killer as munitions, and soldiers who lived in flooded trenches were constantly being exposed to dysentery, typhus, cholera, lice, and fungi that caused "trench mouth" and "trench foot." Displaced civilians, bombed or shelled out of their homes and villages, needed clothing, food, medical care, baths, and beds. Soldiers who had been released from the hospitals but could not care for themselves immediately needed nursing and food. The list of jobs was endless.

After the United States entered the war, the American Red Cross (ARC) was put in charge of all medical relief and organizing. The American Ambulance at Neuilly was appointed Red Cross Military Hospital Number One (Schneider and Schneider, *Into the Breach* 88). The AFFW and ARCH were also absorbed by the Red Cross, along with thousands of other organizations. By centralizing the bureaucracy and organization of the private relief organizations, the American and French militaries and governments hoped to achieve a more efficient and organized system of medical care. Red Cross Hospital Number One became a single piece of a vast medical system that tried to care for millions of wounded men and civilians.

Medical Necessities: The Red Cross, Women Physicians and Army and Navy Nurses

When the U.S. entered the war in 1917, the Red Cross had the distinct advantage of being a civilian organization that was trusted by the militaries of two major Allied Powers: The U.S. itself and France. It had the additional advantage of having organized its own medical relief efforts from the beginning of 1914, when it sent a Mercy Ship containing 400-bed hospital units to both Allied and Axis nations (Schneider and Schneider, *Into the Breach* 87). "The liner carried ten units of medical personnel, each group comprising a medical director, two assistants, and eleven nurses headed by a supervising nurse. A double unit was assigned to each of the great powers — France, England, Germany, and Russia — with one unit each to Austria and Hungary" (Gavin 181).[2] The Mercy Ship was only the start of the Red Cross war relief efforts; their efforts were well-organized and all-encompassing, including nursing at the front and in the hospitals, canteen and communication services for the soldiers, help for the disabled and wounded, assistance for prisoners of war, and domestic hygiene and home nursing, first aid, and nutrition instruction for civilians (Gavin 180–187). Thus, they were put in charge of all of the medical war relief in Europe and authorized to take over any existing organizations:

> In June 1917, the Red Cross was charged by the French and American governments with the major responsibility for distributing funds and supplies for civilian war relief. The private relief agencies were 'invited' to affiliate with the Red Cross as closely as possible. Since the Red Cross controlled so much of the available shipping space and so much money, few of them could afford to refuse [Schneider and Schneider, *Into the Breach* 55].

The vast annexation accomplished by the ARC was not achieved without some mistakes on their part. Women who had poured countless hours and dollars into making their private organizations effective and resourceful were pressed into cooperation with the Red Cross, whose workers were sometimes highly effective, but sometimes arrogant or simply incompetent. There were also power struggles and jurisdiction skirmishes between the Red Cross and other auxiliary organizations like the YWCA, which could often disrupt the services of both organizations involved (Schneider and Schneider, *Into the Breach* 55–56). Still, there were undoubtedly advantages to having a large, centralized bureaucracy that could handle the massive problems created by the constant fighting. The Red Cross could, and often did, utilize the resources of existing institutions to create networks of assistance for women, children, the elderly, and wounded soldiers.

One of the organizations that willingly affiliated itself with the Red Cross was the American Women's Hospitals (AWH), formed by the Medical Women's National Association (MWNA) in June 1917. The AWH was named in honor of the Scottish Women's Hospitals, a similar organization that was already operating in Europe with hospital units staffed by women physicians. While it took time for the AWH to raise money and volunteers for hospital units of its own, they did register over 1,000 women physicians for service in their first year. They sent a group of volunteers to France in August of 1917, including Dr. Esther Pohl Lovejoy, who had been tasked with investigating organizations applying for medical assistance. Since these first volunteers were not officially part of a hospital unit, they divided their services between multiple organizations, including the American Fund for French Wounded and the Children's Bureau of the American Red Cross (Gavin 158).

While the AWH was a formidable organization on its own, like many of its counterparts it needed the shipping space and supplies that the Red Cross was able to procure, and so sought affiliation with the ARC. In March 1918, the AWH came to a sponsorship agreement with the Red Cross; the first AWH unit sailed in June of that year (Gavin 158). However, it is important to note that the Red Cross, in this case, did not provide much financial help; the AWH was almost entirely responsible for its own expenses, and the women who participated in it donated a great deal of their own money as well as doing extensive fundraising to support their activities. In its first two years of operation, the AWH raised $224,000 in support of its units (Gavin 159).

One distinction between the AWH and other hospital units that went overseas was the goal of AWH hospital units to care for both soldiers and civilians under one roof. The Red Cross sent hospital units to the battlefield for the soldiers and set up civilian care units wherever they found civilians in need, even in the middle of an abandoned and destroyed village. The AWH, on the other hand, was looking to serve soldiers and civilians simultaneously and were a private organization that did not fall under the command of the army, something that made it easier for their women physicians and surgeons to practice medicine (Jensen 107–110). The AWH also placed a particular importance upon medical and maternity care for women, and all kinds of care for children (Jensen 107–108).

The advocacy of the MWNA and the independent formation of the AWH was doubly important because of the difficult position that women physicians found themselves in relative to the United States Army. Despite gladly enlisting every male physician available into the Army Medical Corps, women physicians were forbidden to enlist as regular members of the army. Their only option was to go overseas as contract surgeons, "a ploy that deprived the women of military pay, rank, and benefits, but gave the military the advantage of their services. These women minded most the lack of rank, which hampered them in the execution of their duties" (Schneider and Schneider, *Into the Breach* 95–96).

Lack of rank and pay were not the only objections women physicians had to the contract system. Many rightly felt that being asked to work under contract rather than as enlisted physicians was an insult to their professional skills and sexism on the part of the army. Still, fifty-five American female doctors worked under army contract during the war, eleven of them overseas and the rest in military and civilian posts in the States (Jensen 86–87): "Some believed that if contract service was the place where women could push the boundaries of military service, then they would join and push. And a few women found contract service to be the only way that they could circumvent military restrictions and still serve as members of the hospital units that they had joined for overseas work" (Jensen 86).

Those women physicians who could not bring themselves to serve as contract surgeons circumvented the army by serving with the AWH, the Women's Overseas Hospital, the AFFW, the American Ambulance, and the

British and French armies.[3] Despite their lack of rank and the absolute exclusion from their own army, American women physicians found ways to serve the Allies and often found grateful allies in the medical men with whom they served.

Nurses who worked with the Army Nurse Corps (ANC), Army Medical Corps, and the U.S. Navy did not suffer the same exclusion as female doctors, yet stigma against their sex still remained. Nurses held no official military rank, and therefore no enforceable authority over their patients or other military officers and personnel. When they were trying to run hospital wards, provide proper care and recuperation for their patients by demanding physical therapy, sleep, and pill taking, and giving orders to male orderlies, they were often fighting power battles over military authority:

> Male military leaders ... used the idea of selfless female service as permission to maintain nurses in an auxiliary, ambiguous position in the military. Women nurses were subject to military discipline and regulations but had no official rank in a hierarchical system that depended on it. As neither enlisted personnel nor commissioned officers, nurses were "hired extras" in the business of war, invited to accompany the military because they were women practicing the indispensible work of women's nurturing [Jensen 120].

Confusion was increased because of the differences between the Army Nurse Corps and the Red Cross. Many women in the ANC were drawn from the Red Cross nursing enrollment pool, which was the official reserve of the Army Nurse Corps (Gavin 45; Zeiger 107). However, if women chose to stay in the Red Cross as nurses rather than join the ANC, they did not receive any disability benefits if they were injured. On the other hand, women who joined the Army Nurse Corps were, often unknowingly, signing themselves up for service indefinitely, rather than for the two-year term that was standard in the Red Cross (Schneider and Schneider, *Into the Breach* 109). The status of nurses was not clear on either side, and their lack of rank only aggravated the difficulty of working in a predominantly male hierarchy without any official military authority. "In Washington, D.C., where AEF medical policy was established, and in France, on the wards and in the operating rooms, nurses and nurse leaders came into conflict with men and the military establishment in more organized, concrete, and potent ways than did any other servicewomen" (Zeiger 105). Nurses ran daily into the problem of trying to give orders to men who were only used to taking orders from other men, and patient care often suffered because orderlies, male doctors, or surgeons failed to adhere to a nurse's instructions or consider her professional opinion. In the worst cases, a nurse's gender subjected her to sexual harassment and active hostility from her male colleagues (Jensen 123–125).

Military rank for nurses became a long, drawn-out, and only partially won fight with Congress and military leaders, and the fight was taken up by many individuals and groups, both male and female. Suffrage leaders saw military rank for nurses as another issue of citizenship; like the right to vote, military rank for female nurses would demonstrate the equality of female citizens under the law (Jensen 121). The National Committee to Secure Rank for Nurses was organized in 1918, and the House Committee on Military Affairs heard testimony on the need for nurses' rank in April of 1918. Among those who gave testimony were Harriet Stanton Blatch (daughter of Elizabeth Cady Stanton and founder of the Women's Political Union), Jane Delano (director of Red Cross nursing), Surgeon General William Gorgas, and Dr. Franklin Martin, chair of the General Medicine Board of the Council of National Defense (Jensen 122). Despite all of the distinguished professionals who advocated for military rank for nurses, however, the fight went on until 1920, and even then, Congress was only willing to grant nurses relative rank, or rank in name only, without all the benefits, pay, or full authority of their military counterparts (Jensen 121). For every medical professional who desired military rank for nurses, there was one many who questioned its necessity or efficacy in the relations between nurses and medical officers.

The struggles of wartime nurses to achieve full recognition and military rank for their work and the firm opposition of Congress and the military illustrate the ambivalent attitude held by many about the work of women in the war. Critical though their work might be, women were not meant to have an entirely equal footing with "the boys" on the battlefield. Women who worked in other auxiliary organizations to bring home comforts to the soldiers would encounter similar attitudes — not so much from the soldiers or the generals, but from their male supervisors.

Home Comforts for the Boys: The YMCA, the Salvation Army, and the YWCA

In order to lessen the confusion and increase the efficiency of the auxiliary services in the AEF, General John J. Pershing issued General Order No. 26, which gave specific functions to the Red Cross, YMCA, Salvation Army, and YWCA. While the Red Cross tended to the sick and injured, both enlisted and civilian, and provided relatively luxurious recuperation facilities, the YMCA was in charge of the "instruction, amusement, and moral welfare of the troops" (Gavin 130), the Salvation Army was there to tend to soldiers' souls, and the YWCA looked after the women war workers themselves, making sure that female auxiliary workers had any assistance they might need (Schneider and Schneider, *Into the Breach* 121–124 and 139–140). The YWCA also ran Hostess Houses in U.S. military training camps, places where wives, mothers, and sweethearts could come and stay while waiting for their male family members to be shipped out (Zeiger 54). By dividing up the purposes and responsibilities of the welfare organizations attached to the AEF, some conflicts over jurisdiction were automatically avoided. Given the vast needs of the troops at the front, however, any services offered that happened to overlap were inevitably utilized and swallowed up (Schneider and Schneider, *Into the Breach* 50). For example, all three organizations ran their own canteens, which would always serve doughnuts, baked goods, coffee, cocoa, and any other comforts they could obtain. In bigger spaces (an abandoned building, for example) there might be tables and chairs, reading material, or sometimes even a gramophone to keep the troops entertained, as well as the female volunteers who were there to talk to the men and keep up morale. Mobile canteens stationed near the front were often run by a single volunteer or at most a pair (Schneider and Schneider, *Into the Breach* 129; Gavin 130–131).

Many of the functions of the auxiliary organizations had grown out of the work of the Commission on Training Camp Activities headed by Raymond Fosdick. While military officers objected to the Hostess Houses in their camps as well as to movie theaters, theatrical performances, circulating libraries, and recreational huts for the troops, since they viewed such programs as unnecessary, President Wilson and his cabinet were fully behind all of the welfare and morale programs of the CTCA (Zeiger 54–55). When those programs were transported to Europe, most of the military objections to them died away, since military leadership down through U.S. civilians were worried about the corrupting influence of Europe on American troops — particularly France, where wine, Catholicism, and prostitution were thought to run rampant (Zeiger 55). For many of the same reasons, auxiliary agencies employed many more women overseas than they did back home. The presence of American women was thought to be crucial to policing and controlling the morals and behavior of the troops (Zeiger 55, 58 and 59).

The YMCA had by far the largest job and therefore the most extensive operations and the most volunteers. In total, there were about 3,198 women working with the YMCA (Zeiger 52; Gavin 130). In addition to hundreds of canteens near the front and at railroad stations, the YMCA operated 23 leave areas in Europe, catering to thousands of soldiers with food, drink, recreational activities, and dancing. YMCA workers also did a myriad of miscellaneous jobs that came to hand: assisting in operating rooms, mending clothes, writing letters, helping the nurses at the clearing station, cooking, serving food, running a library for the soldiers, going through hospital wards searching for missing soldiers, or anything else that would prove useful. Even helping to run one leave area could be exhausting; the women workers were always outnumbered and always having to be social when they were on duty. Marian Baldwin, one of the workers at Aix-les-Bains, France, wrote that "we have only twenty girls and there are always two thousand or more men! [At the dances] Every time the whistle blows they can 'cut in.' The consequence is that a girl is literally hurled from one man to another while dozens of eager hands try and snatch her away from him ... but how the boys enjoy it!" (qtd. in Schneider and Schneider, *Into the Breach* 127–28).

In contrast to the YMCA, with its 3,200 women workers, the Salvation Army had what may have been the smallest number of women workers for an organized relief effort. There were somewhere between 104 and 200 women overseas for the Salvation Army (Zeiger 53; Schneider and Schneider, *Into the Breach* 122), and while they ran huts and canteens with everyone else, they carved out a unique niche for themselves by staying true to their evangelical principles and coming up with a few unique services. "[The Salvation Army] approached soldiers as candidates for conversion, evaluating the success of its workers by their contributions to the religious life of the troops.... They clung to their peacetime principles, regularly holding religious services and preaching, opening their doors to all, regardless of race or creed..." (Schneider and Schneider, *Into the Breach* 122). Being a spiritual guidepost for men in the armed services was the hallmark of the Salvationists, and one that they performed with kindness and appreciation for every soldier. Spiritual comfort was their primary mission.

Of course, the soldiers were not above appreciating the Salvation Army lassies for more earthly reasons. It was a Salvation Army worker who first made doughnuts for the doughboys, and the treats soon became one of the most popular at all of the wartime canteens. Helen Purviance, a Salvation Army ensign from Indiana, had been looking for something healthier than chocolate to serve the men, and managed to commandeer the ingredients for doughnuts. Originally making crullers in a frying pan, Purviance and Ensign Margaret Sheldon soon had improvised a cutter and were making doughnuts by the hundreds (Gavin 214). Doughnuts soon spread to all of the other AEF organizations, but the Salvation Army lassies were given the credit for them.

Another problem solved by the Salvation Army was much more complicated and important: sending money home. There was no easy way to send money home in those days, and U.S. soldiers often accumulated more than they could spend in a trench or at a canteen. Men who wanted to send money to their families were grateful for the money transfer system that the Salvation Army created. The money would be sent "by money order to New York, from there to the corps officer nearest the soldier's house, and thence to the appropriate family.... The money transfer plan also worked in reverse on occasions when friends at home sent money to soldiers overseas" (Gavin 221). Having the opportunity to send funds back to the States was a welcome relief to soldiers who otherwise would have no way to get their pay to their families.

Salvationist women were in a particularly positive position relative to the armed forces. Women were given an equal footing with men in the Salvation Army, both in terms of the organization's mission and in terms of promotion. The Salvation Army assigned military rankings to all of their workers, men and women, which made it easy for them to fit in with enlisted men. On the other hand, they refused the U.S. Army's offer to give their workers official military officer ranking, as they did not want to put military status between their workers and the soldiers (Schneider and Schneider, *Into the Breach* 122). In other words, Salvation Army workers were ranked within their own organization, and so it was easy for soldiers to place them in the Salvation Army hierarchy, but since they were not of the U.S. armed forces and not affiliated with them, the soldiers did not have to treat them like commanders. While Salvation Army women were not in need of rank the way army nurses were, it surely made their interactions with soldiers more relaxed.

The women of the YMCA and the Salvation Army, as well as the drivers, the nurses, and the doctors, often pushed the parameters of their assignments, sometimes directly challenging military orders to stay away from the front or to leave a fighting unit that was going to the trenches. The negotiation of what was supposed to be an exclusively male space was a tense one for many military commanders and YMCA supervisors, while for women workers the fight was much more crucial: the chance to be helping at the front was why most of them had come overseas. If the soldiers' place was at the front, then their place was at the front as well, serving the men as best they could, often saving their lives. Canteen women were there to keep up the morale of the fighters, a job they took as seriously as the soldiers took theirs:

> The best efforts of the United States Army and the welfare organizations to keep the women canteeners out of danger failed. The military ordered women to stay behind brigade headquarters, but at the front brigade headquarters was easy to lose, even if the women had wanted to find it. Women kept ignoring orders to leave the troops they were looking after, and bobbing up again after they had been sent to the rear. Inevitably the chaotic situation, the women's determination, and the real need for their help eroded the regulations designed to keep them well behind the front [Schneider and Schneider, *Into the Breach* 135–136].

YMCA canteen women were ultimately permitted to stay with the men at the front in three different major drives, while Salvation Army women did everything they could to circumvent military orders and set up wherever they felt they were needed, following regiments to battle and field hospitals and evacuating when necessary (Schneider and Schneider, *Into the Breach* 136–139; Zeiger 75). Even though some of their male supervisors, particularly in the YMCA, and some of the military men felt that the battlefield was no place for women to be, it did not deter the auxiliary workers from performing the services they saw as a duty to the soldiers and to their country.

In contrast to the YMCA and the Salvation Army, the YWCA took upon itself a mission that was not strictly related to caring for the soldiers: caring for the women, both women workers and civilian women. The YWCA sent about 350 women overseas, and they took care of female auxiliary workers and did their best to provide services for French and Russian women workers.

The YWCA's work actually began with the Hostess Houses in stateside training camps. The women of the YWCA were in charge of running these homes, which were set up as places for wives, mothers, and sweethearts to come say goodbye to their soldiers before the men were shipped out. Using the Hostess Houses as a model, the YWCA created similar facilities for women war workers overseas, places where they could relax, write letters, cry, socialize with other women, and simply rest. Similarly, they created "Sunshine Rooms" for nurses who worked at some of the bigger military hospitals and who slept in dormitories with very little privacy. A room with chairs, rugs, magazines, music, and other homelike comforts were a blessing to nurses who were often on their feet for two days at a stretch (Schneider and Schneider, *Into the Breach* 139–141).

The YWCA provided or found living quarters for Signal Corps telephone operators, YMCA workers, Red Cross workers, Army Quartermaster Corps workers, and Army Ordnance Corps workers. They provided canteens, gymnasiums, kindergartens, nurseries, dorms, and a labor bureau for French female munitions workers. They ran practical classes in "English, French, bookkeeping, commercial arithmetic, stenography, choral singing, and gym" in Petrograd and Moscow, in the middle of the Russian Revolution (Schneider and Schneider, *Into the Breach* 145). The sheer magnitude of what the YWCA was able to accomplish with such a small number of workers is impressive:

> ... eighteen hostess houses for soldiers, American women, and war brides; fifteen Signal Corps houses for "hello girls"; three Army Service Corps centers; forty-four nurses' clubs; thirty-one *foyers* for Frenchwomen; six recreation centers; five summer camps; a summer conference; an emergency training school; five refuges for port and transport workers; four cemetery huts, where they offered lodgings, food, and kindness to visitors to remote cemeteries; and three British/American cooperative undertakings [Schneider and Schneider, *Into the Breach* 144].[4]

Creating this number of homes and services for women workers was an extraordinary undertaking when one considers that the YWCA women were serving in foreign countries, with a considerable language barrier between them and many of the women they sought to serve, as well as language barriers between themselves and the officials and civilian volunteers with whom they had to work.

What is even more interesting is that the YWCA participated in the war despite its long tradition of pacifism (Schneider and Schneider, *Into the Breach* 139). Here was an organization that defined itself and its principles in anti-war terms, and yet they still felt compelled to send women into the war zone and to help women affected by the war. While the YWCA's auxiliary support of the war could be construed as a betrayal of principle on one hand, on the other hand its particular mission to support women, and *not* soldiers, held true to its ideal to serve any and all women in need. These women were pushing gender boundaries by being in the war zone, but they were not in direct conflict with military authority the way many canteeners, nurses, and doctors were. The radicalness of their actions lay in their solidarity with other women and their determination to alleviate the detrimental effects of living and working in the midst of a war.

One particular group of women that the YWCA served had access to the front lines and crucial war communications in a way that few other women did: The "Hello Girls" or telephone operators of the Army Signal Corps were well aware of the dangers of the front line and the importance of their duties. Along with the enlisted women of the Navy and the Marine Corps, the Hello Girls were a crucial part of armed forces communication and, with their position on the European front lines, some of the most visible of any women war workers.

The Armed Forces: The Hello Girls, the Navy, and the Marine Corps

If the women of the Great War owe thanks to any men for some of their advances in the armed services and the warfront, those two men are General John J. Pershing and Secretary of the Navy Josephus Daniels. Both men were tireless advocates of women's work in the war, pushing the executive branch and the military to use the services of women in every capacity. While they could not override the stubbornness and prejudice of Secretary of War Baker, Pershing and Daniels saw to it that within their own ranks, women were utilized in every way possible. In the endless fight of women workers to get more equality in the ranks and more access to the front, these two men were in the vanguard of military authorities who saw women's participation in the war as necessary and right.

It was General Pershing who made it possible for so many women to go overseas with the AEF, particularly the YMCA. Pershing backed the national Y's decision to recruit women auxiliary workers, against considerable public pressure and the objections of regional Y branches. He gave his blessing to the Salvation Army's desire to go overseas and serve the men, and he requested female clerical help in the army. Several units of female clerical workers came overseas in 1918 (Gavin 77, 130, 209–210; Zeiger 82).

It was also Pershing who was responsible for the famous corps of bilingual "Hello Girls" who went overseas as part of the Army Signal Corps. These women were charged with translating and passing along some of the most crucial communications of the war. While the army had tried using both female, but untrained, French telephone operators and untrained American army men, they had found both plans to be inadequate. Pershing requested an original contingent of one hundred French-speaking, American telephone operators to be sent overseas to man the army switchboards. Since telephone operators were almost entirely female by 1917, the telephone operators were going to be women by default (Gavin 77; Zeiger 79). The harder job turned out to be finding women who were sufficiently skilled in French; a good number of women who were of French or French-Canadian descent were recruited for their bilingual abilities. Many of these were Catholic, making them some of the few Catholic women to serve in the war (Zeiger 32). Ultimately, five or six units with a total of 223 operators were sent overseas.

The telephone operators served in a number of crucial positions, especially in France, including the U.S. Army headquarters in Paris, the Service of Supply in Tours, General Pershing's office in Chaumont, the battles of St. Mihiel and the Argonne, and seventy-five French and English cities. Many of the calls they handled on the battlefront were in code, relaying troop movements and orders. (Gavin 79, 88–89). All of the women were subject to investigation by Army intelligence, as well as being required to follow Army rules and regulations. If they were out at night, they had to obtain a pass with a time of return. Uniforms were required. There was a ban on any social interaction with privates or civilians. While some women objected vociferously to such rules and even defied them on occasion, most saw it as part of their job and their duty to obey the regulations and perform well (Zeiger 93).

The argument made in war propaganda of the period was that women office workers and telephone operators would free up men to fight, men who would otherwise be running the bureaucracy of the Army while they should be in the trenches. Because this argument is repeated so insistently in both propaganda and armed services reports, it is also repeated in histories of women's war work. However, as Susan Zeiger so adroitly points out, the idea that women who worked in clerical and telephone positions were freeing up men to go to the front was simply untrue. The truth was that office and telephone work were so completely feminized by the time the U.S. entered the war that there was actually a shortage of qualified military *or* civilian men who could fill those positions:

> By 1910, the occupations of telephone operator and stenographer/typist were the fifth and seventh most feminized in the census, composed of 94 percent and 93 percent women, respectively. Women office workers and telephone operators in World War I were not substituting for men in male occupations but rather were stepping into *female* occupations now encompassed by the military [Zeiger 79; emphasis Zeiger's].

In other words, the military had expanded to absorb occupations that were predominantly female. The Navy and the Marines had need of highly skilled clerical workers; therefore they enlisted them. The same was true for nurses; nurses were not substitutes for men, but performed essential functions for the Army in a profession in which they held a large majority.

However, working for the army did not automatically grant women the status of veterans. The Hello Girls discovered after the war that their veteran status was in jeopardy because the Army considered them civilian contract employees, in spite of the fact that they had all taken the enlistment oath. At the time, the majority of Hello Girls understood that they *were* enlisting in the Army. They followed all the rules and regulations the Army prescribed. They were required to purchase their own uniform and wear it while they were on duty. The women were put through military training drills in New York City before they left for the front. Even though the women had been sworn in like soldiers, however (and more importantly, understood themselves to *be* soldiers who had served on the front lines), the Army refused them any military veterans' benefits (Gavin 78, 92; Zeiger 82). Merle Egan Anderson, one of the veteran Hello Girls, was the organizer of the struggle to give the female telephone operators veteran status, and it took her and her fellow operators sixty years to accomplish that goal. Fifty different bills were introduced to try and give the Hello Girls veteran's benefits, but not one of them ever made it through Congress. It was finally achieved with the G. I. Bill Improvement Act of 1977. By that time, only 18 of the Hello Girls were still alive (Gavin 93).

Thanks to Josephus Daniels, women of the Navy and the Marine Corps fared better. Female Navy Yeomen (the navy's term for clerks) were the first women to be enrolled as full-fledged members of the armed forces, and Daniels made clear from the start that he wanted women to be equal in every way to the men — including the rate of their salary (Ebbert and Hall, 3–4; Gavin 2).

The Naval Act of 1916 was what gave Daniels a clear path to enlisting female Yeomen. Part of the act established the Naval Coast Defense Reserve Force, which was open to "'all persons who may be capable of performing special useful service for coastal defense'" (qtd. in Ebbert and Hall 3). The language did not specify or imply any restriction based on gender. In a situation where the Navy needed every available man to staff their warships, Secretary Daniels was more than willing to take the opening.[5] After sending an inquiry through the Bureau of Navigation and the presiding judge advocate general, Secretary Daniels announced in mid–March of 1917 that the Navy would be endorsing the enrollment of women, and the Bureau of Navigation immediately followed his announcement with a letter to all the commandants (regional directors) of naval districts, stating that women could and should be enrolled as Yeomen or in any other capacity they could fill successfully (Ebbert and Hall 3–4). Eventually women were also enlisted as accountants, telephone operators, chemists, pharmacists, draftsmen, couriers, messengers, and radio electricians. Within just a month after the order, by April of 1917, two hundred young women had enlisted, and another 11,680 would follow (Gavin 2; Ebbert and Hall 7 and 10).

The women who enlisted as Yeomen were designated as Yeoman (F) in the written records to distinguish them from their male counterparts. The enlistment requirements were actually quite simple:

> A woman had to be between eighteen and thirty-five years of age, of good character and neat appearance. The Navy preferred high school graduates with business or office experience but did not require a college education. A prospective yeomanette simply presented herself at a recruiting station, was interviewed for qualifications, and filled out application forms. After she passed the perfunctory physical exam, she was sworn in and signed up for a four-year hitch. The entire process often took less than a day [Gavin 3].

The easy process of Navy enlistment made it accessible for women of varying backgrounds from all over the U.S., and earning pay equal to a man's was certainly part of the appeal for women who needed the income. Other women enlisted out of patriotism, a longing for adventure, or as a way to feel closer to the men in their families who were serving in the armed forces (Ebbert and Hall, 17–19 and 25).

Yeoman (F) served everywhere: in naval district offices, navy yards, Washington offices, and overseas in France, Guam, Puerto Rico, and Hawaii (Gavin 5). While many of them served as typists, stenographers, and secretaries, some of them handled responsibilities that were vast and incredibly important. Two Yeoman (F) served as the personal secretary and chief administrative officer for Rear Admiral Samuel McGowan, the Navy's paymaster. "Yeoman (F) Laila Anders assisted the officer in charge of clothing, overseeing manufacturers' production of clothing for a quarter of a million enlisted men. Yeoman (F) Eleanor Griffith, an auditor in the disbursing division, routinely signed four-million-dollar vouchers, while another Yeoman (F) was given authority to assign to railroad officials the priorities by which they were to ship navy supplies" (Ebbert and Hall 42). Other duties of the Yeoman (F) included working at the Bureau of Medicine and Surgery, the naval hospitals, the Naval Medical Supply Depot, the Division of Enlisted Personnel, working as couriers and messengers, working in naval munitions factories, and working in naval intelligence (Ebbert and Hall 43–44).

The latter group of women, those who worked in code breaking, censorship, fingerprint processing, wireless operation, and ship message traffic, handled some of the most critical strategic information of the war. Much of it went directly to President Wilson, Daniels, or Franklin D. Roosevelt, then Assistant Secretary of the Navy. Women in the Naval Intelligence Office in New York monitored cases of actual and possible espionage (Ebbert and Hall 44–46). The accuracy of such messages and information was critical; small mistakes could lead to disastrous consequences in the water. The Yeoman (F) were trusted to be as discreet as possible, and they took that responsibility seriously. Marian Taylor, one of the first two women wireless operators hired by the Navy, was the only woman who knew the positions and movements of all the Allied ships in the Atlantic Ocean. She received reports on a hidden telegraph system inside a steel vault, which she used as an office. According to her obituary, she never even told her husband any of the information connected to her work until the Navy released the ships' movements to the public in 1936 (Ebbert and Hall 45).

Although the Navy had tremendous success with the Yeoman (F), it took the Marine Corps almost a year to request Daniels' approval for drafting women in its own ranks, which meant that it did not even begin to utilize women until four months before the war was over. However, the need for clerical help had grown desperate, since more and more men who worked in Marine Corps offices were needed for the intense fighting overseas. Finally, Major General George Barnett asked Secretary Daniels for the authority to enroll women, which Daniels easily granted (Gavin 25; Ebbert and Hall 13).

As in the Navy, the recruiters who enrolled women were not always enthusiastic about the idea, but they were ordered to enroll women and they did. Their requirements for the women who enlisted were demanding; they were highly selective about who they enlisted. Although the age requirements were the same—18 years old minimum, with the occasional exception made for a 17-year-old who was highly skilled — the skills and references demanded were much stricter than in the Navy: "Each [woman] was to furnish three letters of recommendation and, if possible, to be interviewed by the head of the office where she was to be assigned; some highly promising applicants were even sent to Washington for the interview" (Ebbert and Hall 14). The stenographic test the USMC administered to its female applicants was so difficult that only five women out of two thousand initial applicants at the New York office were enlisted. In total, the Marine Corps enlisted 305 women before the end of the war, mainly as typists, stenographers, and bookkeepers. Some women also handled the correspondence to families that announced casualties; a few others were in public relations and assigned to recruitment. Perhaps the most unusual job was that assigned to Lela Leibrand, a former Hollywood screenwriter who was put in charge of editing films of Marine training drills and endless ghastly footage from the fronts in Europe (Ebbert and Hall 54–55).

Once they were discharged, the women of the Navy and Marine Corps were entitled to all the veterans' benefits that enlisted men also enjoyed, including burial at Arlington National Cemetery, the right to wear a World War I Victory medal, government insurance, veterans' medical care and disability benefits, and a bonus added to their civil service examinations should they wish to take civil service jobs (Ebbert and Hall 100). In this respect they were better off than the Hello Girls or the women physicians, who were regarded as contract workers and denied benefits. Women of the Army Nurse Corps might receive benefits, even though they never received military rank, but women of the Red Cross did not (Schneider and Schneider, *Into the Breach* 109). Secretary Daniels ensured both the status and the equality of his Yeomen (F) and Marine Reserves (F) by enlisting them as actual members of the armed services.

There were other women who performed services that were not within the purview of the military, but that were nevertheless essential to the war effort. While the Yeomen and Marine Reserves (F) worked at home and overseas communicating crucial information to the Allies, other women transported supplies and wounded men, kept up the spirits of the soldiers, and made the war a reality for American civilians.

Others: Drivers, Entertainers, and War Correspondents

Female drivers, or "chauffeuses," are some of the most unsung heroes of women's war work, precisely because they were constantly mobile and continuously changing duties; therefore, they are difficult to trace in the historical record. Most of the medical organizations in Paris and in France had women drivers, including the indefatigable Gertrude Stein and Alice B. Toklas. Women drove for the hospitals, for the Red Cross, for the civilian relief organizations, and for the French Army. Often, they ended up transporting wounded soldiers and refugees as well as supplies.

One difficulty for American women with driving skills was that, like their nursing and Signal Corps counterparts, they could not officially enlist in the U.S. Army. The Army had men for ambulance and motor driving, and, thanks to Secretary of War Baker, refused to take women drivers. Therefore, many of the women affiliated themselves with the French and British Armies, which were happy to have them. One primary example is the Hackett-Lowther Unit, an ambulance unit that was coordinated by the British and attached to the French Army. An American woman, Mary Dexter, was part of the Hacket-Lowther ambulance unit and asserted that "there are heaps of women driving for the English army, and for the French — an American woman spoke to me in the street yesterday who has been chauffing for the French near Amiens for some months" (qtd. in Schneider and Schneider, *Into the Breach* 100). Ambulance drivers often came under direct fire, and women drivers could be the difference between life and death for wounded soldiers and civilians, who depended on the transport and medical supplies they made available.

Entertainers provided a different kind of service entirely. While the army frowned on things that seemed frivolous, they acknowledged the need for good morale among their soldiers, and the entertainers who went overseas with the YMCA and the Over There Theatre League were some of the best morale boosters they could have asked for. Many entertainers who wanted to help even went so far as to organize themselves, calling a meeting for volunteers at New York's Palace Theater in April 1918 and creating the Over There Theater League on the spot. The YMCA agreed to provide uniforms and living expenses as long as the entertainers obeyed their organization's orders overseas, and the theater league provided a salary of two dollars per day (Schneider and Schneider, *Into the Breach* 158).

Out of 828 professional entertainers sponsored by the two organizations, 561 of them were women. "These men and women were augmented by some 500 professionals engaged overseas and by 12,800 soldier actors in staged and costumed plays, circuses, and shows" (Gavin 141; see also Schneider and Schneider, *Into the Breach* 155–161). They gave presentations in or on whatever quarters offered themselves, from tugboats, barns, and trenches to boxing rings and boxes of ammunition. They sang, danced, performed dramatic recitations and comedy skits, presented plays, and carted films and portable projectors from one battlefield to another (Schneider and Schneider, *Into the Breach* 155–161). "The Y professionals played ... for soldier audiences estimated at an astounding eighty-eight million" (Gavin 142). They gave the soldiers laughter, courage, and a little bit of joy in a world that had become hellish.

One of the most famous wartime entertainers was Elsie Janis, a vaudevillian and comedian who combined singing, jokes, and acrobatics in her routines. Janis, interestingly, left a written record of her ambivalence about working with the YMCA.; evidently she initially thought them too prejudiced in their religious doctrine to care for her performances or her associates. She perhaps even thought they would turn away soldiers who were not members of the Y: "[I] was not too keen on being with the Y.M.C.A. It sounded rather like it might cramp my speed—and I asked them quite frankly if my friends could come to the shows whether they were Young Christians or not? They explained that they had only one idea, that was to make the boys happy.... I must say for the Christian Association they have some speed" (qtd. in Schneider and Schneider, *Into the Breach* 155). Janis was one of the most popular performers sponsored by the Y.

A final group of women went to Europe not to drive or entertain, but to report. Women war correspondents were few but nevertheless influential; they attempted to bring the reality of the war in Europe to their readers in the States. They went overseas before the U.S. was officially a part of the war, reported on events in both Allied and Axis countries, and, when it came, reported the Russian Revolution in thorough detail. If female drivers pushed the boundaries of masculine space on the battlefield, women journalists pushed military and intelligence regulations to their limits and beyond; there was little they would not do to get their desired "scoop." Despite the flat refusal of the American military to accredit women reporters and despite the hesitation and obstruction of diplomacy officials, women journalists managed in small numbers to get to Europe and report on the war zones.

For example, both Rheta Childe Dorr and Clara Savage Littledale managed to get to the front—but they took entirely different approaches to getting their stories past their editors. Dorr, who wrote for both the New York *Evening Post* and *Evening Mail*, deliberately avoided military bureaucracy and signed up with the YMCA as a lecturer, making a business arrangement that would allow her to lecture in whatever location she went for her journalism assignments. At the same time, she often wrote sentimental pieces about her observations at the front, stressing maternalism and sentimentality rather than objective reporting of conditions. Littledale, who was a reporter for *Good*

Housekeeping, chafed under the requirements of her editors to such an extent that when she was summoned back to the States, she simply sent a cable that said, "Resigning and Remaining" (Schneider and Schneider, *Into the Breach* 197–200).

Other journalists took their editor's requests for "women's stories" to its literal endpoint: they wrote about women's experiences in the war, as civilians, as nurses, as workers, as mothers, and as refugees. Gertrude Atherton, who was a novelist and magazine writer, spent three months in France in 1916 reporting on the work of French and British women. Jessica Payne did similar writing for the *Brooklyn Eagle.* Writer Inez Haynes Irwin not only covered wartime life in England and France, but also in Switzerland and Italy (Schneider and Schneider, *Into the Breach* 197, 200–201).

One of the most unusual and most active women journalists was Madeleine Zabriskie Doty, a Smith College graduate and trained lawyer who made a name for herself in prison reform and social welfare efforts. During the course of the war she performed some of the most extended and exhaustive wartime reporting in Germany and Russia — a self-assigned beat that, while it did not always endear her to the pro–Allies U.S., earned her commendation for fairness, honesty, and compassion in her reporting. Doty managed to expose the civilian cost of the German war in a way that few others did: "German military strength was being obtained at tremendous cost to its civilians back home, where, in addition to lost lives, severe rationing was causing starvation, especially among the poor, so widespread [Doty] felt there could be a revolt to overthrow the Kaiser's government" (Rhinehart 127). In her own account, Doty highlighted the contrast between the lives of the workers and civilians, which she observed extensively, and the official press tours organized by the German government. While none of the civilians had enough food, milk, or other supplies, the government tour featured luxurious food, elegant transportation, travel to beautiful natural areas, and exhibitions of their rehabilitation hospitals for soldiers. Doty was repeatedly disturbed by the contrast between the "official" picture of Germany and the squalor she observed among ordinary citizens: "The Casino Garden with its lights, its music, and thronging people seemed a fairyland. It wasn't until we left and passed through the iron gates that reality returned. Pressed against the outer railing were the lean and hungry populace. It suddenly became very difficult for me to go on with this life of luxury" (qtd. in Rhinehart 148).

Doty also had to avoid the authorities in both Germany and Russia, particularly the former. Her unpublished memoir recounts several incidents in which she was followed and monitored by German spies, or taken in for questioning by the authorities. In one incident that sounds as though it comes directly from a spy film, Doty had to sew all of her notes into the lining of her coat, so that they would not be confiscated on her way out of Germany (Rhinehart 159–161). Generals and dictators alike did not want the harsh economic conditions of their countries in wartime being publicized in enemy countries.

Journalists like Dorr, Littledale, Atherton, and Doty did their best, sometimes at the expense of their own safety, to report on the war as it was happening, on the battlefield and off. They made Americans aware not only of the official casualties, but the unofficial ones — the poor, the starving, the dispossessed, the workers who spent every day simply trying to survive, and the women who worked all over the world to make conditions just a little better.

Jobs on the Homefront: Railroad Workers, Munitions Workers, Airplane Builders, and Streetcar Conductors

American women did not just fulfill wartime duties overseas. Plenty of women found all kinds of work to do on the homefront — and some of the most important work was in occupations formerly dominated by men. With so many American men in the army, domestic industries were desperate for workers, and no matter how skeptical those industries were about hiring women, keeping up with wartime production demanded workers, lots of them.

Railroad yards hired women for a variety of jobs, from bookkeeping and secretarial work to scrap haulers, coal shovelers, and engine cleaners. "Women throughout the country accounted for thirty-five blacksmiths, six boilermakers, fourteen coppersmiths, sheet-metal workers, and pipe fitters, fourteen electricians, and 370 machinists" (Maurine Greenwald 116). Railroad yards were also one of the few places where both African American and white women worked together, though often they were in different positions. African American women were able to leave domestic positions and become car cleaners, a job that paid more and required fewer hours than being a servant at a private residence. They also worked to distribute linens in Pullman cars and move scrap in the railroad yards (Maurine Greenwald 25–26). White women were outdoor laborers, as well, but they also had jobs as clerks, storeroom workers, and telephone and telegraph operators (C. Brown 161–176).

While it lasted, working for the railroads provided some of the best conditions women workers had ever had. Most women in railroad service earned between seventy and one hundred and five dollars a month, working 48- to 60-hour workweeks. The popularity of railroad work can be seen by the number of women employees: at the peak of the railroads' employment of women during the war, there were 101, 785 women employees (Maurine Greenwald 93).

However, there were limits and problems even with railroad work, which was generally acknowledged to be the best-paying war work available to women. Much of the equality and fairness on the railroads was due to the Women's Service Section of the Railroad Administration, which oversaw wages and working conditions for female railroad workers (Maurine Greenwald 78–80 & 87). Field agents for the WSS tried to address any mistreatment of women workers, and often they succeeded, but even they could not always stop or prevent the sexual harassment that women encountered on the job. Women workers often chose to endure the inappropriate behavior rather than give up the higher wages and shorter hours that railroad work provided (Maurine Greenwald 99–100).

Other homefront workers found a similar mix of the positive and negative in their wartime jobs. Female munitions workers, for example, enjoyed both higher wages and shorter hours, but there was open hostility to their presence in many of the munitions factories, hostility that only increased when the women workers proved that they could turn out munitions at a faster rate than the men. Union men in skilled trades were upset that their jobs were being broken down into smaller tasks and that women did not follow the moderate pace they set on the factory floor. "A gear manufacturing firm where women sandblasted, ground, drilled, and broached metal parts disclosed that women's output averaged 15 to 25 percent more than that of their male co-workers. In a munitions plant making fuses, women drill press and milling machine operatives produced 25 to 50 percent more than men" (Maurine Greenwald 119). Women who worked in seasonal trades like box-assembling, glove-making, and corset-making were often paid by the piece, and they had to earn as much as they could while the work lasted. They applied the same principle to their work in wartime factories, which earned them both the enmity of their male fellow workers and the grudging respect of their male supervisors (C. Brown 127–128).

Some factories and other production areas, like the Recording and Computing Machines Company in Dayton, OH, and the shipyard in Newark, NJ, set up training schools for women or gave them instruction on the floor. Women were taught to operate one kind of machine, in order to get them into production lines more quickly, and other changes were made for their benefit, including social clubs and restaurants that would encourage them to socialize and relax under company auspices. Demand was sometimes so great that the remaining men welcomed the help of the women, if only to keep production up to speed. Once factories discovered that women could indeed be well trained, they willingly hired women, particularly after drafting in the armed forces began for the men (C. Brown 132–135; Maurine Greenwald 55–57).

The aircraft industry offered similar opportunities — and fewer problems — to women workers. Perhaps because the new industry was so small, women worked in all aspects of it, and seem to have met with little resistance. The six thousand women who worked in the industry shaped and varnished wooden parts, soldered and fitted metal ones, painted and applied insignias to the planes, and inspected the final products for any flaws or mistakes before the planes were packed into a crate for shipping. The women worked in forty plants across the country, although fully a third of them worked at the two plants owned by Curtiss Aeroplane and Motor Corporation in Buffalo, NY (C. Brown 142–148). Women filled a unique and small, but ever-growing, niche in the production of airplanes.

Unlike the women in airplane and munitions factories or railroad yards, women streetcar conductors did not participate in a business that, at least on the surface, had a direct impact on the war effort. However, streetcars were essential transportation for many employees in wartime industries, and so any interruption in streetcar and trolley service was seen as a nuisance at best and a catastrophe at worst (Maureen Greenwald 145). Women streetcar and trolley conductors had a significant effect on the workforce in a number of ways. Maurine Greenwald posits that three factors were key in determining how women streetcar conductors were received in any given community by the male streetcar conductors: "the existence of a streetcar union and its ability to define and defend the conditions of labor; the intentions of women to work as conductors on a permanent basis; and the extent of solidarity between men and women wage earners in a community" (141). If male trolley and streetcar workers were unionized, women workers almost universally encountered resistance and hostility when they moved into working as streetcar conductors. Trolley unions saw the presence of women workers as the equivalent of union busting, and so they would close ranks against the trolley companies and the women workers alike. In cities where there was a strong trolley or streetcar workers union, women were usually *not* related to the men already employed, and antagonism was more likely to happen and faster to flare up. In fact, the firm position of the unions against female employees actually prevented female relatives of conductors from becoming employees; an alliance that might have been helpful for both male conductors and unions was lost because of the political position already taken by the union (Maurine Greenwald 146–147).

On the other hand, if a union was *not* present, the acrimony from male carmen was almost nonexistent. Greenwald also points out that many of the new women conductors were related to male employees by blood or marriage, and so there was more inclination to work together. Streetcar companies often advertised for women who were related to carmen; in this way, the women could be seen as (and construct themselves as) employees who were "holding" the jobs for their conscripted male relatives (146–148).

However, women were not always simply "placeholders," nor did they always see their work that way. If women only intended to work on the cars for the duration of the war, their employment was generally accepted and even encouraged (Maurine Greenwald 145). If they sought to continue working on the cars after the war, as many women did, then their presence became an open threat. Union men thought that women conductors meant lost jobs, lowering of wages, and loss of a field of work that they could move in and out of with ease. Women saw working on the trolleycars as a vast improvement in wages, hours, and working conditions. Often, being a conductor was the difference between making ends meet and not having enough money to live on. Generally, women conductors were working to support families and feed their children, either in the absence of their husband or as part of an extended household:

> Most of the women ... worked because they had to, not because they wanted to escape their home routines or earn pocket money for personal luxuries. The women required living wages to meet real responsibilities. Of thirty-three Detroit women interviewed by Department of Labor investigators in December 1918, thirteen were single, ten were married and living with their husbands, six were widowed, three were divorced, and one had been recently deserted by her husband. Eighteen of the thirty-three women supported dependent parents, husbands, or children. In another Detroit survey, it was found that 120 women conductors supported 154 dependents [Maurine Greenwald 155].

Like their counterparts in the railroad yards, munitions factories, and the AEF, women conductors needed wages and were highly aware of their own marketability. Also like the women in these other areas of war work, they fought for their right to keep their new and better-paying jobs, even if they ultimately lost. Protracted struggles between car companies, unions, and women conductors broke out in Detroit and Cleveland, resulting in highly publicized hearings that went all the way to the National War Labor Board. While the NWLB ruled in both cases that the women conductors had a right to keep their jobs, the transit company in Cleveland refused to follow the board's ruling unless the local union consented — and the local union remained firm in their opposition to women conductors. Things went slightly better in Detroit, where the women conductors had agreed to step aside in their positions if war veterans could be hired, but the relationship with their male coworkers was permanently strained (Maurine Greenwald 165–172). The result was different in Kansas City, where there was a long history of cooperation and respect between the Women's Trade Union League and the male trade unions. Women transit workers there cooperated with and supported the male workers, and male employees did the same in return, so that all the workers presented a united front against the transit company. The Kansas City Amalgamated Union accorded women workers membership rights, and sided *with* the women workers rather than against them. When the workers went on a prolonged strike, their continued resistance eventually rendered the transit company financially insolvent (Maurine Greenwald 172–180).

However, class and union solidarity, and even national patriotism and solidarity in the face of war, did not always stop or override racial and religious prejudice. As we have seen, few Catholic women were accepted into any branch of war service save the Army Signal Corps. While African American women took advantage of many of the domestic wartime jobs that opened up in the men's absence, they were routinely rejected for auxiliary work and kept from the front lines of the war. Jewish women, too, were only able to go overseas in very limited capacities and small numbers.

African American and Jewish Women

Prejudice against non-white, non–Protestant soldiers and women workers was rampant during the First World War. Racial prejudice and nativism at home, combined with wartime nationalism, created a difficult political environment for African American women and Jewish women who wished to go overseas. The obstacles they encountered were both similar and different; African American women and soldiers were contending with racial prejudice that had developed over centuries of slavery and segregation, and with the popular "scientific" evidence of eugenics, which painted them as the lowest of the human species, with minimal intelligence and maximum brutality and promiscuity (Russett 14, 50–57, 201–205; A. Stern 13–17). While Jewish people were also lower on the eugenics evolutionary ladder, the hostility of the U.S. government stemmed more from its perception that Jewish immigrants were descended from those who were now political and battlefield enemies, and that Jewish people might still retain more loyalty to their native countries than to their adopted homes.

African American women organized on a large scale to serve the 200,000 black men who went overseas, but their services were repeatedly rejected by the Army Nurse Corps and the Red Cross. The YMCA accepted a few black overseas workers, but they were mostly men. The YMCA also sponsored four of the six black women who are known to have served in Europe. There was also a female concert pianist named Helen Hagan who entertained the troops, and probably a black woman doctor. It is not known how many black women "passed" in order to go overseas and serve, but there may have been hundreds (Schneider and Schneider, *Into the Breach* 169–170). The YMCA hired a few more black women as secretaries once the war was officially over, sending another dozen or so overseas in 1919 (Zeiger 28).

Three of the black women who were YMCA secretaries served in France: Mrs. James L. Curtis, Mrs. Addie W. Hunton, and Miss Kathryn M. Johnson. While the women were initially given separate assignments, they were eventually all sent to St. Nazaire, where they endeavored to meet the needs of 7,000 American black enlisted men, the majority of whom were working as stevedores. There the women set up a YMCA hut and provided the same services as many other canteens: coffee, cookies, doughnuts, pies, company, and conversation. A Sunday evening chat hour was one of the most popular programs they instituted for the men, in which they held conversations about current politics, music, art, religion, higher education, and other topics. They also created a few particular services that may have been unique among Y workers. They set up a schoolroom where they taught over a thousand illiterate black soldiers to read and write, most of them from the South where education for blacks was still scarce. Many of those same men came from towns without library services for African Americans, and the women taught them a system for book lending. Finally, the Y secretaries arranged for a few black soldiers to attend French universities when the war was over (Gavin 139–140; Schneider and Schneider, *Into the Breach* 170–171). They managed to do an amazing amount of work and nurturing with few hands and even fewer resources. Though very few black women were able to get overseas to serve, those that did made a tremendous difference in the lives of soldiers.

Despite their almost wholesale rejection by the military and auxiliary organizations, African American women organized on a large scale on the homefront, eager to prove their willingness and capability to serve. They arranged social services for black enlisted men and their families, knitted, sold war bonds, and took care of health and hygiene in African American communities. Black nurses were particularly important in providing the latter: "When black nurses received no call from the Red Cross, Adah Thoms, an African American nurse leader who had helped to found the National Association of Colored Graduate Nurses, established a separate corps for black nurses under the auspices of the newly formed Negro Circle for War Relief"

(Zeiger 27–28). Two dozen black nurses were finally accepted into the army and assigned to military stations in three states during the influenza epidemic of 1918, when the need for nursing was absolutely desperate and medical facilities and personnel in the States and overseas were overrun with ill patients (Zeiger 28). The three women in St. Nazaire converted their YMCA hut into a sick ward during the epidemic, nursing both black and white soldiers (Schneider and Schneider *Into the Breach* 171–172).

Jewish women found themselves in similarly restricted situations when it came to war service. Their religion and their ancestry subjected them to prejudice and intense scrutiny by the U.S. government, the military, and auxiliary relief organizations. While there has not been much research into or recovery of their domestic activities during the war, Jewish women served overseas primarily with the Jewish Welfare Board, the auxiliary organization that was tasked specifically with caring for the welfare of Jewish troops:

> Early in the war, under pressure from the YMCA, the major auxiliary organizations involved in war service devised a plan whereby soldiers from the three major faiths would be ministered to separately: Protestants by the YMCA, Catholics by the Knights of Columbus, and Jews by the Jewish Welfare Board (JWB).... The JWB, established to support Jewish servicemen socially and advocate for them in matters of military policy, did send almost two hundred welfare workers overseas, more than half of them women [Zeiger 29].

Like their YMCA, Red Cross, AEF, and Army Nurse Corps counterparts, the majority of women workers with the JWB were single and older, averaging 31 years of age (Zeiger 35). Most of them were also educated to some degree; 21 percent were clerical workers, 25 percent were teachers, and 17 percent were social workers (Zeiger 39).

However, despite their age, education, and generally unmarried status, women workers with the JWB had a terrible time getting their applications through the War Department. The process took months, although it was often swift for workers from other organizations, and applications were frequently held up not only by the War Department, but also by the British and French embassies:

> Clearance by the War Department ... was an elaborate and time-consuming process for JWB applicants, ostensibly because Jews were likely to be of "enemy" German or "Bolshevik" Russian ancestry. Applications from the JWB were routed to Military Intelligence and delayed indefinitely. The Military Intelligence branch asked to review the JWB's application form in June 1918; Jewish men and women were required to provide information on immigration, naturalization, and nativity, both for themselves and for their parents, as well as three letters of recommendation.... The French and British embassies routinely turned down JWB applicants on the basis of their "nativity" [Zeiger 29].

Jewish women auxiliary workers were, at bottom, asked to prove their loyalty to the United States before they would be allowed overseas, and even with impeccable credentials and recommendations, there was no guarantee that the government would process their applications in a timely manner. Even if the U.S. finally granted them permission to leave the country, France or England might refuse to give them papers. All things considered, it was impressive that the JWB managed to send as many women as they did. Like their African American counterparts, Jewish soldiers had to make do with the smaller amount of services allotted to them, as prejudice followed them and their female peers over the Atlantic.

Despite the restrictions on and prejudice against their wartime service, African American and Jewish women were able to make a substantive contribution to the war effort, one that was all the more impressive because of the greater obstacles they encountered. While the legal and social status of African Americans in the U.S. remained more or less the same as it had been before the war, African American men and women who served overseas were able to make a lasting positive impression on European allies, who treated them with more kindness and equality than they received at home. For Jewish-Americans, their position as American citizens became more precarious with the entry of the U.S. into the war. During and immediately following the conflict, many Jewish people were deported from the country for their political beliefs and activism. In that sense, the service of Jewish men and women in the Allied cause may have served as a way to demonstrate their loyalty to their adopted home.

Gains and Losses

The service of American women during the Great War had uneven and sometimes unpredictable results. While women undeniably showed their mettle and served their country in a myriad of ways, they still encountered prejudice and obstruction from Congress, the Cabinet, all branches of the military, and male members of wartime auxiliary organizations, as well as male civilians. For some men, like Secretary of War Newton Baker, women did not belong on a battlefield or near a regiment, full stop. For those men, women's wartime contributions both at home and abroad were crimes against the natural order. Women's newfound freedoms — in work, in travel, through their participation in what had formerly been an all-male arena — rankled and disgusted many. Even the members of Congress, who were willing to acknowledge women's countless contributions to the war, refused to provide many of those same women with military rank or veterans' benefits.

Women, however, embraced the challenges the Great War set forth for them, in most cases going far above and beyond what was thought possible in their care for the troops, the civilians, and each other. Through the many, many auxiliary organizations that they organized to help the war effort, through employment in wartime and domestic industries, through journalism, through enlistment in the branches of the armed services that would accept them, women proved their patriotism, capability, and toughness in a worldwide crisis. Often, they defied orders from their superiors in order to serve the troops, rescue the wounded, or scoop a story. Despite all of the heartbreak and the horror that they saw, they were also able to find the "fun" in their new adventures and experiences, relishing the independence and autonomy that came with war work. Women employed stateside took full advantage of the higher wages and job mobility offered by the wartime economy, while at the same time taking pride in the work that they knew was contributing to the war effort. When peace was declared, women fought against returning to the status quo; they tried every way possible to keep their jobs, keep their wages, to stay enlisted in the military, and to continue providing relief from the devastation the war had left in its wake. Although they lost most of those battles, the lives of individual women were changed forever. Some of them found new careers and vocations through their war work; some of them carried a newfound sense of independence and pride. Though it was delayed and fought over, women were given a new level of citizenship when they were granted the right to vote in 1920. Though peace brought with it many of the old gendered restrictions, American women as a whole were never the same.

Girls' series fiction was never the same, either. The war demanded a new kind of heroine, but the portrayal of women's war work in series fiction was just as uneven as women's real-life experiences. Heroines in established series like the *Outdoor Girls*, *Grace Harlowe*, and *Ruth Fielding* stayed at home to work for the YMCA and Red Cross, went overseas as hospital or auxiliary volunteers, or became nurses and ambulance drivers. Other series were written specifically to capitalize on the wartime fervor, including the *Red Cross Girls* and the *Khaki Girls* books. Patriotism was heralded, ethnic and racial prejudice were exploited, and daring and bravery became the birthright of American women as well as men. While all of the books championed women's patriotic service, exactly what constituted that service and how much of it was appropriate for women was clearly open to cultural debate. Women had changed — and girl readers and girl heroines were changing with them.

Notes

1. Estimating the number of women who participated in the war both at home and overseas is extraordinarily difficult. Records are incomplete, missing, and sometimes inaccurate for the women working overseas. Women changed jobs on the homefront by the thousands, and it is impossible to trace every woman who traded a job in the garment industry for one in a munitions factory. While the numbers for individual organizations are sometimes possible to come by (the Navy, Marine Corps, and the American Expeditionary Forces, for example), there is no way to completely verify how many women performed war work of some kind. There were simply too many women and too many possible occupations.

2. Historians are not quite clear about the personnel in these Mercy Ship units. While Lettie Gavin says the units were composed of eleven nurses, a medical director, and two assistants (181), Dorothy and Carl Schneider say the units contained twelve nurses and three surgeons each (*Into the Breach* 87).

3. The Women's Overseas Hospital was a mobile hospital unit fully staffed by U.S. women physicians. Organized by the New York Infirmary for Women and Children and the National American Woman Suffrage Association, the unit originally offered its services to the American Army, which refused them. The unit then approached the French Army, which took the women gladly. There were at least thirty female physicians in the unit, perhaps more, and they worked in French hospitals, treated many French refugees, and eventually established a 100-bed French military hospital (Schneider and Schneider, *Into the Breach* 90).

4. This is another case where numbers differ. Zeiger states that there were twelve Signal Corps houses for the telephone workers, but that the YWCA was also responsible for housing the AEF stenographers who were working overseas (92).

5. Daniels was an avowed suffragist; Susan Godson notes that "[Daniels held] a firm belief in woman's suffrage, and he worked tirelessly for passage and ratification of the Nineteenth Amendment. Generally sympathetic toward women's aspirations and aware of their efficient clerical service in government agencies, Daniels had no difficulty justifying a role for them in the U.S. Navy" (60).

Six

Running the Gamut and the Gauntlet
World War I Series Fiction as a Catalyst for Change in the Cultural Landscape of American Girlhood

The entry of the United Sates into the Great War meant that book publishers had to do a rapid about-face in their series plotlines and priorities. Given that the U.S. had done its best to stay out of the war, few American publishers had paid any attention at all to the conflict raging overseas, at least not in their publications for adolescents. When the political mood of the time was demanding isolationism and peace, it was bad business to drum up patriotism and wartime ardor. However, as hostilities between the U.S. and the Central Powers increased, public support for the war became more visible, and a declaration of war seemed imminent, publishers must have felt the turning tide as much as any other group of citizens.

John C. Winston of Philadelphia was one of the only publishers to address the war before the U.S. was officially a part of the Allied Powers; he began publishing the *Red Cross Girls* series in 1916. Most other publishers, Edward Stratemeyer included, waited until the U.S. had declared war before addressing it in their fiction — but that meant they had some catching up to do in writing, profit-making, and propaganda creation. As most ongoing series of the time addressed the war in one way or another, it seems safe to assume that most publishers supported U.S. entry into the war, as did the majority of the American public. Publishers had a large audience, and they would have seen it as their duty as loyal citizens to promote patriotism among American young people. Even if they *did* disagree with the war, it would have been reckless to say so in print, as individuals and companies were being prosecuted under the federal Espionage Act for publications or products that were deemed seditious, disloyal, or treasonous.

Creating wartime fiction specifically for *girls*, however, seems to have been regarded with some ambivalence by series book publishers. While some embraced the wartime fervor and came up with ways for their heroines to participate in the war, others ignored it entirely, or could not find ways to continue a series after the war ended. Wartime volumes often ended a series, though it is hard to say why this might have been; perhaps publishers found it difficult to return the characters to homefront life, much like the actual soldiers and workers who came home. Having placed their girl heroines into such harrowing adult situations, publishers could not convincingly make them happy, carefree girls again. Some examples include: the *Betty* books by Alice Hale Burnett, which ended with *Betty and the Red Cross*; the *Girls of Central High* series, which ended with *The Girls of Central High Aiding the Red Cross*; a rare Campfire Girls series by Harriet Rietz and Helen Hart that finished with *The Campfire Girls' Red Cross Work*; and the *Aunt Jane's Nieces* series that ended with *Aunt Jane's Nieces in the Red Cross*. A handful of publishers like Winston created new series as a result of the war, including the *Red Cross Girls*, the *Khaki Girls*, and the *Somewhere Series*, but once the Armistice was declared, the series were discontinued as rapidly as their plot threads could be tied up and ended. The last of the wartime volumes in most series were published in 1920. Another possibility lies in the change in cultural attitudes during the twenties; most Americans wanted to put the war behind them as quickly as possible, and series books followed suit. The serious, life-and-death nature of the war and related service activities probably did not appeal to girls who were being immersed in imagery of the carefree flapper.

In this chapter I have addressed series that show a range of cultural responses to women's war work. In some cases, well-established series like the *Outdoor Girls* and *Ruth Fielding* are the best mechanism for this kind of examination; since the main characters return to more or less "normal" lives after the war, the books provide a glimpse into how women may or may not have advanced as a group both during the war and after it was over. Series that address the war in more depth, like *Grace Harlowe* and the *Khaki Girls*, are also useful because their heroines undergo a wide range of wartime adventures and responsibilities. These series allow an assessment of how accurately fiction was reflecting women's participation in the war effort. Admittedly, however, my examination is incomplete; the scarcity of these volumes even among sellers, collectors, and university libraries makes it difficult to do a complete canvassing of wartime series. More scholarship is needed on these fascinating volumes before their full effects on series' fiction and girls' culture can be understood.

The girls' series fiction of the First World War is particularly adept at portraying both the service of women and their idealization, simultaneously encouraging young women to go out into the workforce in the name of patriotism, to maintain their role as the traditional caretakers of men, and, occasionally, to expand their horizons and engage in more daring occupations. The books were filled with patriotic propaganda clearly intended to encourage young women to support the war and the men overseas, but the work the vast majority of the fiction encouraged was of a very limited and "feminine" type, although it may be argued that the kinds of caretaking demanded of women during the war undercuts the very idea that they were dependent on anyone. As I have shown, even women who were engaged in war work at home were often taking care of and providing for elderly relatives or siblings. However, the class and occupational diversity of women war workers is not reflected in wartime series fiction. The girls of the U.S. were being called on in mass numbers to do work for their country, but the women who worked in traditionally "masculine" occupations were generally not profiled in the contemporary series fiction. I have not found one series that focuses on a female reporter, munitions worker, Yeoman (F), Marine Reserve (F), or telephone operator, even though the latter, nicknamed "Hello Girls," were some of the most celebrated female war workers. The girls in these books are, for the most part, YWCA volunteers and Red Cross workers. This kind of occupational stereotyping is particularly true of the series published by the Stratemeyer Syndicate, but two notable exceptions to the norm can be found outside of the Stratemeyer collection, in the *Grace Harlowe* and *Khaki Girls* series. Grace begins as a Red Cross worker, but eventually becomes an ambulance driver, while the Khaki Girls, Valerie Ward and Joan Mason, join the Liberty Motor Corps and then join a company of female ambulance drivers.

Two important stipulations need to be made here. First, it needs to be said that women's caretaking, whether in nursing or canteen work, is in no way a lesser occupation than ambulance driving, telephone operating, doing clerical work in the Navy, or any of the many other services that women took it upon themselves to perform. It was precisely this perception that female nurses and doctors fought against for the duration of World War I, and it was why, in the end, women nurses were not given official military rank. No matter how necessary their presence, women encroaching on the male military establishment made Secretary of War Baker, Congress, and much of the general public nervous and uncomfortable, and those with federal authority often went out of their way to make distinctions between women's and men's wartime service. Women's caretaking has always been a crucial part of any wartime enterprise, for without it many more men would die or be permanently injured. However, because *women* were traditionally wartime caretakers, precisely because of their gender, their essential work was often dismissed as unequal. They could and should nurse, but they could "never" fight or serve as men do. Nursing and other forms of caretaking maintain cultural gender distinctions about women and men that are still not easily shaken in the present day.

As women engaged in more traditionally "male" wartime occupations, however, the story changed. When women entered the Navy and Marine Corps, when they drove ambulances and handled firearms, when they became welders or railroad yard workers on the home front, the cultural commentary was loud and vociferous. These women were directly challenging the idea that certain jobs and arenas were only for men, and unless and until they proved their competency and fitness for those arenas, cultural perception was against them. This may be why so many girls' series held to the idea that their heroines were most useful as YMCA and Red Cross workers — although they were part of the war machine, they were participating as caretakers, in a role that was culturally familiar and accepted. Only a few heroines were permitted to push cultural boundaries far enough to be on the battlefield itself, saving lives and taking lives as necessity dictated.

However, even in their "female" occupations, Stratemeyer's Ruth Fielding and Outdoor Girls manage to transcend some of the typical gender roles. The war put these heroines in the public realm and allowed them to make a place for themselves because war work was accepted and encouraged by the American public. This is even acknowledged occasionally by the authors:

> Here is told how two of America's best little women, withdrew from everything attractive at home, not excluding the very worthiest war work, that they might 'get across' and do full time service on the fields of France ... the really marvelous exploits of the girls include such experiences as could not have been accurately put down in a book of girls' adventures before the war gave them new and remarkable opportunities [E. Brooks, *Windsor Barracks* 3].

Here, the narrator explicitly states that the war has opened up new vistas for women, and that women were eager to go overseas and participate. While real women encountered considerable resistance to their participation in the war, fictional young women encounter almost none. Although their level of participation varies — on the homefront or overseas, in the Y or in the Red Cross — their parents or guardians almost never object to their war work, if indeed they are present at all. (Mr. Mason, Khaki Girl Joan Mason's father, is the exception to this rule, and Joan's quest to obtain his permission to go overseas will be examined below.) Participating in the war is seen as a patriotic duty; what changes with each series is how far girl heroines push cultural boundaries in order to fulfill that duty.

The second stipulation that needs to be taken into account when examining wartime series fiction is that the heroines in no way represent the diverse classes and races of real women war workers. In all of the series that I analyze here, the heroines are white, Protestant, and middle- to upper-class. None of them are engaging in war work because they need the increase in wages or because they are supporting family members. Working-class war work, like munitions production and railroad maintenance and repair, is never motioned. The girls in these series are driven to serve through patriotism and loyalty, and they take full advantage of their privileged race and class positions in order to do so. They, their parents, or other members of their families finance and support their endeavors. The same racial and social prejudices that led to the exclusion of African American, Jewish, and Catholic women from wartime service hold true in series fiction, and like much wartime propaganda, series fiction only features white, Protestant, and educated American girls.

Although series fiction can only claim to represent a narrow segment of women war workers, girls' series heroines *do* illustrate the tension between wartime freedom and traditional gender roles, the constant negotiation of individual autonomy and cultural proscriptions for young women. The mixed messages of girls' series fiction from this period demonstrate the changing nature of women's roles in the culture at large. American women were more educated and politically active than ever before, but in order to achieve their goals, they often had to circumvent restrictions put in place by a male bureaucracy. Fictional wartime heroines face this same set of difficulties.

Sending Heroines to War

In order to send heroines into the war zone at all, series writers had to find solutions to a number of problems. American girls were supposed to be pure and wholesome; how could series heroines stay wholesome on the battlefield or in any part of the war zone? How could writers justify women's participation in the war? Given that American women were doing all kinds of male work, what kinds of work were suitable for series heroines?

The answer to the first question is that series writers made heroines fit into a combination of cultural types. As Martha Banta points out in *Imaging American Women*, the New Woman that had emerged shortly before the war was a conglomeration of three variations — the Beautiful Charmer, the Outdoors Pal, and the New England Woman. The Beautiful Charmer is exactly what her name implies — a pretty girl who is used to having her own way and determined to get what she wants, but at the same time is practical, socially adept, and unquestionably chaste. The Outdoors Pal was the physically active girl who had the free spirit expected of American women, both freedom of body and freedom of mind (but who, of course, still upheld the morality of America). The New England Woman is conscientious and spiritual, passionate, intelligent, and industrious, always doing what is expected of her. Merging these three types led to the image of the New Woman. Once the United States entered the war, the New Woman was translated into the Protecting Angel and the Amazon Warrior on World War I propaganda posters. Soldiers fought to protect and save the Angels and looked to the idealized figurehead of the Warriors for inspiration (Banta 46–53, 85–88, 484–94). War workers were also a conglomeration of all of these types, at least when they were on duty—they were the Charmer and the Pal to the soldiers, bringing American beauty and wit to the battlefield, while they were the industrious New England Woman in their work, constantly toiling to make the battlefield a little more bearable.

Even though their work excited them and made them feel useful, living up to so many different images was frequently exhausting for real women war workers. Series fiction heroines, on the other hand, achieve the balance with little effort. While different series emphasize different aspects of war work and often favor one cultural type over another, there are elements of all the types in wartime heroines, and their capacity to be many different people at once is seemingly endless. Writers endowed them with an almost infinite adaptability and a wide range of skills; they could be a Red Cross inventory worker in one moment and an Intelligence agent the next, then turn around and be charming to a general or a convalescent soldier.

Those skills were one way to justify women's participation in the war, and indeed, the Navy, the Marine Corps, and the Red Cross all *did* point out women's capabilities as a reason for enlisting them in the war effort. There were things that women could do that either were not done by men or did not require a man to do them, including nursing, medical supply and inventory, and secretarial work. The most frequent employment for a series heroine was as a YWCA or Red Cross Girl. However, even when series heroines took on the more unconventional roles of ambulance drivers or intelligence workers, authors could justify the plot by pointing out that there were plenty of Allied women doing that particular kind of work. American women had to work much harder to attain this kind of position (and often went to other Allied organizations to do it), given the adamant opposition of the U.S. Army and Secretary of War Baker. However, even Baker would have had difficulty denying that such occupations were good propaganda for the war effort. Ambulance driving was exciting, dangerous, necessary, and useful. It was certain to appeal to some of the most adventuresome American women.

Six. Running the Gamut and the Gauntlet

Of course, most fictional women stayed closer to the center of "acceptable" wartime activities. While ambulance driving offered perhaps the most liberating and progressive form of war work, there was a wide range of possibilities and new roles for young women. The *Outdoor Girls*, *Ruth Fielding*, *Grace Harlowe*, and the *Khaki Girls* series run the gamut of conservative to liberal interpretations of women's wartime contributions.

The Outdoor Girls: Holding Down the Home Front

The *Outdoor Girls* series provides a glimpse of the kinds of work that upper-middle-class women did on the home front. The very name "Outdoor Girls" suggests that the four girl friends from Deepdale — Betty, Mollie, Amy, and Grace — are modeled on the variation of the American Girl that Banta calls the Outdoors Pal. These girls are energetic, cheerful, full of life, and have no scruples about joining their male friends — Allen, Will, Roy, and Frank — in sports or other physical activities. Banta describes the dynamic this way:

> Fun between the sexes was predicated on an instant recognition of everyone's gender.... All the figures are alike in the physical zest they display and in their readiness to mug, and no pronounced cultural distinctions separate feminine from masculine, but which are women and which are men is easy enough to determine.... The image of the girl who went cycling might not raise a finger to urge the vote for women, but her *image* as the type of the American Girl became part of the process that altered social perceptions and formed new conceptions of what it was possible for females to do and to be [88, 258].

In the books before the war, Betty, Mollie, Amy, and Grace are part of a slowly evolving new picture of female intelligence, strength, and usefulness. They are happy to compete on a field with the boys, claim intelligence equal to a man's, and do their bit in the war effort, but gender distinctions of clothing and behavior remain fairly intact. The *Outdoor Girls* series is the most conservative of all the series examined here. It is the least unusual because the four protagonists stay within acceptably feminine boundaries and do not challenge the conventional role of women very much. However, the merits of the Outdoor Girls' war work lies in the fact that women working in a formal auxiliary role for the armed forces was something new, different, and exciting. Although they do not go overseas to the battle zone, the girls participate in auxiliary work based in the U.S. The Outdoor Girls are ready to take advantage of the new image of young women and do their part in the war effort. They do so in *The Outdoor Girls in Army Service* and *The Outdoor Girls at the Hostess House*, dividing their work between the Deepdale Red Cross and the YWCA.

In the first book, the girls hold a large lawn party as a fundraiser for the Red Cross and put on a play with the help of the boys. Then they repeat the performance for the YWCA and come up with the idea of setting up a Hostess House at Camp Liberty, where the boys are training. As detailed in the previous chapter, the Hostess Houses were facilities where mothers, wives, fiancées, and other family members could stay while they waited for the soldiers in their families to be shipped out. They were intended as a comfortable, private space for goodbyes. The Outdoor Girls' work at their fictional Hostess House is the focus of the second book detailing their war work, as one might guess from the title. The girls perform such duties as helping the foreign soldiers learn English, writing letters for soldiers who cannot write, entertaining relatives who are waiting for their boys to get off duty, setting up entertainment in which the soldiers participate, and canvassing area residents for rooms when the camp is full and more lodgings are needed.

These two books hold the best examples I have found of patriotic propaganda aimed at "women's work." Betty, Mollie, Amy, and Grace do not really step out of the female mold. They are doing work for men and for the families of men, only now they are doing it in a patriotic context. There is not much male supervision in either book, but there does not need to be. The girls are still in their typical roles, acting them out in a different setting. They are being set up as perfect examples of American womanhood, as combinations of the Beautiful Charmer and Outdoors Pal types that the soldiers leave behind. However, it is the war that makes it possible for the four girls to break into a public setting and make themselves and their duties useful to the outside world. At one point, the girls' YWCA director, Mrs. Wilson, commends them for their work at the Hostess House, saying:

> It isn't a small thing, you know — sending thousands of our boys away cheered and strengthened, armed to meet the future — better men, just for having met you. And the mothers and wives and sweethearts who have been entertained so royally and permitted to say goodbye to their loved ones under the very best and cheeriest conditions possible ... that's the spirit that has made your work here such a wonderful success [Hope, *Hostess House* 165].

In some ways, this passage is straight war propaganda. Girl readers might have been inspired to turn around and volunteer at a Hostess House, a YMCA office, or a local Red Cross. It also lends a great deal of romanticism to war work, which was necessary and fulfilling but also grueling and repetitive for the women who undertook it. Thinking of hosting as romantic work also helps disguise the fact that it is already culturally assigned as *women's* work: entertaining, comforting, and taking care of the soldiers' families and the soldiers themselves. Like nursing, hosting and entertaining soldiers' families can be culturally categorized as highly necessary but somehow less valuable than men's contributions to the war because they are a traditional and expected part of women's roles in wartime. However, the text tries to remove that devaluation by saying "it isn't a small thing, you know"— trying to make it self-evident that women's war contributions are equally important to men's. The passage also offers an interesting nod to female solidarity, in the sense that the girls are helping other women like themselves who have to send their boys off to war. The narrator acknowledges that war affects everyone, of both sexes, not simply the men who must go fight.

In *The Outdoor Girls in Army Service*, the girls discuss their place in the war and come to some interesting and conservative conclusions that actively discourage girls from doing anything out of the ordinary realm of service. The quartet briefly considers going overseas as nurses, in order to be near their male counterparts, but dismisses the option almost instantly. As Betty says, "'We'd probably be sent to another part of the field entirely, and probably wouldn't see them from the beginning of the war to the end. No, I guess we'll just have to keep on knitting for them'" (Hope 105). This discussion sends mixed signals on a number of levels: for starters, the motivation behind the girls' desire to be nurses is sincere but dubious. They want to be near their own boys from home, but do not seem to feel any commitment to the other soldiers. Familial and romantic attachment drives them to the idea of nursing, rather than patriotism, a desire for adventure, professional advancement, or simply better wages, which were all frequent reasons for real women's service. The author of this volume may have been trying to dissuade girls who wanted to be overseas purely because they were close to enlisted men; as we have seen, many of the auxiliary organizations refused to accept women who had relatives or fiancés in the service. Unfortunately, by having Betty voice this argument, the narrative belittles not only the real contributions that women could make to the overseas war effort, but also the contributions of the Outdoor Girls themselves, who do considerably more than just knit for the soldiers at Camp Liberty.

It should be noted that the entire discussion is out of keeping with Betty's character. Betty is the "Little Captain" of the foursome and leads the girls in almost every instance, whether they are trying to catch a thief, bring a spy to justice, or simply walk a few more miles during a day of hiking. She is always the one to push the girls a step further and remind them of their duty. Betty's statement is double-edged; while it reinforces the idea that war work should be based in a patriotic desire to serve the soldiers and the country, it also furthers the idea that women are most useful when they are at home and knitting, even during wartime. Betty, Mollie, Amy, and Grace do not take on either the Protecting Angel or Amazon Warrior personas. They remain on the homefront as the quintessential American Girls who the boys are fighting for, as an ultimate ideal for men to both long for and take comfort in.

It is possible that the Stratemeyer Syndicate was trying to use this series to appeal to the girls who did have to stay at home, those without means to go overseas. Marketing was Stratemeyer's forte, and he was surely aware that the vast majority of young women did not have the resources to engage in work in the war zone, despite the significant number that managed to go. Others were prevented from going through their relation to men in the service or through the age restrictions enforced by the auxiliary organizations. From a profits and publishing point of view, it would have been simply common sense to create a scenario in an existing, well-established series where familiar characters chose *not* to go overseas, just like all of the girl readers who were unable to.

During the Great War, women were able to travel farther and in greater numbers than they ever had before, thanks to the advances in technology that brought steamships and automobiles into existence. All the women who went over to France and other parts of Europe went by steamship. The Outdoor Girls between them had two automobiles that would have been immensely valuable in a motor corps or an ambulance unit. Had the writers wished it, they certainly could have sent the girls to the battlefield. By marketing a series that specifically wrote overseas war work out of the range of possibility, Edward Stratemeyer seemed to be pushing a conservative agenda for girls, one that encouraged patriotism but not adventure or independence.

However, Stratemeyer became somewhat more daring with the *Ruth Fielding* series, taking the war work of women a step farther and beginning to push the boundaries of what was acceptable. Before the war, Ruth is educated at the fictional Ardmore College[1] and begins a career for herself as a screenwriter and director of moving pictures. When the war breaks out, Ruth becomes a Red Cross volunteer and goes to France as a hospital supply worker. There, not only does she perform the female duties of nursing, comforting, etc., but also she finds herself caught up in mysteries of wartime profiteering and espionage.

Ruth Fielding: Expanding the Limits of Women's Service

Ruth Fielding was the heroine of one of the longest-running and most successful series prior to Nancy Drew, and while the series in full will be examined in the next chapter, Ruth's wartime adventures are notable for several reasons. One, unlike the Outdoor Girls, Ruth serves both at home *and* overseas with the Red Cross. Two, Ruth solves several mysteries related to army intelligence while she is overseas, using little more than her own observational skills. Three, although she does not delve into the more daring occupations of the war, Ruth pushes both literal and metaphorical borders when she ventures into enemy territory in search of her best friend and love interest, Tom Cameron. Although Ruth downplays her own contributions to the war effort, often allowing male supervisors, law enforcement officials, or army officers to dictate her actions, she is nevertheless determined to serve her country in some capacity that makes a difference. As a fictional character, Ruth balances the new and unusual idea of women actively participating in the war with the more traditional view that men are the real decision-makers on the battlefield.

Interestingly enough, the first wartime plot that Ruth uncovers centers around a woman and her two male conspirators. Ruth, as a steadfast and patriotic American woman, is set up as a foil to a woman who has neither patriotism nor scruples, who sees the war as a tool to be used for her own gain. In *Ruth Fielding in the Red Cross*, Ruth is working at the Red Cross State Headquarters in Robinsburg when she is assigned to go overseas with a base hospital supply unit. She is eventually sent to the base hospital in Clair, France. While there, she obtains and inventories all the hospital supplies, she watches the recovery wards when the wounded men come in, provides basic nursing, and writes letters for the soldiers.

Over the course of her work at home and abroad, she grows suspicious of her supervisor, Rose Mantel. Ruth first encounters Mrs. Mantel at a Red Cross meeting in her hometown, where the "woman in black," as Ruth thinks of her, is spreading rumors that the Red Cross is actually selling items that local women have knitted for the soldiers. When Ruth asks her to back up her assertions with proof, Mrs. Mantel is unable to offer any evidence that what she says is true. Ruth immediately becomes suspicious of her motives for slandering the auxiliary organization.

When Ruth is recruited from her local Red Cross offices to go work in the supply department at State Headquarters, she is startled to discover that Mrs. Mantel is the chief bookkeeper for the state office. It is at State Headquarters that she first notices Mrs. Mantel's associates, a Frenchman named Mr. Legrand and a Mexican man known as Mr. Jose. While Ruth does not care for either of the men, she does not have any proof that they are doing anything suspicious until one evening when she sees Jose cleaning or repairing the fire extinguishers in the office. Shortly afterward, a fire in the office destroys all of the ledgers — which had been left out of their safe by Mrs. Mantel. When one of the workers attempts to use a fire extinguisher on the blaze, it is ineffective, and Ruth realizes that Jose must have tampered with the devices.

Ruth suspects then that the fire was set on purpose to cover discrepancies in the books, particularly because Red Cross donations for the month seem particularly small. However, there is no proof of Mrs. Mantel's involvement, and Mr. Legrand disappears after the fire. Ruth is then accepted to go overseas with a Red Cross hospital supply unit to be stationed in Lyse, France. During the ocean voyage, Ruth sees both Jose and Legrand on the ship and realizes that the men have disguised themselves and are traveling under aliases. Mrs. Mantel is subsequently assigned as the chief of the supply unit, which only heightens Ruth's suspicions further. Once they all arrive in Lyse, Mrs. Mantel recommends Ruth for a position at another hospital in Clair. Ruth surmises that the woman in black hopes to get her out of the way.

After supply problems occur at the hospital at Lyse, Ruth hears about the situation from her colleagues and deduces that Mrs. Mantel is part of a ring of thieves that has been diverting medical supplies from the hospital and selling them for profit to private, black market dealers in France. Despite the clearly despicable nature of the thieves' activities, however, Ruth does have some fears about telling her suspicions to the police. She does not want to interfere where she is not wanted. None of her adventures defy the military organization of the war or the patriarchal organization of society. Ruth walks a careful line between being patriotic and responsible and breaching the lines of male authority. She is continuously conscious of where those lines are: "Yet [Ruth] naturally shrank from getting her own fingers caught in the cogs of this mystery that the French police were doubtless quite able to handle in their own way, and all in good time" (Emerson, *Red Cross* 172). Ultimately, once Ruth amasses enough suspicions, she writes a lengthy letter to the French police chief in Lyse, and the authorities deal with Mrs. Mantel and her accomplices. Ruth provides the intelligence, but the French police still provide the muscle and legal rights to deal with the criminals.

While Mantel's nationality is never made clear, it is revealed eventually that her real name is Rosa Bonnet, and she was married to an American bank robber. Although none of the criminals are proven to be German, Ruth suspects the Mexicans of having German sympathies: "[The old servant, Bessie] might easily be of the same nationality as José— Mexican. And the Mexicans are largely pro-German" (Emerson, *Red Cross* 178). Even though Ruth is sorting through her suspicions in this passage, clearly there is a moment of editorializing in the text, where being Mexican is conflated with being sympathetic to the Central Powers. This is likely a result of the Zimmerman Telegram, in which the German foreign secretary, Arthur Zimmerman, sent a coded message to the German ambassador to Mexico, asking for a Mexican alliance in the event of war with the United States. Germany offered significant U.S. territory to Mexico in exchange for their political and military support. While Mexico rejected the offer, the telegram outraged the American public, and mass support for declaring war began to increase rapidly. Just over a month after the telegram was sent, the U.S. declared war on the Central Powers. The relationship between the U.S. and Mexico was already tense due to the Mexican Revolution, and the Zimmerman telegram only exacerbated anti-Mexican sentiment in the States (Katz 350–367). Making a Mexican and a Frenchman two of the villains in *Ruth Fielding in the Red Cross* not only reinforces U.S. xenophobia and hostility toward Mexico, but also reminds every reader that even civilians from Allied nations cannot be trusted, that everyone is vulnerable to corruption and betrayal.

Mrs. Mantel and her male accomplices are, according to the thinking of the time, of the small-minded class of people that put profit over patriotism. Their alleged pro-German sympathies make them morally suspect from the outset. There is not any sort of "unmasking" of individuals who were thought to be upstanding and respectable; it is made clear from the beginning that these men and their female leader are not worthy of respect or sympathy. Ruth is made to share the ethnic prejudices of her contemporaries; being a patriotic heroine means knowing who your enemies are. As a fictional example for others, she cannot fall into the No Man's Land of universal sympathy for the soldiers, as real nurses and female pacifists often did. Ruth feels compassion for the men who fight on the winning side and dislikes anyone who does not fight for the Allied cause. She does not hesitate to turn in Mantel and her collaborators because she believes them to be innocent; she only hesitates to put herself forward because she does not want to interfere with the jobs or the professionalism of legitimate law enforcement.

Thus, on the one hand, Ruth acts as a patriotic American female by serving as a hospital volunteer and nurses' aide of sorts, supporting the soldiers without actually being on the battlefield. On the other hand, she defies the typical "helper" role of women in wartime, using her intelligence to help catch a group of black market thieves. She is not the active agent of catching them but the passive one, the observer who provides enough information for police to make the arrests. With such careful limits placed on female empowerment, the *Ruth Fielding* series does not manage to completely defy the gender roles assigned to women and men.

However, even within the proscribed limits of male authority, Ruth breaches the boundaries of the battlefield, the most important space designated as male. Ruth comes closest to assuming a man's role in *Ruth Fielding at the War Front,* when she is forced to undertake a mission of espionage to save her best friend and love interest, Tom Cameron. Tom is accused of betraying the American troops and giving information to the German Army. Ruth learns that her French friends Allaire and Henri Marchand, both high up in the French Army, are spies behind the lines who send information to the U.S. Army. Through them, she finds out not only that Tom has in fact been spying for the U.S. Army in Germany, but also that he has been arrested by the Germans and is being held as a suspect. Ruth decides to try and rescue him with the help of the Marchand brothers. She takes on several disguises, both male and female, to get through the Allied lines and across No Man's Land into Germany. At first she dons a trench helmet and is taken right into the American trenches in France — masculine territory if there ever was any. Then she dons a soldier's waterproof suit to go through a swamp, crossing into the German lines. Once there, she becomes a male Sub-Leutnant of the German Army in order to pass through the security checks in the German trenches. Finally, she puts on the traditional dress of a German female in order to be disguised as the sister of "Captain von Brenner," Tom's alias in Germany. Ultimately, she succeeds in her mission to rescue Tom.

How is it, though, that Ruth's disguises and her venture into "male" territory are not seen as a threat to the male establishment? She goes much further into the public, "male" sphere than any of the Outdoor Girls, and no objection is offered. She disguises herself as male and works her way through both Allied and Central battlegrounds, yet her actions are commended. There are several carefully constructed plot elements that make this possible. One of these, as aforesaid, is the *motive* for Ruth's adventure across the lines. She is not attempting to be a soldier, but to save one; not attempting to become a female spy, but to save a male one. In a greater sense, she is working for the American cause by saving a man who is one of its sources of information. Once again, much like her intelligence gathering for the French police, Ruth is performing a service for the sake of male individuals, male organizations, and male causes. She is helping Tom Cameron, the soldiers who make up the U.S. Army, the U.S. Army as an organization, and the male-directed-and-organized Allied cause. Another element is that, in order to accomplish her mission, Ruth is assisted completely by men. She is still within patriarchal boundaries because there are men guiding her actions. Finally, Ruth's assumption of a male disguise *and her re-emergence as a woman* serves to confirm her femininity and brands it more deeply on the minds of those who read about her. Her last disguise as Mina Von Brenner is perhaps the most important because it cements in the minds of readers that Ruth has no intentions of becoming a man. She returns to her own female clothes, her own gender behavior, and is only a man for as long as it takes to save the soldier who means the most to her.

Impersonation and gender-switching were not uncommon amusements during the turn of the century. There were several men who became stars of the stage doing female impersonations, including actor Julian Eltinge. Actresses Vesta Tilly and Florenze Tempest, among others, were famous for their performances in which they dressed as men. Novels such as *The Princess Passes* by C.N. and A.M. Williamson played with the idea of women disguising themselves as boys and entering the male world. Photograph studios of the day would take pictures of girls dressed in men's clothing (Banta 250–75). As long as all characters involved became their "rightful" selves by the end of the story, it was amusing and non-threatening. As Banta says:

> Those who did not really mind the advent of the New Woman and those who only mildly disliked the type were free to enjoy inversion narratives; in either case not much was at stake when switches in gender roles were shown as essentially silly.... For those who were at ease with the changes taking place on every side, stories that inverted gender signs simply confirmed that men were men and women (old or new) were females after all [280].

Male clothing was also a necessity in more practical settings; women who worked in factory, railroad, and agricultural labor during the war often wore pants or heavy coveralls to protect their bodies. In short, during wartime it was not at all uncommon for a woman to don men's clothing. For those who were comfortable with women of Ruth's type, her adventures were enjoyable, and for those who were not, the fact that she assumes her "correct" role as a woman in the end served to calm their fears about women overthrowing patriarchal society. Combined with the patriotic fervor that gripped America during the war, the necessity of the work women were doing, and the number of women who were working overseas, some temporary transgressions involving gender roles and boundaries were easily overlooked.

Then again, Ruth's adventure into enemy lines may be more subversive than it appears at first glance. It cannot be overlooked that Ruth's mission to save Tom reverses the fairy tale roles of the knight and the damsel in distress. Despite all of the careful qualifiers (read: male supervisors) placed around her undertaking, Ruth is the hero in this particular story arc, rescuing the "damsel" who needs saving. It is Ruth who must undergo physical and mental tests of endurance, strength, and adaptability as she travels the Allies' and the Central Powers' trenches in disguise, works her way through a swamp to get from one side of the battlefield to the other, and passes security checks in enemy territory. Ruth is reenacting the hero's journey, enduring trials and tribulations to reach the one she loves. Only once she has proven herself by passing through all of the obstacles is she allowed to reach Tom, the prisoner in the tower who needs her help to escape. In this reading, the Marchand brothers might be seen as Ruth's allies or fairy godmothers, providing her with whatever she needs to accomplish her goal, whether those needs are papers, necessary costume changes, or male military authority. Ruth is triumphant in her quest to bring Tom back to safety, and in so doing she saves crucial intelligence for the Allied forces, intelligence that could save many lives. Her victory is twofold: she saves the man she loves and the lives of many others.

None of the episodes from these two *Ruth Fielding* volumes illustrate situations that females would have ordinarily found themselves in, yet Ruth's resourcefulness and patriotism are praised. Her actions are necessary and noteworthy in wartime, so the fact that they might be threatening to the male establishment is overlooked in the text. This threat is also circumvented because Ruth is put into these positions by circumstances outside of her control; she is not intentionally trying to do any work that would ordinarily be done by males. Saving Tom Cameron is the possible exception to this, but even here we are given to understand that Ruth undertakes to save him for the purely feminine morals of love, friendship, and patriotism, not because she has any wish for adventure or power. Ruth is allowed to take on this "masculine" work for the sake of love and country. In both volumes, her atypical adventures allow her to transcend gender roles and prove her worth. Her forays into war work and masculine territory provide new areas of empowerment for young women.

While Ruth's venture into the trenches is only temporary, and she is eventually brought back behind the battle lines and to safety, there were publishers and writers outside of the Stratemeyer Syndicate who dared to cross the gender boundaries and have their female characters come completely into the public, masculine sphere of the battlefield. The *Khaki Girls* series by Edna Brooks and the *Grace Harlowe* series by Jessie Graham Flower are two cases in point.

Grace Harlowe: International Woman of Mystery

Grace Harlowe is one of the best examples of an intelligent and resourceful female in girls' fiction. She has her share of exciting adventures, but she uses brain power more often than physical strength to solve the problems and mysteries she encounters. However, she is not at all afraid to question authority, venture into enemy territory, or directly disobey her superiors if it means helping the Allied cause in any way. Grace answers to her conscience first and her supervisors second, dealing with any conflicts of authority after the fact — and the authorities usually concede that her actions have been correct. Unlike Ruth, Grace immediately acts when she sees any suspicious conduct or any illegal activity connected to the war. An accomplished driver, Grace does not hesitate to put herself in the line of fire for wounded men. She is more bold and self-reliant than Ruth, unflinchingly invading male space and male authority. Also unlike Ruth, by this point in her series Grace is married to her sweetheart Tom Gray, who is enlisted in the Army.[2]

Grace *does* share with Ruth the same beginnings of her war work: The Red Cross. Grace serves with the Red Cross as part of the Overton College Red Cross Unit. Overton is Grace's alma mater, and many of her friends are members of the unit. This is also based in historical fact; five of the Seven Sisters colleges, as well as Sophie Newcomb College, either sponsored groups of alumnae or sent over whole relief units to serve in various ways. The Smith College Relief Unit was the largest of them, containing seventeen women who worked together for the duration of their time overseas (Schneider, *Into the Breach* 71–78). Like several of their historical counterparts, the Overton girls are eventually split up and their talents divided among different organizations. Grace ends up stationed at Base Hospital Number Three, still assigned to the Red Cross. In *Grace Harlowe Overseas*, Grace helps the French Bureau of Information capture two enemy spies, although their ringleader Andre manages to escape the authorities (Flower, *Red Cross* 18–19). In the next volume, *Grace Harlowe with the Red Cross in France*, Grace almost immediately finds herself in a dangerous situation when the ambulance she is riding in, as part of an army ammunition and supply line, is shelled and overturned at the side of the road. Her driver, Jimmie Wellington, is injured in the blast, and when Grace attempts to drive him out of the area under fire, they are both overturned in the ambulance. Grace tends to Jimmie as well as she can and hitches a ride to Hospital Number Three, meeting her supervisor for the first time when she walks in to request help in reaching Wellington and bringing him in for treatment. The supervisor refuses her request and locks Grace up for insubordination. Grace promptly climbs out the window, borrows an ambulance, and goes to fetch Wellington, bringing him back to the hospital. He receives much-needed surgery for a skull fracture, and Grace's prompt action saves his life.

Grace not only goes through another round of enemy fire in order to reach Corporal Wellington, but she is promptly dismissed from service by her supervisor once she returns. It is not until she is summoned by Major Clowes, the man in charge of the entire hospital, that she gets the chance to tell her story in full. The Major commends Grace for her actions, but rebukes her for her behavior to her supervisor:

> Mrs. Gray, you have done a very fine thing, but you have set a bad example in discipline, and for this I must rebuke you and warn you that it must not occur again. Corporal Wellington has you to thank for saving his life ... but remember that in an institution the size of this one, and especially in wartime, military discipline is necessary [Flower, *Red Cross* 56].

Grace accepts the rebuke, but does not promise to obey orders, merely saying that she will "'try to heed [the major's] advice, and you may depend upon me to do what I believe is right, at all times'" (Flower, *Red Cross* 57). Even after being forced to defend her actions to a military authority figure who could have punished her quite severely, perhaps ended her war work altogether, Grace makes it clear that she will obey her conscience above all else. Military authority comes second for Grace when she is in the war zone; the lives of the soldiers and their well-being come first. Much like the Salvation Army women and YMCA canteeners who put their regiments first and their orders second, Grace does everything she can to contribute to the war effort, orders or no orders.

Another instance of Grace's dedication to the men is when the hospital is subjected to bombing raids by the Germans. Grace and another hospital worker, Virginia Coates, do their best to comfort the wounded men during the raids, even though their presence in the wards is against hospital regulations:

> On each of the four following raids, Grace and Virginia had done splendid service in quieting and entertaining the men. Everyone in the hospital knew of it, and the superintendent had been to see the major about the matter, demanding that both young women be dismissed, for the sake of the discipline of the institution. The major said that, on the face of things, there could be no doubt that they had violated direct orders, but that on the other side, both women were well entitled to honorable mention in reports.... Grace determined to do her duty as she saw it, and meet the consequences afterwards [Flower, *Red Cross* 86].

This is the second instance in which Grace is kept on in her position *in spite of the fact* that she has violated military discipline and direct orders. The superintendent, a woman, is more outraged over Grace's behavior than Major Clowes, who clearly puts the morale of the men above rules and regulations, particularly during a bombing raid. While this appears unrealistic, an attitude that might have been invented for the sake of fiction, it was in fact not uncommon for military commanders to overlook or conveniently ignore women on the battlefield. For example, when YMCA canteeners followed a particular regiment to battle in violation of military orders, the commanders often let them stay. Military men in the field had to weigh the happiness and comfort of their troops against the danger of the women being at the front; more often than not, troop morale won the day. Grace and Virginia are allowed to stay with the men not only during a normal day at the hospital, but also in a battlefield situation. Giving recovering soldiers peace of mind is of primary importance.

Comforting troops, of course, is not Grace's only talent. As it turns out, she also has a knack for solving military intelligence mysteries. Grace gets caught up in a signaling mystery during her tenure at Hospital Number Three. One night when Grace is up late, she notices a green light shining from the chateau roof. A short time after, on a different night, she sees a red light. Then a report of a green and white light together is circulated. Grace begins to suspect that the lights are signals to the Germans, letting the enemy planes know when to bomb the hospital. The green light means a raid on the hospital, and the red light stops the raid. Grace also eventually realizes that the green and white lights together target her specifically, for there are two separate occasions when the bombs are aimed at her tent, and the second time the tent is hit and demolished. Grace's only suspect is Sergeant Binet, a hospital sergeant for the French patients. Grace recognizes his voice but cannot place his face, although he seems simultaneously curious about and hostile to Grace. Binet talks to Virgina Coates about Grace several times: "The sergeant asked many questions about Grace, inquiring particularly if she had said anything about him, or asked questions regarding him.... He suggested mildly that Mrs. [Grace] Gray was soon to be sent away..." (Flower, *Red Cross* 95). Virgina, of course, tells Grace about the sergeant's curiosity, and Grace continues to be plagued by the feeling that she should recognize him.

Grace decides to test her theory about the lights on the roof, and one night she climbs up to the hospital roof with a red lantern, hoping to stop an oncoming raid. She is caught by Sergeant Binet and Corporal Stevenson and taken to Major Clowes for a hearing. During this hearing, Grace realizes that Sergeant Binet is André, the famous enemy spy from her first case, the third man who worked with the two enemy spies she helped to capture. She never saw his face in that investigation, only overheard him speaking, and he escaped the authorities. Grace uncovers his identity during the hearing and clears herself in the process; she, along with Corporal Stevenson and Major Clowes, finds incriminating evidence in "Binet's" quarters. André is arrested by Corporal Stevenson, who is actually from the Intelligence Bureau. All of this is done without a great deal of physical work and little violence of any kind. Grace simply observes and puts together the facts as one might put together puzzle pieces. As a result of this case, not only does Grace win accolades in army intelligence reports, but she is given her much-desired commission as an ambulance driver.

Grace's mental and observational powers also come in handy in another volume, *Grace Harlowe with the American Army on the Rhine*. First, Grace observes carrier pigeons that are being flown toward enemy lines. Then an ammunition dump is blown up in the village where she is staying, and the explosion ruins the canteen building where Grace has been working. Next, a fire breaks out in one of the army barracks. Grace becomes suspicious of Dr. Klein, the German in whose house she is staying (along with several other war workers) while the army occupies the village. Once she confides her suspicions to Captain Boucher, another member of the Intelligence Department, she is given official status as an intelligence operative and reports directly to Boucher (Flower, *On the Rhine* 193–94).

The characterization of Dr. Klein in this story is, as one might expect from war propaganda, prejudiced and hostile, even xenophobic. When Grace first learns about the doctor, her friend Elfreda tells Grace that Klein is not a typical German, that he in fact disagrees with his country's position on the war. Grace dismisses the possibility out of hand:

> "... Dr. Klein, a scientific, studious-appearing fellow, and apparently very friendly to Americans. He says the Germans have been in the wrong in this war and—"
>
> "I should be suspicious of that man, Elfreda. Either he is not a German or else he isn't telling the truth...." [Flower, *On the Rhine* 177].

Klein's assistance to the Americans makes him untrustworthy in Grace's mind because, for her, all Germans are rude, antagonistic, and arrogant. In the world Grace inhabits, it is not possible for a German to legitimately disagree with Germany's participation in the war. Even Klein's impeccable manners offend Grace: "He was altogether too smooth, too polite and courteous for a Hun..." (Flower *On the Rhine* 189). This is one case where the narrative divorces itself from reality; like Ruth's prejudice against Mexicans, Grace's views reflect American prejudice and aggression against the Central Powers in general and Germans in particular, rather than attempting to diminish hostilities between the warring countries. There were in fact plenty of women who worked to attain some kind of peaceful settlement between the Allied and Central Powers, but those women were also frequently branded as unpatriotic at best, treasonous at worst. Since Grace is always characterized as patriotic and loyal (one of her nicknames is Loyalheart), her feelings and opinions are presented as the one "true" perspective on the war. In addition, Grace's intuition and intelligence rarely lead her wrong on a case, and they do not fail her in this instance, either. Dr. Klein turns out to be the central villain in a German spy ring.[3]

Six. Running the Gamut and the Gauntlet

Grace repeatedly hears voices coming from Klein's cellar through the floor of her room. For three nights running she catches bits of conversation between Klein and others, and she becomes determined to listen more closely. She borrows an auger from Captain Boucher and bores a small hole through the floor of her room. By listening through the hole, without the interference of the floorboard, she gathers a good deal of information on a group of German spies who are planning to blow up the town's second ammunition dump and burn the army barracks to the ground, thereby killing many members of the U.S. Army and driving the rest out. Dr. Klein, whose real name is Carl Schuster, and his partner Rosa von Blum are the coordinators of the scheme. Grace discreetly notifies Captain Boucher of the plot she has discovered, and Boucher meets her in her own room to hear for himself. After Boucher spends an evening listening in to Klein's telephone conversations in the cellar, his men capture both the doctor and his accomplice and prevent the destruction of the entire village (Flower, *On the Rhine* 246–255). Captain Boucher commends Grace for her intelligence, resourcefulness, and discretion, giving her all of the credit for the successful arrests.

In her many types of work for the war effort, Grace manages to cross most of the gender boundary lines that are present in the armed forces and on the battlefield. Grace experiences every part of war, doing work that is both "masculine" and "feminine." She starts out as a Red Cross worker, works her way up to becoming an ambulance driver at the front, does canteen work, and is made a member of the U.S. Intelligence Department, a field that is almost completely male-dominated. She is absolutely determined to do what she perceives to be right and just, even when it goes against the orders of those ranked higher than she. She takes her concerns to her superiors no matter whether they are male or female, and if their answers or actions do not satisfy her, she takes matters into her own hands until the problem resolves itself. In the end, she wins approval for her actions through what she has accomplished. She holds nothing back, and the men in the books, from majors to privates, openly admire her integrity and intelligence.

One of the most interesting passages in *Grace Harlowe with the Red Cross in France* is one where Grace questions her independent spirit and wonders whether it is an appropriate female trait, telling her friend Elfreda that she wonders "if [she hasn't] too much self-reliance, if such a trait is unwomanly."

> "Unwomanly!" exclaim[s] Elfreda. "That would be impossible. If all the women I know possessed your sweet womanliness, your gentle heart and manner, they surely would grace their little worlds. However, so long as you please Tom and are true to yourself you will be all that any man or woman could desire" [227–28].

In two instances in the last sentence, it is the men who are put first. Does Elfreda's comment imply that Grace should please Tom *before* she is true to herself? By saying that Grace will be all that any *man or woman* could desire, in that order, the author seems to suggest that it is most important to please the men; however, Grace's actions throughout the books suggest otherwise. She does what she believes to be right and deals with the consequences afterward. Ultimately, this course of action wins her commendation, which is noteworthy for two reasons. One, it shows instances where what is right takes precedence over someone's authority and wins the day. Two, this is a case where both male and female authority is defied by a female, and in the end, that female is rewarded for her actions. Grace is "all that any man or woman could desire" *because* she follows her heart and her instincts, because she stands up for what is right. Neither men nor women find her wanting; Grace's character and courage speak for themselves.

As a wartime heroine, Grace proves herself to be skilled on all fronts and in all situations. She provides comfort to the soldiers, utilizes her driving skills near the battle lines, and is a highly adept intelligence operator. The one area she does not venture into is actual armed confrontation; Grace's weapons are those of mental intelligence, not physical force. In the *Khaki Girls* series, the final boundary that separates male soldiers and women workers is crossed. Valerie Ward and Joan Mason are two wartime heroines who combine all the positive qualities of the Beautiful Charmer, the Outdoors Pal, and the New England Woman with a firm determination to defend themselves and their country. Their intellects and driving skills serve them well, they earn the respect of their female and male peers and superiors, they cross into and through the battle lines of the trenches, and they are willing to shoot.

The Khaki Girls: Leveling the Battlefield

Published in four volumes between 1918 and 1920, the *Khaki Girls* series bridges the final gap between the young women working at the front lines and the young men on the battlefield. Valerie Ward and Joan Mason begin their war work in *The Khaki Girls of the Motor Corps* by joining the Liberty Motor Corps and serving as drivers in the United States. The two girls become fast friends, and both of them excel in ambulance driving and Secret Service work, ultimately helping to round up a group of Central Powers spies known as the Bund.

Whether the Liberty Motor Corps was modeled after an actual woman's unit of drivers is difficult to determine. I have found no historical record of a female motor corps under that name or any other, but once again, proper records are limited. If the Liberty Motor Corps was completely made up for story purposes, the fact still remains that American women were serving as drivers in many places in and around the front. Valerie and Joan go through a number of obstacles to both join the Motor Corps and attain their coveted positions overseas.

Surprisingly, the biggest initial obstacle for Joan is her age. When the two girls meet in the first volume, Valerie is twenty-two, almost twenty-three when the story begins, but Joan is only nineteen, technically too young to enlist in any kind of motor work, since the minimum age requirement given in the story is twenty-three. Joan's father, Mr. Mason, is adamantly opposed to Joan going to France; he is willing for her to do war work in the States, but he is afraid of what she would encounter if she went overseas. Despite all of his objections, however, he makes a deal with Joan that if she can prove she is capable enough to do overseas work, he will let her go. The difficulty becomes finding war work she can do that will prove both her driving skills and her resourcefulness.

Enter Valerie Ward. Valerie proves to be the human catalyst who sets all of Joan's dreams into motion. The two girls meet at an auto show, where they are both exclaiming over the latest ambulance model. Valerie also wishes to join the Motor Corps, and unlike Joan, she does not have an overprotective father but an encouraging older brother as her guardian: "'He's one of the few men who look at things from the right angle. He says it's spirit, not sex that counts. Isn't that bully in him?'" (Brooks, *Motor Corps* 44).

Valerie and Joan's conversation is one of the most interesting in the first volume, because it deliberately juxtaposes parents with other family members and finds parents wanting in their judgment of their daughters' ambitions. While Valerie's brother commends her desire to go to France, Joan points out the double standard inherent in her father's attitude: "'If I were his son instead of his daughter he'd be the first to urge me to enlist in the Army or Aviation Corps or whatever branch of the service appealed to me.... He thinks this is just a whim on my part; that I only want the glory of doing something unusual in the war for a girl'" (Brooks, *Motor Corps* 46). If Joan were a boy, her patriotism and eagerness to serve would be praised; since she is girl, those same emotions are seen as an exercise in vanity or self-aggrandizement. Valerie points out that her parents would have reacted the same way: "'If my father and mother were alive today it would be the same with them'" (Brooks, *Motor Corps* 46). Parents are hindrances rather than enablers, and the girls pledge to help each other rather than looking to others. Valerie's brother becomes the exception that proves the rule; he is one of the "few," like Secretary Daniels and General Pershing, who are willing to allow women into the war and praise them for their service.

Valerie and Joan find another woman ally in Captain Katherine Bartram, head of the Liberty Motor Corps. Although she questions the girls thoroughly about their motor and repair skills, she is willing to help them speed up the process of joining the Corps. As Valerie and Joan both have chauffeur and mechanic's licenses from the state, Captain Bartram arranges for them to take an exam at a nearby automobile school without actually attending the classes. Valerie and Joan pass their tests with flying colors, and undergo a physical exam as well as an Oath of Allegiance at the local federal office.

Once they are officially part of the Motor Corps, Captain Bartram tells Valerie and Joan that they will frequently be doing work for the Department of Justice as drivers—and reinforces prejudice against the Germans at the same time:

> Thanks to German propaganda, Truth has had a hard pull to struggle free of the network of lies that held it down. Hundreds of German spies and sympathizers with the Fatherland are still doing their bit for the Kaiser.... In the work which you will frequently be asked to do for the Department of Justice you will be brought into contact with enemy aliens at least. As to spies — who can say? They are likely to crop up quite unexpectedly [Brooks, *Motor Corps* 92–93].

Unlike Grace Harlowe, Valerie and Joan do not have to earn their way into intelligence work or prove their fitness for it. By virtue of their position as drivers, they are automatically enlisted as secret-keepers; they must keep their eyes and ears open and their mouths closed if they hope to make good in the Corps. Like Grace and Ruth Fielding, however, the girls and Captain Bartram share the automatic suspicion and condemnation of the Germans. Patriotic fervor does not allow for shades of gray; these heroines must know who their enemies are.

Knowing one's enemies is sometimes easier than fighting one's friends, however. Joan has a hard struggle to convince her father that she can satisfactorily drive and perform war work. She does not tell him that she has joined the Motor Corps until it is already *a fait accompli*, fearing his disapproval or being denied permission. Having passed all of her tests and her oath and been formally inducted into the Corps, Joan tells her father at dinner. Mr. Mason is curt to her, but does not try to argue with her, and it is then that he realizes how determined she is:

> It was too late now to oppose her. It had suddenly dawned upon him that he did not wish to do so. Something far deeper than a girlish whim had actuated her plea to go to France as an ambulance driver. His daughter was a true patriot. She was not of the stay-at-home order. She was one to dare all for the sake of a prin-

Six. Running the Gamut and the Gauntlet 193

ciple. She was of the sort that was needed over there [Brooks, *Motor Corps* 99–100].

Mr. Mason's fears were surely shared by many parents who watched their daughters go off to perform war service, and the *Khaki Girls* series is perhaps the only one where those fears are actually mentioned and discussed. Most series heroines who perform war work are slightly older than Joan; Grace Harlowe and Ruth Fielding are both through college and have careers of their own before war breaks out, and while the Outdoor Girls do not attend college, they are also well out of high school when the war starts. Joan is an anomaly, and she becomes the conduit for allowing parental fears to be expressed and overcome. Mr. Mason grows to be very proud of his daughter and her abilities, recognizing that she is just as capable of contributing to the war as any man.

Joan and Valerie's skills as war workers are proven through several incidents later in the book. In the first, Captain Bartram asks Joan to take an article to the local newspaper office for her, an update on the activities of the Corps. As Joan enters the office building, she is almost run down by a man hurrying away. Looking around after he has left, Joan spots a bundle behind the door and deduces that it must have been placed there by the mysterious man. Suspecting foul play, she alerts one of the office workers, who goes to fetch some of the editors. They discover the package is a bomb, and in the confusion, Joan delivers her note to the city editor and slips out, hoping to remain unnoticed (Brooks, *Motor Corps* 199–125).

Of course, Joan is tracked down by the determined reporters, and after she tells them her version of events, she explains the entire incident to Captain Bartram, including her suspicions about the man who ran her down. The Captain advises her to make a report at the Department of Justice, which she does. When Joan is later taken to identify a potential subject, however, she firmly asserts that they have the wrong person. Though the suspect and the man she saw look alike, they had different eye colors and slightly different features. The man, whose name is Hoffman, is released because they have nothing to hold him on, and the next day, an explosion occurs at the local railroad yard.

The agents at the Department of Justice suspect Hoffman's involvement, but he has disappeared. However, the entire situation comes to a head a few nights later, when Valerie and Joan are returning home from a play. A black touring car follows them from the theater, and the two men inside hold up the girls. It turns out there are two Hoffmans, brothers, who planned and carried out the bombings at the church and railroad yard, and attempted the bombing at the newspaper office. They follow Joan and Valerie intending to get rid of them, but the girls surprise them with their fearlessness — and their willingness to use firearms.

Women handling firearms was a controversial subject during the war, and the *Khaki Girls* books attempt to address that in several ways. There were many women in the United States who deliberately enrolled in military preparedness and shooting courses, seeing it as their right to arm and defend themselves as citizens:

> At rifle ranges and armories around the country in the war years women joined existing rifle clubs and formed their own rifle and gun organizations in what contemporaries considered dramatic numbers. Thousands joined women's paramilitary organizations designed to promote women's defense and military skills. Many of these women were motivated by a belief in the importance of women's equal rights and the need for equal opportunities with men. Their activities were part of the negotiation for women's full citizenship rights in the context of the suffrage campaign. They hoped to become an official part of the citizens' preparedness army or the military itself and in so doing would perform the citizen's obligation to defend the state. For some women, claiming the right of preparedness was also an assertion of their right to defend themselves against male violence, whether in the context of war or in a broader definition of "home defense" against domestic violence or other assault [Jensen 40–41].

Women who learned to shoot, whether at home or in service to the military, saw it as part of their rights and duty as citizens to wield the same weapons as their male contemporaries, in defense of themselves and their country. Valerie and Joan share this same perspective; when they first join the Motor Corps, they eagerly take on the task of learning to use a revolver. Captain Bartram tells the girls that they must learn to shoot in case they go to France, as all of the ambulance drivers carry revolvers. She emphasizes that shooting may be the difference between life and a miserable, tortuous death: "I sincerely trust that you will never have to defend yourself in that way.... But if you ever have it to do be sure and shoot straight. You can expect no mercy from fiends who make war on women and children." Joan relishes the chance to learn to shoot, and foreshadows a later encounter with the Germans when she says, "If any hateful Boches ever attack an ambulance I'm driving, I'll certainly know how to shoot sharp" (Brooks, *Motor Corps* 104). Captain Bartram and Joan categorize all Germans as aggressive males who will not hesitate to harm, perhaps even rape and kill, a woman ambulance driver. Basing their assessment on the attacks on women and children in Belgium, Captain Bartram and Joan see shooting as *both* necessary self-protection and part of their rights as American citizens. Since they are in the unique position of being women who serve the U.S. Army and the Intelligence Bureau, the ability to shoot is a necessity *and* an obligation.

Six. Running the Gamut and the Gauntlet 195

The first test of Valerie and Joan's newly acquired shooting skills comes in their final confrontation with the Hoffman brothers. When the brothers chase the girls in their touring car and attempt to capture them, Valerie fearlessly shoots one of their would-be captors in the thigh, while Joan keeps the other brother at a standstill with her own revolver. In this way, the bombers are captured, with the girls receiving accolades for their part in capturing the spies.

Nor is their encounter with the bombers the last time they are forced to defend themselves with firearms. In *The Khaki Girls Behind the Lines*, the two girls are permitted to join the "Trusty Twenty" ambulance corps, made up of girls from the fictional Windsor College. There is no record of an ambulance corps made up entirely of female ambulance drivers, so it was probably a useful adaptation for the book. The vacancies in the "Trusty Twenty" are due to one girl being killed and another being injured and sent home. Due to their previous experience and exceptional work back home, the Khaki Girls are sent to France to fill those places.

Over the course of their work in the French village, the girls have their hands full. Joan grows suspicious of a girl known as the "Crossroads Princess," a member of the English Auxiliary Army Corps who directs traffic between the village and the barracks. When Joan's ambulance gets a flat after a detail to the trenches, she stops a passing government limousine. The passenger refuses to allow her chauffeur to help, but Joan recognizes the woman as the "Princess." Later, she hears a story from Marcelle, the ambulance corps' cook and maid, that connects the Princess to a local wealthy family. The Princess had been staying with the wealthy woman and her children while the husband was off fighting. While the Princess was there, the house was raided and the family killed by the Germans. Everything of value was taken, including a hidden casket of jewels, and the house burned down. Marcelle suspects that the Princess is the one who told the Germans the location of the casket, but no one could prove that she had anything to do with the actions of the Germans.

Finally, on her way back to the corps barracks one night, Joan is waylaid for help by a woman covered in a shawl. The woman wishes Joan to take her aunt, who has a broken arm, to the hospital. Joan, however, is suspicious of the woman's behavior, and when the woman climbs into Joan's ambulance, Joan puts on extra speed and attempts to drive on, bringing the woman with her. The woman begins to strike Joan, attempting to take control of the ambulance herself. In the ensuing struggle she falls out of the ambulance and is knocked unconscious. Joan retrieves her, and it is then that she learns that the mysterious woman in the shawl is in fact the Crossroads Princess. She decides to take her back to the barracks. Before she can do so, however, a man drives up to her ambulance and jumps in, trying to capture her. Joan pulls her revolver from its holster and shoots him through the shoulder, incapacitating him and allowing her to bring him to the hospital for both treatment and arrest. Eventually, it is discovered that the "Princess" is a German noblewoman and highly placed spy, and that the man is her cousin. While he is captured and imprisoned, thanks to Joan and her quick shooting, the "Princess" escapes, evading the Khaki Girls and the authorities.

As indicated in *The Khaki Girls of the Motor Corps* (and true to Joan's prediction in that volume), the Khaki Girls and their peers in the "Trusty Twenty" carry revolvers as a matter of course and use them when necessary. Joan ends up shooting a man who is trying to harm her, an action that is equal in every way with those of the men on the battlefield. Had Joan not been capable of using the weapon she carried, she might very well have lost her life or been taken prisoner indefinitely. One of the other girls in the ambulance corps, Georgia Stevens, recounts to Valerie and Joan a time when she got lost and ran into a German patrol. One of the men climbed up into the ambulance to try to capture her, and she shot and killed him in order to get away. She completely defends her right to do so, while admitting she did not like having to do it: "'It was either his life or a prison camp for me.... I was glad I killed him, but sorry I had to do it. It doesn't *seem* just right for women to kill, even in self-defense. It *is* right, though'" (E. Brooks, *Behind the Lines* 132–133). The use of firearms becomes not only a measure of women's competence on the battlefield, but a measure of their equality with men and their rights as citizens of the U.S. If American boys can shoot on the battlefield in defense of themselves and their country, then American girls can and will, too.

In the next volume of the series, *The Khaki Girls at Windsor Barracks*, Valerie and Joan are both wounded while they are trying to get information to the front. A wounded soldier they pick up has important information for the Allies about the next attack, and he gives the information to Valerie and Joan, trusting them to meet the courier. The pair are informed by the courier, who is also hurt, that the advance patrol is missing. He tells them where to take the information, and they continue on. When they reach the woods, the two girls are hit by shrapnel from the stray shell of an enemy plane. It wounds Joan's shoulder and Valerie's ankle, but they find a member of the advance patrol who is able to signal an Allied plane and send the message to the front, as well as get help for the three of them.

Valerie and Joan's experiences temporarily put them on a completely equal footing with the men in the war zone. They are forced to shoot and wound or kill a man in order to protect themselves. They have no one else around to protect them, male or female, and they must rely on their own wits and resources in order to survive. In addition, when they are wounded, it is just as any soldier at the front might have been, with a shell from an enemy plane. They are cited for saving the Allied offensive with the coded message they carried. They are completely independent, free of any sort of constraint, and admired for their own work and merits.

It is worth noticing, too, that Valerie and Joan have no men in their own lives to influence them. The only mentions of men are references to the girls' brother and father, respectively, and Every Soldier, who the girls work for but are not attached to in any romantic sense. If one examines the range of series in this chapter, from conservative to liberal, one can see the presence of significant others declining more and more. The four soldiers who belong to the Outdoor Girls are present in every book, and the girls tend to focus on what is happening to their soldiers, rather than what is happening to them. This is also somewhat true of the *Ruth Fielding* books, although to a lesser degree. Tom is present in each volume, but Ruth does not center her life around him. Her life is centered on her work, and it is only when Tom needs her, and/or when he is in life-threatening danger, that the focus shifts to him.

The *Grace Harlowe* series goes a step farther. Grace's significant other becomes a ghost figure. She is married, and it is acknowledged that her husband, Tom Gray, is in the army, but in the novels I have examined, he does not make any sort of appearance. He is only mentioned occasionally, when Grace receives correspondence from him or happens to encounter someone who has seen or heard news of him. The final step, once again, is taken by the *Khaki Girls* series. Valerie and Joan are not attached to any men at the outset of the book, aside from their relatives, and they make a point of not becoming attached to any, since it is against the regulations of their work to become involved with soldiers. Only in the last book, *The Khaki Girls in Victory*, which shows the girls returning home in the aftermath of the war, are there suggestions that the girls might be willing to entertain the idea of romance, now that their war work is drawing to a close. Their work for the Allied Cause is their first priority, and that work requires freedom from the male ties that formerly restrained them.

This type of independence was celebrated and enjoyed by women who were working in the war and was later lamented when the war ended. It was not the end of the war women workers were sorry for, but the end of the freedom that the war had brought to them. Having acted under the assumption of that freedom for so long, the lack of it made it difficult for some women to adjust back to the old pattern when they came home. In May 1919, novelist Mary Lee wrote in a letter: "I wish something would *happen*. This is the last little gasp of war, and it *is* fun if you are right up where things are happening. I suppose the Germans will sign peace tomorrow and life will start again on the dull slothfulness of another era of peace and prosperity." Journalist Elizabeth Shepley Sergeant, in her published journal about her two years in a hospital during the end of the war, summed up the feelings of the women war workers: "The almost fourth-dimensional sense of power and service which sustained such women is gone. They are physically and mentally drained to the dregs; yet they don't dare to stop and rest; that means reflection" (qtd. in Schneider and Schneider, *Into the Breach* 279).

Sadness over the loss of their work and independence is not felt nearly as deeply by the heroines of girls' fiction. When the Outdoor Girls are sent home for a furlough, Amy and Mollie do express their boredom and their wish to be back at Camp Liberty doing their work at the Hostess House. Before they are able to return, though, the house is burned in a fire, and a few months later the war is over. Ruth Fielding, too, is sent home shortly before the end of the war, having been wounded. She expresses sincere regret at leaving her work, but a letter from home tells her that she is also needed there, to help nurse the elderly housekeeper who is almost like a mother to her. The Khaki Girls are called home once the armistice is signed, although there are hints that, if their series had been allowed to continue, they would not have given up their war work so easily. The phantom title given at the end of *The Khaki Girls in Victory* is *The Kahaki Girls in Camp; Or Volunteers in the Land Army*. The intent clearly was to have the girls working with the Women's Land Army at home, so that their participation in war work might continue even after the armistice. So the girl workers, for one reason or another, are called back to their regular lives, and while they express some regret, they do not seem discontent. They simply turn to the next task at hand, find other work to do, and are grateful when the war finally ends and their men come home.

In reality, not all of the women workers went back to domestic life, although a good number of them did. The women of the U.S. Army were all released by July 1919, and the female Marines were all disenrolled by 1922. The physical therapists were given the choice of resigning or being assigned to an army hospital in the States. (Gavin 16, 35, 116). The female factory and clerical workers on the homefront had an experience that would be reenacted in larger numbers after WWII. Their jobs were either phased out until they did not exist or given back to the men who came home (Schneider and Schneider, *Progressive Era* 228). However, a few women here and there managed to stay on as civilian employees of the government or continued their careers as physicians and nurses. The suffragists saw their highest ambition realized when American women were given the vote in 1920.

In a similar fashion, the heroines of girls series' fiction were allowed to have the new and exciting experiences that the war made possible, and those experiences encouraged a younger generation of women to make their way into the public realm. Granted, the fictitious adventures were somewhat narrow in scope, for the books did not cover half of the ways that women actually participated in the war. Nevertheless, the books brought women's work in the war to the forefront and showed what an important contribution women could make in the public sphere if they were given the chance. For the short time that the United States participated in the Great War, a substantial number of American women were on an equal footing with men and earned the respect of the soldiers, the government, and the world at large through their service: "In area after area, risk-taking women had gained more control and more confidence. They had moved from women who shouldn't to women who could" (Schneider and Schneider, *Progressive Era* 246). This new confidence and control were communicated to wartime schoolgirls through fiction, further encouraging them to pursue work and recognition in the public realm. The cultural inheritance of these girl readers would become evident in the next decade, when they would grow up to become the ambitious and assertive flappers of the 1920s.

Notes

1. The Outdoor Girls are not the "College Girls" that Shirley Marchalonis details so clearly in *College Girls: A Century in Fiction*. Even here, the Outdoor Girls stay closer to the conservative end of the spectrum and do not pursue higher education.

2. Without the entire set of *Grace Harlowe* war volumes at my disposal, I do not know if Grace made it to Europe before the official military order that banned military relatives from going overseas. Despite inquiries with the National Archives and the Military History Institute at the U.S. Army War College, I have been unable to locate the original order issued by the War Department. However, historians' accounts and contemporary documents indicate that it was issued in July or August of 1917 and was later amended in August of 1918 to allow the service of women with brothers in the military. See Schneider and Schneider, *Into the Breach* pages 124–127, and the contemporary wartime references included in footnotes 21–23 and 29. Mrs. Teddy Roosevelt Jr. is one example of a woman who made it overseas before the order took effect; she set sail for France three weeks before it was issued, and she set up the first YMCA canteen in Paris during the summer of 1917. Her husband was the commander of the First Battalion, Twenty-Sixth Infantry, First Division of the AEF (Gavin 130–131).

3. Series heroines have a penchant for always picking out the villain, and they are rarely, if ever, sympathetic to that villain and his motives. Grace, like both her contemporaries and her successor Nancy Drew, has this same talent and the same lack of sympathy. On the other hand, I felt that this situation was more complex than a typical series mystery. Were the U.S. not at war, Grace would be predisposed to be friendly to Dr. Klein. He is Western European, educated, white, and intelligent, exactly the kind of foreigner that Americans emulate and admire. In wartime, however, Klein is a citizen of an enemy country, and so everything about him becomes suspect. Conscientious objection or pacifism is not tolerated, even in the States, and genuine political consciousness in an enemy is completely dismissed as a possibility in the text. Grace might have reacted to a U.S. pacifist with the same hostility, but she probably would not have suspected that person of being a spy.

SEVEN

Taking Advantage of New Markets
Ruth Fielding as a Motion Picture Screenwriter, Producer, and Executive

Once both fictional and actual American women returned home from the war, there was more than a little adjusting to be done. While women war workers struggled to fit back into domestic life, and soldiers returned from the front with both internal and external scars and injuries, most Americans celebrated the end of the war and looked for ways to forget its horrors as quickly as possible. An economic upswing and renewed emphasis on leisure time and consumption aided the rapid arrival of the Roaring Twenties, the advent of the flapper, and the new carefree sexual attitudes demonstrated by writers like novelist F. Scott Fitzgerald and Lois "Lipstick" Long of *The New Yorker* (Zeitz 39–70; 87–103). Ready-to-wear fashions for women assisted them in looking like Parisian models, motor cars only increased in popularity, and popular culture emphasized youth, vitality, and fun.

The motion picture was perhaps the one commodity and leisure attraction that most embodied the glamour and playfulness of the twenties. Hollywood had perfected its silent film formula before the war, making stars out of Mary Pickford, Norma and Constance Talmadge, Lillian and Dorothy Gish, Theda Bara, Gloria Swanson, Greta Garbo, and Marion Davies, among others. The young industry of silent film had also fostered the talents of many female screenwriters (known then as "scenario writers") and directors, many of whom had long and distinguished careers in motion pictures. Frances Marion began her scenario writing during the silent era and became one of the most famous and highest paid screenwriters in filmmaking. The new entertainment of film, in other words, opened up possibilities for women to create careers. Motion pictures were a highly profitable business that made a great deal of money. Women were already excelling in that field as actresses, screenwriters, and directors before the war, and many more young women dreamed of fame, success, and Hollywood stardom.

No fictional heroine rides out the turbulent transition from wartime to peacetime with more determination and success than Ruth Fielding. The *Ruth Fielding* series began in 1913 and was already up to its twelfth volume by the time the United States declared war with Germany. Ruth is perhaps the earliest example of a series heroine who becomes a professional woman, participating and succeeding fully within a capitalist market dominated by men. Although many series heroines both before and after Ruth attend college, not many of them graduate to become full-time professionals producing marketable goods. Ruth takes advantage of the expanding business of motion pictures and the new culture of leisurely consumption in order to make a career for herself. Unlike most other series heroines, she does not stay solely in the role of discerning consumer; she also plays an active role in producing items to be consumed by others.

The Beginning of a New Profession

Ruth is perfectly poised to take advantage of the opportunities presented by film: she attends a boarding school called Briarwood Hall and completes the college preparatory curriculum there, graduating with her close friend Helen Cameron. She then goes to Ardmore College and works for the Alectrion Film Corporation both before graduation and after. The war interrupts Ruth's rising career, but she resumes film work when she returns from France (albeit with some difficulty) and eventually forms a production company of her own. Through her higher education and several fortuitous occurrences, Ruth becomes a major player in movie production.

It is while at Briarwood that Ruth has her first encounter with motion pictures. Ruth and Helen, along with Helen's brother Tom, happen upon a film crew when they witness the company's lead actress falling from a tree and into the river. Tom rescues her from the current, and Ruth takes her home to get dry clothes and rest. Ruth confesses to the actress, Hazel Gray, that she would like to try writing a film scenario, but does not know how to get it read or receive criticism on it. Hazel promises to give the scenario to the head of her film company, a Mr. Hammond. As luck would have it, Mr. Hammond comes himself to collect Miss Gray and is interested in filming a picture at Ruth's home, the Red Mill. The Red Mill is old and surrounded by farmland,

Seven. Taking Advantage of New Markets

very scenic and pretty, and the setting catches Mr. Hammond's eye. He promises to read Ruth's scenario if she attempts to write one, and he gives her an address to send the manuscript to. Ruth writes her first scenario in the beginning of her senior year at Briarwood, a little "allegorical comedy" called "Curiosity" (Emerson, *Moving Pictures* 61).

Before Ruth knows the fate of her scenario, however, a calamity befalls Briarwood Hall. The West Dormitory where Ruth and her friends live is burned to the ground and is uninsured. While the school's headmistress, Mrs. Tellingham, is trying to come up with a plan to raise funds for a new dorm, Ruth finds out about the acceptance of her scenario. Mr. Hammond has written to her and paid her for the one-reel scenario.[1] Ruth realizes, in that moment, that she could write a screenplay involving Briarwood Hall, one that would feature the campus and students and raise money to replace the burned building. Ruth contacts Mr. Hammond, and he is enthusiastic about the idea, promptly coming to Briarwood to make arrangements with the headmistress. Mrs. Tellingham will receive a percentage of the picture's profits for the dormitory fund (Emerson, *Moving Pictures* 124). Ruth is also determined to get as many of the girls as possible involved in the film, so they will all feel they have contributed something to the new dorm. Mr. Hammond asks Ruth to act in the picture, as the best friend of the heroine, and it is discovered that Ruth has a talent for screen acting as well as writing.

The Briarwood girls, eager to help in any way possible, even take a hand in the advertising of the picture — yet another indication that Stratemeyer's heroines were as aware of consumer culture as he was. In order to promote the film and hopefully raise more money for the dormitory, the girls come up with a poster and caption for the film, "Heart of a Schoolgirl," that is used in all the local towns in order to attract viewers. The poster reads, "The Briarwood Girl with Her Best Foot Forward" (Emerson, *Moving Pictures* 189). Ruth and her friends find out at their graduation that the film brought in a good amount of the funding needed for the new dormitory.

Even more importantly, Ruth receives a letter from Mr. Hammond with a check, asking her to send him any more writing that she might do for the screen. Due to the success of "Curiosity" and "Heart of a Schoolgirl," he would like first consideration of any of her screenplays. Ruth thus forms a professional connection that will be of increasing importance in her career (Emerson, *Moving Pictures* 198).

After Briarwood, Ruth and Helen continue their education at Ardmore College. Ruth, in the summer before her first year, writes the scenario for Mr. Hammond that will be shot at the Red Mill. By the following summer, Ruth completes a picture scenario called "The Forty-Niners" and travels out West with Mr. Hammond and his film company for the shooting. The film tells the story of the California Gold Rush. This film is also when Ruth begins investing in motion pictures — she has an interest in the product and outcome rather than receiving advance payment for her writing:

> Instead of being paid outright for her work as the writer of the scenario, some of her own money was to be invested in the picture. Having taken up the making of motion pictures seriously and hoping to make it her livlihood [sic] after graduating from college, Ruth wished her money as well as her brains to work for her.
>
> Nor was the president of the Alectrion Film Corporation [Mr. Hammond] doing an unprecedented thing in making this arrangement. In this way the shrewd capitalists behind the great film-making companies have obtained the best work from chief directors, the most brilliant screen stars, and the more successful scenario writers. To give those who show special talent in the chief departments of the motion picture industry a financial interest in the work, has proved gainful to all concerned [Emerson, *In the Saddle* 7].

It is also revealed, in *Ruth Fielding in the Red Cross*, that Ruth has bought stock in the Alectrion Film Corporation (Emerson 40). Someone in Stratemeyer's company clearly knew enough about motion pictures to be able to provide commentary about investment practices. Silent film stars and writers routinely invested money in their pictures, including Mary Pickford, Douglas Fairbanks, and Charlie Chaplin. Francis Marion also invested a considerable amount of her own earnings in the pictures she wrote and helped to produce and direct. It was not at all unusual for those involved in motion pictures to invest in them for the profits. Marion had plenty of money to invest; in 1915, she landed a contract for ten thousand four hundred dollars a year at World Films in New York, becoming their head scenario writer and the highest-paid writer in the business. By 1917, she had moved to the Famous Players Lasky studio with Mary Pickford and was making fifty thousand dollars a year (Beauchamp 51–70). She also invested fifty thousand dollars in a biographical film of Abraham Lincoln, agreeing to write the scenario for its producers, brothers Al and Ray Rockett, for a share of the future profits. While *The Dramatic Life of Abraham Lincoln* did not make a great deal of money, it won awards and much critical praise, and both the Rocketts and Marion were pleased (Beauchamp 143–44 and 158–59). Mary Pickford's 1916 contract with Famous Players created a production company solely for her films, the Pickford Film Corporation, and stipulated that Mary took home half a million dollars a year or fifty percent of the profits from her pictures, whichever was larger (Whitfield 144–145). Investing in one's own films was good business; having a share of the profits was often far more lucrative than being given a studio salary.

The other unusual aspect of the early motion picture industry was the many roles played by each individual involved in a picture. Actors routinely had a hand in staging and scene development, if not outright production. Mary Pickford was the ultimate example of this; the same contract with the Famous Players studio that gave her such a large profit share and her own production company also gave her the authority to choose her own directors, final approval of a film's supporting cast and advertising campaign, and one of three votes for the final cut of a film (Whitfield 144–145). Writers often helped with producing, directing, or acting. Frances Marion had both a short acting career in the silents and occasionally a stint as a director or assistant director, even though her primary earnings and accolades were through writing. Her initial contract at Bosworth Inc., signed in 1914, was as an actress, under the tutelage of the director Lois Weber. She worked as Weber's assistant, learned to cut film, was a stunt and riding double, an extra, and an occasional supporting actor in front of the camera. In 1920, she directed her husband Fred Thompson and Mary Pickford in *The Love Light*, and in 1922 she co-directed *The Song of Love* with Norma Talmadge (Beauchamp 36–43, 128–131, and 147–48.) Directors and cameramen often experimented with the technical side of filmmaking and made the biggest strides in film technology and cinematography. D. W. Griffith was perhaps the greatest example of the latter; he had begun his career as an actor and then moved into directing. He was the first director to make extensive use of the close-up, among other innovations (Brownlow 114, 178). Being able to perform multiple roles, in a studio or at one's own company, was essential to survival in the Hollywood of the teens and twenties. Marion, Pickford, Griffith, and others had perfected this talent and used it to their advantage.

Ruth's multifaceted work with the Alectrion Film Corporation is quite accurate for the time. The combination of writing, acting, and investing in films would not have been at all uncommon. Stratemeyer would have seen the advantage immediately in choosing the movies as a field for Ruth's talents. He was once again able to capitalize on a new and liberating technology in order to enthrall his readers.[2] Motion pictures were about illusions, escapism, and glamour, but they were also a product that relied heavily on fantasy and advertising, things Stratemeyer understood very well. Since Ruth is college-educated, she is highly qualified to write for the movies, and she becomes part of a new and exciting field of work in which women excelled. She is tailor-made as a heroine to attract girl readers who are fascinated with motion pictures.

Of all the women who worked in motion pictures, starting in silents and through the transition to talkies, Ruth is most like Mary Pickford and Frances

Marion. Indeed, she seems like a perfect combination of the legendary female friends: like Marion, she begins as a scenario writer and actress, winning success in both areas. Like Pickford, Ruth is financially savvy about her films and eventually is able to form her own film company. She is a more involved director than either Marion or Pickford; Pickford would direct herself and others in front of the camera, but never officially directed a picture, while Marion only directed a handful of films (Brownlow 140–141; Beauchamp 128–131 and 147–148). Ruth makes scenario writing and directing her twin passions, seeing the latter as the natural outgrowth of the former.

Also like Frances Marion, Ruth's career is interrupted by the outbreak of war. Ruth and her friends leave Ardmore in the middle of their sophomore year to dive into war work (Emerson, *Red Cross* 6). Marion sought an appointment overseas as a war correspondent and was granted one through the federal Committee of Public Information. Marion took a cameraman and director with her to Europe, all of them under orders to film the work of Allied women. She also frequently involved herself in nursing (Beauchamp 92–98). Ruth takes a more typical path to war work through the Red Cross, though she is able to use her filmmaking skills for a patriotic cause. When Ruth first joins the Red Cross, she uses her skill in the film industry to create a fundraising film for the organization. Ruth comes up with the idea for a scenario called "The Boys of the Draft," following a new regiment of soldiers through their training, travel, and experiences overseas, and demonstrating how the Red Cross helps the soldiers on the battlefield. A portion of all the profits from the film are donated to the Red Cross, and although the production is rushed, the film is a smash success (Emerson, *Red Cross* 40–48). However, after that, Ruth sets her heart on going to France and spends the duration of the war as a Red Cross worker, as detailed in the previous chapter.[3]

When Ruth finally returns home, however, she has an advantage in returning to civilian life because she *has* a profession to come home to. Women war workers were most often thrown out of their professional positions or discharged from their military posts once the war was over, and they had difficulty finding new work when they were competing against returning soldiers. In a pattern that would be repeated in later wars, most women were expected to step aside from their better-paying clerical and industrial jobs to make way for the returning men. They were often forced to return to jobs that paid lower wages or leave their humanitarian work to marry. Ruth, however, has no such trouble. Motion pictures were one of the few professions that welcomed women at all times, in wartime or peacetime, economic prosperity or depression, and so women of Hollywood could return to their jobs with little difficulty. Since Ruth is already established in motion pictures, and since films were more popular than ever, Ruth has the perfect outlet once she is back in the States, something on which to focus and help her transition back into everyday life. In *Ruth Fielding Down East*, the first volume where Ruth is actually back on U.S. soil, we find that her "Seaside Idyl" [sic] scenario that she wrote before the war is already in production and being filmed. Although Ruth claims that she "'wasn't taking much interest in this particular picture'" because she has been concentrating on a new scenario, clearly the filming has not escaped her attention, either (Emerson, *Down East* 27). Four weeks after setting foot in her home country, Ruth is back to movie work and scenario writing.

This is not to say that Ruth's transition to post-war life is easy or without flaws. Interestingly, Ruth is one of the series characters that has some emotional difficulty with her return home. Ruth is still suffering from a wounded shoulder, the result of a bombing raid on the French hospital where she was working. In addition, her normally cheerful and complacent attitude has become somewhat depressed and nervous, like many actual women who came home. She has endured physical injury, exhausted herself in the service of her country, and feels simultaneously relieved and regretful that she is no longer in France. Her injury keeps her from serving the soldiers any longer, yet her mind is still on the battlefield when she is not occupied with film work. She even admits to Helen, Tom, and her Aunt Alvirah that she does not feel like having fun or being cheerful while peace has still not been declared (Emerson, *Down East* 24–34).

Aggravating the problems surrounding Ruth's reassimilation is the loss of her newest scenario, which disappears off the porch of her home at the beginning of *Ruth Fielding Down East*. Convinced that her new scenario is the best story she has ever created, Ruth keeps the details of it secret from everyone, and when her manuscript pages disappear, she cannot reconstruct it. Nor, if the thief should try to sell the story, would Ruth have any proof that the story was originally hers. Ruth is despondent and cheerless after the loss, unable to regard it as anything less than disastrous. It is not until she goes on a motor trip with Helen, Tom, their friend Jennie Stone, and Jennie's fiancé Henri Marchand, that Ruth truly realizes how much she has been affected:

> She must steady her own nerves.... She had allowed the loss of her scenario to shake her usual calm. She knew she had not been acting like herself during this automobile journey and that she had given her friends cause for alarm.
> Then and there Ruth determined to talk no more about her loss or her fears regarding the missing scenario. If it was gone, it was gone. That was all there was to it. She would no longer worry her friends and disturb her own mental poise by ruminating upon her misfortune [Emerson, *Down East* 92–93].

There are several different ways to read this particular episode in Ruth's life, one that seems out-of-character with her usual resourcefulness, quick thinking, and calmness in the face of emergency. Ruth does not become hysterical, but she does become nervous, withdrawn, and depressed. The intent of the writer is not clear. Is Ruth's character change meant to be read as a warning? On the one hand, her depression and nervousness might be seen as an effect of her war work, a sign of female weakness and an argument against women in the battle zone. In some ways it echoes the same old arguments of cultural commentators in the nineteenth century, who bewailed the effects of higher education of women, claiming that women were damaging their nerves, brains, and reproductive systems through excessive mental and physical exertion.

On the other hand, it is entirely possible that the author was doing his or her best to represent some of the suffering and unequal treatment that women war workers went through. Plenty of women suffered injury, illness, and trauma as a result of their time in the war zone. Often, they were not entitled to veteran's benefits or medical care. Even if they were, their treatment was not always successful. Many Navy women, for example, contracted influenza during the epidemic of 1918, and some developed tuberculosis from the illness. The Navy's Bureau of Medicine and Surgery struggled to find facilities to care for these women long-term; as members of the Navy, they were entitled to the care, but naval hospitals were not set up to accommodate women (Ebbert and Hall 76–85). While Ruth does not come down with any kind of physical illness or lose her job, her depression over leaving the war zone and her distress at the setback to her civilian career (in her case, through the loss of her scenario) were common problems among women war workers. The feeling of being useful and productive was addictive and empowering to most women who participated in the war.

Ruth becomes herself again *through* participating in a crisis, supporting the idea that she is not permanently damaged from her overseas work. Toward the end of *Ruth Fielding Down East*, Ruth and her friends are out for a sail when they get caught in a storm and have engine troubles. Ruth takes over the steering of the boat in the midst of the storm, while Tom and the crew do their best to get the engine working again. Ruth is perfectly calm and even a bit thrilled by the danger: "The girl of the Red Mill smiled at them. She had done something! Nor did she feel at all overcome by the effort. The danger through which they had passed had inspired rather than frightened her" (Emerson, *Down East* 192). Ruth needs a cause to work for that is greater than herself, whether that is helping soldiers in France or saving her friends during a storm. She feels that she can be useful again, and so becomes cheerful Ruth once more.

As for the lost scenario, after many twists and turns that problem is solved as well. Ruth discovers the stage actor who stole the work from her front porch, whose name is John Pike. Eventually he confesses to stealing the scenario, hoping to make some money for himself and his daughter Arabella by selling it. Among other things, Ruth gains both Pike and his daughter steady employment in motion pictures, so that they are able to work for their living (Emerson, *Down East* 195–207). Yet again, this was frequently true in real life; France Marion was notorious for trying to give her out-of-work actor friends jobs, whether behind the camera or in front of it. Mary Pickford continually found roles for her two siblings in films, even when they took advantage of her celebrity and status (Beauchamp 201–204, 249, 254; Whitfield 170–72, 224, 279). Ruth sees potential in the old man and his daughter; Pike works for Mr. Hammond as a character actor, and Arabella begins her film career in a comedy.

Climbing the Ladder of Success

After her transition back to the homefront and films, Ruth takes an ever-larger role in the Alectrion Film Corporation and her own motion pictures. In "Brighteyes," a Western filmed during *Ruth Fielding in the Great Northwest*, Ruth not only writes the scenario and finds her own star, the Native American girl Wonota, but she also puts up fifty percent of the money for the picture (Emerson 45). She spends a great deal of time with Mr. Hammond and Jim Hooley, the film's director, making sure that her writing translates well into camera shots and a completed film: "...she stood practically at Jim Hooley's elbow when the story was being filmed. So, with the author working with the director, the picture was almost sure to be a success" (Emerson, *Great Northwest* 142). Ruth's expertise in scenarios combined with the skill of a seasoned director results in a successful picture. Like Frances Marion, Ruth gets the chance to oversee her work as it is turned into a visual product.

In *Ruth Fielding on the St. Lawrence* and *Ruth Fielding Treasure Hunting*, Ruth takes the next big step forward in her career, forming the Fielding Film Company and assuming responsibility for her own motion pictures from start to finish. Her decision comes primarily from professional dissatisfaction; she wants more control over the final product of a picture than she can have as an actress and scenario writer. Even though she works closely with Mr. Hooley to come up with successful shots and an engaging film, the final decisions about how, when, and what to shoot and cut are not hers:

> Why should she be tied to certain agreements that cramped her? Especially in a case of this kind. For the sake of saving expense, Mr. Hammond was likely to

insist that the artistic part of "The Long Lane's Turning" should be sacrificed.... "I am going to be in a position some time where I shall have the say as to every detail of the picture," [Ruth] told herself. "I want to be my own manager and my own producer. Otherwise I shall never be happy — nor will I ever be sure of making worth-while pictures" [Emerson, *St. Lawrence* 152–53].

Ruth becomes determined to have more power over a picture's outcome than she will ever have as a scenario writer. In the next volume, *Ruth Fielding Treasure Hunting*, she is attempting to put together financing for a picture that would be written, directed, and produced by herself. Mr. Hammond agrees to let her borrow Wonota and the director/cameraman Jim Hooley from the Alectrion Film Corporation. Ruth struggles to secure the financial backing, however, until an anonymous benefactor comes to her aid and agrees to be her business partner. Under the agreement, Ruth receives complete control over all her pictures and the financing for her opening picture, for which she has already begun the scenario. Although Ruth does not know her financial backer, her lawyer assures her that everything is in order, and so the Fielding Film Company is born. Ruth's first picture, "Treasure Trove," is a success, and Ruth's days as an independent filmmaker begin. Her next picture, "Snowblind," is made during *Ruth Fielding in the Far North* and once again written, directed, and produced by herself.

Being a woman director carries its own difficulties. While Ruth has an established rapport with the members of her company, people who have worked with her many times and are loyal to her, it is harder to create a good film with a different crew and team of actors. In *Ruth Fielding in Alaska*, Mr. Hammond asks Ruth to step in and direct one of Alectrion's films, "The Girl of Gold," when the original director is lured away by a rival film company. While some of Mr. Hammond's people are familiar with Ruth's skills and respect her, others are not. Raymond Howell, the casting director, Gerard Bolton, the assistant director, and one of the actors, Joe Rumph, all vocally express their skepticism about Ruth's ability to make a success out of the complex film (Emerson 36–37, 76–77, 82–83). Ruth herself worries that her gender will be seen as a liability by the men in the group:

> A woman director is at a disadvantage with a man because the men in the company always seem to go on the assumption that she's no good until she proves the contrary. There are good woman directors in the moving picture business.... But they have always had to work twice as hard to prove their ability as a man in the same position [Emerson, *In Alaska* 67].

Conveniently, all of the individuals who doubt Ruth in this particular volume are men. However, the text is making a point here that was lived out by many women in motion pictures. Even in a profession as egalitarian as movies (and early Hollywood was, by all accounts, a field open to anyone and everyone), women were at a disadvantage because of their gender. They were accepted as actresses, as dancers, as writers, but it was harder to be a cameraman, director, or producer when those aspects of filmmaking were male-dominated. Only an extremely successful woman would be able to work her way into the higher echelons of movie production. Frances Marion and Mary Pickford are two prime examples of these kinds of women, and it is no coincidence that they were close friends and highly supportive of each other's careers; they each owed a significant amount of their success to working with one another. Still, profits were the key indicator of success, and for a woman moviemaker to be taken seriously, her films had to make money.

Ruth has great confidence in her abilities, but she is very aware of the fact that her pictures are triumphs only if they are deemed so by the moviegoing public. While she strives for artistic, quality films, her company can only continue to function if those films make money, if they are eagerly consumed by movie audiences. Before the premier of "Snowblind," Ruth is fretting about this uncertainty:

> Also, though she was sure in her own mind that "Snowblind" was a good picture, felt that she had put the best of her art into making it, there was always the doubt as to just how it would be received by that fickle thing, an American audience.
> The latter, besides being fickle, was pitiless. Where it condemned, it condemned so heartily that the object of its displeasure might just as well be sent at once to the darkest corner of the director's room of discarded plays. It was done for — a complete failure. This, unless there was the possibility of practically remaking the whole thing. And in the case of Ruth Fielding's "Snowblind," where the scenes had actually been filmed amid the snow and ice of the far North, retakes would be an impossibility [Emerson, *Golden Pass* 2].

Ruth, as a professional writer, director, and producer, wields control over her products and the market in ways that women consumers could not always do. Women consumers pick and choose out of the products that are available to them, searching for items that will bring the most benefit to their households or that will express their personality in ways distinct from their peers. Ruth, on the other hand, is trying to *create* an artistic product that will generate the most profit. She does her best to control all the variables related to the quality of her films: her crew, the actors in her films, the locations of the shooting, the pace of the story and its plot, the authenticity of the action. All of these things, hopefully, add up to a skillfully made film that the public will pay to see. Ruth is engaging in the game of quality vs. quantity; longer, higher quality films that take more care to make should, in theory, make higher profits than shorter, shoddily made films. However, Ruth does not control the consumers themselves, and she recognizes that if they do not like the film despite all of her careful work, it will be a failure. Her money will be lost and her business will be in jeopardy. This is the difficult balance she has to strike on the production side of a consumer economy: she can do a great deal to control the quality of her product, but she cannot ever guarantee that consumers will want to buy (or in Ruth's case, pay to see) that product. In that sense, movie production is more than a bit of a gamble. Movies are produced for entertainment, for pleasure; they are not staples like food and clothing — and even selling staples does not guarantee a profit. Ruth is hoping that her own preferences as a writer, director, and viewer will match those of the majority of the film-viewing public. Her artistic and personal expression happens through the creation of her films; her skill as a producer comes with understanding her audience's expectations as well as her own. While making motion pictures was a new and glamorous profession for women, it also entailed a lot of risk, and not every woman who tried to make a living in Hollywood succeeded.

Of course, having financial and administrative supporters always helps, whether those supporters come from a movie studio, one's family, or professional connections. In Ruth's case, it is the person closest to her who makes the Fielding Film Company a reality. It is revealed, at the end of *Ruth Fielding Treasure Hunting*, that Tom Cameron is in fact Ruth's financial backer. He made the arrangements, through his lawyer, to give Ruth the capital she needed and incorporate the film company. In this way, he puts himself into the business side of the Fielding Film Company, Inc. While he initially makes this decision simply due to his belief in Ruth, he soon takes all of the administrative details off of her shoulders, becoming a working partner in the business. Tom has been searching for something to take up as a profession since he returned from the war, and he finds that motion pictures suit him almost as well as they do Ruth. While he does not share her creative abilities, he enjoys the unexpected travel and has a good feel for finance, having been trained at his father's dry goods company.

Ruth objects to the plan initially, hating the idea of being beholden to one of her oldest friends (and her acknowledged suitor), but Tom declares that he invested in the company as much for his own interest as for Ruth's success. He is determined to make the new venture profitable, and he knows that handling the business transaction side of pictures for Ruth will make her work much easier to do. As long as Tom is worrying about bills, acting contracts, film distribution, and the thousand other details that come with getting pictures successfully made and shown, Ruth can focus all of her energy on the films themselves (Emerson, *St. Lawrence* 85–88, 107–108; *Treasure Hunting*

105–107 and 205–206). However, Ruth's success is guaranteed only so long as she can keep up with the rapid changes in the filming industry. Later in the series, all of Ruth's gains are threatened with the advent of "talkies."

The Problem of "Talkies"

Like many real actors, writers, and studios, Ruth is overwhelmed by the change to sound in her pictures and is not at all sure that the new medium will be lucrative or rewarding. In the world of motion pictures, talkies caused a great deal of upheaval. Many actors and actresses who had been wildly popular in silents could not adapt to the new filming and sound style. Some had voices which simply did not record well; others struggled with the new atmosphere on a set. Kevin Brownlow notes that on the set of a silent picture, because there was no sound recording, there was often a lot of noise during filming. The director would talk to the actors as the cameras were grinding. There were musicians playing to create the mood of a scene. Carpenters would be working on a nearby set. When sound became a factor, a set had to be absolutely silent for the recording equipment, and it made many experienced actors and directors feel awkward: "When the talkies came, the director could no longer direct during a shot. The musicians went, the megaphone went, the improvisation went. An icy, ghostly silence descended during shooting — a silence that was, ironically, to kill many talkies" (Brownlow 83). Early talkies often seemed stilted and artificial, with awkward action and stiff acting, precisely because the adjustment to the new technology was so difficult. While sound was a novelty, the quality of the films themselves went down considerably.

Early recording equipment was another problem. It altered the timbre of many actors' voices, rendering their speech unsuitable for sound film: "An unfortunate tendency of early recording was its habit of raising voices by an octave or two; the best results came from booming baritones. Tenor voices ... sometimes recorded as a high-pitched squeak, suggestive more of Mickey Mouse than Don Juan" (Brownlow 665). Famous silent actors were ruined by sound, not from lack of talent but from primitive technology.

Jeanine Basinger points to another possible reason for the difficulty that silent stars had in transitioning to sound films: their voices did not match the images they had created on the screen or the voices that fans had created for them: "Their voices had already been 'heard' in the heads of the moviegoing public who had met *them* in the silence, with only a piano or orchestra to intrude. To hear their favorites suddenly speak was a shock for fans. To hear them speak without the voices that had been mentally supplied for them wasn't acceptable" (Basinger 470; emphasis Basinger's). If fans had created a soprano voice for Greta Garbo, she might never have become famous in sound films.

Ruth struggles with all of these same difficulties in her first attempt at a talkie, detailed in *Ruth Fielding in Talking Pictures*. The business risk is great; equipping studios for sound is expensive and time-consuming, and both Ruth and Tom worry that Alectrion and the Fielding Film Company will be out of business whether they jump into talking pictures or not. Tom notes: "'If [Mr. Hammond] ignores the talkies, rival companies may put him out of business; if he attempts a talking picture and fails to make a good one, he's likely to be face to face with bankruptcy'" (Emerson, *Talking Pictures* 4). When Mr. Hammond asks Ruth to turn her next scenario, "The Girl of the Border," into a talkie for Alectrion, Ruth agrees with trepidation. She is also in charge of directing the film, and in the transition to sound, the atmosphere at the studios is tense, cutthroat, and stressful. Ruth has written the scenario for her picture, but finds she is not skillful at writing the dialogue necessary for a talkie. Already a proven actress, Ruth is persuaded by Mr. Hammond to take the lead role in the film, but she is terrified that her sound test might prove her unfit for work in front of the camera. Even worse, she is putting all of her regular actors through sound tests and is forced to fire a number of them because their voices will not record. One of these is actress Viola Casselle, who has a suitable voice but cannot enunciate properly for the microphones: "...the actress stammered her words and made ugly hissing sounds through her teeth. To be quite fair with her, Ruth had permitted Miss Casselle several tests, but as there was no improvement, she had regretfully told the actress that she could not use her in the picture. The young directress had been obliged to let other actors go, but none had protested as bitterly as Miss Casselle" (Emerson, *Talking Pictures* 23).

Miss Casselle is lucky to have multiple chances. Many real actors were thrown out of their studios after one bad voice test. Late-twenties Hollywood went into a panic over talkies; *The Jazz Singer*, with Al Jolson's few spoken lines, had turned the film profession on its head. Some silent actors scraped a living as extras and some had a creative renaissance working on the production side of the camera, but many lost their jobs permanently at the height of their popularity and skill. A few were fortunate enough to make good voice tests and make sound films; Greta Garbo, with her deep alto, was immediately popular in talkies—although M-G-M had delayed putting her into them precisely because they were afraid of the audience's reaction. Her first sound film was not until 1930, when *Anna Christie* was released (Brownlow 664; Basinger 471).

Viola Casselle is not the only actor Ruth has to fire; there are also three Mexican cowboys who protest vehemently when Ruth cannot give them contracts because of their voices. Ruth is genuinely sorry not to hire them because of their skill with horses: "'They speak English fairly well, but they do not have screen voices. I hated to let them go because they are exceptionally good horsemen, but I had to replace them with American cowboys who can speak the vernacular of the Southwest'" (Emerson *Talking Pictures* 47). Not having a "screen voice" is a problem across the acting profession, and it costs the studio time, money, and resources to sort out the good screen voices from the bad. While Ruth regrets having to fire so many people, she is only doing her best to make a successful picture.

Not only does Ruth have problems with voice testing, but also the initial shooting of the film does not go well. Like the real silent actors who had to adjust to microphones and silent stages, Ruth's actors are tense and nervous, uncomfortable in the new medium: "At once a deathlike silence came over the room. Whispers ceased. Immediately the cameramen, in their class booths, flashed lights to signify that they had threaded their films and were ready.... The knowledge that the microphones were recording the slightest noise as well as their voices, made [the actors] self-conscious and nervous" (Emerson, *Talking Pictures* 64–66). Everyone has trouble adapting to the new methods and the demands of the new technology, and Ruth is afraid that their picture is a failure almost before it has begun.

Slowly, however, problems are solved. Ruth's voice test goes well, so her part in the picture is assured. She asks playwright Franklin Foote to assist her with dialogue in the scenario, and later on Foote is hired by the studio to coach the actors in speaking their lines. Over the course of a month, the indoor scenes that initially went badly are re-filmed and come out satisfactorily. Even the outdoor scenes are completed successfully, though it is much harder to control noises coming from the surrounding environment than it is in a studio. Ruth and her company manage to concede to the new demands of talkies, turning out a motion picture that is artistically superior as well as profitable. Like other producers and marketers, Ruth is forced to concede to the public's demands in order for her film company to survive, but she stays on top of her profession by refusing to sacrifice the quality of her productions. Her devotion to detail is rewarded when "The Girl of the Border" brings in large returns.

Ruth's success in motion pictures, beginning in the silents and through the transition to talkies, is important for several reasons. First, as a heroine she demonstrates exactly how much women's lives had changed since the 1860s, when marriage was usually the only economically viable option. Ruth has the advantages of higher education and a profession that allows her to remain economically independent. While she no longer has the kind of religious and familial influence that was wielded so effectively by Elsie Dinsmore, the Marches, and the Chautauqua Girls, it is possible to argue that Ruth's work in the movies gives her an even wider cultural influence than her benevolent foremothers. Through the production of films, Ruth is helping to shape the choices of movie viewers in many areas — choices about material goods, as the movies demonstrate what is fashionable and stylish, choices about work ethic and social behavior, and choices about love, romance, and gender norms.[4] Ruth is blazing a trail for women by claiming professional equality with men, excelling in her chosen area of work, and by creating products that not only entertain, but also question and create social norms.

Second, Ruth's professional achievements showcase women's economic possibilities. Motion pictures were one of the few fields where women could rise through the ranks with relatively few obstacles, and so their creative and business acumen was allowed to develop unimpeded. Through her skills both in front of and behind the camera, Ruth builds her own company that flourishes in a competitive capitalist market. In financial terms, she is just as successful as any of the men who surround her, and so she breaks gender barriers by proving women's ability to succeed in a way that influences the economy. She exemplifies women's contributions to the market as producers, not just as consumers.[5]

Third, Ruth's path to economic independence in 1920s Hollywood reveals some of the compromises and choices that women of the Progressive Era were forced to make when it came to having both a profession and intimate relationships. While Ruth's rise to fame is exhilarating and empowering for both her and her readers, Ruth finds that the balance between work and love is not so easy to negotiate.

Balancing Work and Love

Ruth's success in motion pictures combined with her business partnership with Tom Cameron brings up new and difficult problems for her. Being a producer (both in the economic sense and in her literal capacity as a film producer) takes a toll on Ruth's love life. Ruth and Tom Cameron have been close friends for most of their lives, and while neither Ruth nor Tom ever shows a preference for anyone else, they are not even engaged for most of the series and do not get married until the twenty-fourth volume of thirty.[6] Ruth hesitates to bind herself to anyone, even Tom, for fear that it will hinder the work that she thrives on: "Ruth was well aware of Tom's feeling for her and, though she was fond of the young fellow, strove to keep Tom and his emotions as much in the background as possible. Ruth had no intention of marrying and 'settling down' until she had proved to her own complete satisfaction just how far she could go in her chosen line of work" (Emerson, *Golden Pass* 16). As Ruth progresses from scenario writer, to actress, to director and producer, her determination to become a formidable force in motion pictures only grows, and it becomes harder and harder for her to give Tom any sort of definite commitment or timeline for their marriage. She feels guilty about it repeatedly (in the later volumes of the series it is mentioned early on in almost every book), but professional success and independence are extremely important to Ruth, and she has difficulty saying no to projects that will increase her skills and stature in the movies.

Very much in love with her fiancé and yet unwilling to give up her career for Tom or to compromise her own need for personal fulfillment, Ruth's efforts to reconcile her romantic relationship and her job correspond to an extent with the history of white, college-educated women in the twenties. Some middle- and upper-class career women had a choice about whether or not to marry. For some, their jobs gave them economic independence; others were independently wealthy and could create reform careers for themselves. Companionate marriage was the new ideal, a union based in friendship and sharing of responsibilities, but even with the changes in marriage there were women who felt that the benefits of being single and successful outweighed the potential benefits of marriage: "Some women no longer thought of marriage as their inevitable destiny. And marriage freely chosen differs from marriage necessitated by economic helplessness. Some professional women, convinced that marriage and career didn't go together, chose careers" (Schneider and Schneider, *Progressive Era* 146). Upper-class female reformers, especially, often chose not to marry because it seemed to them that they could not properly tend to families while trying to ameliorate social ills. The immigrants, children, and others whom they were trying to help became their families. Eric Rauchway points out that reformers saw immigrants and the lower classes as needing material comfort and education to be proper U.S. citizens, and women reformers were in a unique position to provide this kind of help: "Nobody could better supply these needs than the well-educated, well-connected, and unmarried daughters of a professional class whose universities were open to them but whose professions were not. These women invented careers of their own, serving evident social needs. But mothering whole communities precluded ... mothering one's own children" (Rauchway 6). Although women had been going to college for decades by the turn of the century and went in ever-increasing numbers throughout the twenties, many professions that were traditionally only open to men (law, medicine, business) kept their ranks closed to women.

Of course, there were plenty of women who still chose to marry and pursue careers simultaneously. In *The Refuge of Affections*, Rauchway profiles Progressive Era couples who made a point of developing reform careers both together and individually, while still creating functioning families: Charles and Mary Ritter Beard, Willard and Dorothy Whitney Straight, and Wesley Clair and Lucy Sprague Mitchell (31–122). Christine Stansell reinforces Rauchway's observations by showing that among the Greenwich Village elite of the oughts and teens, the ideal partnership (whether the individuals were married or not) was supposed to contain shared work and intellectual interests as well as sexual passion: "With the supposed emergence of a sphere where men and women mingled in all sorts of meaningful ways, work no longer obviated the possibility of heterosexual love. Rather, the release of female expression in work, feminists believed, could create playful, inventive partnerships" (Stansell, *American Moderns* 249). Marriage at the turn of the century was supposed to be a partnership of equals, where both partners nurtured each other intellectually, emotionally, and sexually.

However, for the women involved, satisfying their own ambitions *and* their desire for love and families sometimes proved to be a difficult and draining task. Ida Rauh and Max Eastman, for example, struggled to make their relationship work after they were married. Rauh had completed law school at New York University, but she could not practice because law as a profession was so opposed to women. Instead, she made a career as an actress and a supporter of suffrage and the Women's Trade Union League. Eastman was a journalist and the editor of *The Masses*. The longer they were married, the more stifled Rauh felt, particularly after the birth of her son. She and Eastman eventually divorced (Stansell, *American Moderns* 262–266). Max's sister Crystal Eastman was another NYU law graduate who threw herself into suffrage, labor struggles, and peace organizations. She also married twice and had two children with her second husband (Schwarz 54–55, 76, 119; Stansell, *American Moderns* 244–245, 259–260). Although her second marriage was apparently happy, Crystal Eastman was one of the few to openly acknowledge that marriage could smother both partners intellectually and sexually: "Marriage can become such a constant invasion of [one's] very self that it amounts sometimes to torture" (qtd. in Stansell, *American Moderns* 260).

The care of children was, perhaps, the ultimate problem in modern marriage. Contraception allowed women to delay their childbearing, but when children were born, women inevitably found themselves taking care of their offspring while their husband's careers flourished. It was true of Raugh and Eastman, of writers Hutchins Hapgood and Neith Boyce, and perhaps most famously, true of Charlotte Perkins Gilman and her first husband, Charles Stetson. After her marriage and the birth of her daughter, Gilman suffered from acute depression for years, and her marriage to Stetson ended after a decade (Stansell, *American Moderns* 261–266, 290–294; Schwarz, 77). No matter how egalitarian turn-of-the-century couples strived to make their marriages, women devoted more time to childrearing than men, and women who had previously enjoyed stimulating careers often found themselves depressed, overwhelmed, or resentful. Without children, it was difficult but sometimes possible to balance two careers; with children in the picture, couples who managed to keep both their careers flourishing were the exception.

Ruth continually weighs this choice between career and marriage as she becomes more involved in filmmaking. Marriage is not a necessity for her; she has enough money and professional skills to be independent for as long as she wishes. Tom is already her best friend and business partner, and she hesitates to add family responsibilities to her life: "As Ruth grew, her ambition grew also. The temptation to determine just how far her talent would carry her in the motion picture business was too great for her to resist. So while returning Tom's affection, the girl put him off time and time again, pleading her career as an excuse" (Emerson, *In Alaska* 14). The tone of the text is a little ambivalent here; implying that Ruth's career is an "excuse" for not marrying Tom makes it seem as though 1) Ruth doesn't really love him and 2) the author, perhaps, does not take Ruth's career very seriously. "Temptation" also has a connotation of sinfulness or distraction; Ruth's career could be dismissed as a distraction from her duty to herself and Tom. Being the professional woman that she is, however, Ruth is surely well aware of what it means to get married and have children; marriage could significantly impede her ability to pursue her ambitions.

Tom, for his part, is willing to wait for Ruth and says so on multiple occasions, but even he feels impatience at times. When Ruth takes on a new project in *Ruth Fielding in Alaska*, for example, she is hesitant to accept the directing job without consulting Tom. Tom tells her to go ahead, despite his own reservations about the delay in their relationship:

> He had a moment of wondering how he had ever found the courage to ask a girl like this to marry him and give up a profession in which she was making good so royally. It would be too bad to waste her talent; even Tom realized that.
> But despite his good sportsmanship and his acknowledgement of Ruth's genius, Tom knew that this new work for Mr. Hammond that she had just pledged herself to undertake would postpone their marriage indefinitely. Despite

the fact that he had tacitly given his consent, Tom was sore at heart and found it a distinct effort to join in the spirited conversation.... [Emerson, *In Alaska* 25].

Tom is wise enough to see that Ruth is incredibly talented; he even indirectly acknowledges that her skill and determination in her work are two of the things that he loves about her. However, he experiences frustration over being Ruth's business partner, her best friend, her fiancé, and yet not her husband. As much as he admires Ruth's acumen in her chosen profession, and as caught up as he himself is in the motion picture business and all that it entails, Tom still wants a home and family with Ruth.

Still, Tom is an exception among men of the twenties because he is willing to have Ruth continue her work after they are married. Paula Fass, in her extensive exploration of marriage and sexual behavior among 1920s youth, notes that while women often planned to work outside the home after marriage, men usually did not approve of their wives working: "Most young women expected to work during the early years of marriage in order to put the family on a stable economic foundation. Men, however, usually disapproved of their wives working and could rarely believe that their wives might want to work after marriage.... Only one of nine men would give the wife a choice of working after marriage" (Fass 81). Tom knows that Ruth will want to continue her work and in fact encourages her to do so; it is Ruth who fears that she will no longer be successful if she marries. Tom openly recognizes how long and arduously Ruth has worked for her achievements: "'You've worked hard to make a name for yourself, and I want you to keep it. I don't mind if the public knows you as Ruth Fielding, as long as I know you're Mrs. Cameron'" (Emerson, *Clearing Her Name* 1–2).

Ruth is successful even after she marries, of course. In the fictional world of series books, this happy outcome is entirely possible. With a supportive husband who is also her business partner, Ruth is able to find the balance that eluded so many real women. As Ruth Fielding (rather than Mrs. Cameron), she attains so much financial success in moving pictures that she could stop working if she chose to, yet she keeps on working for the joy of it: "'I work because I love it, Tom. Work doesn't seem hard when you're absorbed in it'" (Emerson, *Clearing Her Name* 2). Ruth is also fortunate in her choice of career; as aforesaid, Hollywood was genuinely open to women in many ways that most professions were not; in the days of silents and early talkies, climbing up the financial and business ladder was something that women frequently did — and something they often helped each other achieve. Ruth finds happiness in both her work and her spouse (and eventually, her daughter) without compromising too much of herself.

Ruth Fielding is, ultimately, one of the most fully developed heroines in early twentieth- century series fiction. Reaping the benefits of education and new social norms that allow her to pursue a profession, Ruth becomes a force to be reckoned with in the Hollywood of silent films and early talking pictures. She crosses the divide between being a self-aware, independent consumer and creating merchandise for profit. She successfully produces consumer entertainment for a capitalist market, weighing artistic merit and accuracy against public taste and demand. Though she never verbalizes the cultural influence of her films, Ruth's fierce devotion to quality motion pictures suggests that she understands how much sway they hold over the public imagination. In addition, the films reflect her competence and skill as a woman professional in a new field; she is constantly aware that her output is being judged and evaluated by others, and women filmmakers as a whole are being measured by her products. Ruth is both a part of her era and ahead of it, on the leading edge of successful, entrepreneurial women who made careers for themselves in the early part of the century and foreshadowed women's participation in a much wider array of vocations.

On a personal level, Ruth's relationship with Tom Cameron is one of the only ones in series fiction that demonstrates both the ideal of companionate marriage and the difficulty of negotiating what feminists later named the "double shift" of work and family. Ruth and Tom create a working romance, a relationship that is equal parts friendship, business, and love, and they spend a long time trying to understand and accommodate each other's needs and wants. While Ruth has found an incredibly supportive partner in Tom, someone who is her best friend and business partner as well as her beau and then fiancé, she is still highly aware of the restrictions that marriage could place on her independence. As guilty as she feels about continuously delaying her marriage, Ruth's career is her priority for most of the series. Once she has established herself in films and finally marries Tom, she has the satisfaction of knowing that even if she completes fewer projects, her films will be greeted with anticipation by Hollywood and the moviegoing public. After years of ambition, work, and negotiation, she has it all. The long road to get there only makes Ruth more endearing as a heroine; readers see the striving and the flaws that make Ruth more human.

In more ways than most series heroines ever accomplish, Ruth finds fulfillment. She builds an international career on work that she loves. She is financially successful. She has a husband who supports her and shares in her work, and a child whom she and Tom raise together. She is the best representation of the New Woman found in series fiction, the culmination of a long arc of U.S. women's history and literary development that begins with social reform and benevolence and develops through higher education, women's rights, consumerism, and suffrage. Up through the early thirties, she is the ideal heroine for the fully modern, twentieth-century girl.

And then Nancy Drew changes everything.

Notes

1. Silent films were often categorized by the number of reels of film it took to film the entire picture. One reel of film was about 10–12 minutes long and was all that an early projector could hold. Many early pictures were one-reelers. Feature films were about five reels long. See Tim Dirks, "Early Cinematic Origins and the Infancy of Film, Part 2."

2. Stratemeyer was well known for incorporating new technology into his series books. Tom Swift is constantly on the move with new inventions, including motorboats, motorbikes, automobiles, radios, moving picture cameras, and airplanes. In addition to Ruth Fielding, there were four separate series that dealt explicitly with moving pictures: the Moving Picture Boys, the Motion Picture Chums, the Motion Picture Comrades, and the Moving Picture Girls. Dave Dashaway and Ted Scott are both aviators. See Deidre Johnson, *Edward Stratemeyer* 50–63.

3. Ruth's filmmaking for the war effort is also true to life; numerous silent stars made wartime films and supported the war effort by appearing at fundraisers and selling war bonds. Pickford, Fairbanks, and Chaplin were especially active and were credited with selling millions of dollars worth of war bonds for the government. See Beauchamp 82–86 and Whitfield 174–180.

4. Film historian Lary May discusses the ways in which turn-of-the-century vice crusaders and Progressive Reformers saw the potential for movies to be a positive force for social good. Movies could promote American, middle-class, Angle-Saxon values to the working classes and the large new population of immigrants. Ultimately, the support for releasing moral and uplifting films led to the formation of the National Board of Review, "the first national censorship board for the movies" (May 54). See May, *Screening Out the Past*, 52–59.

5. Beverly Gray, a series heroine from the 1930s and '40s, follows in Ruth's footsteps in creating marketable entertainment commodities. Beverly is a journalist initially, eventually combining that career with other lucrative ventures as a screenwriter, playwright, and novelist. Her college friends develop fine art careers as well: Shirley Parker becomes a theater and film actress, Lois Mason is an artist, and Lenora Whitehill decides on a career in photography. All of them are successful in selling their various forms of art to appreciative audiences.

6. There is some inconsistency in the series about Ruth and Tom's engagement. In the wartime volumes (*In the Red Cross* and *At the War Front*), we are told that Ruth and Tom are not officially engaged. In volume twenty-four, *Ruth Fielding at Cameron Hall*, the text says that Ruth accepted Tom's ring before the war, which is not true if one actually reads the early volumes. This discrepancy is probably due to the fact that the series had multiple ghostwriters, and those who wrote some of the later volumes may not have read the earlier books.

Conclusion
Nancy Drew and a New Era

Much has been written about the cultural influence of Nancy Drew.[1] The sixteen-year-old girl detective, with her blond hair and her blue roadster, is the star of the most successful and longest-running girls' series in history. Her adventures began in 1930 and continue to the present day. The mysteries have been released in hardback, in paperback, and as graphic novels. They have been written in third-person and first-person. Nancy has gone from sixteen to eighteen, from blond to "titian-haired." Most of Nancy's adventures are with her two best friends, Bess and George, or her boyfriend Ned Nickerson, but she has also shared books with the Hardy Boys, the other highest-selling series in the Stratemeyer Syndicate's publication list. She is an icon, a casual reference in countless articles about every subject, and a pastime for millions of girl readers.

Of course, at the time of Nancy's publication, not even Edward Stratemeyer anticipated how much she would change the world of series. He was ill with pneumonia during the winter of 1930, when the first three books were being edited, and he died in May, just twelve days after the books were released by Grosset & Dunlap. While he had overseen the initial outlining of the books, assigned the ghost writer (Mildred Wirt Benson), and done the editing for the first two volumes, the third was read and edited by his longtime assistant, Harriet Otis Smith (Rehak 114–122). He did not know whether his new sleuth would be successful; as it turned out, she captured the world of juvenile books in a way that has never been surpassed.

One of the driving impetuses behind this project was the need to understand Nancy's predecessors, the heroines who shaped girls' series just as that genre was coming into being and made Nancy's creation possible. While Nancy's forerunners may be less enduring than she in terms of marketing and profits, it is also true that they are more real, more grounded in their times, their social mores, their historical conflicts, and the rapid changes of the world around them. American girls' series from 1865 to 1930 reflect the gradual historical progression of a number of interrelated cultural developments: 1) the expectation that girls would be community symbols of morality and proponents of familial and community well-being, 2) the cultivation of reading as a genteel activity for girls that was used for both self-education and the reinforcement and challenging of social norms surrounding gender, and 3) the changing nature and meaning of consumerism and leisure for young women.

Postbellum series books emphasize the power of girl heroines to create change within their families and communities through individual charity, benevolence organizations, and reform networks. These narratives create a proto–New Womanhood that expands on antebellum ideas of benevolence and social reform without sacrificing the moral high ground of domesticity. Protestant faith is a crucial part of this equation; Protestantism and benevolence combine to signal a heroine's conformity to middle-class ideals of faith and respectability. Heroines then become guiding moral forces in their communities, conveying proper moral and social behavior to their kin and neighbors.

This is not to say that considerations of wealth, class, and consumerism are absent in postbellum texts; in fact they show up almost continuously. The March women are a prime example of characters who retain their precarious place in the middle class through piety and benevolence; were they missing either one, they would lose their class standing altogether and become objects of charity themselves. The girls are not immune to material desires; Meg and Amy especially must learn to give up their individualistic wants for pretty clothes and other nice things as part of learning to "be good." Alcott uses moments of material self-indulgence to teach the March girls about the consequences of selfish behavior.

Elsie Dinsmore's socioeconomic status is much higher than the Marches'; her staggering wealth can easily sustain her family's luxurious lifestyle and still leave plenty of money to give away to others. What is interesting about Elsie and her children is their belief that wealth makes their charitable obligations even greater and more important. In order to fulfill their duty as good Christians, they must use most of the wealth God has placed in their hands to alleviate the privations and sufferings of others. In addition, because the Dinsmores are Evangelical Protestants (in contrast to the more liberal Protestantism of the Marches), they must do their best to win over souls who have not yet converted to Protestantism; failure in either duty means failing God. Because of their economic standing, the Dinsmores are able to practice top-down, large-scale benevolence in a way that the Marches would never be capable of. Elsie can move a mother and child to a new house, finance a new business, donate to local charities, and support church missions with scarcely any impact on her lifestyle. At the same time, Elsie's constant example of good Christian behavior exerts an almost measureless influence on those around her; she is able to convert even the most ill-behaved and misguided to the Christian faith, including her own father. In contrast, the Marches extend their help to the community through smaller acts of kindness, like feeding poor families and tending others who are sick.

Isabella Alden's Chautauqua Girls combine the Marches' lessons of "being good" with Elsie's unequaled ability to convert and minister to others; they take their faith and their moral convictions one step further into the public sphere. Flossy Shipley and Ruth Erskine both learn to overlook class differences of education, clothing, speech, and work. Flossy becomes actively involved in social reform. She does not simply donate money to organizations, but also helps to organize city-wide charity networks and visits poverty-filled slums. Ruth eventually becomes a speaker and advocate for the Woman's Christian Temperance Union, moving into local politics thanks to her religious and moral convictions about the use of liquor. Ruth's character is part of the biggest national reform movement and women's organization of the nineteenth century.

When consumerism becomes the dominant cultural ethos in series books at the turn of the twentieth century, religion disappears quickly, but concerns about class and morality do not. Girl heroines learn responsible consumption through lessons that teach them not to overindulge their desires for material things. Patty Fairfield, for example, becomes a responsible consumer through the lessons of her Aunt Alice, a woman who is a perfect mix of the old and new ideas about womanhood. Alice knows how to balance work and leisure and manage the consumption of food and goods for her family's home. At the same time, she is highly familiar with the new world of consumption and makes her way through department stores and their abundance of goods with ease, choosing judiciously from all of the offerings. Finally, Alice still performs charity work, which ties her to the older tradition of nineteenth-century benevolence. She trains her niece to be both a domestic manager and a conscientious consumer. Patty understands that this balance between careful spending and household management is the key to being a good consumer.

Although girl heroines are no longer religiously obligated to give money away to others, too much spending on oneself can still lead to moral degeneration. Like their postbellum counterparts, early twentieth-century heroines learn that excessive spending can lead to awful consequences. Marian Barber of the *Grace Harlowe* series becomes so attached to the status brought to her through expensive clothes and disposable income that she resorts to theft and speculation to try and maintain her standing. Patty Fairfield's cousins are spoiled, selfish people who have become accustomed to buying anything they want and who use their wealth to try and climb ever-higher into their social circle.

On the other hand, consuming can also be a pleasurable activity for girls, one that allows them to develop individual taste and personality as well as responsible spending habits. While the emphasis in postbellum series is undoubtedly on denying oneself for the sake of others, turn- of-the-century texts allow more latitude for the enjoyment of material goods. Patty Fairfield delights in choosing her own clothes as well as goods for her home with her father. She both gives and receives gifts from abroad that create individual taste and social standing for herself and her friends. Grace Harlowe's friend Anne Pierson finds that her first silk party dress gives her confidence and self-esteem because, unlike her everyday clothes, it does not display her family's poverty to the world. Grace and her group of friends enjoy a round of hot chocolate at their local drugstore and thereby utilize public space for their social interaction, a space that is not controlled by parents, teachers, or older siblings. Girl heroines suddenly have an unprecedented amount of choice in what to wear, what to eat, and what to buy. Most of their choices are made in new and pleasurable public establishments, whether drugstores or department stores. Sometimes parents are present, but more often they are not, and series girls cheerfully revel in their own ability to pick and choose what they like.[2]

Perhaps no other luxury item features so prominently in turn-of-the-century series fiction as the automobile. Patty Fairfield, the Outdoor Girls, Grace Harlowe, and many others eventually get their own autos and driving licenses, enabling them to venture farther and farther away from home and into public spaces where they are strangers and tourists. Series heroines use the automobile to go everywhere, to unfamiliar towns and cities as well as to the homes of relatives and friends. The automobile is also the item that frequently allows them to physically enter the battlefields of World War I.

Consumption of any kind is notably absent from World War I series fiction for several reasons. The focus on manufacturing military supplies in the U.S. had drawn many farmers and their workers to more lucrative factory jobs, leaving a desperate shortage of farm labor to bring in the harvest. Food shipments to the Allied forces drove up prices at home, resulting in food riots in New York City, Philadelphia, and Chicago. Food shortages were a very real problem, and farmers and their sons were not exempt when the draft was instituted (Weiss 23–28). Manufacturers could neither produce as many domestic goods, nor produce them as cheaply with such a shortage of labor. Moreover, excessive consumption was seen as unpatriotic; extra supplies and comforts were much more necessary for the soldiers than for people at home. However, automobiles were still useful tools that performed crucial functions in the military, and those who had the means to buy them and the skill to use them could make valuable contributions to the war effort. Series girls, like their historical counterparts, drive cars and ambulances to bring food, water, and nursing supplies to destroyed villages. They pick up wounded soldiers from the battlefield and the field hospitals and transport them to safer locations. They use their driving and nursing abilities in the patriotic service of their country and manage to catch a few wartime spies along the way. The Great War, more than any other historical event of this period, encouraged independence and ambition in series heroines and real women alike.

Nineteenth- and early twentieth-century women provided a large amount of the workforce that produced items for the consumer marketplace. However, if they were working in a factory, mill, or sweatshop, it was nearly impossible for women to wield any power over the conditions of production or have any input about the items they were creating. After the conclusion of the Great War, consumerism returned to the economy, but this time historical women and girl heroines gained a stronger hand in the creation and production of items for the commercial market, particularly in the world of movies. Women like Mary Pickford, Marion Davies, and Frances Marion immersed themselves in the Hollywood studios, creating screenplays, character portrayals, and films that audiences flocked to see. Ruth Fielding is the most compelling fictional counterpart to these Hollywood legends. She follows the same pattern of other series heroines by going through high school and college, and she spends the war years as a nurse and intelligence gatherer overseas. She then comes home and embraces a career as a motion picture writer, actress, director, and finally film company executive. Ruth has tremendous professional success and, despite some arguments with her husband Tom Cameron about her priorities, she always emerges triumphantly from any difficulties. She is intelligent, resourceful, incredibly ambitious, and profoundly human, learning through trial and error how to balance her career and her romantic relationship.

No such balancing act is necessary in Nancy Drew's life. Part of readers' continuous fascination with Nancy lies in her ability to effortlessly handle any situation. She has the same confidence, intelligence, and resourcefulness of Ruth Fielding without any of the doubts or insecurities. She is always calm, always collected, even when she is locked in closets, rendered unconscious, or in a high-speed car chase. She can be dirtied and bloodied one minute and in a perfect party dress the next, with her devoted boyfriend Ned on her arm. Nancy's independence and self-sufficiency have earned her praise from feminists and readers alike. As Melanie Rehak notes: "What we remember is

Nancy: her bravery, her style, her generosity, and her relentless desire to succeed linger long after the last page has been turned, the villain sent to jail, the trusty car put in the garage" (xiii).

What needs to be understood is that Nancy's immortality as a heroine was the result of many developments that came before her, many cultural evolutions and many lessons learned by juvenile book publishers in general and the Stratemeyer Syndicate in particular. The morality and community-mindedness of postbellum series is not absent in Nancy Drew mysteries, but it is based in secular rather than religious values. Nancy's faith lies in the law and the justice system rather than in God. Like her foremothers, Nancy is a keen judge of character — she always knows when someone's behavior is morally or socially unacceptable or actually criminal. Her amateur sleuthing rids the community of immoral persons, those who would lie and steal their way to material prosperity. The law punishes thieves and frauds for their crimes, but Nancy always gets to outsmart them first.

Also like the heroines who came before her, consumption is always present in Nancy's life. Nancy is a consumer in spades, even during her debut at the beginning of the Great Depression. She is the ultimate independent consumer, with her roadster and her easily-expanded wardrobe that holds clothes for any occasion. Her father Carson, a successful lawyer, is a doting parent and always makes sure that Nancy has financial resources. Nancy can often be found shopping with her friends Bess and George or meeting them for a meal in a River Heights diner or restaurant. Nancy and her friends take pleasure in consumption as a social activity, and they assume that public spaces are theirs to occupy and enjoy.

In contrast, Nancy's cases are often on behalf of those who *lack* money and resources, even if they are ethical middle-class citizens in every other way. In her very first mystery, *The Secret of the Old Clock*, Nancy helps the Horner girls regain their rightful inheritance from their relative Josiah Crowley, thereby keeping the money from the snobbish and already wealthy Topham family. Many of Nancy's subsequent crime-solving adventures have to do with restoring property to the disinherited, dispossessed, or less fortunate who aspire to be successful and productive (and therefore consuming) members of society.

However, there is one big difference between Nancy and the postbellum and Progressive Era series heroines who predated her. Nancy does not grow up, marry, have children, or grow old. She finishes high school, we are told at the beginning of the series, but she does not go on to college. She presides over her father's house with the help of maid-turned-housekeeper Hannah Gruen. She perpetually dates Ned without ever allowing their relationship to get too serious or committed. History goes by the wayside in River Heights—

Nancy is not touched in any immediate way by the Depression, World War II, the Korean War, the civil rights movement, or Vietnam. Nancy never contemplates going overseas for anything except a vacation and often a case; in fact, the historical events that pass her by are scarcely ever acknowledged.[3]

There are aspects of the books that change — the Stratemeyer Syndicate did major updates of Nancy Drew in 1959 and again in 1979, altering the plots and shortening some of the earlier books, and changing the fashions, cars, and social attitudes in new volumes to conform to contemporary values.[4] Instead of a roadster, Nancy drives a blue convertible; instead of being a blond, she is "titian-haired," often depicted in illustrations as reddish-blond or auburn. While in the original series she is sixteen, her age is changed to eighteen, though she never gets any older in the many cases that come after that. Her clothes, too, are modernized, updated in illustrations to reflect current fashion trends. In other words, although Nancy's accessories change, her age, her unfailing instincts, social graces, and her ability to catch villains do not. While the attitudes toward race and class evolve over the eighty years of the series, Nancy never consciously reflects on any of them — the current attitudes are presented as the correct ones, with no explanation for the change. Nancy, as always, is never in the wrong.

The absence of historical specificity in a girls' series was something new, and it was not true of many other series that came both before Nancy and after her.[5] As this study has shown, early heroines had adventures that often corresponded with historical events. Their debates, discussions, and actions often centered on contemporary religious, political, and social questions. Often these debates are openly acknowledged by the characters and the author uses their discussions to instruct readers; in other cases, the writer offers commentary on the novelty of girl heroines doing new things. For Nancy, doing new and exciting activities and displaying her limitless array of talents is an everyday occurrence. She does not worry about politics or social revolutions. She never compromises her independence through marriage or children; in fact she is scarcely old enough to contemplate them. Nancy never outgrows her readers; she is simply refashioned for each new generation. She was the next successful evolution in girls' series heroines: an independent, confident, multitalented detective who was old enough to keep company with adults and be successful in her "amateur" sleuthing. However, she was never too old to lose her appeal, never dependent on romance or children or even a career for self-definition. Young readers adored her, and continue to adore her, for all of her admirable qualities.

On the other hand, the static nature of Nancy's life makes Nancy less appealing to older readers; despite her maturity and self-sufficiency, she does not develop a career, familial ties, or more complex problems that we associate with adulthood. Perhaps she is not meant to. As a series heroine, Nancy exemplifies for girl readers the kind of girl they could grow up to be, but at a certain point, she demands the same independence of her readers that she possesses. Once they have caught up to her, they must make their own decisions and plow ahead with the same unshakable focus. She is only there to point the way, rather than telling readers how to live their adult lives.

Many more series girls have come after Nancy, including Beverly Gray, Judy Bolton, Cherry Ames, Trixie Belden, Elizabeth and Jessica Wakefield, Kristy Thomas, Mary Anne Spier, Lyra Silvertongue, Bella Swan, Tally Youngblood, and Gemma Doyle, to name just a few. Series writers and publishers continue to dream up new heroines to appeal to modern girl readers, and all of those heroines deserve examination as part of the ongoing social discourse about girlhood. Series books both reproduce and challenge our culture's ideas about what it means to grow up female in the United States and elsewhere. They reflect our fears, hopes, and dreams for young women, as well as the strictures we place upon them and the paths to empowerment that are open to them. If we hope to understand how girls think about the world around them and how they are socialized into expectations for adulthood, there can be no better place to start than by searching their bookshelves for clues.

Notes

1. There are so many articles and examinations of Nancy Drew that it would be impossible to list them all here, but some of the most crucial include Deidre Johnson, *Edward Stratemeyer and the Stratemeyer Syndicate*; Bobbie Ann Mason, *The Girl Sleuth: On the Trail of Nancy Drew, Judy Bolton, and Cherry Ames*; Carol Billman, *The Secret of the Stratemeyer Syndicate: Nancy Drew, the Hardy Boys, and the Million Dollar Fiction Factory*; Sherrie Inness, *Nancy Drew and Company: Culture, Gender, and Girls' Series*; and Caroline Stuart Dyer and Nancy Tillman Romalav, eds., *Rediscovering Nancy Drew*.

2. Real young women also engaged in this kind of public, group consumption, as well as consumption that helped define their tastes and personalities. I examine one group of historical girls who follow this pattern of behavior in "The Girls of 83 Round Hill Road: Boarding Houses, Social Interaction, and the Culture of Consumption at Smith College, 1892–1895," *Journal of the History of Childhood and Youth* 5.3 (Fall 2012).

3. One interesting exception to this is Nancy Drew #64, *Captive Witness*, published in 1981. The plot involves a documentary stolen from the Vienna Film Festival, and Nancy just happens to be taking a tour of Europe that ends in Vienna, along with Ned, Bess, and George. The documentary details many of the abuses perpetuated in Eastern Europe behind the "Iron Curtain" during the Cold War. In the process of recovering the film, Nancy also gets involved in helping to smuggle ten orphaned

children out of Hungary so that they may be reunited with their nearest relatives. The villains of the piece all have German names and speak German; one presumes that readers are supposed to think of them as Eastern Germans.

4. For more information about the Syndicate's updating of the Nancy Drew and Hardy Boys books, see James Keeline, "Who Wrote Nancy Drew? Secrets from the Syndicate Files Revealed"; Marilyn S. Greenwald, *The Secret of the Hardy Boys*, 245–249; Deidre Johnson, *Edward Stratemeyer*, 145, 152–53; and Melanie Rehak, *The Girl Sleuth*, 246–251. This is one element of Nancy Drew that is extraordinarily difficult to research; the different editions not only had changes made to the plots, but also the original ghostwriters were not responsible for the changes. The Syndicate was highly secretive about the identities of their ghostwriters to begin with, so determining who wrote which books and who made what changes to the later editions is an enormous task.

5. Nancy's predecessors are talked about in this study, but her successors are not. There were many girls' series published after Nancy Drew that were historically specific and showcased heroines who were of their times. Just to name a few: Cherry Ames, who among other things is a nurse during World War II; Judy Bolton, who solves mysteries from the 1930s through the 1960s and does grow up and get married; and Vicki Barr, who is a flight stewardess in the 1950s and '60s.

Appendix: Series Books in Order of Publication

Note: While in some cases I have not consulted or quoted every volume of a series, it is helpful to see them listed in the order they were published, to get a sense of the continuity of events and the maturity of the characters. All the volumes I have used and consulted are listed here.

Alcott, Louisa May. *Little Women.* 1868–69. New York: Modern Library–Random House, 2000. Print.
_____. *Little Men.* 1871. New York: Signet Classic–Penguin, 1986. Print.
_____. *Jo's Boys.* 1886. New York: Bantam Books–Bantam Doubleday Dell, 1995. Print.
Alden, Isabella Macdonald. *Four Girls at Chautauqua.* 1876. Wheaton, IL: Living Books–Tyndale House, 1996. Print.
_____. *The Chautauqua Girls at Home.* 1877. Wheaton, IL: Living Books–Tyndale House, 1997. Print.
_____. *Ruth Erskine's Crosses.* 1879. Wheaton, IL: Living Books–Tyndale House, 1997. Print.
_____. *Judge Burnham's Daughters.* 1888. Wheaton, IL: Living Books–Tyndale House, 1996. Print.
_____. *Ruth Erskine's Son.* 1907. Bessemer, MI: Keepers of the Faith, 2003. Print.
_____. *Four Mothers at Chautauqua.* 1913. Wheaton, IL: Living Books–Tyndale House, 1997. Print.
Brooks, Edna. *The Khaki Girls of the Motor Corps.* New York: Cupples & Leon, 1918. Print.
_____. *The Khaki Girls Behind the Lines.* New York: Cupples & Leon, 1918. Print.
_____. *The Khaki Girls at Windsor Barracks.* New York: Cupples & Leon, 1919. Print.
_____. *The Khaki Girls in Victory.* New York: Cupples & Leon, 1920. Print.
Champney, Elizabeth W. *Three Vassar Girls Abroad.* Boston: Estes and Lauriat, 1883. Print.
_____. *Three Vassar Girls on the Rhine.* Boston: Estes and Lauriat, 1886. Print.
_____. *Witch Winnie.* New York: Dodd, Mead, 1889. *Google Books.* Web. August 2009.
_____. *Witch Winnie's Mystery.* New York: Dodd, Mead, 1891. Print.

Emerson, Alice B. *Ruth Fielding of the Red Mill.* New York: Cupples & Leon, 1913. Print.
———. *Ruth Fielding at Briarwood Hall.* New York: Cupples & Leon, 1913. Print.
———. *Ruth Fielding at Snow Camp.* New York: Cupples & Leon, 1913. Print.
———. *Ruth Fielding at Lighthouse Point.* New York: Cupples & Leon, 1913. Print.
———. *Ruth Fielding at Silver Ranch.* New York: Cupples & Leon, 1913. Print.
———. *Ruth Fielding on Cliff Island.* New York: Cupples & Leon, 1915. Print.
———. *Ruth Fielding at Sunrise Farm.* New York: Cupples & Leon, 1915. Print.
———. *Ruth Fielding and the Gypsies.* New York: Cupples & Leon, 1915. Print.
———. *Ruth Fielding in Moving Pictures.* New York: Cupples & Leon, 1916. Print.
———. *Ruth Fielding Down in Dixie.* New York: Cupples & Leon, 1916. Print.
———. *Ruth Fielding at College.* New York: Cupples & Leon, 1917. Print.
———. *Ruth Fielding in the Saddle.* New York: Cupples & Leon, 1917. Print.
———. *Ruth Fielding in the Red Cross.* New York: Cupples & Leon, 1918. Print.
———. *Ruth Fielding at the War Front.* New York: Cupples & Leon, 1918. Print.
———. *Ruth Fielding Homeward Bound.* New York: Cupples & Leon, 1919. Print.
———. *Ruth Fielding Down East.* New York: Cupples & Leon, 1920. Print.
———. *Ruth Fielding in the Great Northwest.* New York: Cupples & Leon, 1921. Print.
———. *Ruth Fielding on the St. Lawrence.* New York: Cupples & Leon, 1922. Print.
———. *Ruth Fielding Treasure Hunting.* New York: Cupples & Leon, 1923. Print.
———. *Ruth Fielding in the Far North.* New York: Cupples & Leon, 1924. Print.
———. *Ruth Fielding at Golden Pass.* New York: Cupples & Leon, 1925. Print.
———. *Ruth Fielding in Alaska.* New York: Cupples & Leon, 1926. Print.
———. *Ruth Fielding and Her Great Scenario.* New York: Cupples & Leon, 1927. Print.
———. *Ruth Fielding at Cameron Hall.* New York: Cupples & Leon, 1928. Print.
———. *Ruth Fielding Clearing Her Name.* New York: Cupples & Leon, 1929. Print.
———. *Ruth Fielding in Talking Pictures.* New York: Cupples & Leon, 1930. Print.
———. *Ruth Fielding and Baby June.* New York: Cupples & Leon, 1931. Print.
———. *Ruth Fielding and Her Double.* New York: Cupples & Leon, 1932. Print.
———. *Ruth Fielding and Her Greatest Triumph.* New York: Cupples & Leon, 1933. Print.
Finley, Martha. *Elsie Dinsmore.* New York: Dodd, Mead, 1867. Chicago: Saalfield [circa 1920]. Print.
———. *Elsie's Holidays at Roselands.* New York: Dodd, Mead, 1868. *Project Gutenberg.* Web. 2009.
———. *Elsie's Girlhood.* New York: Dodd, Mead, 1872. *Project Gutenberg.* Web. 2009.
———. *Elsie's Womanhood.* New York: Dodd, Mead, 1875. *Project Gutenberg.* Web. 2009.
———. *Elsie's Motherhood.* New York: Dodd, Mead, 1876. *Project Gutenberg.* Web. 2009.
———. *Elsie's Children.* New York: Dodd, Mead, 1877. *Project Gutenberg.* Web. 2009.
———. *Elsie's Widowhood.* New York: Dodd, Mead, 1880. Print.
———. *Grandmother Elsie.* New York: Dodd, Mead, 1882. *Project Gutenberg.* Web. 2009.
———. *Elsie's New Relations.* New York: Dodd, Mead, 1883. *Project Gutenberg.* Web. 2009.
———. *Elsie at Nantucket.* New York: Dodd, Mead, 1884. *Project Gutenberg.* Web. 2009.
———. *The Two Elsies.* New York: Dodd, Mead, 1885. *Project Gutenberg.* Web. 2009.

_____. *Elsie's Kith and Kin*. New York: Dodd, Mead, 1886. *Project Gutenberg*. Web. 2009.
_____. *Elsie's Friends at Woodburn*. New York: Dodd, Mead, 1887. Print.
_____. *Christmas with Grandma Elsie*. New York: Dodd, Mead, 1888. *Project Gutenberg*. Web. 2007–2009.
_____. *Elsie and the Raymonds*. New York: Dodd, Mead, 1889. Print.
_____. *Elsie Yachting with the Raymonds*. New York: Dodd, Mead, 1890. Print.
_____. *Elsie's Vacation and After Events*. New York: Dodd, Mead, 1891. *Project Gutenberg*. Web. 2007–2009.
_____. *Elsie at Viamede*. New York: Dodd, Mead, 1892. Print.
_____. *Elsie at the World's Fair*. New York: Dodd, Mead, 1894. *Project Gutenberg*. Web. 2007–2009.
_____. *Elsie at Home*. New York: Dodd, Mead, 1897. *Project Gutenberg*. Web. 2007–2009.
Flower, Jessie Graham [Josephine Chase]. *Grace Harlowe's Plebe Year at High School*. Philadelphia: Altemus, 1910. Print.
_____. *Grace Harlowe's Sophomore Year at High School*. Philadelphia: Altemus, 1911. Print.
_____. *Grace Harlowe's Junior Year at High School*. Philadelphia: Altemus, 1911. Print.
_____. *Grace Harlowe's Senior Year at High School*. Philadelphia: Altemus, 1911. Print.
_____. *Grace Harlowe's Second Year at Overton College*. Philadelphia: Altemus, 1914. Print.
Flower, Jessie Graham [Frank G. Patchin]. *Grace Harlowe with the Red Cross in France*. Philadelphia: Altemus, 1920. Print.
_____. *Grace Harlowe with the American Army on the Rhine*. Philadelphia: Altemus, 1920. Print.
Hope, Laura Lee. *The Outdoor Girls of Deepdale*. New York: Grosset & Dunlap, 1913. Print.
_____. *The Outdoor Girls at Rainbow Lake*. New York: Grosset & Dunlap, 1913. Print.
_____. *The Outdoor Girls in a Motor Car*. New York: Grosset & Dunlap, 1913. Print.
_____. *The Outdoor Girls in Florida*. New York: Grosset & Dunlap, 1913. Print.
_____. *The Outdoor Girls in Army Service*. New York: Grosset & Dunlap, 1918. Print.
_____. *The Outdoor Girls at the Hostess House*. New York: Grosset & Dunlap, 1919. Print.
_____. *The Outdoor Girls at Bluff Point*. New York: Grosset & Dunlap, 1920. Print.
_____. *The Outdoor Girls at Wild Rose Lodge*. New York: Grosset & Dunlap, 1921. Print.
_____. *The Outdoor Girls Along the Coast*. New York: Grosset & Dunlap, 1926. Print.
_____. *The Outdoor Girls at New Moon Ranch*. New York: Grosset & Dunlap, 1928. Print.
_____. *The Outdoor Girls on a Hike*. Racine: Whitman, 1929. Print.
_____. *The Outdoor Girls in the Air*. Racine: Whitman, 1932. Print.
Wells, Carolyn. *Patty Fairfield*. New York: Dodd, Mead, 1901. Print.
_____. *Patty at Home*. New York: Dodd, Mead, 1904. Print.
_____. *Patty in the City*. New York: Dodd, Mead, 1905. Print.
_____. *Patty's Summer Days*. New York: Dodd, Mead, 1906. Print.
_____. *Patty in Paris*. New York: Dodd, Mead, 1907. Print.
_____. *Patty's Friends*. New York: Dodd, Mead, 1908. Print.
_____. *Patty's Pleasure Trip*. New York: Dodd, Mead, 1909. Print.

———. *Patty's Success.* New York: Dodd, Mead, 1910. Print.
———. *Patty's Motor Car.* New York: Dodd, Mead, 1911. Print.
———. *Patty's Butterfly Days.* New York: Dodd, Mead, 1912. Print.
———. *Patty's Social Season.* New York: Dodd, Mead, 1913. Print.
———. *Patty's Suitors.* New York: Dodd, Mead, 1914. Print.
———. *Patty's Romance.* New York: Dodd, Mead, 1915. Print.
———. *Patty's Fortune.* New York: Dodd, Mead, 1916. Print.
———. *Patty Blossom.* New York: Dodd, Mead, 1917. Print.
———. *Patty—Bride.* New York: Dodd, Mead, 1918. Print.
———. *Patty and Azalea.* New York: Dodd, Mead, 1919. Print.

Bibliography

When multiple ghostwriters are known to have contributed to a series, I have done my best to identify the ghostwriters for particular volumes. The work of James Keeline and Deidre Johnson has been especially helpful in this regard. Information on Stratemeyer Syndicate ghostwriters is scarce and difficult to obtain, and author information for each series is being continually revised as more research is done.

Abelson, Elaine. *When Ladies Go A-Thieving: Middle-Class Shoplifters in the Victorian Department Store.* New York: Oxford University Press, 1992. Print.
Adickes, Sandra. *To Be Young Was Very Heaven: Women in New York Before the First World War.* New York: St. Martin's Griffin, 1997. Print.
Alcott, Louisa May. *Eight Cousins.* 1874. New York: Grosset & Dunlap: 1927. Print.
_____. *Jo's Boys.* 1886. New York: Bantam Books–Bantam Doubleday Dell, 1995. Print.
_____. *Little Men.* 1871. New York: Signet Classic-Penguin, 1986. Print.
_____. *Little Women.* 1868–69. New York: Modern Library–Random House, 2000. Print.
Alden, Isabella Macdonald. *The Chautauqua Girls at Home.* 1877. Wheaton, IL: Living Books–Tyndale House, 1997. Print.
_____. *Four Girls at Chautauqua.* 1876. Wheaton, IL: Living Books–Tyndale House, 1996. Print.
_____. *Four Mothers at Chautauqua.* 1913. Wheaton, IL: Living Books–Tyndale House, 1997. Print.
_____. *Judge Burnham's Daughters.* 1888. Wheaton, IL: Living Books–Tyndale House, 1996. Print.
_____. *Ruth Erskine's Crosses.* 1879. Wheaton, IL: Living Books–Tyndale House, 1997. Print.
_____. *Ruth Erskine's Son.* 1907. Bessemer, MI: Keepers of the Faith, 2003. Print.
Andrews, William L., ed. *Sisters of the Sprit: Three Black Women's Autobiographies of the Nineteenth Century.* Bloomington: Indiana University Press, 1986. Print.
Antler, Joyce. *The Journey Home: Jewish Women and the American Century.* New York: The Free Press, 1997. Print.
Association of Collegiate Alumnae. *Health Statistics of Women College Graduates.* Boston: Wright and Potter Printing, 1885. *Google Books.* Web. 14 April 2010.
Babb, Valerie. *Whiteness Visible: The Meaning of Whiteness in American Literature and Culture.* New York: New York University Press, 1998. Print.
Banham, Rob. "The Industrialization of the Book 1800–1970." *A Companion to the History*

of the Book. Ed. Simon Eliot and Jonathan Rose. Malden, MA: Blackwell, 2007. 273–290. Print.

Banta, Martha. *Imaging American Women: Ideas and Ideals in Cultural History.* New York: Columbia University Press, 1987. Print.

Baker, Paula. "The Domestication of Politics: Women and American Political Society, 1780–1920." *Women, the State, and Welfare.* Ed. Linda Gordon. Madison: University of Wisconsin Press, 1990. 55–91. Print.

———. *The Moral Frameworks of Public Life: Gender, Politics, and the State in Rural New York, 1870–1930.* New York: Oxford University Press, 1991. Print.

Basinger, Jeanine. *Silent Stars.* Hanover, NH: Wesleyan University Press, 2000. Print.

Baxter, Kent. *The Modern Age: Turn-of-the-Century American Culture and the Invention of Adolescence.* Tuscaloosa: University of Alabama Press, 2008. Print.

Baym, Nina. *Woman's Fiction: A Guide to Novels By and About Women in America 1820–1870.* 1978. Urbana: University of Illinois Press, 1993. Print.

Beauchamp, Cari. *Without Lying Down: Frances Marion and the Powerful Women of Early Hollywood.* Berkeley: University of California Press, 1998. Print.

Bederman, Gail. *Manliness & Civilization: A Cultural History of Gender and Race in the United States, 1880–1917.* Chicago: University of Chicago Press, 1995. Print.

Bendroth, Margaret Lamberts. *Fundamentalism & Gender, 1875 to the Present.* New Haven: Yale University Press, 1993. Print.

Benson, Susan Porter. *Counter Cultures: Saleswomen, Managers, and Customers in American Department Stores, 1890–1940.* Urbana: University of Illinois Press, 1986. Print.

Berg, Barbara J. *The Remembered Gate: Origins of American Feminism.* Oxford: Oxford University Press, 1978. Print.

Billman, Carol. *The Secret of the Stratemeyer Syndicate: Nancy Drew, the Hardy Boys, and the Million Dollar Fiction Factory.* New York: Ungar, 1986. Print.

Blodgett, Jan. *Protestant Evangelical Literary Culture and Contemporary Society.* Westport, CT: Greenwood Press, 1997. Print.

Bobiniski, George S. *Carnegie Libraries: Their History and Impact on American Public Library Development.* Chicago: American Library Association, 1969. Print.

Bordin, Ruth. *Woman and Temperance: The Quest for Power and Liberty, 1873–1900.* 1981. New Brunswick, NJ: Rutgers University Press, 1990. Print.

Boydston, Jeanne. "The Pastoralization of Housework." *Women's America: Refocusing the Past.* 6th ed. Ed. Linda K. Kerber and Jane Sharron DeHart. New York: Oxford University Press, 2004. 153–164. Print. Excerpt from *Home and Work: Housework, Wages, and the Ideology of Labor in the Early Republic.* New York: Oxford University Press, 1991. Print.

———, Mary Kelley, and Anne Margolis. *The Limits of Sisterhood: The Beecher Sisters on Women's Rights and Women's Sphere.* Chapel Hill: University of North Carolina Press, 1988. Print.

Boylan, Anne M. *The Origins of Women's Activism: New York and Boston, 1797–1840.* Chapel Hill: University of North Carolina Press, 2002. Print.

Brackett, Anna C., ed. *The Education of American Girls.* New York: G.P. Putnam's, 1874. *Google Books.* Web. 14 April 2010.

Braude, Ann. "The Jewish Woman's Encounter with American Culture." *Women and Religion in America, Vol. 1: The Nineteenth Century.* Ed. Rosemary Radford Ruether and Rosemary Skinner Keller. San Francisco: Harper & Row, 1981. 150–192. Print.

Brekus, Catherine A. *Strangers and Pilgrims: Female Preaching in America, 1740–1845.* Chapel Hill: University of North Carolina Press, 1998. Print.

Brodhead, Richard. *Cultures of Letters: Scenes of Reading and Writing in Nineteenth-Century America.* Chicago: University of Chicago Press, 1993. Print.

Brooks, Edna. *The Khaki Girls at Windsor Barracks.* New York: Cupples & Leon, 1919. Print.

---. *The Khaki Girls Behind the Lines.* New York: Cupples & Leon, 1918. Print.
---. *The Khaki Girls in Victory.* New York: Cupples & Leon, 1920. Print.
---. *The Khaki Girls of the Motor Corps.* New York: Cupples & Leon, 1918. Print.
Brooks, Geraldine. *March.* New York: Penguin, 2006. Print.
Browder, Laura. *Slippery Characters: Ethnic Impersonators and American Identities.* Chapel Hill: University of North Carolina Press, 2000. Print.
Brown, Carrie. *Rosie's Mom: Forgotten Women Workers of the First World War.* Boston: Northeastern University Press, 2002. Print.
Brown, Janet E. "The Sage of Elsie Dinsmore: A Study in Nineteenth Century Sensibility." *University of Buffalo Studies* 17.3 (1945): 75–131. Print.
Brownlow, Kevin. *The Parade's Gone By.* Berkeley: University of California Press, 1976. Print.
Brumberg, Joan Jacobs. *The Body Project: An Intimate History of American Girls.* New York: Vintage, 1998. Print.
---. *Fasting Girls: The History of Anorexia Nervosa.* New York: Vintage, 2000. Print.
Cane, Aleta Feinsod, and Susan Alves, eds. *"The Only Efficient Instrument": American Women Writers and the Periodical, 1837–1916.* Iowa City: University of Iowa Press, 2001. Print.
Carnes, Mark C. *Secret Ritual and Manhood in Victorian America.* New Haven: Yale University Press, 1989. Print.
---, and Clyde Griffen, eds. *Meanings for Manhood: Constructions of Masculinity in Victorian America.* Chicago: University of Chicago Press, 1990. Print.
"Carolyn Wells, Novelist, Dead." *New York Times* 27 Mar. 1942: 23. *ProQuest Historical Newspapers: The New York Times.* Web. 21 Mar. 2010.
Cawelti, John G. *Adventure, Mystery, and Romance: Formula Stories as Art and Popular Culture.* Chicago: Chicago University Press, 1976. Print.
Champney, Elizabeth W. *Three Vassar Girls Abroad.* Boston: Estes and Lauriat, 1883. Print.
---. *Three Vassar Girls on the Rhine.* Boston: Estes and Lauriat, 1886. Print.
---. *Witch Winnie.* New York: Dodd, Mead, 1889. *Google Books.* Web. August 2009.
---. *Witch Winnie's Mystery.* New York: Dodd, Mead, 1891. Print.
Cherland, Meredith. *Private Practices: Girls Reading Fiction and Constructing Identity.* Oxon, England: Taylor & Francis, 1994. Print.
Chinn, Sarah E. *Inventing Modern Adolescence: The Children of Immigrants in Turn-of-the-Century America.* New Brunswick, NJ: Rutgers University Press, 2009. Print.
Clark, Beverly Lyon. *Kiddie Lit: The Cultural Construction of Children's Literature in America.* Baltimore: Johns Hopkins University Press, 2003. Print.
---, ed. *Louisa May Alcott: The Contemporary Reviews.* Cambridge: Cambridge University Press, 2004. Print.
Coolidge, Susan [Sarah Chauncey Woolsey]. *What Katy Did.* 1872. New York: Puffin-Penguin, 2004. Print.
Cott, Nancy. *The Bonds of Womanhood: "Woman's Sphere in New England," 1780–1835.* 1977. New Haven: Yale University Press, 1997. Print.
---. *The Grounding of Modern Feminism.* New Haven: Yale University Press, 1987. Print.
Cox, J. Randolph. *The Dime Novel Companion: A Source Book.* Westport, CT: Greenwood Press, 2000. Print.
Curtis, Susan. *A Consuming Faith: The Social Gospel and Modern American Culture.* Baltimore: Johns Hopkins University Press, 1991. Print.
Denning, Michael. *Mechanic Accents: Dime Novels and Working-Class Culture in America*, rev. ed. London: Verso, 1998. Print.
Dirks, Tim. "The History of Film, The Pre-1920s: Early Cinematic Origins and the Infancy of Film, Part 2." *AMC Filmsite.* American Movie Classics. Web. June 2012.
Dodd, Mead, and Co. Advertisement. *American Literary Gazette and Publisher's Circular* 1 Dec. 1870: 151. *American Periodicals Series Online.* Web. 3 Mar. 2010. PDF file.

Dodd, Mead, and Co. Advertisement. *The Literary World: A Monthly Review of Current Literature* 27 Mar. 1880: 116. *American Periodicals Series Online.* Web. 3 Mar. 2010. PDF file.
Dodd, Mead, and Co. Advertisement. *The Critic: A Weekly Review of Literature and the Arts* 31 Mar. 1894: I. *American Periodicals Series Online.* Web. 3 Mar. 2010. PDF file.
Dodd, Mead, and Co. Advertisement. *Century Illustrated Magazine* 98.6 (Oct. 1894): 16–17. *American Periodicals Series Online.* Web. 3 Mar. 2010. PDF file.
Douglas, Ann. *The Feminization of American Culture.* New York: Noonday Press, 1998. Print.
Dublin, Thomas, ed. *Women at Work: The Transformation of Work and Community in Lowell, Massachusetts, 1826–1860.* New York: Columbia University Press, 1979. Print.
_____. *Farm to Factory: Women's Letter's, 1830–1860*, 2d ed. New York: Columbia University Press, 1993. Print.
Duffey, Eliza B. *No Sex in Education, or an Equal Chance for Both Boys and Girls.* Philadelphia: J.M. Stoddart, 1874. *Google Books.* Web. 14 April 2010.
Dyer, Carolyn Stuart, and Nancy Tillman Romalov, eds. *Rediscovering Nancy Drew.* Iowa City: University of Iowa Press, 1995. Print.
Ebbert, Jean, and Marie-Beth Hall. *The First, The Few, The Forgotten: Navy and Marine Corps Women in World War I.* Annapolis: Naval Institute Press, 2002. Print.
Edwards, Rebecca. *Angels in the Machinery: Gender in American Party Politics from the Civil War to the Progressive Era.* New York: Oxford University Press, 1997. Print.
Emerson, Alice B. *Ruth Fielding and Baby June.* New York: Cupples & Leon, 1931. Print.
_____. *Ruth Fielding and Her Double.* New York: Cupples & Leon, 1932. Print.
_____. *Ruth Fielding and Her Great Scenario.* New York: Cupples & Leon, 1927. Print.
_____. *Ruth Fielding and Her Greatest Triumph.* New York: Cupples & Leon, 1933. Print.
_____. *Ruth Fielding and the Gypsies.* New York: Cupples & Leon, 1915. Print.
_____. *Ruth Fielding at Briarwood Hall.* New York: Cupples & Leon, 1913. Print.
_____. *Ruth Fielding at Cameron Hall.* New York: Cupples & Leon, 1928. Print.
_____. *Ruth Fielding at College.* New York: Cupples & Leon, 1917. Print.
_____. *Ruth Fielding at Golden Pass.* New York: Cupples & Leon, 1925. Print.
_____. *Ruth Fielding at Lighthouse Point.* New York: Cupples & Leon, 1913. Print.
_____. *Ruth Fielding at Silver Ranch.* New York: Cupples & Leon, 1913. Print.
_____. *Ruth Fielding at Snow Camp.* New York: Cupples & Leon, 1913. Print.
_____. *Ruth Fielding at Sunrise Farm.* New York: Cupples & Leon, 1915. Print.
_____. *Ruth Fielding at the War Front.* New York: Cupples & Leon, 1918. Print.
_____. *Ruth Fielding Clearing Her Name.* New York: Cupples & Leon, 1929. Print.
_____. *Ruth Fielding Down East.* New York: Cupples & Leon, 1920. Print.
_____. *Ruth Fielding Down in Dixie.* New York: Cupples & Leon, 1916. Print.
_____. *Ruth Fielding Homeward Bound.* New York: Cupples & Leon, 1919. Print.
_____. *Ruth Fielding in Alaska.* New York: Cupples & Leon, 1926. Print.
_____. *Ruth Fielding in Moving Pictures.* New York: Cupples & Leon, 1916. Print.
_____. *Ruth Fielding in Talking Pictures.* New York: Cupples & Leon, 1930. Print.
_____. *Ruth Fielding in the Far North.* New York: Cupples & Leon, 1924. Print.
_____. *Ruth Fielding in the Great Northwest.* New York: Cupples & Leon, 1921. Print.
_____. *Ruth Fielding in the Red Cross.* New York: Cupples & Leon, 1918. Print.
_____. *Ruth Fielding in the Saddle.* New York: Cupples & Leon, 1917. Print.
_____. *Ruth Fielding of the Red Mill.* New York: Cupples & Leon, 1913. Print.
_____. *Ruth Fielding on Cliff Island.* New York: Cupples & Leon, 1915. Print.
_____. *Ruth Fielding on the St. Lawrence.* New York: Cupples & Leon, 1922. Print.
_____. *Ruth Fielding Treasure Hunting.* New York: Cupples & Leon, 1923. Print.
Enstad, Nan. *Ladies of Labor, Girls of Adventure: Working Women, Popular Culture, and Labor Politics at the Turn of the Twentieth Century.* New York: Columbia University Press, 1999. Print.

Epstein, Barbara Leslie. *The Politics of Domesticity: Women, Evangelism, and Temperance in Nineteenth Century America*. Middletown, CT: Wesleyan University Press, 1981. Print.
Erenberg, Lewis A. *Steppin' Out: New York Nightlife and the Transformation of American Culture, 1890–1930*. Chicago: University of Chicago Press, 1984. Print.
Ewans, Mary. "The Leadership of Nuns in Immigrant Catholicism." *Women and Religion in America, Vol. 1: The Nineteenth Century*. Ed. Rosemary Radford Ruether and Rosemary Skinner Keller. San Francisco: Harper & Row, 1981. 101–149. Print.
Fass, Paula S. *The Damned and the Beautiful: American Youth in the 1920s*. Oxford: Oxford University Press, 1977. Print.
Finley, Martha. *Christmas with Grandma Elsie*. New York: Dodd, Mead, 1888. *Project Gutenberg*. Web. 2007–2009.
_____. *Elsie and the Raymonds*. New York: Dodd, Mead, 1889. Print.
_____. *Elsie at Home*. New York: Dodd, Mead, 1897. *Project Gutenberg*. Web. 2007–2009.
_____. *Elsie at Nantucket*. New York: Dodd, Mead, 1884. *Project Gutenberg*. Web. 2009.
_____. *Elsie at the World's Fair*. New York: Dodd, Mead, 1894. *Project Gutenberg*. Web. 2007–2009.
_____. *Elsie at Viamede*. New York: Dodd, Mead, 1892. Print.
_____. *Elsie Dinsmore*. New York: Dodd, Mead, 1867. Chicago: Saalfield [circa 1920]. Print.
_____. *Elsie Yachting with the Raymonds*. New York: Dodd, Mead, 1890. Print.
_____. *Elsie's Children*. New York: Dodd, Mead, 1877. *Project Gutenberg*. Web. 2009.
_____. *Elsie's Friends at Woodburn*. New York: Dodd, Mead, 1887. Print.
_____. *Elsie's Girlhood*. New York: Dodd, Mead, 1872. *Project Gutenberg*. Web. 2009.
_____. *Elsie's Holidays at Roselands*. New York: Dodd, Mead, 1868. *Project Gutenberg*. Web. 2009.
_____. *Elsie's Kith and Kin*. New York: Dodd, Mead, 1886. *Project Gutenberg*. Web. 2009.
_____. *Elsie's Motherhood*. New York: Dodd, Mead, 1876. *Project Gutenberg*. Web. 2009.
_____. *Elsie's New Relations*. New York: Dodd, Mead, 1883. *Project Gutenberg*. Web. 2009.
_____. *Elsie's Vacation and After Events*. New York: Dodd, Mead, 1891. *Project Gutenberg*. Web. 2007–2009.
_____. *Elsie's Womanhood*. New York: Dodd, Mead, 1875. *Project Gutenberg*. Web. 2009.
_____. *Elsie's Widowhood*. New York: Dodd, Mead, 1880. Print.
_____. *Grandmother Elsie*. New York: Dodd, Mead, 1882. *Project Gutenberg*. Web. 2009.
_____. *The Two Elsies*. New York: Dodd, Mead, 1885. *Project Gutenberg*. Web. 2009.
Finnegan, Margaret. *Selling Suffrage: Consumer Culture & Votes for Women*. New York: Columbia University Press, 1999.
Flower, Jessie Graham [Frank G. Patchin]. *Grace Harlowe with the American Army on the Rhine*. Philadelphia: Altemus, 1920. Print.
_____. *Grace Harlowe with the Red Cross in France*. Philadelphia: Altemus, 1920. Print.
Flower, Jessie Graham [Josephine Chase]. *Grace Harlowe's Junior Year at High School*. Philadelphia: Altemus, 1911. Print.
_____. *Grace Harlowe's Plebe Year at High School*. Philadelphia: Altemus, 1910. Print.
_____. *Grace Harlowe's Second Year at Overton College*. Philadelphia: Altemus, 1914. Print.
_____. *Grace Harlowe's Senior Year at High School*. Philadelphia: Altemus, 1911. Print.
_____. *Grace Harlowe's Sophomore Year at High School*. Philadelphia: Altemus, 1911. Print.
Foote, Stephanie. "Resentful *Little Women*: Gender and Class Feeling in Louisa May Alcott." *College Literature* 13.1 (2005): 63–85. *MLA International Bibliography*. Web. 27 August 2008.
Foster, Frances Smith, ed. *A Brighter Coming Day: A Frances Ellen Watkins Harper Reader*. New York: The Feminist Press, 1990.
Fox-Genovese, Elizabeth. *Within the Plantation Household: Black and White Women of the Old South*. Chapel Hill: University of North Carolina Press, 1988. Print.

Gaines, Kevin K. *Uplifting the Race: Black Leadership, Politics, and Culture in the Twentieth Century*. Chapel Hill: University of North Carolina Press, 1996. Print.

Garvey, Ellen Gruber. *The Adman in the Parlor: Magazines and the Gendering of Consumer Culture, 1880s to 1910s*. New York: Oxford University Press, 1996. Print.

Gaskell, Philip. *A New Introduction to Bibliography*. Oxford: Oxford University Press, 1972. Print.

Gavin, Lettie. *American Women in World War I: They Also Served*. Niwot: University Press of Colorado, 1997. Print.

Gilmore, Glenda. *Gender & Jim Crow: Women and the Politics of White Supremacy in North Carolina, 1896–1920*. Chapel Hill: University of North Carolina Press, 1996. Print.

Ginzberg, Lori D. *Women and the Work of Benevolence: Morality, Politics, and Class in the Nineteenth-Century United States*. New Haven: Yale University Press, 1992. Print.

Girls' Series Books: A Checklist of Titles Published 1840–1991. University of Minnesota Libraries. 1992. http://special.lib.umn.edu/clrc/girlsseriesbook.html.

Godson, Susan H. *Serving Proudly: A History of Women in the U.S. Navy*. Annapolis: Naval Institute Press, 2001. Print.

Gordon, Linda. *The Moral Property of Women: A History of Birth Control Politics in America*. Urbana: University of Illinois Press, 2002. Print.

Gordon, Lynn D. *Gender and Higher Education in the Progressive Era*. New Haven: Yale University Press, 1990. Print.

Goulden, Nancy Rost, and Susan Stanfield. "Leaving Elsie Dinsmore Behind: 'Plucky Girls' as an Alternative Role Model in Classic Girls Literature." *Women's Studies* 32.2 (2003): 183–208. *MLA International Bibliography*. Web. 27 August 2008.

Grammer, Elizabeth Elkin. *Some Wild Visions: Autobiographies by Female Itinerant Evangelists in Nineteenth-Century America*. Oxford: Oxford University Press, 2003. Print.

Grayzel, Susan R. *Women and the First World War*. London: Longman-Pearson Education, 2002. Seminar Studies in History. Print.

Greenwald, Marilyn S. *The Secret of the Hardy Boys: Leslie McFarlane and the Stratemeyer Syndicate*. Athens: Ohio University Press, 2004. Print.

Greenwald, Maurine Weiner. *Women, War, and Work: The Impact of World War I on Women Workers in the United States*. Ithaca: Cornell University Press, 1980. Print.

Greer, Jane, ed. *Girls and Literacy in America: Historical Perspectives to the Present*. Santa Barbara, CA: ABC-CLIO, 2003. Print.

Gregory, W.F. Letter to Edward Stratemeyer. 21 February 1901. Microfilm. Reel 1, Incoming Correspondence. Stratemeyer Syndicate Records. Manuscripts and Archives Division. The New York Public Library. Astor, Lenox and Tilden Foundations.

Gross, Robert A. "Building a National Literature: The United States 1800–1890." *A Companion to the History of the Book*. Ed. Simon Eliot and Jonathan Rose. Malden, MA: Blackwell, 2007. 315–328. Print.

Hall, G. Stanley. *Adolescence: Its Psychology, and Its Relations to Physiology, Anthropology, Sociology, Sex, Crime, Religion, and Education*. 2 vols. New York: D. Appleton, 1904. Print.

Hall, Joan Wylie. "'The Book I Couldn't Have': The Perilous Attractions of *Elsie Dinsmore*." *Eudora Welty Newsletter* 23.2 (1999): 28–33. Print.

Hamilton-Honey, Emily. "The Girls of 83 Round Hill Road: Boarding Houses, Social Interaction, and the Culture of Consumption at Smith College, 1892–1895." *Journal of the History of Childhood and Youth* 5.3 (2012): 261–392. Print.

Hardesty, Nancy A. *Women Called to Witness: Evangelical Feminism in the Nineteenth Century*, 2d ed. Knoxville: University of Tennessee Press, 1999. Print.

_____. *Your Daughters Shall Prophesy: Revivalism and Feminism in the Age of Finney*. New York: Carlson, 1991. Print.

Hardman, Pam. "The Steward of Her Soul: Elsie Dinsmore and the Training of a Victorian Child." *American Studies* 29.2 (1988): 69–90. Print.
Harris, Marla. "'A History Not Then Taught in History Books': (Re)Writing Reconstruction in Historical Fiction for Children and Young Adults." *The Lion and the Unicorn* 30.1 (2006): 94–116. *Project Muse.* Web. 12 August 2008.
Henkin, David M. *City Reading: Written Words and Public Spaces in Antebellum New York.* New York: Columbia University Press, 1998. Print.
Hoganson, Kristin L. *Consumers' Imperium: The Global Production of American Domesticity, 1865–1920.* Chapel Hill: University of North Carolina Press, 2007. Print.
Hope, Laura Lee. *The Outdoor Girls Along the Coast.* New York: Grosset & Dunlap, 1926. Print.
____. *The Outdoor Girls at Bluff Point.* New York: Grosset & Dunlap, 1920. Print.
____. *The Outdoor Girls at New Moon Ranch.* New York: Grosset & Dunlap, 1928. Print.
____. *The Outdoor Girls at Rainbow Lake.* New York: Grosset & Dunlap, 1913. Print.
____. *The Outdoor Girls at the Hostess House.* New York: Grosset & Dunlap, 1919. Print.
____. *The Outdoor Girls at Wild Rose Lodge.* New York: Grosset & Dunlap, 1921. Print.
____. *The Outdoor Girls in Army Service.* New York: Grosset & Dunlap, 1918. Print.
____. *The Outdoor Girls in Florida.* New York: Grosset & Dunlap, 1913. Print.
____. *The Outdoor Girls in a Motor Car.* New York: Grosset & Dunlap, 1913. Print.
____. *The Outdoor Girls in the Air.* Racine: Whitman, 1932. Print.
____. *The Outdoor Girls of Deepdale.* New York: Grosset & Dunlap, 1913. Print.
____. *The Outdoor Girls on a Hike.* Racine: Whitman, 1929. Print.
Hoppenstand, Gary, ed. *The Dime Novel Detective.* Madison: Popular Press–University of Wisconsin Press, 1982. Print.
Horowitz, Helen Leftkowitz. *Alma Mater: Design and Experience in the Women's Colleges from Their Nineteenth-Century Beginnings to the 1930s*, 2d ed. Amherst: University of Massachusetts Press, 1993. Print.
____. *The Power and Passion of M. Carey Thomas.* Urbana: University of Illinois Press, 1994. Print.
____. *Rereading Sex: The Battle Over Sexual Knowledge and Suppression in Nineteenth Century America.* New York: Alfred A. Knopf, 2002. Print.
Howard, Anne Bail. "Louisa May Alcott on the Chautauqua Trail." *Children's Literature* 34 (2006): 186–192, 265–66. *Literature Online.* Web. 30 July 2008. http://lion.chadwyck.com.
Howe, Julia Ward, ed. *Sex and Education.* Boston: Roberts, 1874. *Google Books.* Web. 14 April 2010.
Hunter, Jane H. *How Young Ladies Became Girls: The Victorian Origins of American Girlhood.* New Haven: Yale University Press, 2002. Print.
Hunter, Tera. *To 'Joy My Freedom: Southern Black Women's Lives and Labors After the Civil War.* Cambridge: Harvard University Press, 1997. Print.
Inness, Sherrie A.. *Intimate Communities: Representation and Social Transformation in Women's College Fiction, 1895–1910.* Bowling Green, OH: Bowling Green State University Popular Press, 1995. Print.
____, ed. *Delinquents and Debutantes: Twentieth Century American Girls' Cultures.* New York: New York University Press, 1998. Print.
____, ed. *Nancy Drew and Company: Culture, Gender, and Girls' Series.* Bowling Green, OH: Bowling Green State University Popular Press, 1997. Print.
Jackson, Jacqueline, and Philip Kendall. "What Makes a Bad Book Good: Elsie Dinsmore." *Children's Literature* 7 (1978): 45–67. Print.
Jacobson, Lisa. *Raising Consumers: Children and the American Mass Market in the Early Twentieth Century.* New York: Columbia University Press, 2004. Print.

Jensen, Kimberly. *Mobilizing Minerva: American Women in the First World War.* Urbana: University of Illinois Press, 2008. Print.

Johannsen, Albert. *The House of Beadle and Adams and Its Dime and Nickel Novels.* Vol. 1. University of Oklahoma Press, 1950. Print.

Johnson, Deidre. *Edward Stratemeyer and the Stratemeyer Syndicate.* New York: Twayne, 1993. Print.

_____, ed. "Isabella MacDonald Alden (Pansy)." *19th Century Girls' Series.* Web. 2008–2009. http://www.readseries.com/auth-pansy/pansybio.htm.

_____, ed. "Martha Finley." *19th Century Girls' Series.* Web. 2008–2009. http://readseries.com/auth-dm/finley1.html.

_____. "Nancy Drew — A Modern Elsie Dinsmore?" *The Lion and the Unicorn* 18.1 (1994): 13–24. Print.

_____. *Stratemeyer Pseudonyms and Series Books: An Annotated Checklist of Stratemeyer and Stratemeyer Syndicate Publications.* Westport, CT: Greenwood Press, 1982. Print.

Jones, Jacqueline. *Labor of Love, Labor of Sorrow: Black Women, Work, and the Family, from Slavery to the Present.* 1986. New York: Random House-Vintage, 1995. Print.

Jones, Martha S. *All Bound Up Together: The Woman Question in African American Public Culture, 1830–1900.* Chapel Hill: University of North Carolina Press, 2007. Print.

Kaestle, Carl F. *Pillars of the Republic: Common Schools and American Society, 1780–1860.* New York: Hill and Wang, 1983. Print.

Katz, Friedrich. *The Secret War in Mexico: Europe, The United States, and the Mexican Revolution.* Chicago: University of Chicago Press, 1981.

Keeline, James. "Booming the Books: Innovations in Book Promotion by Edward Stratemeyer." Unpublished conference paper. PCA/ACA Conference, San Francisco, CA, 2008. Web. PDF file.

_____. "Comments on Emily's Prospectus." Microsoft Word File. Received in "Re: Emily Honey's Prospectus." Message to the author. 13 April 2008. 11:42 A.M. E-mail and Microsoft Word file.

_____. "Edward Stratemeyer: Author and Literary Agent, 1876–1906." Unpublished Conference Paper. PCA/ACA Conference, 1999. Web. PDF file.

_____. "Re: 'Booming the Books' and Sales Figs." Message to the author. 27 June 2008. E-mail.

_____. "Re: Emily Honey's Prospectus." Message to the author. 13 April 2008. 11:41 A.M. E-mail.

_____. "Syndicate 101, or Where Did All Those Books Come From?" Unpublished paper. Web. PDF file.

_____. "Who Wrote Nancy Drew? Secrets from the Syndicate Files Revealed." Web. PDF File. 27 June 2012. http://www.keeline.com/Nancy_Drew.pdf

Keene, Carolyn [Mildred Wirt Benson]. *The Secret of the Old Clock.* 1930. Bedford, MA: Applewood Books, 1991. Print.

Keene, Carolyn [Richard Ballad]. *Captive Witness.* New York: Wanderer–Simon & Schuster, 1981.

Kelley, Mary. *Learning to Stand and Speak: Women, Education, and Public Life in America's Republic.* Chapel Hill: University of North Carolina Press, 2006. Print.

_____. *Private Woman, Public Stage: Literary Domesticity in Nineteenth-Century America.* 1984. Chapel Hill: University of North Carolina Press, 2002. Print.

Kent, Kathryn R. *Making Girls into Women: American Women's Writing and the Rise of Lesbian Identity.* Durham, NC: Duke University Press, 2003. Print.

Kerr, Andrea Moore. *Lucy Stone: Speaking Out for Equality.* New Brunswick, NJ: Rutgers University Press, 1992. Print.

Kessler-Harris, Alice. *Out to Work: A History of Wage-Earning Women in the United States.* New York: Oxford University Press, 1982. Print.

Kett, Joseph F. *Rites of Passage: Adolescence in America 1790 to the Present.* New York: Basic Books, 1977. Print.

Kilde, Jeanne Halgren. "The 'Predominance of the Feminine' at Chautauqua: Rethinking the Gender-Space Relationship in Victorian America." *Signs* 24.2 (1999): 449–486. *JSTOR.* Web. 27 August 2008.

Kraditor, Aileen S. *The Ideas of the Woman Suffrage Movement, 1890–1920.* New York: W.W. Norton, 1981. Print.

Kunzel, Regina G. *Fallen Women, Problem Girls: Unmarried Mothers and the Professionalization of Social Work, 1890–1945.* New Haven: Yale University Press, 1993. Print.

Leach, William. *Land of Desire: Merchants, Power, and the Rise of a New American Culture.* New York: Vintage, 1994. Print.

Lears, T. Jackson. *Fables of Abundance: A Cultural History of Advertising in America.* New York: Basic Books, 1994. Print.

_____, and Richard Wightman Fox. *The Culture of Consumption: Critical Essays in American History, 1880–1980.* New York: Pantheon, 1983. Print.

LeBlanc, Edward T. "A Brief History of Dime Novels: Formats and Contents, 1860–1933." *Pioneers, Passionate Ladies, and Private Eyes: Dime Novels, Series Books, and Paperbacks.* Ed. Larry E. Sullivan and Lydia Cushman Schurman. New York: Haworth Press, 1996. 13–21. Print.

Litwin, Rory, ed. *Library Daylight: Tracings of Modern Librarianship, 1874–1922.* Duluth: Library Juice Press, 2006. Print.

Long, Elizabeth. *Book Clubs: Women and the Uses of Reading in Everyday Life.* Chicago: University of Chicago Press, 2003. Print.

Lowe, Margaret A. *Looking Good: College Women and Body Image, 1875–1930.* Baltimore: Johns Hopkins University Press, 2003. Print.

MacLeod, Anne Scott. *American Childhood: Essays on Children's Literature in the Nineteenth and Twentieth Centuries.* Athens: University of Georgia Press, 1994. Print.

_____. "From Rational to Romantic: The Children of Children's Literature in the Nineteenth Century." *Poetics Today* 13.1 (Spring 1992): 141–153. *JSTOR.* Web. 4 Apr. 2008.

Marchalonis, Shirley. *College Girls: A Century in Fiction.* New Brunswick, NJ: Rutgers University Press, 1995. Print.

Mason, Bobbie Ann. *The Girl Sleuth: On the Trail of Nancy Drew, Judy Bolton, and Cherry Ames,* 2d ed. Athens: University of Georgia Press, 1995. Print.

Matteson, John. "An Idea of Order at Concord: Soul and Society in the Mind of Louisa May Alcott." *A Companion to American Fiction, 1865–1914.* Ed. Robert Paul Lamb and G.R. Thompson. Malden, MA: Blackwell, 2005. 451–467. Print.

Mattingly, Carol. *Well-Tempered Women: Nineteenth-Century Temperance Rhetoric.* Carbondale: Southern Illinois University Press, 1998. Print.

May, Lary. *Screening Out the Past: The Birth of Mass Culture and the Motion Picture Industry.* New York: Oxford University Press, 1980. Print.

McGovern, Charles F. *Sold American: Consumption and Citizenship, 1890–1945.* Chapel Hill: University of North Carolina Press, 2006.

Michie, Helena. "'Dying Between Two Laws': Girls Heroines, Their Gods, and Their Fathers in *Uncle Tom's Cabin* and the *Elsie Dinsmore* Series." *Refiguring the Father: New Feminist Readings of Patriarchy.* Ed. Patricia Yaeger and Beth Kowaleski-Wallace. Carbondale: Southern Illinois University Press, 1989. 188–206. Print.

Miller, Susan A. *Growing Girls: The Natural Origins of Girls' Organizations in America.* New Brunswick, NJ: Rutgers University Press, 2007. Print.

Mink, Gwendolyn. "The Lady and the Tramp: Gender, Race, and the Origins of the American Welfare State." *Women, the State, and Welfare.* Ed. Linda Gordon. Madison: University of Wisconsin Press, 1990. 92–122. Print.

Mintz, Steven. *Huck's Raft: A History of American Childhood*. Cambridge: Belknap Press of Harvard University Press, 2004. Print.
Mitchell, Sally. *The New Girl: Girls' Culture in England, 1880–1915*. New York: Columbia University Press, 1995. Print.
Mollo, John. *Military Fashion: A Comparative History of the Uniforms of the Great Armies from the 17th Century to the First World War*. New York: G.P. Putnam's, 1972. Print.
Monahan, Evelyn M., and Rosemary Neidel-Greenlee. *A Few Good Women: America's Military Women from World War I to the Wars in Iraq and Afghanistan*. New York: Alfred A. Knopf, 2010. Print.
Morrison, Toni. *Playing in the Dark: Whiteness and the Literary Imagination*. Cambridge: Harvard University Press, 1992.
Murolo, Priscilla. *The Common Ground of Womanhood: Class, Gender, and Working Girls' Clubs, 1884–1928*. Urbana: University of Illinois Press, 1997. Print.
Nash, Ilana. *American Sweethearts: Teenage Girls in Twentieth-Century Popular Culture*. Bloomington: Indiana University Press, 2006. Print.
Nelson, Claudia, and Lynn Vallone. *The Girls' Own: Cultural Histories of the Anglo-American Girl, 1830–1915*. Athens: University of Georgia Press, 1994. Print.
Newman, Louise. *White Women's Rights: The Racial Origins of Feminism in the United States*. New York: Oxford University Press, 1999. Print.
Odem, Mary E. *Delinquent Daughters: Protecting and Policing Adolescent Female Sexuality in the United States, 1885–1920*. Chapel Hill: University of North Carolina Press, 1995. Print.
Painter, Nell. *The History of White People*. New York: W. W. Norton, 2010. Print.
Palladino, Grace. *Teenagers: An American History*. New York: Basic Books, 1996. Print.
Palmieri, Patricia Ann. *In Adamless Eden: The Community of Women Faculty at Wellesley*. New Haven: Yale University Press, 1995. Print.
Parille, Ken. "'Wake up, and be a man': *Little Women*, Laurie, and the Ethic of Submission." *Children's Literature* 29 (2001): 34–51. Project Muse. Web. 14 April 2010.
Peiss, Kathy. *Cheap Amusements: Working Women and Leisure in Turn-of-the-Century New York*. Philadelphia: Temple University Press, 1986. Print.
Quimby, Karin. "The Story of Jo: Literary Tomboys, Little Women, and the Sexual-Textual Politics of Narrative Desire." *GLQ: A Journal of Lesbian and Gay Studies* 10.1 (2003): 1–22. MLA International Bibliography. Web. 14 April 2010.
Radway, Janice A. *Reading the Romance: Women, Patriarchy, and Popular Literature*. Chapel Hill: University of North Carolina Press, 1991. Print.
Rauchway, Eric. *The Refuge of Affections: Family and American Reform Politics, 1900–1920*. New York: Columbia University Press, 2001. Print.
Rehak, Melanie. *Girl Sleuth: Nancy Drew and the Women Who Created Her*. Orlando: Harcourt, 2005. Print.
Repplier, Agnes. "Little Pharisees in Fiction." *Scribner's Magazine* 20 (Jul.-Dec. 1896): 718–724. Rpt. in *19th Century Girls' Series*. Ed. Deidre Johnson. 11 Dec. 2009. Web. 28 Mar. 2010. http://www.readseries.com/auth-dm/phar1.html.
Rhinehart, Alice Duffy, ed. *One Woman Determined to Make a Difference: The Life of Madeleine Zabriskie Doty*. Bethlehem: Lehigh University Press, 2001. Print.
Rieser, Andrew C. *The Chautauqua Moment: Protestants, Progressives, and the Culture of Modern Liberalism*. New York: Columbia University Press, 2003. Print.
Robbins, Sarah. *Managing Literacy, Mothering America: Women's Narratives on Reading and Writing in the Nineteenth Century*. Pittsburgh: University of Pittsburgh Press, 2004. Print.
Robinson, Jenny. "How Katy Lied: Pictures of Joy and Pain in *What Katy Did* and Other American Girls' Stories." *The Radiant Hour: Versions of Youth in American Culture*. Ed. Neil Campbell. Exeter, England: University of Exeter Press, 2000. 88–114. Print.

Rodgers, Daniel T. *Atlantic Crossings: Social Politics in a Progressive Age.* Cambridge: Belknap Press of Harvard University Press, 2000. Print.
Roediger, David. *Working Toward Whiteness: How America's Immigrants Became White; The Strange Journey Form Ellis Island to the Suburbs.* New York: Basic Books, 2005. Print.
Romalov, Nancy Tillman. "Mobile and Modern Heroines: Early Twentieth Century Girls' Automobile Series." *Nancy Drew and Company: Culture, Gender, and Girls' Series.* Ed. Sherrie A. Inness. Bowling Green, OH: Bowling Green State University Popular Press, 1997. 75–88. Print.
Rostenberg, Leona. "The Discovery of Louisa May Alcott's Pseudonym." *Pioneers, Passionate Ladies, and Private Eyes: Dime Novels, Series Books, and Paperbacks.* Ed. Larry E. Sullivan and Lydia Cushman Schurman. New York: Routledge, 1997. 193–196. Print.
Rotundo, E. Anthony. *American Manhood: Transformations in Masculinity from the Revolution to the Modern Era.* New York: Basic Books, 1993. Print.
Ruether, Rosemary Radford, and Rosemary Skinner Keller, eds. *Women and Religion in America, Vol. 1: The Nineteenth Century.* San Francisco: Harper & Row, 1981. Print.
Russett, Cynthia Eagle. *Sexual Science: The Victorian Construction of Womanhood.* Cambridge: Harvard University Press, 1989. Print.
Ryan, Mary P. *Cradle of the Middle Class: The Family in Oneida County, New York, 1790–1865.* Cambridge: Cambridge University Press, 1981. Print.
Sanchez-Eppler, Karen. *Dependent States: The Child's Part in Nineteenth-Century American Culture.* Chicago: University of Chicago Press, 2005. Print.
Saxton, Martha. *Being Good: Women's Moral Values in Early America.* New York: Hill and Wang, 2003. Print.
Schneider, Dorothy, and Carl J. Schneider. *American Women in the Progressive Era, 1900–1920.* New York: Facts on File, 1993. Print.
_____, and _____. *In Their Own Right: The History of American Clergywomen.* New York: Crossroad, 1997. Print.
_____, and _____. *Into the Breach: American Women Overseas in World War I.* New York: Viking-Penguin, 1991. Print.
Schultz, James R. *The Romance of Small-Town Chautauquas.* Columbia: University of Missouri Press, 2002. Print.
Schwarz, Judith. *Radical Feminists of Heterodoxy: Greenwich Village 1912–1940.* Norwich, VT: New Victoria, 1986. Print.
Scott, John C. "The Chautauqua Vision of Liberal Education." *History of Education* 34.1 (2005): 41–59. *MLA International Bibliography.* Web. 27 August 2008. Print.
Shepherd, Allen. "Sweet Little Ways: Elsie Dinsmore." *The Markham Review* 11(1982): 57–59. Print.
Smith-Rosenberg, Carroll. "The Female World of Love and Ritual: Relations Between Women in Nineteenth-Century America." *Signs: Journal of Women in Culture and Society* 1.1 (1975): 1–29. Rpt. in *Disorderly Conduct: Visions of Gender in Victorian America.* Carroll Smith-Rosenberg. New York: Oxford University Press, 1986. 53–76. Print.
Solomon, Barbara Miller. *In the Company of Educated Women.* New Haven: Yale University Press, 1985. Print.
Soltow, Lee, and Edward Stevens. *The Rise of Literacy and the Common School in the United States: A Socioeconomic Analysis to 1870.* Chicago: University of Chicago Press, 1981. Print.
Stansell, Christine. *American Moderns: Bohemian New York and the Creation of a New Century.* New York: Henry Holt, 2000. Print.
_____. *City of Women: Sex and Class in New York, 1789–1860.* 1982. Urbana: University of Illinois Press, 1987. Print.

Stern, Alexandra Minna. *Eugenic Nation: Faults & Frontiers of Better Breeding in Modern America*. Berkeley: University of California Press, 2005. Print.
Stern, Madeleine B. "Dime Novels by 'The Children's Friend.'" *Pioneers, Passionate Ladies, and Private Eyes: Dime Novels, Series Books, and Paperbacks*. Ed. Larry E. Sullivan and Lydia Cushman Schurman. New York: Routledge, 1997. 197–214. Print.
_____, ed. *Critical Essays on Louisa May Alcott*. Boston: G. K. Hall, 1984. Print.
Stoneley, Peter. *Consumerism and American Girls' Literature, 1860–1940*. Cambridge: Cambridge University Press, 2003. Print.
Stratemeyer, Edward. Letter to Arthur E. Bostwick. 21 February 1905. Microfilm. Reel 12, Outgoing Correspondence. Stratemeyer Syndicate Records. Manuscripts and Archives Division. The New York Public Library. Astor, Lenox and Tilden Foundations.
_____. Letter to Arthur E. Bostwick. 24 February 1905. Microfilm. Reel 12, Outgoing Correspondence. Stratemeyer Syndicate Records. Manuscripts and Archives Division. The New York Public Library. Astor, Lenox and Tilden Foundations.
_____. Letter to Arthur E. Bostwick. 23 March 1905. Microfilm. Reel 12, Outgoing Correspondence. Stratemeyer Syndicate Records. Manuscripts and Archives Division. The New York Public Library. Astor, Lenox and Tilden Foundations.
_____. Letter to W.F. Gregory. 19 February 1901. Microfilm. Reel 1, Incoming Correspondence. Stratemeyer Syndicate Records. Manuscripts and Archives Division. The New York Public Library. Astor, Lenox and Tilden Foundations.
_____. Letter to Gabrielle E. Jackson. 18 October 1906. Microfilm. Reel 12, Outgoing Correspondence. Stratemeyer Syndicate Records. Manuscripts and Archives Division. The New York Public Library. Astor, Lenox and Tilden Foundations.
_____. Letter to Gabrielle E. Jackson. 26 October 1906. Microfilm. Reel 12, Outgoing Correspondence. Stratemeyer Syndicate Records. Manuscripts and Archives Division. The New York Public Library. Astor, Lenox and Tilden Foundations.
_____. Letter to the Librarian of Congress. 25 February 1905. Microfilm. Reel 12, Outgoing Correspondence. Stratemeyer Syndicate Records. Manuscripts and Archives Division. The New York Public Library. Astor, Lenox and Tilden Foundations.
_____. Letter to the Librarian of Congress. 14 March 1905. Microfilm. Reel 12, Outgoing Correspondence. Stratemeyer Syndicate Records. Manuscripts and Archives Division. The New York Public Library. Astor, Lenox and Tilden Foundations.
_____. Letter to Evelyn Raymond. 7 November 1906. Microfilm. Reel 12, Outgoing Correspondence. Stratemeyer Syndicate Records. Manuscripts and Archives Division. The New York Public Library. Astor, Lenox and Tilden Foundations.
_____. Letter to Evelyn Raymond. 10 November 1906. Microfilm. Reel 12, Outgoing Correspondence. Stratemeyer Syndicate Records. Manuscripts and Archives Division. The New York Public Library. Astor, Lenox and Tilden Foundations.
_____. Letter to Evelyn Raymond. 17 November 1906. Microfilm. Reel 12, Outgoing Correspondence. Stratemeyer Syndicate Records. Manuscripts and Archives Division. The New York Public Library. Astor, Lenox and Tilden Foundations.
_____. Letter to Evelyn Raymond. 6 December 1906. Microfilm. Reel 12, Outgoing Correspondence. Stratemeyer Syndicate Records. Manuscripts and Archives Division. The New York Public Library. Astor, Lenox and Tilden Foundations.
_____. Letter to Evelyn Raymond. 10 December 1906. Microfilm. Reel 12, Outgoing Correspondence. Stratemeyer Syndicate Records. Manuscripts and Archives Division. The New York Public Library. Astor, Lenox and Tilden Foundations.
_____. Letter to Evelyn Raymond. 5 February 1907. Microfilm. Reel 12, Outgoing Correspondence. Stratemeyer Syndicate Records. Manuscripts and Archives Division. The New York Public Library. Astor, Lenox and Tilden Foundations.
Sullivan, Larry E., and Lydia Cushman Schurman, eds. *Pioneers, Passionate Ladies, and Private Eyes: Dime Novels, Series Books, and Paperbacks*. New York: Routledge, 1997. Print.

Susman, Warren I. *Culture as History: The Transformation of American Society in the Twentieth Century*. 1973. Washington, D.C.: Smithsonian Institution Press, 2003. Print.
Tarbox, Gwen Athene. "American Children's Narrative as Social Criticism, 1865–1914." *A Companion to American Fiction, 1865–1914*. Ed. Robert Paul Lamb and G.R. Thompson. Malden, MA: Blackwell, 2005. 428–448. Print.
_____. *The Clubwomen's Daughters: Collectivist Impulses in Progressive Era Girls' Fiction, 1890–1940*. New York: Garland, 2000. Print.
Terborg-Penn, Rosalyn. *African-American Women in the Struggle for the Vote, 1850–1920*. Bloomington: Indiana University Press, 1998. Print.
Thayer, William M. *The Good Girl and True Woman; Or, Elements of Success Drawn from the Life of Mary Lyon and Other Similar Characters*.1858. Boston: Gould and Lincoln, 1863. Print.
Tompkins, Jane. *Sensational Designs: The Cultural Work of American Fiction 1790–1860*. New York: Oxford University Press, 1985. Print.
Turner, Patricia. *Ceramic Uncles and Celluloid Mammies: Black Images and Their Influence on Culture*. New York: Anchor, 1994. Print.
Tyack, David, and Larry Cuban. *Tinkering Toward Utopia: A Century of Public School Reform*. Cambridge: Harvard University Press, 1995. Print.
Wadsworth, Sarah A. "Louisa May Alcott, William T. Adams, and the Rise of Gender-Specific Series Books." *The Lion and the Unicorn* 25.1 (2001): 17–46. Project Muse. Web. 30 July 2008.
Waller, Altina L. *Reverend Beecher and Mrs. Tilton: Sex and Class in Victorian America*. Amherst: University of Massachusetts Press, 1982. Print.
Weiss, Elaine F. *Fruits of Victory: The Woman's Land Army of America in the Great War*. Washington, D.C.: Potomac Books, 2008.
Wells, Carolyn. *Patty and Azalea*. New York: Dodd, Mead, 1919. Print.
_____. *Patty at Home*. New York: Dodd, Mead, 1904. Print.
_____. *Patty Blossom*. New York: Dodd, Mead, 1917. Print.
_____. *Patty—Bride*. New York: Dodd, Mead, 1918. Print.
_____. *Patty Fairfield*. New York: Dodd, Mead, 1901. Print.
_____. *Patty in Paris*. New York: Dodd, Mead, 1907. Print.
_____. *Patty in the City*. New York: Dodd, Mead, 1905. Print.
_____. *Patty's Butterfly Days*. New York: Dodd, Mead, 1912. Print.
_____. *Patty's Fortune*. New York: Dodd, Mead, 1916. Print.
_____. *Patty's Friends*. New York: Dodd, Mead, 1908. Print.
_____. *Patty's Motor Car*. New York: Dodd, Mead, 1911. Print.
_____. *Patty's Pleasure Trip*. New York: Dodd, Mead, 1909. Print.
_____. *Patty's Romance*. New York: Dodd, Mead, 1915. Print.
_____. *Patty's Social Season*. New York: Dodd, Mead, 1913. Print.
_____. *Patty's Success*. New York: Dodd, Mead, 1910. Print.
_____. *Patty's Suitors*. New York: Dodd, Mead, 1914. Print.
_____. *Patty's Summer Days*. New York: Dodd, Mead, 1906. Print.
Welter, Barbara. "The Cult of True Womanhood, 1820–1860." *American Quarterly* 18 (Summer 1966): 151–175. JSTOR. Web. 2008–2009.
Whitfield, Eileen. *Pickford: The Woman Who Made Hollywood*. Lexington: University Press of Kentucky, 1997.
Wiegand, Wayne A. *"An Active Instrument for Propaganda": The American Public Library During World War I*. Westport, CT: Greenwood Press, 1989. Print.
Winship, Michael. "The National Book Trade System, Part I: Distribution and the Trade." *A History of the Book in America, Vol. 3: The Industrial Book 1840–1880*. Ed. Scott E. Casper et al. Chapel Hill: University of North Carolina Press, 2007. 117–130. Print.

Woloch, Nancy. *Women and the American Experience*, 3d ed. Boston: McGraw Hill, 2000. Print.
"Youths' Author Dies at 46." *New York Times* 11 Feb. 1931: 22. *ProQuest Historical Newspapers: The New York Times.* Web. 21 Mar. 2010.
Zeiger, Susan. *In Uncle Sam's Service: Women Workers with the American Expeditionary Force, 1917–1919.* 1999. Philadelphia: University of Pennsylvania Press, 2004. Print.
Zeitz, Joshua. *Flapper: A Madcap Story of Sex, Style, Celebrity, and the Women Who Made America Modern.* New York: Three Rivers Press, 2006. Print.

Index

abolition 3, 31, 35–36, 43, 52, 63
Adams, William Taylor 86–87, 89
adolescence 1, 9, 11, 13–21, 23, 25, 27, 30, 51, 88, 92–93, 96–97, 99, 169
advertising 18–20, 45, 85, 99, 103–106, 125, 129, 203, 205
African Americans 11, 21, 23, 33, 49, 66, 70–71, 83, 137–138, 159, 163–165, 166, 173
agency 3, 5, 27, 30, 49, 61, 64, 96, 107
airplanes 6, 130–131, 161, 222
Alcott, Louisa May 9, 12, 23, 43, 49, 55–60, 67, 69, 80–81, 93–95, 102, 224; *see also Eight Cousins; Jo's Boys; Little Men; Little Women*
Alden, Isabella 10, 12, 46–50, 53–55, 73, 77, 79–80, 83; *Esther Reid* 46; *see also The Chautauqua Girls*
Alger, Horatio, Jr. 12, 84, 89; *Ragged Dick* 12, 89
ambulance drivers 136, 156–157, 167, 171–172, 174–175, 188–190, 194–195, 227
American Ambulance Hospital at Neuilly 140–141, 143
American Expeditionary Forces (AEF) 136–139, 144–147, 151, 162, 165, 168, 199
American Fund for French Wounded (AFFW) 137, 140–143
American Library Association 97
American Red Cross (ARC) 7, 136–137, 141–145, 149, 155–156, 164–165, 167, 170–172, 174–176, 178–181, 185, 189, 204, 206, 222
American Relief Clearing House (ARCH) 137, 140–141
American Women's Hospitals (AWH) 142–143
Anne of Green Gables 10
Army 85, 128–129, 135–136, 139, 143, 148–149, 151–152, 156, 159, 165, 168, 174, 179, 182, 185, 188–189, 191, 194, 198–199
Army Medical Corps 143–144
Army Nurse Corps (ANC) 139, 144, 155, 164–165
Army Signal Corps 135–136, 149–151, 156, 163, 168
Atherton, Gertrude 158–159
automobiles *see* motor cars

Baby-Sitters Club 1
Baker, Newton (Secretary of War) 135, 150, 156, 166, 171, 174
Banta, Martha 129, 173–175, 183
Barnard, A.M. *see* Alcott, Louisa May
Basinger, Jeanine 23, 213–214
battlefield 6–7, 26, 143, 145, 149, 157, 159, 163, 166, 172–175, 178–179, 181–184, 186–187, 189–190, 196, 206–208, 226–227
Beadle and Adams 85–86
Beautiful Charmer 173, 176, 190
benevolence 2–4, 11–12, 26–33, 35–36, 39, 49, 51, 54–55, 58–60, 64–67, 69–70, 72, 76, 80, 83, 108, 111, 113, 118, 216, 221, 224–225
Benson, Mildred Wirt 223; *see also Nancy Drew*
Berg, Barbara 27–29, 31–32, 59
Beverly Gray 1, 222, 230
Billman, Carol 92, 230
Blackwell, Alice Stone 43
Blackwell, Antoinette Brown 31, 52
Blackwell, Henry 43
Bobinski, George S. 97
Bordin, Ruth 38–41, 48
Boston Public Library 96–97
Bourne, Randolph 16
Boylan, Anne 29–30
Brooks, Edna 184; *see also The Khaki Girls*
Brownlow, Kevin 23, 205–206, 213–214
Bunyan, John 56, 58; *see also Pilgrim's Progress*

Calvinism 61–62
Catholicism 12, 51–53, 61, 66, 68, 81, 118, 137, 146, 151, 163, 165, 173
Cawelti, John 88
Champney, Elizabeth 20, 49–50, 53; *see also The Three Vassar Girls; Witch Winnie*
The Chautauqua Girls 2–3, 10, 46, 53–55, 73, 84, 93, 109, 113, 116, 216; Erskine, Ruth 72, 77–80, 225; Roberts, Evan 74–76; Shipley, Flossy 72–80, 225; Wilbur, Marion 72, 78, 117; *see also* Alden, Isabella
Chautauqua Institute 2–3, 32, 35, 37–41, 46–49, 53–54, 73–74, 77, 79–80

Index

Chautauqua Literary and Scientific Circle 38
Cherland, Meredith 22
Chinn, Sarah 15–17, 133
Clark, Beverly 19, 56–57
Clarke, Edward 17, 23, 130, 133
Commission on Training Camp Activities (CTCA) 146
consumerism 2, 5–6, 8–9, 15, 18–19, 21, 23, 39, 44, 83, 100, 104–117, 119–122, 124–126, 129, 131–133, 201–203, 211–212, 216, 221–222, 224–228, 230
conversion 16, 25, 27, 30–31, 34, 51, 61–62, 64–65, 66, 71, 73, 78–79, 82, 147
Cott, Nancy 22, 32–33
Cox, J. Randolph 85–86, 100
Curtis, Susan 83

Daniels, Josephus (Secretary of the Navy) 135–136, 139, 150, 152–155, 168, 191
Davies, Marion 8, 23, 201, 227
Denning, Michael 43–44, 85, 87, 89, 100, 102
department stores 15, 68, 100, 104–106, 110, 113–114, 122, 125, 131, 225–226
dime novels 4–5, 43–44, 84–90, 92–95, 100, 102
Dodd, Mead, and Company 19–20
domestic fiction 88, 92–93
Dorr, Rheta Childe 157, 159
Doty, Madeleine Zabriskie 158–159

Eight Cousins 94–95; *see also* Alcott, Louisa May
Elsie Dinsmore 2–3, 20, 46–47, 52–53, 55, 75–77, 82–84, 93, 113, 116; Dinsmore, Elsie 11, 54–55, 60–65, 67–73, 79–82, 104, 109, 118, 216, 224–225; Dinsmore, Horace 60–65, 73–74, 81–82, 126; *see also* Finley, Martha
Emerson, Alice B. *see Ruth Fielding*
Enstad, Nan 44, 85, 93, 132
Epstein, Barbara 22, 30, 37, 61–62
eroticism 81–82
espionage 7, 154, 170, 178, 181–182, 184, 187–190, 227
eugenics 11, 163
Evangelical Protestantism 3, 26, 30, 45, 47–48, 60, 64–67, 69, 74, 79, 82–83, 147, 224

Fass, Paula 220
film *see* motion pictures
Finley, Martha 12–13, 21, 46–50, 63–64, 66–67, 69–70, 73, 80–83; *Mildred Keith* 20, 47; *see also Elsie Dinsmore*
Finney, Charles 31, 52
firearms 172, 190, 194–196
First Great Awakening 31
First World War *see* World War I
Flower, Jessie Graham 120–122, 132, 184; *see also Grace Harlowe*

Garbo, Greta 201, 214
gender roles *see* masculinity

ghostwriters 4–5, 9, 87, 90, 222, 231
Ginzberg, Lori 3, 22, 28–29, 54–55, 59, 67, 77
Girls of Central High 6, 170
Goldman, Emma 16
Grace Harlowe 5–7, 116–117, 167, 170–171, 175, 184, 199; Barber, Marian 119–121, 131, 225; Briggs, Elfreda 188–190; Clowes, Major 185–187; Coates, Virginia 186–187; Gray, Tom 185, 189–190, 197; Hammond, Henry 119–121; Harlowe, Grace 117–121, 131–132, 185–190, 192–193, 197, 200, 226; Nesbit, Miriam 117; Pierson, Anne 117–119, 121–122, 131, 226; *see also* Flower, Jessie Graham
Great War *see* World War I
Greenwald, Marilyn S. 89, 231
Gregory, W.F. 95–97
Grosset and Dunlap 108, 223

Hall, Granville Stanley 16–17, 23, 130, 133
Hello Girls 149–152, 155, 171
Henkin, David 45
Henry Altemus Company 117, 133
Hoganson, Kristin 114–115, 132
Hope, Laura Lee *see The Outdoor Girls*
Hostess Houses 146, 149, 176, 198
Hunter, Jane 3, 13–15, 34–35, 43–44, 53, 133

immigrants 11, 15–17, 21, 28, 33, 44, 51, 55, 137, 163, 217, 222
Inness, Sherrie 10, 230

Jackson, Gabrielle E. 91, 102
Jacobson, Lisa 18
Janis, Elsie 157
Jewish Welfare Board (JWB) 165–166
Johannsen, Albert 85, 89, 100
Johnson, Deidre 23, 46–47, 81, 86–88, 90, 95–96, 222, 230–231
Jo's Boys 56, 59–60; *see also* Alcott, Louisa May
Judaism 51–53, 68, 137, 163, 165–166, 173

Keeline, James 85, 90, 92, 99–100, 102–103, 132, 231
Kett, Joseph 3, 13–14, 27–28
The Khaki Girls 7, 167, 170–171, 175, 184, 190, 198; Bartram, Captain Katherine 192–194; Mason, Joan 7, 172, 190–197; Mason, Mr. 172, 191–193; Ward, Valerie 7, 190–197; *see also* Brooks, Edna

Leach, William 68, 83, 105, 132
LeBlanc, Edward T. 85–86
Leibrand, Lela 155
librarians 5, 42–43, 93–99, 102–103
literacy 4, 11, 22, 41–42, 44, 49, 84, 164
Little Men 56, 59; *see also* Alcott, Louisa May
Little Women 3, 9, 55–57, 81, 95; Bhaer, Friedrich 56, 94; Laurence, Laurie 56, 59–60; March, Marmee 57–58, 81, 94, 225;

March girls 54–60, 65–67, 79–80, 94, 104, 113, 216, 224–225; *see also* Alcott, Louisa May
Littledale, Clara Savage 157, 159
Lothrop, Lee & Shepard 95–96
Lyon, Mary 26, 35

MacLeod, Anne Scott 12, 14–15, 23
Marine Corps 135, 137–139, 150, 152, 154–155, 168, 172, 174, 198
Marion, Frances 8, 23, 201, 204–206, 209, 211, 227
Martha Washington Society 37
masculinity 7, 14, 52–53, 57, 63, 124, 128–131, 171–173, 175, 179–184, 189, 197, 210, 224
Mathiews, Franklin 95
Matteson, John 58–60
Mattingly, Carol 48, 53
McGovern, Charles 105–106, 132
Mead, Margaret 16–17
Medical Women's National Association (MWNA) 142–143
Michie, Helena 63–64
Moody, Dwight 68
Mormonism 12, 33, 52, 66
motion pictures 8, 23, 104, 178, 201–202, 204–206, 209–210, 212–213, 215–217, 219–222, 227; scenario writing 201–212, 214–215, 217, 227; sound 213–215; voice tests 213–215
motor cars 6, 21, 104, 123–127, 130–131, 140, 178, 191, 201, 222, 226–227, 229
motorboat 130–131, 208, 222
movies *see* motion pictures

Nancy Drew 1–2, 8, 10, 19, 81, 90, 178, 200, 222–223, 227–231; *see also* Benson, Mildred Wirt; Stratemeyer Syndicate
Nash, Ilana 17–18
National War Labor Board (NWLB) 162
Navy 135, 137–139, 141, 144, 150, 152–155, 168, 171–172, 174, 208; Naval Act of 1916 153
New England Women 173–174, 190
New Womanhood 4, 32–33, 55, 72, 80, 84, 129, 173–174, 183, 221, 224
New York Public Library 98, 103
Newark Public Library 93, 95, 98
nurses 26, 65, 135–136, 138–141, 144, 146, 148–150, 152, 158, 167–168, 171–172, 174, 176–179, 181, 198–199, 206, 227, 231; African American 164–165; military rank 144–145, 155, 171

Optic, Oliver *see* Adams, William Taylor
The Outdoor Girls 5, 7, 90, 123, 127–128, 130–131, 133–134, 167, 170, 172, 175–179, 182, 193, 197–199, 226; Billette, Mollie 127, 129–130; Blackford, Amy 127, 129; Ford, Grace 127, 129; Nelson, Betty 127–131, 177; *see also* Stratemeyer Syndicate
Outdoors Pal 173–176, 190
Over There Theatre League 156

Palladino, Grace 17–18
Patty Fairfield 2, 5–6, 107–108, 116–117, 123; Barlows 111–112; Elliott, Aunt Alice 112–114, 225; Elliott, Marian 114, 131; Fairfield, Fred 113, 116, 125–127; Fairfield, Patty 110–116, 124–128, 130–132, 225–226; Farringtons 116, 124, 126–127; Flemings 110–111; St. Clairs 108–112; *see also* Wells, Carolyn
Peiss, Kathy 15, 132–133
Pershing, Gen. John J. 135–136, 145, 150–151, 192
Pickford, Mary 8, 23, 201, 204–206, 209, 211, 222, 227
Pilgrim's Progress 56–57, 81; *see also* Bunyan, John
postbellum series 2–4, 12, 19, 21, 25, 46, 49, 55, 59, 224, 226, 228
printing technology 4–5, 84, 87, 93, 100–102
Progressive Era 2, 21, 33, 49, 55, 72, 107, 111, 132, 198, 216, 218, 228
Prohibition 40
prostitution 28–29, 45, 146
Protestantism 3, 11–13, 25, 27–29, 32, 38–39, 42, 46, 49–51, 53, 60, 66, 68, 72, 83, 117–118, 137, 163, 165, 173, 224
pseudonyms 4, 46, 89–90, 94, 98, 102, 132–133
public libraries 42–43, 53, 164

race relations 11, 29–30, 45, 69–71, 83–84, 123, 137–138, 159, 163, 173, 180–181, 188, 229
Radway, Janice 22
Rauchway, Eric 132, 217–218
Raymond, Evelyn 91–92, 102
Reconstruction 2, 11, 13, 83–84
Red Cross *see* American Red Cross
Red Cross Girls 7, 167, 169–170
Rehak, Melanie 93, 227–228, 231
Reiser, Andrew 3, 38–39, 53, 55, 83
Repplier, Agnes 47, 81
reproduction 16–17, 19, 208
republican motherhood 42, 58
Robbins, Sarah 41–42
Romalov, Nancy 123, 129, 133
Ruth Fielding 6–7, 167, 170, 172, 175, 178, 181, 197, 201; Alectrion Film Corporation 202, 204–205, 209–210, 214; Cameron, Helen 202–203, 207; Cameron, Tom 7, 179, 182–184, 197, 202, 207–208, 212, 214, 216–217, 219–222, 227; capitalist production 202, 211–212, 215–217, 221, 227; Fielding, Ruth 8–9, 179–185, 192–193, 198, 202–217, 219–222, 227; Fielding Film Company 209–210, 212, 214; Hammond, Mr. 202–204, 209–

Index

210, 214, 219; Mantel, Rose 179–181; marriage 216–217, 219–221
Ryan, Mary 29

Salvation Army 137, 145, 147–149, 151, 186; military rank 148; money transfer system 147–148
Sanchez-Eppler, Karen 48, 82
Saxton, Martha 58
Schneider, Carl 35, 132, 168, 199
Schneider, Dorothy 35, 132, 168, 199
school reform 13–14, 17, 41, 84, 133, 208
Second Great Awakening 27, 31, 73
Sergeant, Elizabeth Shepley 198
Seven Sisters colleges 17, 49, 185
Shepherd, Allen 82
Smith-Rosenberg, Carroll 22, 113, 132
Sons and Daughters of Temperance 37
Sophie Newcomb College 185
Stone, Lucy 43, 52
Stoneley, Peter 21, 106–107
story papers 4, 43–44, 84–87, 89–90, 93–95, 100, 102
Stratemeyer, Edward 4–5, 9, 21, 84–87, 89–90, 93, 95, 99–100, 102, 104, 108, 133, 169, 178, 203–205, 222–223; correspondence 5, 91–92, 95–98, 103; *Rover Boys* 89–91, 99; see also Stratemeyer Syndicate
Stratemeyer Syndicate 4–5, 23, 89–90, 92–93, 96–97, 99, 102, 108, 127, 132, 171–172, 178, 184, 223, 228–229, 231; *Bobbsey Twins* 90; *Dorothy Chester* 92, 102; *The Happy Hollisters* 90; *The Hardy Boys* 90, 223, 231; *Tom Swift* 89, 222; see also Nancy Drew; *The Outdoor Girls*; Stratemeyer, Edward
Street & Smith 85–86, 91
subscription libraries 53
suffrage 3–4, 40, 45, 49, 84, 128–129, 145, 167–168, 194, 199, 218, 222
Sunday School 27, 31, 35, 38–39, 52, 74, 76, 80; libraries 42, 53, 56–57
Susman, Warren 104–105, 132
Sweet Valley High 1

Talmadge, Norma 201, 205
temperance 3–4, 29, 31, 35, 37–41, 45, 48, 52–55, 72, 78–80, 82, 84
temperance fiction 48, 82
Thayer, William 26
The Three Vassar Girls 2, 119; see also Champney, Elizabeth
Tompkins, Jane 22, 88

True Womanhood 2, 21, 27, 32–33, 39–40, 50, 54–55, 60, 64–66, 72, 80, 84

Uncle Tom's Cabin 63
Unitarianism 30, 61

Vincent, John Heyl 38–40

Wanamaker, John 68–69, 104
war correspondents 155, 157–158, 206
wartime entertainers 156–157
wartime industry 138–139, 159–162, 171–175, 177–178, 181, 183, 197–199, 206, 208
Washington Society 37
Wells, Carolyn 108–111, 115, 120–121, 124, 132; see also Patty Fairfield
Welter, Barbara 2, 22, 32
Wiegand, Wayne 97
Willard, Frances 35, 52
Wilson, Woodrow 136, 146, 154
Winston, John C. 169–170
Witch Winnie 2, 20, 49, 119; see also Champney, Elizabeth
Woloch, Nancy 32–33
Woman's Christian Temperance Union (WCTU) 2–3, 32, 35, 37–41, 48–49, 53, 55, 78–80, 225
Woman's Crusade 37–39
Woman's Temperance Publishing Association 48
women physicians 135, 140–144, 148, 150, 155, 168, 199; military rank 143
Women's Land Army of America 135, 137, 198
Women's Overseas Hospital 143, 168
women's public speaking 3, 34–37; preaching 3, 31, 34, 40, 52, 79, 147
women's rights 17, 36, 59, 222
Women's Service Section of the Railroad Administration (WSS) 160
World War I 2, 6–8, 92, 132, 135–169, 171, 174, 178, 199, 226–227

Young Men's Christian Association (YMCA) 68, 136–137, 139, 145–151, 156–157, 164–165, 167, 172, 176, 186, 199
Young Women's Christian Association (YWCA) 7, 137, 142, 145–146, 149–150, 168, 171, 174–176

Zeiger, Susan 152

www.ingramcontent.com/pod-product-compliance
Lightning Source LLC
Chambersburg PA
CBHW051215300426
44116CB00006B/588